HOW TO SAIL AROUND THE WORLD

Overleaf: *What is blue-water sailing really like? Here we see a tiny boat out on the limitless ocean. There's enough wind so that both sails are reefed as the sloop drives westward at 5 knots. The captain—dressed in oilskin bottoms and wearing a sweater and a warm hat against the chill of November—looks things over. On deck is the usual clutter aboard a cruising yacht: a life raft capsule, a sailbag, a folded-up rubber dinghy, and a long oar. A wind-vane steering device mounted on the transom guides the boat. At the back of the cockpit is a solar panel that generates electricity for lights and a radio. In case of bad weather, a storm trysail is stowed in the dark-colored bag at the base of the mast. An anchor hangs over the bow. The mast has triangular steps fitted to its sides to enable the captain to climb aloft for repairs or to see ahead. This yacht is called a Contessa 26; she displaces less than 3 tons; her mast is 33 feet high. She was designed by English naval architect Jeremy Rogers and built in Canada. This photograph was taken sixteen miles east of New York City on November 6 and shows 20-year-old Tania Aebi at the conclusion of her single-handed voyage around the world. Though this picture was taken in 1987, it could just as well have been made today or 50 years hence because the ocean and the winds change very little. The challenges and the rewards of long-distance sailing are very great.*

ALSO BY HAL ROTH

Pathway in the Sky
Two on a Big Ocean
After 50,000 Miles
Two Against Cape Horn
The Longest Race
Always a Distant Anchorage
Chasing the Long Rainbow
Chasing the Wind
We Followed Odysseus

HOW TO SAIL AROUND THE WORLD

Advice and Ideas for Voyaging Under Sail

Hal Roth

with photographs and illustrations by the author

INTERNATIONAL MARINE / McGRAW-HILL

CAMDEN, MAINE • NEW YORK • CHICAGO • SAN FRANCISCO • LISBON •
LONDON • MADRID • MEXICO CITY • MILAN • NEW DELHI •
SAN JUAN • SEOUL • SINGAPORE • SYDNEY • TORONTO

The McGraw·Hill Companies

3 4 5 6 7 8 9 0 DOC DOC 0 9 8 7 6 5 4

Library of Congress Cataloging-in-Publication Data
    Roth, Hal, 1927–
  How to sail around the world : advice and ideas for
  voyaging under sail / Hal Roth.
     p.   cm.
  Includes bibliographical references and index.
   ISBN 0-07-142951-4 (hard : alk. paper)
  1. Yachting. 2. Voyages around the world. I. Title.
  GV813.R635 2004
  797.1'264–dc22   2003016128

Questions regarding the content of this book should be addressed to
International Marine
P.O. Box 220
Camden, ME 04843
www.internationalmarine.com

Questions regarding the ordering of this book should be addressed to
The McGraw-Hill Companies
Customer Service Department
P.O. Box 547
Blacklick, OH 43004
Retail customers: 1-800-262-4729
Bookstores: 1-800-722-4726

Acknowledgments for photographs and illustrations not by the author begin on page 457.

To Margaret,
the love of my life
for forty-five years,
and who made it
all possible.

Contents

Frigate bird, South Pacific

Illustrations

Drawings (19)

Preface

Aquarter-century ago I wrote a technical sailing book called *After 50,000 Miles*. The book sold 62,000 copies in English and foreign translations, which suggests that there are plenty of potential small-boat sailors out there. I know from letters and comments made to me personally that the book helped many owners of small yachts who had their eyes on distant sailing goals. For that I am thankful.

This book is based on the same plan as the earlier volume. That is, its emphasis is on the easy, the simple, and the achievable, rather than on the overly ambitious and impossible. My goal is to discuss each aspect of long-distance sailing and to reduce it to the essentials. To pass along what has worked well for me and for other sailors. To eschew trivia, and to be practical and realistic at all costs. To tell the good and the bad free from the pressures of advertising. Of course, my prejudices and foibles show up, but that's what makes us individuals.

Margaret and I have always operated on a shoestring, and my sympathies are for the beginner and the little guy with stars in his eyes and not much money. In fact, too much money may actually work against you, but more about this later.

I've learned that sailing to the far corners of the world takes a yeasty combination of desire and reality, of planning and scheming and hope. Yet one day most of us have to return from Tahiti or Bermuda or Ithaca. Sometimes we need to leaven our big ideas with a sprinkling of common sense. The people you meet away from home will help you, but only if you have something to give in return, whether it's an idea, a skill, a shared experience, or the glimpse of another kind of life. In the long term, material advantages mean little. It's the spirit of giving and adventure that counts.

This book is full of technical information and is based on yachts from 25 to 55 feet in overall length. I express opinions frequently. I name people and products. My standards are demanding because I use marine gear for years, not for one quick trip. Sometimes I must make repairs in out-of-the-way places, so I carry lots of tools, spare parts, and fastenings. If I seem exasperated at times, it's because I believe that some trends in ocean-cruising yachts are self-defeating.

We can begin the list with cockpits that are too large for safety, paltry anchors, overdependence on electricity and too many gadgets. I do not like inaccessible engines, the lack of suitable dinghies for taking out anchors, and keel designs that make yachts difficult or impossible to haul out of the water in remote places. I think that some people lose much of the pleasure of long-distance voyaging by trying to sail yachts that are too big and too complicated.

I'm not a fan of cockpits that are swathed with dodgers, biminis, side curtains, scratched-up plastic windows, and tricky little shelters and enclosures that restrict a helmsman's vision and hide him from the real world. I like to breathe raw air. I like to reach up and touch the mainsail. I like to feel the breeze on my face and to hear the sounds of the sea. My shelter from the sun is sunscreen lotion, a wide-brimmed hat, and a pair of sunglasses. If there's spray flying around, I put on oilskins. If it's cold at night, I have a selection of long johns, sweaters, and quilted oilskins. It's not that I'm trying to be a tough guy, but sailing is my life; I feel closer to the wind and stars and sky and birds if I'm really in the out-of-doors.

In addition, I believe that I can run the vessel better with firsthand visual, auditory, and tactile clues. While there's occasional spray and more rarely a boarding sea, modern yachts are extremely buoyant. My cockpit is dry 90 percent of the time, particularly because I try (not always successfully) for passages with reaching and running winds.

In my judgment there's entirely too much emphasis on engines and motoring, which completely destroys the purity and delight of sailing. Being becalmed occasionally is a normal part of sailing. What's wrong with waiting a few hours for wind? Personally, I'm tired of hearing people say: "There was no wind, so we had to motor." What they really mean is: "There was no wind, so we *chose* to motor."

People with their hands on the throttle completely miss the wonder of light-weather sailing, that blissful state when your vessel glides across a calm and quiet sea hour after hour while the big light-weather sails swish and fill and magically pull you along.

Finally, a word about the health of the waters on which we sail: It's not enough to leave a clean wake behind us. We must work actively to keep plastic out of the sea. Regrettably, the amount of this junk is increasing because modern packaging is made mostly of plastic instead of cardboard or paper. Unfortunately, business decisions are made on the basis of advertising messages, not concern for the environment. In the meantime, Styrofoam and the other ugly stuff apparently float forever.

You and I must carry plastic ashore, where it can be incinerated or buried in a landfill or disposed of otherwise. We must all speak up and demand that everyone does the same. Otherwise, our lovely oceans and shorelines will become dumps for plastic garbage, fit only for sliding across like shoes on a greasy floor. Japan's Inland Sea and places along the coasts of Italy, Greece, and Turkey are a disgrace. Some of the waters and harbors around the United States and Canada don't look too good either. We must all work together to halt the spread of plastic in the sea.

1

THE PLEASURE AND THE FREEDOM

This book is for people who dream of taking small sailing yachts across oceans, who hope to make extended blue-water passages, and who plan to live aboard for long periods. Or said another way: it's for people who want to become high-mileage sailors and to exchange the near and safe for the distant and unknown.

Margaret and I have had a wonderful sailing life for more than thirty-five years. We've crossed all the oceans of the world and have sailed to a thousand foreign ports and anchorages. Yet it seems only yesterday that we elected to sail and earn our way with words and pictures while living aboard a 35-foot yacht.

The people we know in the business world have made far more money, but their riches could never buy the satisfaction that's come to us from all our experiences and the pleasure of making friends in so many places. I think of watching all those sunsets at sea and the excitement of putting together a small shelf of books about our voyages.

On our first trip we traveled across the Pacific from California to Tahiti, Samoa,

Whisper *sailing into Attu, the westernmost island of the Aleutians.*

1

the Gilbert Islands, and through the four main islands of Japan. Then to the Aleutian Islands, southeast Alaska, Canada's Queen Charlotte Islands, and back to California. Another time we sailed to the Galápagos Islands off the coast of Ecuador. Next we went to Peru, the Strait of Magellan, Tierra del Fuego, and Cape Horn. Finally to Buenos Aires, Uruguay, a dozen places in Brazil, a stop in Bermuda, and on to Nantucket Island.

On a great voyage in the 1980s, we sailed from Maine to the Caribbean and through the Panama Canal to French Polynesia. We spent a month in the Tuamotu Archipelago, 72 gorgeous palm-clad slivers of coral and sand barely above the sea, where the people seem to be half fish, half human because they live so close to the water. We continued on to Vanuatu in the western Pacific, a place where kinky-haired Melanesian men wore little more than penis sheaths but spoke four languages and knew more about world politics than I did.

Sailing ever westward, we glided along the coast of the immense, rust-colored deserts of Northern Australia. We stopped at Thursday Island and bustling Darwin, where we met Australians and Aborigines. Two months later, on a silky Indian Ocean, we tiptoed along Indonesia's necklace of islands. We took public buses across lovely Bali, an oasis of green hills and oh-so-gentle people, where the driver would stop and worship at a roadside shrine for a few minutes while his passengers sat quietly. Margaret and I stopped at tiny Keeling-Cocos in the middle of the Indian Ocean. Then to the tropical Seychelle Islands off the east coast of Africa and on to Somalia and Yemen, our introduction to the Arab world.

The sail north in the Red Sea was hot, hard, and dusty. We stopped in Port Sudan to fill our water tanks, and 10 days later we passed through the Suez Canal into the Mediterranean.

We rested in Cyprus during a mild winter, and the following summer spent a month each sailing along the coasts of Turkey, Greece, Italy, and Spain. Finally we crossed the Atlantic to Martinique in the Caribbean and headed north to Maine. We had gone entirely around the world in our little yacht, *Whisper*.

I had long wanted to try sailing single-handed to see if I had enough guts and technical skills to do it by myself. So in 1986–87, I set off and made a voyage east-about around the world by way of the Southern Ocean in a competition called the BOC Challenge. I sailed in an engineless 50-footer, and for the first leg traveled from Newport, Rhode Island, to Cape Town, South Africa. Then around the Cape of Good Hope and across the Southern Ocean to Sydney, Australia. Next past New Zealand and across more of the Southern Ocean until I reached Cape Horn. In the Atlantic once again, I sailed north to Rio de Janeiro, across the equator, and back to the United States. Margaret served as my shore support crew and met me at each of the three stops. I made the same journey in 1990–91, and once more my wife helped me.

In 1995, Margaret was again on board, and we were back to a 35-footer, a boat size we liked better. We sailed from the Chesapeake to Gibraltar and thence to northwest Turkey to begin a project to trace the voyages of Odysseus.

In addition to these six major voyages, Margaret and I have made dozens of shorter cruises: from California to British Columbia; Maine to Rhode Island; Maine to Maryland; and Maine to Florida and the Bahamas. In 2000 and again in 2001, we sailed from Maryland to Canada's Cape Breton Island at the eastern end of Nova Scotia. We circled the big island of Newfoundland twice, and in 2001 we made a long run northward along the coast of Labrador among the great icebergs that drift south from Greenland.

At 5 or 6 knots it takes a good many years to accumulate a significant total of sea miles. It's easy to exaggerate one's sailing or to claim a lot of miles as part of a big crew on a long voyage. It's quite a different game sailing with one or two. Our experiences include 5 trips across the Pacific, 11 runs across the Atlantic, and 3 jaunts past Cape Horn. In all, I have sailed 200,000 miles. Margaret has sailed 120,000 miles.

During our years at sea we've been on the yacht continuously, in winter and in summer, and we've visited parts of the earth that a tourist never sees. We've had moments of sublime pleasure and nerve-jarring agony. We've run before the gentlest of trade winds for a month; other times we've bashed into severe headwinds.* Once we blew ashore in a frightful storm; another time we hit a coral reef because of an error on a new chart. But the bad times were few, and the good times were many.

I think back to some of our wonderful anchorages: the ethereal turquoise of tropical lagoons; the charming, butterflylike fishing villages along the southeast coast of Japan; the nose-tingling fragrance of cedars and spruces in the bays of southeast Alaska; the rose-colored flamingos flying overhead in southern Peru; yellow and green parrots chattering in the tropical jungles of Brazil next to the yacht; the chilling immensity of frosty, ice-blue glaciers that loomed above us in Beagle Channel in southern Chile; the storybook village of Bonifacio, hidden among the limestone cliffs of southern Corsica in the Mediterranean.

My mind becomes a kaleidoscope of twisting colors, out-of-focus landscapes, storms and calms, sail changes and anchoring. My ears ring with the babble of strange languages, sea sounds in the night, and the hooting of big ships in distant harbors. I hear the shrill sounds of the crier—the muezzin—who calls the faithful to prayer five times a day in the coastal towns and cities we sailed to in Tunisia, Turkey, and Yemen.

I smell the cloying sweetness of drying copra in the tropics. I turn my head to sniff the iodine seashore at low water in the far north. I think of dolphins

---

*According to Chilean sailors, the wind always blows from the bow.

breathing alongside the yacht at night; of boobies plummeting into the ocean after fish; of frigate birds circling ever higher at the far edge of my eyesight. Of dozens of humpback whales spouting and jumping outside the port of St. Anthony in New-foundland. I think of pleasant, lingering meals with new friends; the fun of shop-ping in strange markets with curious money. . . . All these thoughts make up the essential stuff of a happy lifetime at sea.

But half the magic of voyaging under sail is the wonderful journey itself. Yet when I tell people about being at sea and out of sight of land for a week or a month or even two months, they can't wait to ask questions. "How do you pass the time?" they say. "Aren't you lonely? What happens all day? How do you stand it?"

I stand it very well because I love the sailing. I spend hours in the cockpit or in the main companionway watching the yacht slip through the water. The boat glides across the sea effortlessly, quietly, day after day, while the water murmurs along the hull and the invisible wind and the white sails drive the boat forward.

It's all so easy and beautiful. I cherish the peacefulness and the simplicity.

The sailing is my dream, my goal, everything I want, and I secretly wish that the journey could go on forever.

The sun comes up in the morning, rises high at noon, and slips below the blue of the horizon in the evening. The days pass quickly and I have to look in the ship's logbook to see whether it's Tuesday or Friday. . . . We eat. We sleep. We fix things. We read. We reef and unreef the sails. We're becalmed. We deal with storms. We look around for ships. We try to keep her going day and night.

This is supposed to be a technical book. Yet I'm already wandering from the mark. You see I am an incorrigible romantic; who else would travel at a snail's pace in an era of speedy air transport?

The birch-bark canoe of the American Indian and the creaking, six-horse stage-coach of 150 years ago belong to another age. The small sailing yacht is hopelessly antiquated, too. These boats are slow, often intolerably uncomfortable, difficult to build, and expensive to maintain. Yet the popularity of sail for long-distance travel-ing is increasing at a surprising rate. How can we explain this? By any rational analy-sis, a sailing vessel should be tucked away like a museum replica of an extinct bird. Can you imagine taking three or four weeks to sail from Boston to Gibraltar when a jet plane can do the trip in a few hours and at far less cost?

The answer is that life under sail—especially in your own vessel—is highly

View from aloft on a modern sloop-rigged yacht during an Atlantic crossing from the Canary Islands to the Bahamas in 1997. Here Whisper *runs easily before the fair trade wind with an eased mainsail and a poled-out headsail. The line at top left is the star-board running backstay. The other line is a trailing fishing line. The standing backstay is hard to see.*

appealing because it is simple, basic, and infinitely challenging. Your existence goes back to first principles. At a stroke, you erase 90 percent of the trivia of modern life. You travel to new places at your own pace and can linger as much or as little as you wish. In no other activity except perhaps mountaineering are you so independent and so accountable for your own actions.

You alone put food on board. You alone bend on the sails and adjust them. You alone choose your sailing waters. You alone are responsible for finding your way on the sea. You alone select the anchorages. You alone are in charge of the upkeep of the yacht. If you get into trouble, it's generally you alone who must bail yourself out. The business of solving your own problems, making your own repairs, and looking after yourself is satisfying and grows into nice feelings of independence, confidence, and self-respect.

It was my friend, the late Hawaii-based sailor Bob Griffith, who spoke of "the pleasure and the freedom" inherent in world cruising. What a lovely phrase: the pleasure and the freedom.

However, before we hypnotize ourselves with words, we need to be realistic. Listen to this wise counsel from Guy Cole:

> . . . for every one engaged in long-distance cruising there are probably a thousand others who dream about it. The trouble with many of these dreamers is that they seek to project themselves from an environment which they find completely unsatisfactory, into one which they regard as wholly desirable, without considering the steps which come between. Therein lies many a personal tragedy. Much of this can be laid directly as a charge against the people who write books about long-distance cruises. They make it all sound fatally easy. "The wind had now worked up to Force Eight and we pulled down a couple of reefs in the main. . . ." Impatiently, the reader flips over the page to see what happened next. Yet, concealed within that careless sentence, is half an hour of bitter struggle, wrestling with refractory canvas, in the blackness of a rain-squall, while being thrown around the decks of a small boat pitching and tumbling in an ocean swell.
>
> Worse still are those who write books describing how they simply bought a boat, and sailed away—just like that—without any knowledge of seamanship or navigation, or anything else. It has been done. There is no denying it. But in order to survive for long enough to enable them to acquire the necessary knowledge to carry on with their cruising, these people must have been extraor-

dinarily lucky. And we hear nothing of those who failed miserably, or never got started, through inexperience.[1]

Cruising under sail is a hundredfold more complex than merely buying a suitable yacht. We know this because the marinas and harbors of the world are dotted with private pleasure craft, most of which go nowhere at all. There are tens of thousands of boatowners but very few sailors. Pay attention to this phrase: *lots of boatowners but few sailors*. And a sailor you must be if you're going to try ocean voyaging. You need a modicum of sailing aptitude, some ability to fix things, and the willingness to pitch in and work.

Most veteran long-distance small-boat sailors are free spirits who fall into the classification of restless adventurer and who are always looking at distant horizons

Dictionary woes. "Excuse me. Is góhan *cooked rice? Is* komé *raw grain rice? Or do I have the words mixed up?" Margaret shopping in Yamagawa, Japan.*

and trying new things. These spooky engineers usually lack fancy certificates, but they've all served fairly intensive apprenticeships and have learned a good bit about the sea, the care of their vessels, and the management of themselves.

To learn the fundamentals of sailing you need to go to a special school for a few weeks. You will be taken out in a dinghy or small vessel for instruction in sail handling, tacking, gybing, docking, maneuvering in restricted waters, and following safety procedures. Then you must practice as often as possible and serve as crew for friends on their yachts.

In the beginning you will be only a grunt, but little by little it will come to you. Every time you sail on a different vessel you learn a thing or two because each captain has his own way of doing things. You need to practice stitching sails, to find out about anchors and rigging, and to get some notion of sanding and painting and fixing things because life under sail is a never-ending round of maintenance, modifications, and large and small repairs.

To master celestial navigation requires specialized study and practice, although the mysteries of the sextant and related calculations are much exaggerated.

I know that global positioning system (GPS) instruments are far easier to use and more accurate than sextants for keeping track of your position. I use a GPS device and it's wonderful. However, I believe that you should be able to navigate with a sextant as well. Suppose your GPS unit (and the spare) stops working, you have a battery problem, or the system itself is shut down. At least take a sextant, a book of instructions, a small, portable shortwave radio (for time signals), and a current nautical almanac with you.

Celestial navigation is fascinating, and it gives you a good feeling to find your way by measuring the angles of the sun, moon, stars, and planets. When you shoot stars with a sextant, you soon learn to identify some of the constellations; it's fun to sail your way through the night sky by identifying a few pinpricks of white light. (Of course, everybody knows that stars aren't stars. They're tiny openings into the vault of heaven itself. . . .)

You must have patience to learn the craft of sailing, which has set and orderly ways of doing each operation, schemes of success that have been polished and refined for generations. Even the nautical vocabulary is specialized because sailors must be able to describe every part of a vessel and talk about each maneuver and action with unmistakable precision.

You can pick up the fundamentals quickly, but half a lifetime is scarcely enough to perfect your techniques. A good sailor is always studying and learning and asking questions. Fortunately, the people who travel on the sea tend to be literate souls who often write books, and there's an astonishing pile of publications out there. These fall into three categories:

1. Technical books that show you how to tie knots, identify sea-birds, adjust a compass, bake a halibut, or make sense out of a radar screen.
2. Cruising guides—usually with maps and sketches—that tell about Vancouver Island or the Portuguese coast or where to anchor in the Turks and Caicos Islands.
3. Accounts of voyages. Recollections of the joys, triumphs, heart-aches, and disasters of small-boat sailors. There are hundreds of these books—some excellent, some middling, some dreadful.

You can hurry along your learning process with selective reading, but in spite of the help and pleasure from books, you must find out about sailing firsthand. You do not become a seaman by reading. You need practice. You need to pry your eyes open at 0200. *You need to get your hands dirty.*

Age is no barrier. My dear friend, Colin Darroch, fulfilled his lifetime ambition by single-handing a small vessel from San Francisco to Hawaii and back when he was 68. The Frenchman Jean Devogué circumnavigated the globe when he was 69. I have read many accounts by sailors who paused in the midst of great nautical adventures "to celebrate [their] 75th birthday," or "to take note that [they were] 79 today."

At the other end of the age scale, Robin Lee Graham began his fine circumnavigation when he was 16. More recently, a plucky 21-year-old young woman named Tania Aebi completed a trip around the world that she started when she was 18.

In 1895–98, Joshua Slocum sailed around the world in his famous *Spray*. Harry Pidgeon, who was 51 when he began, circumnavigated in *Islander* in 1921–26. The *Spray* was 36 feet, 9 inches in length; *Islander* was 34 feet. Both yachts were home-built, and both men were simple, salt-of-the-earth sailors whose direct and pithy accounts of their trips seem eternally fresh. Think for a moment of the astonishment that Slocum and Pidgeon would exhibit if they were alive to view some of today's cruising vessels. These pioneer small-boat sailors would marvel at plastic hulls, masts constructed of aluminum or carbon tubes, superstrong sails woven of fibers made from chemicals, small auxiliary engines that run on oil taken from the ground, devices called radios that enable one to talk at a distance, and navigation schemes that use mysterious signals sent by orbiting mini-moons.

Slocum and Pidgeon would have shaken their heads in disbelief.

The two captains rigged their vessels as gaff yawls and hand sewed their sails from bolts of cotton cloth. Both boats had plenty of sail area for their size, and Slocum and Pidgeon could make their vessels steer themselves by adjusting the sails (usually the small mizzen). Both yachts had no engine, both were easy to beach for

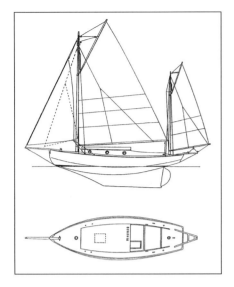

The 34-foot Islander *yawl was built by Harry Pidgeon on the Los Angeles waterfront in 1917–18 from plans sold by the old* Rudder *magazine. Pidgeon constructed the yacht entirely by himself, took her on a trial voyage to Hawaii, and sailed west-about around the world via Panama and South Africa from 1921 to 1925. He learned to make the yacht steer herself by adjusting the mizzen sail. Pidgeon taught himself celestial navigation and partially paid for the trip by selling articles and photographs.*

bottom cleaning, both were built for very little money, and both made outstanding ocean passages.[2]

Recently I visited the little waterfront museum in San Pedro, California, that has mementos from *Islander*'s voyages. I saw the grain grinder and the vernier sextant that Harry Pidgeon carried on his trip around the world three generations ago. I thought of Harry grinding dry corn into meal and wheat into flour that he baked into bread on his wood-burning stove. In my mind's eye I could see him using his sextant to shoot a morning sun line and a noon sight. I reflected on the fun and the satisfaction that show in his writings.

These two sailors and their vessels of the past underscore the wonderful simplicity that's possible with voyaging yachts. Of course, in today's world, we use modern materials (plastics, epoxy glues, stainless steel fastenings, glass and carbon fibers, polyurethane paints) to build and finish our vessels. However, in outfitting and execution, Slocum and Pidgeon can teach us a lot. Their key word is *simplicity*.

Again and again Margaret and I have confirmed the lessons that we have learned from these earlier sailors: a yacht must be easy to handle, sail well, and have balanced steering. The boat needs plenty of sail area for moving in light airs and should be easy to shorten down when it breezes up. The job of poling out a headsail or a spinnaker for downwind sailing should be quick and simple. A yacht needs a reasonable draft (say, 6' for a 35' length) to help her to sail to weather. Self-steering arrangements are important.

Below, the vessel needs a snug seagoing sleeping berth for each person, a small galley in which the cook can work safely, and a table (with a comfortable seat for the navigator) large enough to spread out a chart. World-ranging sailors chase away the damp and cold with a heating stove and carry enough water and supplies to last two months or more.

These days, a small engine is useful to help with anchoring procedures, to enter

Much of the fun and excitement of long-distance sailing is seeing what people do in far-off places. Here seven young Micronesian men and a 16-year-old girl sing and play their hearts out on a beach in Tarawa simply for the joy of making music.

a complex marina system, and to generate electricity. Certainly electricity is handy to run a GPS device and to power reading and navigation lights, but it should be possible to get along with very little—perhaps a few amps from a solar panel or two.

We don't need queen-size beds, turbocharged engines, auxiliary power plants, large fuel tanks, washer-dryers, and tents over the cockpit.

Can it be that in this new century, a hundred years after Slocum, we have fallen into the trap of trying to make some of our beamy cruising vessels into shoreside apartments? Do we need shag rugs, upholstered chairs, microwave ovens, icemakers, TV sets, and fancy restaurant-type dining with vases of flowers and long-stemmed wine glasses?

Some of these things are all very well at anchor or in a fancy marina, but at sea they're a bust. I've been in engine rooms of 50-foot cruising yachts that reminded me of the engine room of a diesel submarine. Air-conditioning may be nice at times, but why pay the price of machinery and engine time? Why not go where there's some wind and open a hatch?

It's obvious from their products that many builders who make cruising yachts have done little sailing themselves. They're interested not in cruising, but in selling so many units per month. Marketing experts know that a woman's vote is important, so the builders have become more concerned with decorator styling in the main saloon than with draft for windward ability. Salespeople would rather talk more about refrigeration than adequate anchors. The builder's specifications of one 33-foot yacht show a freshwater capacity of 20 gallons but offer "hot water with pressure water system and shower" for an extra $1,117. How long do you suppose 20 gallons of water will last?[3]

Yet some of these people mumble about world-cruising capability in the same breath that they discuss bank financing. Perhaps the truth is that most yachts will never unplug their yellow electrical umbilical cords and go anywhere anyway, so the dockside apartment marine fantasy is more realistic.

I hope I'm wrong.

The uneasiness between many owners of monohulls and multihulls is discouraging. We should remember that we're all sailors and can learn much from each other. Even the most mossbacked monohull fan is generally astonished at the acceleration and speed of multihulls when he goes for his first ride. And there is the advantage of the easy beaching of such vessels. True, multihull capsizes are horrifying, but instead of endless criticizing and holier-than-thou pontificating by monohull owners, all of us should encourage naval architects to come up with improved schemes of self-righting for oceangoing catamarans and trimarans. This is a problem of first priority. Certainly if naval architects like Dick Newick can design such brilliant, eye-catching, high-performance trimarans as *Three Cheers*, *Gulfstreamer*, and *Val*, they can invent a system of righting an upside-down craft. They must.

Finally, do yachts have to look so alike? A splendid variety of rigs and hulls is available. There are five hundred years of traditional designs from which to choose. We have the gaff ketch, the staysail schooner, the Chinese lugsail rig, the cat ketch, the lateen—the list goes on and on. We have bluff-bowed hulls from Holland; long, slender hulls from Sweden; double-enders from Norway; and those lovely hulls with their curving lines that John Alden used to draw for his Malabar schooners. Consider the popularity of the Nonsuch design (six hundred boats!) with its single unstayed mast and a sail that's controlled with a wishbone boom.

My favorite freethinker among naval architects is Philip Bolger, whose designs are novel, fresh, and outstanding. (Look at his books *The Folding Schooner* and *Boats with an Open Mind*.) Recent advances in carbon-fiber spar fabrication make freestanding masts increasingly possible. It may be within our grasp to do away with all standing rigging and a hundred or more highly stressed fittings and have better and safer sailing, as the yachting writer and designer Garry Hoyt has shown with his brilliant Freedom designs. (See chapter 7.)

What I'm saying is that a cruising yacht can be distinctive, nice to look at, sail reasonably well, and still be simple and moderately priced. The more complex a vessel is and the more maintenance she requires, the less an owner will enjoy her voyages because too much of his time will be locked into upkeep and repairs.

Remember when we started out to see the world and to meet people in different lands, we spoke of the delight and independence that an ocean-cruising yacht can give? Let's not forget that magical phrase: the pleasure and the freedom.

Sometimes birds flutter on board and visit with us for an hour or two. This storm petrel—a small, graceful, quiet creature—came to see us in the Indian Ocean. However we've seen storm petrels all over the world. They seem to dance just above the waves while they pick up minute scraps of food.

No one has more patience than the builder of a wooden yacht, who must methodically fit together thousands of pieces of specially selected and shaped wood to form his masterpiece. Here Cliff Niederer of Inverness, California, works on the 42-foot wooden hull of a Howard Chapelle design.

2
THE CORPUS ITSELF

The hulls of sailing yachts are made of wood, steel, aluminum, ferro-cement, or fiberglass. Each material has advantages and disadvantages. None is perfect and none is simple or cheap. Great voyages have been made in hulls of each type.

We know that the cost of a hull is roughly 20 percent of her total no matter what the material, so a saving of 10 or 20 percent on the hull (so widely discussed) is really only an economy of 2 to 4 percent on the finished boat. This is not a large consideration because the hull, after all, is the heart of a vessel. The costs for the ballast, mast, rigging, interior woodwork, tanks, machinery, and sails don't vary no matter what hull material is used.

Based on a building scheme that has evolved over thousands of years, a traditional hull of wood or metal is constructed around a central backbone made up of three structural members: the stem, keel, and sternpost. Curved athwartship frames are erected above and on each side of this central backbone. The frames are let in or welded to the keel and stem; to add to the strength of the frames and to tie opposite frames to each other and to the keel, transverse floors are laid across the frames just above the keel. These athwartship floors bind the frames and keel into a unit of great strength. (The floors are structural members and have nothing to do with the cabin floor or sole.)

The ballast keel is usually a massive lead or iron molding that's bolted to the wooden or metal keel. With steel and aluminum, the lead ballast is sometimes melted into place inside the hull. In the case of fiberglass construction, the ballast (in small blocks) is often put inside the bottom of the hull and glassed over. However, a much better practice with a fiberglass hull is to through-bolt the ballast keel to the outside of the bottom. This way the lead takes any knocks instead of the more delicate fiberglass, which is troublesome to repair.

The hull is planked or plated with longitudinal wooden planks or plates of metal. Stringers are fore-and-aft wooden or metal strengthening pieces that are fastened inside the frames from the stem to the stern. The clamp (or shear clamp) is a structural member that runs fore and aft on the inside and just below the tops of the frames. A second structural member called the shelf is bolted to and above the clamp (sometimes one piece of wood or metal is used for both) and takes the athwartship deck beams that support the deck. Boatbuilders often install triangular braces called knees to reinforce right-angle joints. All throughout the construction, each piece is screwed, glued, bolted, or welded to its neighbor to make a strong and rigid structure.

WOOD

There are five ways to build with wood: carvel planking, clinker planking, strip planking, plywood, and cold-molded.

The most traditional wooden construction (still widely used in many countries for work and fishing craft) is *carvel planking*. In this scheme, longitudinal planks, say 1⅜ by 5 inches (for a 38' vessel), are nailed, riveted, or screwed to transverse frames erected on heavy fore-and-aft timbers that make up the stem, keel, and sternpost. After construction, the seams between the planks are caulked to make the hull watertight. Such a hull relies on strong fastenings to hold its hundreds of separate pieces together, each of which has been named and had its function carefully worked out during centuries of trial and error.

A carvel-planked hull requires many skilled hand operations and long planks of high quality, preferably of air-dried wood. Unfortunately, the forests from which boatbuilding timbers used to come are mostly gone; suitable wood is not available in large quantities, and what's left is priced out of sight. This means that today, few woodworkers learn to dress timbers with an adze or to spile planking. Instead they become expert joiners and use their skills to construct fine wooden interiors in hulls built by other means.

Clinker planking is a second way to build with wood. This scheme, sometimes called clench or lapstrake, is similar to carvel construction except that the planks are

A boatbuilder in Alanya, Turkey, lifts a wide plank of carefully seasoned wood while he endeavors to keep four new fishing boats on schedule.

overlapped slightly and through-fastened. This makes an extremely strong hull that requires no caulking and is quite watertight. Unfortunately, the hull is not smooth because of the projecting plank edges. Varnished clinker planking is common in Scandinavia. The original Folkboat was clinker-built.

Strip planking is a scheme of wooden hull construction in which the planks are generally square (perhaps 1 or $1\frac{1}{2}$" on each side). The top of each strip is cut slightly concave and the bottom is a little convex so that each plank will fit nicely into the next when working up or down the curves of the hull (although this may not be necessary with epoxy glue). Every plank is glued and edge-nailed to its neighbor, which results in a rigid, watertight, strong monocoque (one-piece) hull that is well suited to amateur construction. Since small sizes of wood air-dry more rapidly, it is easier to find suitable wood for strip planking than for carvel planking.

Plywood can be bent only one way, so its use is limited to a hard-chine hull with parallel topsides and a V-bottom. The sides of the V are sometimes split and angled outward a second time, which results in a double chine or a more rounded hull section. This type of building is good for amateurs except that the rabbet in the chine logs (the longitudinal pieces that take the edges of the plywood) is difficult to cut. Many yachts with hard-chine hulls are superb sailing vessels, especially the famous Grumete and Cadete designs of Germán Frers Sr. of Argentina. Eric Tabarly's *Pen*

Duick VI, the winner of many races, has a hard-chine hull form, although she was built of aluminum.

The fifth type of wooden boatbuilding is *cold-molded*, in which thin layers of wood (say ⅛" thick × 5" wide) are formed over a male mold. The hull is built upside down, and initially a single laminated piece that forms the stem, keel, and sternpost is put into place along the top of the mold. The first layer of planking over the male mold is followed by the second, carefully glued and stapled, with the grain of the wood aligned in a different direction. The grain of each succeeding lamination crosses at a different angle, resulting in a plywoodlike, one-piece hull of great strength and lightness. From three to nine laminations are built over the form before the hull is removed from the mold and the internal framing installed. The famous yachts *Stormvogel*, *Windward Passage*, *Outlaw*, *Gipsy Moth IV*, and *Gipsy Moth V* all were constructed with the cold-molded process. An advantage of cold-molding is that wafer-thin planks are used and the wood can be seasoned quickly. The hulls are costly, however, because craftsmen of great skill and integrity are needed.

The strength of wood is reduced significantly when wet. The American Plywood Association notes that stiffness, for example, is lessened about 11 percent with a moisture content of 16 percent or more. Allowable stress in bending is reduced 25 percent and compression as much as 39 percent. The West System of the Gougeon Brothers—in which various kinds of wood construction are saturated with thin epoxy glue to make an almost new material—is excellent and has much to recommend it. West epoxy has become a standard fixture in boat construction and repair for both wood and fiberglass.

All five types of wooden construction require frames (steam-bent, sawed, grown, laminated, or made of metal), floors of wood or metal, a clamp and shelf, and stringers.

Builders often construct decks of several layers of plywood with their joints carefully scarfed and staggered. The plywood is screwed or nailed to the deck beams, which are bolted to the shelf, which in turn is bolted to the clamp, as we have seen. Usually builders cover a plywood deck with a layer or two of fiberglass cloth (to seal the deck and prevent leaks) followed by several coats of paint sprinkled with sand. Decks are sometimes planked with selected teak, which looks nice and gives excellent footing. A good scheme for steel and aluminum decks is to glue down large pieces of a carefully fitted rubberlike covering such as Treadmaster, which comes in various colors. Light colors are cooler in the tropics, but white is no good because it causes too much glare for the crew.

Wood is much subject to rot, especially wood of poor quality that's improperly seasoned. Careful design, however, together with adequate ventilation and chemical treatment, can minimize such deterioration. Wood immersed in the sea is attacked by marine borers, which can destroy unprotected timbers in less than a year. Shipworms *(Teredo* and *Bankia)* and gribble *(Limnoria)* can be kept away either by tacking sheets of thin copper over the wood or by covering the hull with heavy (and expensive) toxic paint. With strip-planked, plywood, and cold-molded hulls you can get perfect protection from marine borers by putting a single layer of fiberglass cloth and polyester or epoxy resin (preferred) on the hull. This is generally not possible with carvel construction because of the expansion and contraction of the planks.[4]

STEEL

Steel is excellent for larger yacht hulls, say 35 feet and up. The metal is by far the strongest of all hull materials, and it can be easily and positively fastened by welding. The welder should be certified and his work checked by independent experts who sometimes X-ray welding samples. Steel is cheap, and careful design and modern painting systems deal effectively with rust and corrosion. Either hard-chine or conventionally curved hulls are possible. The procedure starts with steel frames

Steel is tough, strong, and cheap. Alex Jacubenko tack welds a bow plate into position on a 46-foot Buchanan cutter in an outdoor yard in California.

being erected on the stem, keel, and sternpost pieces, which are also cut from steel. Longitudinal stringers fair out the hull and form the substructure. The plating (say $^3/16"$ for a 42-footer) goes on in large, rectangular pieces that can be rolled, pounded, and forced into the necessary curves.[5]

It's impressive to see a metalworker build a new vessel. After raising a plate (say $3 \times 6'$) into position over the framework, the builder clamps one or two edges and fastens them down with tack welds. Then with powerful clamps, purchases, bars, and much ingenuity, the metalworker begins to bend the plate little by little until, after several hours or a day's work, the plate is pulled and pushed into its final curve.

I remember watching a builder named Alex Jacubenko at work in Sausalito, California. "A steel plate is like a woman," he joked. "It will yield only to a stronger mind and a superior force." Then Alex would grunt a little as he wrestled a hydraulic jack into position against a heavy piece of steel.

After all the plates are tacked into place, they are welded together into a structure of tremendous strength, the only sort of hull that has a real chance on a coral reef. The decks can be made of steel (heavy) or plywood (lighter). Poor building techniques or light plating sometimes results in hulls whose topsides look like the rib cage of a hungry horse. However, reasonable plating thicknesses and good work can produce a handsome hull even without the use of fillers (which generally fall off after the yacht leaves the boatyard).

Unprotected steel rusts quickly. It needs to be sandblasted or cleaned with acid, and zinc-sprayed or painted with zinc compounds, followed with an epoxy or tar-based paint system. The metal on the *inside* of a steel hull also needs careful cleaning and attention; otherwise, rust and corrosion will destroy the hull from the inside out. It's a good idea to make the frames and deck beams of flat-bar stock (erected on edge) instead of angle iron or T-bar stock because at a stroke this scheme eliminates hundreds of impossible-to-protect metal faces. In a few areas where rust is a problem, builders use stainless steel: for chainplates, the top of the bulwarks (underneath a wooden rail cap), winch bases, and around the windlass where the anchors are handled and the paint gets chipped.

A builder must be careful not to mix metals during construction. It's unwise, for example, to use bronze through-hull fittings because galvanic action—which affects any two nearby dissimilar metals immersed in an electrolyte—begins at once in salt water. The steel hull, "the giver" or less noble metal, begins to decay, and in time, holes will be eaten in the plating next to the bronze fittings, or "the takers." (Steel hulls made today generally have iron or plastic valves.) It's customary to attach small sacrificial plates of zinc to the propeller shaft and any underwater fittings made of metal different from the hull. The zincs, being anodic, or least noble, are eaten away before the underwater fittings. It's simple to replace the zincs during a haulout.

These points suggest that a steel hull requires a lot of maintenance. This is true to some extent, but if a builder pays attention to the things I mentioned above and the owner keeps current with painting, the upkeep should be little more than that of a carvel-planked wooden hull of comparative size.

Because of their weight, steel yachts are usually designed as heavy-displacement yachts and require large rigs for good performance. Their advantage is great strength. The bottom of the keel can be made of 1-inch steel plate if you wish; the heavy plate acts as both ballast and an indestructible bumper. A steel hull is easy and fast to repair because you can find competent welders all over the world. The metallic shell has watertight integrity, and an owner has no problems at all with shipworm.

Many yachtsmen are wary of steel yachts. This is unfortunate because properly handled, steel is an excellent building material. I've seen many steel yachts that have the appearance of molded fiberglass vessels. Certainly with the costs of yachts escalating to incredible heights, steel may come into more favor, particularly for yachts of medium and heavy displacement more than 40 feet in length.

In Holland, the clever designers at E. G. van de Stadt have come up with a simplified multichine hull based on four longitudinal pieces on each side. Such a hull comes close to one with rounded sections but can be built quickly and at reduced cost. (See overleaf.)

The problem with hard-chine construction for amateur builders has always been the accurate lofting and cutting out of the side pieces. If this work is sloppy, the result is slipshod construction with wavy lines, uneven welding surfaces, and a terrible appearance. With computers, however, the Dutch designers have been able to plot the shape of each hull piece with great precision. Then, using the computer files, a specialist shop can cut out the plates with a laser device to an accuracy of $\frac{1}{2}$ millimeter or 0.019 inch (slightly more than $\frac{1}{64}$"). Reference lines for the bulkheads, floors, engine bed, keel position, and various reinforcements can be marked on the plates at the same time. An amateur builder can buy a kit of these parts. The assembly is quick and the building times can be measured in weeks instead of months. Such hulls can be built in steel, aluminum, or marine plywood. The same computer technique can be adapted to bulkheads and interior furniture cut from sheets of plywood or solid wood. Cleverly used, this technology makes it possible to reduce waste and, incredibly, even to match grain patterns.

ALUMINUM

Aluminum weighs only 34 percent as much as steel, and the alloy generally used for boatbuilding stays quite free of rust and corrosion. It's less strong, however, so designers specify greater thicknesses, often 1.66 times that of steel. Even so, the net saving in weight is a significant 44 percent or so.

The alloy used for boatbuilding is generally grade 6061, which contains small

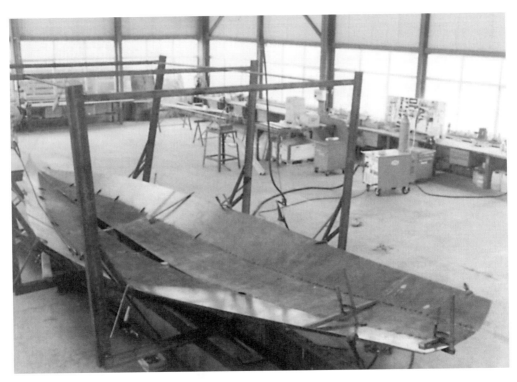

A new steel hull in 15 days? These three photographs show part of the quick assembly method of constructing a multichine hull developed by E. G. van de Stadt of Wormerveer, Holland. The engineers use a computer to calculate the templates for the eight side and bottom pieces for the hull. Not only can these shell pieces be plotted with remarkable precision, but the deck, coachroof, cockpit, bulkheads, engine beds, floors, and so on can be drawn at the same time. Even reference lines for joining the separate pieces can be marked on each part. Specialized firms use plasma torches that follow the computer templates to cut the parts to exact sizes. Because of the accuracy of each piece, a shell with fair lines can be built without frames. Assembly is quick, and an extremely strong basic hull can be constructed in a few weeks. This hull has three chines per side.

amounts of magnesium and silicon. Naval architect Tom Colvin, who has much experience with aluminum and used it for his personal cruising yacht *K'ung Fu-ste*, writes that "it is extremely easy to work with and requires very little maintenance."[6]

Fabrication is similar to building with steel except that curved sections of the hull plating are often formed with simple roller devices. Aluminum can be welded with special equipment and seems ideal for yacht hulls. For a 45-foot vessel, designers generally specify $5/16$-inch plating for the topsides, with lighter material for the decks and increasingly heavier stock in the underwater areas.

A typical 34-foot design in steel displaces 11,900 pounds. In aluminum or wood, the same boat displaces 9,900 pounds and requires an increase in ballast from 4,000 to 4,400 pounds.

Aluminum's main drawbacks are higher cost and the greater expense of welding. However, these items are partially offset by easier fabrication and less rigorous painting requirements than for steel. A downside consideration is that few boatyards are set up to repair aluminum vessels. Note that in all parts of the world outside the United States, this lightweight metal is called *aluminium* (with an extra *i*) and is pronounced *al-u-MINN-e-um*.

In the early 1950s, Tom and Ann Worth circumnavigated in *Beyond*, a Laurent Giles–designed 43-foot cutter that was constructed of riveted Birmabright, an aluminum alloy. For a long time, aluminum was used mostly for large, custom racing yachts. However in the last few years, two sets of my friends—Sally Schroeder and Craig and Linda McKee—have had aluminum yachts built in Holland. So far, both report complete satisfaction.

In good hands, an aluminum hull can be a thing of great beauty, besides being lightweight, tight, and dry. (One owner reports using a whisk broom in the bilge.) It's possible to skip deck and topside painting altogether, though these areas are normally painted for cosmetic reasons (after careful degreasing and acid etching). Paint with lead, copper, or mercury compounds must not be used. Tin-based antifouling paint is generally put on the bottom.

Sound tends to reverberate in metal-hulled vessels ("tin drums"), and condensation can be annoying. To deal with these problems, builders usually insulate steel and aluminum hulls with a few inches of fireproof, sound-deadening polyurethane material.

Most sailors know that removing a stainless steel bolt from an aluminum mast can be a daunting business. This is because electrons flow from the aluminum (the anode, or giver), which corrodes and seizes the threads of the stainless bolt (the cathode, or receiver). The process is *galvanic corrosion*. Similarly, the owner of an aluminum yacht should studiously avoid bronze and copper plumbing parts and bronze deck fittings. If mixing metals is unavoidable, a good procedure is to place a

Aluminum is strong and lightweight and can be easily cut with a band saw and formed into complex shapes. On this hull, temporary girders have been tacked into place to maintain a smooth hull during welding. Aluminum topsides are sometimes left bare, although they are usually painted for aesthetic reasons. Copper bottom paint causes a galvanic couple between the copper and aluminum, so bottom paints with tin or arsenic are generally used. Care needs to be taken with electric wiring and exposure to steel docks and shore power. In spite of these problems, aluminum is popular for custom hulls because of its strength, light weight, and freedom from rust.

thin plastic or rubber gasket or Tufnol washers and sleeves or a special compound between, say, a stainless steel winch and an aluminum cockpit coaming to isolate the metals. Builders using aluminum customarily slip a thin plastic sleeve between the stainless steel engine shaft and the aluminum alloy propeller.

An excellent practical solution to problems of mixed metals is to put a little anhydrous lanolin on both the bolt or fitting and its mounting hole. You can buy a pound of anhydrous lanolin from a pharmacy for twenty dollars. It will last you for the rest of your life, besides being a good hand cream.

A second problem, *electrolysis*, is the corrosion caused by stray electrical currents seeking a ground. This can be serious in a steel yacht and catastrophic in an aluminum hull, whose electrical wiring must be faultless. Most engineers favor a well-insulated two-wire, nongrounded system. Taking aboard electric power from the shore must be done with care.

"Confusion often exists between electrolytic and galvanic corrosion," writes naval architect Nigel Warren. The difference is quite simple: galvanic corrosion is caused by an electric current generated by two different metals in a conducting medium such as salt water (a seawater battery). Electrolytic corrosion, or electrolysis, is caused by a current from an *external* source, often the boat's battery or a shore supply.

"The current that causes electrolytic action is called 'stray current' and usually emanates from a poorly installed electrical circuit or a bad earthing arrangement—on power tools or a radio for instance. . . . " continues Warren. "The rate of electrolytic corrosion can be quite frightening because the stray current may be anything from a trickle (because of damp, for instance) to a deluge from a short circuit; there is no inherent limitation as with galvanic corrosion."[7]

You can often spot an aluminum yacht when she comes into a harbor or marina because the captain invariably hangs a zinc on a wire (grounded to the hull via a big alligator clip) over the side at the bow and the stern. Dangling a zinc in the water and connecting the wire is easy and takes only a minute. The zincs are more active than the aluminum of the hull and will help protect the underwater plating. If after a few weeks the captain notices that his zincs are disappearing, he can replace them or move the boat elsewhere.

Incidentally, using one or more zincs in a crowded harbor is a good plan for *all* vessels, no matter what the hull material. These problems with metal corrosion are not new. A century ago when a giant New York racing yacht with an all-bronze hull (!) was moored with a group of its rivals (perhaps with iron cables to a common iron buoy), the other yacht captains began to complain that their underwater iron was disappearing.

To sum up: aluminum is excellent for yacht hulls, but like sex when you're sixteen, you should take a few precautions. P.S. Don't tie up an aluminum yacht alongside a metal dock or steel pilings for the winter.

FERRO-CEMENT

A few years back there was a great flutter of excitement about *ferro-cement* hull construction. In one system, frames of iron pipe are erected on a metal backbone. Longitudinals of $\frac{1}{4}$-inch iron rods (or high-tensile steel) are tacked into place about every 4 inches from the keel to the bulwarks to make the hull form. Then layers of square welded mesh (or chicken wire) are laid over the hull on both the inside and the outside and tied to one another and to the longitudinal metal rods with thousands of small wires. The entire hull is then plastered with a dense, cement-rich concrete mix.

This all sounds fast and cheap, but the amount of handwork is enormous. Care is necessary with the lofting, the setting up of the frames, and at every other step.

The plastering is critical and expensive, and unless a first-class hull results, the amateur builder will be quite disappointed and own a product that is not only unsatisfying but completely unsalable.

Ferro-cement yachts tend to be real icebreakers. They often weigh a good deal more than their designers and builders admit, and the sailing performance suffers because the vessel is under-rigged for her weight. Because of its inherent heaviness, ferro-cement construction is best for large yachts, say 45 to 55 feet long. In particular, ferro-cement decks and bulkheads are disastrous because of their great weight, which robs the usual iron ballast (lead is better) of much of its effect. The desperate novice owner then installs a big engine and large fuel tanks, whose weight handicaps the sailing even more.

A ferro-cement hull must be insulated for cold-weather sailing; painting is not easy, and sometimes the wavy lines in a hull are enough to make even the strong weep. It's important to get complete penetration of the metal armature when the vessel is plastered; otherwise the hull will be in trouble from the beginning.

To guard against voids, uneasy builders often drill hundreds of holes and pump in epoxy or grout under pressure. The sum of these various problems frequently overwhelms amateur builders; many have abandoned their ferro-cement projects in fields and city parks and along highways.

In spite of these difficulties, a ferro-cement hull built by an expert can take an owner a long way. The voyages of Bob and Nancy Griffith in their 53-foot *Awahnee* were exemplary, although the hull was later fiberglassed to reduce rust bleeding, cracking, and peeling. Over the years I have seen beautiful ferro-cement yachts from New Zealand, Canada, and England. All, however, were constructed by experts who would have done a good job in any medium.

Naval architect Bruce Bingham, who made an intensive study of ferro-cement and even wrote a book on the subject, has been very critical:

> When it gets down to laying mesh, applying rods, twisting wires and fairing out the ferro-cement armature, the inexperienced amateur may be in for a further shock. The process takes untold patience, much more than the proponents dare to admit. A comparable strip-planked hull, for instance, may be constructed and faired in about one fourth the time required for ferro-cement, and a one-off fiberglass hull can usually be completed in slightly more than half the time of ferro-cement, using a male mold process. Aluminum construction is well beyond the amateur capability, but construction of a hard chine plywood or steel hull can still beat ferro-cement on the time scale.[8]

Ferro-cement building—which at one time may have had a reasonable future—suffered enormously from the misleading publicity of a few unscrupulous promoters. They implied (in magazine advertisements that should never have been printed) that a beginner could easily build a yacht with ferro-cement that could sail around the world. Many gullible people dutifully bought plans, building materials, engines, and so on, often from the promoters, and started construction. Perhaps 1 in 500 completed his dream yacht, but the other 499 hopefuls lost everything, including years of time and lots of money.

At the beginning of this chapter, I wrote that the cost of a hull is roughly 20 percent of the total budget no matter what the hull is made of. A saving of 10 or 20 percent on hull costs is really an economy of only 2 to 4 percent on the cost of the finished boat. The other 80 percent goes to the ballast, mast, rigging, interior woodwork, tanks, winches, anchors, engine, sails, and so forth. However, according to the promoters, all the round-the-world dreamers needed were a few bits of iron pipe, some iron rods, a little chicken wire, and a few bags of cement. Ridiculous!

In the 1950s and 1960s, another promoter, who was pushing trimarans, promised the same sort of pie in the sky. A born salesman who could have sold ice to Eskimos, Arthur Piver claimed that with a few sheets of plywood, a little glue, and a few odds and ends that you probably have in your garage, you could put together a multihull in which you could sail off into the blue and retire from the world.*

This was manifestly untrue, as many innocent people discovered after wasting large amounts of time and money. It's not possible to build any sort of reasonable yacht with bits and scraps unless you're resourceful and ingenious to an extraordinary degree and are willing to put up with considerable discomfort and hardship. It's notable that Piver didn't go around the world in one of his vessels, nor did the ferro-cement promoters.

Though there are some first-class ferro-cement yachts around, the boats in general have such a poor reputation (heavy, slow, hard to fix, abysmal resale value) that most yacht brokers, surveyors, and insurers won't touch them with a boat hook. In general, ferro-cement yachts have faded away, not because the hull scheme is inherently bad, but because hype and false promises poisoned the name. It's a shame, because they were overpromoted to the gullible, who suffered.

Naval architect Bill Garden got so fed up with ferro-cement boats that in the budgets he prepared, he cynically included demolition and burial costs, including a bottle of whiskey for the bulldozer driver and a box of grass seed for the back garden after the abandoned monster was broken up and buried.

Next: the fiberglass revolution.

---

*Arthur Piver disappeared in 1965 after setting out on an ocean voyage in one of his trimarans from a port in Southern California.

How a little artistic endeavor helps the look of a yacht! Without this cleverly designed red stripe and the name of the boat, Ia Ora *would be just another white hull in the harbor. But the graceful lines and sweep of the stripe and integrated name make this aluminum-hulled French boat distinctive and unique.*

3

THE MAGIC PLASTIC

According to Dan Spurr's fine book *Heart of Glass*, the first fiberglass boat was not an instant discovery, like Alexander Graham Bell's telephone or the polio vaccine of Dr. Jonas Salk. Instead, it took many people and companies years of experimenting and tinkering with exotic glues and resins (urea formaldehyde, for instance) and all sorts of reinforcing materials (cotton cloth, brown paper, unbleached muslin) before the dream of a plastic boat turned into a real product.

The magic moment, says Spurr, may have been in 1942 when a research engineer

Myth of Malham was designed by Laurent Giles for John Illingworth and built lightly but strongly of double-skinned mahogany with intricate internal framing of metal and wood. Launched in 1947, with a 50 percent ballast ratio and without an engine, she was the terror of ocean racing for 15 years. I wonder how she would go with today's high-tech sails instead of the canvas of half a century ago. Here she slides along in smooth water in the south of England with her cutter rig pulling to perfection. Note the double hatches in the companionway and how the staysail is sheeted inside the upper and intermediate shrouds. Her measurements are 39 feet overall with a waterline length of 33.5 feet, a beam of 9.3 feet, and a draft of 7.2 feet.

named Ray Greene received a gallon of cold-setting polyester resin from the American Cyanamid Company. At the time, Greene was working on experimental rocket tubes for the U.S. Army using fiberglass products from the Owens Corning Company. Greene tried mixing the resin with glass fibers and—presto!—the era of the long-dreamed-of instant boat was born.[9]

The first boats to utilize glass fibers and polyester resin on a commercial basis were a series of 14-foot skiffs built in 1944 by the Universal Molded Products Company of Bristol, Virginia. By 1948 Ray Greene was constructing 8-foot fiberglass dinghies and a 16-foot daysailer called the Rebel.

Greene sold five thousand Rebels and thought he'd discovered boatbuilders' heaven. Think of the rewards! Plastic boats could be built quickly and cheaply; they were strong and light and free from the rot and leaks of wood. Perhaps plastic boats would last forever. Maybe Greene could sell a Rebel to every family in the United States!

But according to veteran boatbuilder and author Allan Vaitses, in his book *The Fiberglass Boat Repair Manual*,[10] the predecessors of the fiberglass boat were the glass-fiber radar domes molded by the General Electric Company toward the end of World War II. A man named Carl Beetle, whose family had built whaleboats for generations, saw the radar domes and decided to transfer the technique to small vessels. Beetle introduced one-piece molded fiberglass boats at the New York Boat Show during the winter of 1946–47.

The truth is that both authors are correct. Man had dreamed of one-piece, leak-proof boats for centuries, but like alchemists trying to make gold from iron, no one knew how to do it. During the early 1940s a number of experimenters found that liquid resin, when catalyzed with heat and pressure, becomes a solid, almost indestructible material. But as Vaitses writes, "It is not very impressive, being rather brittle, and it is hard to imagine what anyone would want with a material physically similar to amber-colored hard candy, yet unfit to eat."[11]

However, when this useless resin is brushed into a bundle of floppy strands of ultrathin glass fibers and cured, the resin binds the fibers into a tough material with more tensile strength for its weight than steel. In a twinkling you have a remarkable new substance. It doesn't rust. It doesn't rot. It's strong and tough, and it lasts for a very long time.

My introduction to fiberglass was in 1958 when I met a builder named Fred Coleman who was making the 41-foot Bounty sloop (or yawl) of designer Phillip

I took this photograph in 1958, but it could just as well have been yesterday. Note the usual problems going to weather with a 150 percent genoa in a 15- to 20-knot headwind. The crew is busy reefing the mainsail. A little water is flying around, and one man is without boots. It's encouraging to see that the Phillip Rhodes design has no weather helm. It's unusual for the helmsman to kneel.

Rhodes at a company called Aeromarine Plastics. The glass-reinforced plastic boats were constructed in a beat-up, corrugated iron Quonset hut on the waterfront of Sausalito, California. The company seemed a hand-to-mouth operation, but the hulls were smooth and impressive and the builder even made a few fiberglass masts. I wrote a story about the new Bounty for *Popular Science* magazine and took the photograph on the previous page of a Bounty under sail.

From time to time I see Bounties sailing. They may need painting, and some of the fittings may be a little shabby and out-designed, but the vessels are still afloat and have probably outlived their original owners. When I think back to 1958 and reflect on the Bounty, the remarkable thing is how similar the vessel is to yachts built today. Of course there have been improvements. The interiors, finishing details, and engineering numbers of yachts constructed in the 21st century are very much better. But from a boat length away, you'd be hard-pressed to tell the difference. A slicked-up Bounty would fit right into this year's Annapolis or London boat shows.

Fiberglass vessels are constructed of thin glass filaments that are made into various kinds of fabrics. When a hull is laid up, usually in a female mold, these fabrics, one or two layers at a time, are saturated with a liquid material, generally polyester resin that has been catalyzed with small amounts of methyl ethyl ketone peroxide (MEKP). You can compare a fiberglass laminate with the steel and cement of reinforced concrete. In a laminate the amount of strengthening glass filament runs about 30 percent, a good deal more than the percentage of steel in reinforced concrete.

Fiberglass (often called FRP for fiber-reinforced plastic) is a remarkable material. It is strong and stable, unaffected by marine borers, and in heavier thicknesses will stop bullets fired from a gun. The material has a useful life of forty years (perhaps much more) and is ideal for molding complex shapes that are difficult and costly to construct in wood. FRP is light (in suitable design and execution), and repairs are easy. You need a dry environment, heat, and a disk sander or rasp to grind and taper the edges of the repair to maximize the bonding area.

Some 90 percent of all U.S. sailing yachts use fiberglass for their hulls. For cruising yachts worldwide, the figure is less—my guess is 60 percent—though the number is increasing. There is much talk of fiberglass, but away from the United States you see many wooden- and metal-hulled yachts.*

Fiberglass also has drawbacks. The materials are expensive, and FRP weighs about 95 pounds per cubic foot. (Hence the emphasis on thin, well-engineered con-

---

*The May 2000 issue of the Dutch magazine *Zeilen* surveyed 134 yachts between 28 and 80 feet that were sailing in the Caribbean. Fifty-three percent were FRP, 26 percent steel, 9 percent aluminum, 8 percent wood, 3 percent ferro-cement, and 1 percent composite (glass over wood).

If you think that fiberglass is the ultimate hull material, you might ponder this photograph of a wrecked yacht on the Caribbean island of Tortola. Two three-strand anchor or mooring lines have sawed right through the supposedly impregnable hull. Could the fiberglass layup have been poorly done and resin-starved? I find it amazing that the lines didn't chafe through before slicing into the hull.

struction.) The usual polyester resin is neither fireproof nor completely waterproof. Abrasion resistance is poor. The work is a messy, smelly business. When you use a disk sander on fiberglass, the resulting dust is extremely irritating, and the hell of fiberglass itch is well known. Generally, a costly female mold is needed for a hull, although one-offs can be made with simple male molds. Finally, an FRP hull and deck need to be carefully insulated to prevent condensation if the vessel is to be used in cold weather.

In addition to fiber materials made of superfine strands of glass, there are light and heavy cloths and rovings constructed of Kevlar or carbon threads that are used where high strength or other properties are required. Kevlar, a proprietary invention of Dupont, is well known because of its use in bulletproof vests and super-strong rope. Carbon fibers add impressive strength to a hull or mast and are sometimes used in place of metal castings in winch bases.

There are several kinds of resins employed with these materials. The most common is polyester resin, which is used in 90 percent of marine work for both new work and repairs. Polyester resin is divided into two types: finishing resin and laminating or air-inhibited resin. Finishing resin is the better choice when you're applying a few layers of fiberglass or repairing a hole in a dinghy. The finishing resin has wax in it that floats to the surface as it cures and creates a hard surface that you can sand. (If you want to add additional fiberglass to a glass surface that's already hard, you will have to sand or grind the surface to ensure a good bond.)

Laminating resin is the choice for bigger jobs and dries to a sticky, nonsandable surface. Unlike with finishing resin, you can add additional layers to the surface of laminating resin without sanding or grinding. You can make finishing resin from laminating resin by adding a few drops of a widely sold wax solution called tack-free additive (TFA) that comes in little bottles.

While polyester resin is good, *epoxy resin* is a superior bonding material for both fiberglass and wood. Epoxy makes stronger bonds and is significantly more resistant to penetration and degradation by water. The best-known epoxy is the West System product made by the Gougeon Brothers company of Bay City, Michigan, which also produces excellent repair manuals for boatowners. Most cruising yachts carry a quart or two of West epoxy with both regular and slow hardeners, which are used at different temperatures. This glue—which keeps indefinitely—is excellent for small repairs where bonding is a problem or the surfaces are slightly damp. Once you begin with an epoxy, however, you must continue with epoxy. While epoxy will bond to underlying polyester, you cannot glass to an epoxy surface with polyester resin, nor does polyester gelcoat work over epoxy.

The extra utility of epoxy comes at a price. In 2003, a quart of West epoxy and hardener cost $39, compared with a quart of polyester finishing resin and catalyst at $11, about one-quarter as much. Vinylester resin, often favored in new construction because of its greater resistance (relative to polyester) to moisture penetration and blistering, cost $16 a quart. All are much cheaper in bulk.

A problem with epoxies is that they are more toxic and cause skin rashes on some people. After long exposure, a small percentage of boatbuilders become allergic to these substances and are forced to use other kinds of adhesives. It helps to wear disposable gloves and throwaway clothing and to work outdoors or in a well-ventilated place.

Let's walk quickly through the construction phase of a 35-footer.

These days practically all plastic boats are built in a female mold. The first step in making a mold is to construct the hull of the yacht in wood. This can be done quickly and cheaply by making a strip-planked hull of inferior pine, nailing and gluing it together, and plastering it with fairing compound to make a supersmooth, fair hull that faithfully follows the drawings of the naval architect. This wooden hull is called a plug.

Shipwrights coat the plug with wax and then lay large amounts of fiberglass and exterior reinforcements over the plug to make a rigid female mold. The plug is discarded, often by forcing it up and out of the mold with water pressure. The resulting mold is carefully polished and waxed and mounted on wheels or rollers so it can be moved around the shop. Sometimes the mold is made in two halves that are bolted together so that a newly laid-up fiberglass hull can be removed by taking the mold apart.

To begin a new sailing yacht, an expert sprays the inside of the mold with a thick layer (20 mils or ½ mm) of gelcoat. Fiberglass hulls and decks are almost always coated with gelcoat, a tough, lustrous, pigmented polyester resin that's available in white and a dozen attractive colors. The gelcoat wraps the hull and deck in a handsome, highly polished finish that protects the surfaces from the weather, sun, and ultraviolet rays. Gelcoat will last fifteen to twenty years on the topsides, depending on how it is treated.

The glass workers or laminators then climb inside the mold and press a layer of

A workman laying up a new Valiant 42 hull at the factory in Gordonville, Texas. Isophthalic resin is mixed in 1-gallon increments (with the catalyzer dyed for proper mix control) and is used with alternate layers of mat and roving fiberglass. This is the traditional scheme of fiberglass construction and has hardly changed in forty-five years. This is a big hull—42 feet long, with a beam of 12.75 feet and a draft of 6 feet. Usually all the fiberglass materials for a single hull are cut to length and marked. Then they're weighed as a unit to make certain that nothing has been left out.

light fiberglass cloth against the gelcoat. They work from a scaffolding lowered into the hull. Or they may incline the mold or take it apart and lay up the hull in halves.

The workers saturate the first layer of cloth with catalyzed resin and use small metal rollers to work out all the air bubbles. Then they begin the main construction. This is a layer of heavy mat—a material with short fibers in random directions—followed by a layer of roving, which is bundles of continuous fibers woven into a sort of coarse, superthick cloth. Mat has superior bonding properties but moderate strength. Roving is a very strong material, but its bonding qualities are poor. The workers put in alternating layers of mat and roving and saturate each layer with resin and roll out any air bubbles until a suitable hull thickness is built up, say from $\frac{5}{16}$ to $\frac{5}{8}$ inch, depending on the location.

Even with fans and air ducts, it's unpleasant to work with strong chemicals and irritating glass materials deep inside a hull. For this reason and because it's difficult to supervise workers you can't see, some companies build fiberglass hulls in two halves that are later joined with many layers of mat and roving. Two-piece hulls are usually strengthened with substantial athwartship floors, which are a good idea for one-piece hulls as well. A few custom builders, such as Frers and Cibels in Buenos Aires, construct a longitudinal I-beam inside the hull along the entire length of the stem, keel, and sternpost to reinforce the hull for high rigging tensions. If the design uses a fin keel, floors are necessary to take the keel bolts.

In any case, some sort of interior structure is necessary for a foundation for the interior joinery; such structures might as well serve as useful strengthening members. This may sound obvious, but a surprising number of builders construct the hulls and interiors separately and merely tack the furniture in place instead of strongly glassing in settee fronts, partial bulkheads, shelves, and so on.

Some builders believe that a hull together with all its stiffeners and reinforcements should be molded at one time (primary bonding) and claim that it is stronger. They believe that glasswork that comes later—even though the surfaces are roughed up by grinding and done by experts (so-called secondary bonding)—is less satisfactory. However, I've personally seen many major hull repairs done with secondary bonding and polyester resin (epoxy is better) that were completely satisfactory.

In the United States there's a phobia about hull thickness ("How thick is she?"), which, though important, is not the whole answer. Fiberglass is a costly and heavy

A fiberglass grid installation for a 46-foot Beneteau yacht. This lightweight grid, which is bonded to the full with polyester putty and FRP tape, greatly strengthens the lower hull and forms a base for the interior bulkheads, joinery, and engine. Additional advantages are a better distribution of keel and rigging loads and a cleaner interior and bilge area. It's been customary to make such grids from wood, but they're heavy and subject to rot in the damp environment. The downside is that a mold for such a fiberglass structure is difficult and expensive to make and is only effective costwise for a series production.

material in massive layups. The hull, of course, varies from the deck to the keel, but as I said earlier, an average topside thickness of $\frac{5}{16}$ or $\frac{3}{8}$ inch (keel $\frac{5}{8}$ to $\frac{3}{4}$"), plus floors, internal stiffening, and a sturdy hull-to-deck joint seem adequate for the size of boats we're discussing. Naval architects have taught us that thin, better-made laminates are more satisfactory than thick, resin-rich layups. Our yachts can be lighter and sail faster with smaller, easier-to-handle rigs.

Years ago a California company made a double-ended sloop called the Westsail 32 and in an unprecedented marketing blitz sold eight hundred boats. The hull was laid up in thicknesses approaching 1 inch (2 layers of gelcoat plus 12 layers of mat and roving). This made an extremely strong hull, much boasted of by owners, but the weight was excessive. ("A combination of armor plate and millstone," wrote one buyer.) The result was that these yachts sail poorly, particularly in light airs, even though naval architect Bill Crealock made a heroic effort to update and enlarge the rig.[12]

This is why a J-35 can sail figure eights around a Westsail 32. One is on the light side; the other is too heavy. An icebreaker needs a colossal rig to move her, and she's dead in light airs. For world cruisers and all their gear, we need a middle road.

Fiberglass yachts built in the United States generally have thick skins, bulkheads, and minimal internal framing. Vessels constructed in Europe and the United Kingdom tend to have thinner skins with more internal longitudinal and transverse stiffeners. Large, unsupported flat areas of a hull are vulnerable to oilcanning, and if an American-style hull is fractured, the damage can extend as far as a bulkhead. Internal framing and smaller panel sizes help localize damage and maintain the shape of the hull.

Internal framing is simple to install when the hull is molded. If $1\frac{1}{2}$-inch-diameter softwood dowels are sliced lengthwise, tacked in place to make a latticework of 12- or 15-inch squares, and covered with three or four layers of glass, the gain in hull rigidity is surprising. The bottom parts of a hull should have adequate floors. Lloyd's scantling rules specify a 9-inch-deep floor spaced every 16 inches for a 35-foot hull. Each floor should have two limber or drainage holes.

For areas that need to be extra strong, perhaps around the chainplates, rudder, mast partners, and keel, the naval architect may specify special materials such as unidirectional roving, biaxial or triaxial fabric, Kevlar cloth, S glass, or carbon fibers. If the weight of the hull is important, these high-strength materials may be employed throughout, though at considerable cost.

It's possible to fuse fiberglass materials together in a perfect bond by using a professional technique called vacuum bagging. In this procedure, the materials to be laminated are laid up, coated with resin, and covered with (1) a piece of nonstick release fabric and (2) a sheet of breather material (which keeps a slight air space between the air bag and the laminate). A clear plastic sheet is then placed over the work and the edges secured with a special mastic sealant. A hose from a vacuum pump is attached to the plastic sheet and the air underneath the plastic is drawn out. The result is that the atmosphere outside the plastic pushes down with a steady, uniform pressure of 14.7 pounds per square inch on every part of the plastic. This forces the materials together, squeezes out all air bubbles and excess resin, and produces a first-class laminate.

An even more exotic scheme employs fiberglass materials that are uniformly charged with resin (prepregs), kept refrigerated until use, and set off by heat. There have been amazing improvements in prepregs, core materials, and construction techniques. The high priest of all this is boatbuilder Eric Goetz (pronounced *Gertz*) of Bristol, Rhode Island, who has put together many America's Cup boats and racing one-offs. His costly, superlight boats are breathtaking in execution, but not in the real world of ordinary sailors and knockabout cruising boats.

Nevertheless, some of the ideas these high-tech experts come up with gradually filter down to the broader market. For example, Goetz molds chainplates of carbon fiber directly into the sides or deck of a hull when he builds a new yacht. At a stroke this eliminates fabricating, polishing, and installing separate stainless steel chainplates. This not only saves weight but eliminates a series of bolts and possible leaks. The carbon-fiber chainplates are strong enough to lift the entire yacht, and my guess is that their final cost is less. This is the sort of thing that the mass market builders may adopt.

But to return to our new hull in the mold. After the basic hull is completed, longitudinal stiffeners, perhaps athwartship floors, a shear clamp, engine mounts, and bulkheads are glassed into place. Because the new boat is "green" and not entirely rigid, it's a good idea to keep the boat in the mold for a day or two until the stiffeners and bulkheads have set up, so the hull will maintain the exact form of the mold. The metal chainplates are now installed to make it easy to lift the boat.

When the chain hoist is finally hooked up and the hull is taken from the mold, the new boat seems a miracle, particularly in a drab and colorless boat shop. Suddenly in front of you is a boat that's glossy and brilliant and almost seems alive in her gorgeous new coat. (Where will she go? Who will sail on her? What will she be named? How will she cleave through the seas?)

How could such a beauty be made from those dreary drums of chemicals and rolls of scratchy fibers? The finish looks even better than the paint on a new car or a refrigerator just out of the box. You can comb your hair in your shiny reflection on the side of the hull.

So far we've talked of single-skin fiberglass construction. Another popular FRP building scheme involves putting a core material between layers of fiberglass. The core material can be end-grain balsa or polyvinyl chloride (PVC) closed-cell foam produced by various companies. Three prominent brands of foam core are Airex, Klegecell, and Divinycell. Each material has different characteristics that the architect and builder balance against cost, durability, and convenience.

Generally in foam-core construction, a female mold is sprayed with gelcoat, as with single-skin building. Then a light outer skin of fiberglass is laminated into place. Next large sheets of flexible core material ($\frac{1}{2}$ to 1" thick) are glued to the laminate with resin. Finally, additional layers of mat and roving are laminated to the inside of the core. This results in a sandwich construction of, say, $\frac{5}{32}$ inch of glass on the outside, $\frac{1}{2}$ inch of core material, and $\frac{3}{32}$ inch of glass on the inside. More glass is always put on the outside of the sandwich because of the bangs and bumps that all boats receive.

Because of the thickness of the sandwich, the fiberglass laminates resist bending strains very well because one skin is under compression while the opposite skin is under tension. The core takes the shear stress.

"Cores make the hull of the boat stiff and light," writes naval architect Eric Sponberg. "Lightness means less weight to move through the water, so the speed is faster. In addition, cores insulate the hull against heat and cold, dampen vibration from slamming seas, and deaden the sound of chugging engines. Thanks to cores, boats have better performance and enhanced creature comfort."[13]

The downside of sandwich construction is that through-hull and through-deck fastening areas need a solid layup, metal spacers, or structural epoxies to keep bolts, for example, from crushing the foam and allowing water to leak into the sandwich. Properly dealing with fastenings and fastening areas demands builders of great integrity; if water migrates into a cored hull made of end-grain balsa and saturates the wood, the balsa rots and turns into a sort of white Jell-O in the way of the leak. If water saturation continues, the entire hull can be ruined and the owner's investment destroyed. Yacht surveyors know all about balsa-cored hulls and take fiendish delight in telling one horror story after another.

Owners of vessels with fiberglass sandwich construction should be aware of these fastening problems, learn how to preserve watertight integrity when they add new fittings or equipment, and be on the lookout for possible leaks into the laminate. If owners can't handle these problems, they should either hire a professional to deal with through-deck and through-hull issues or choose another kind of hull construction.

In spite of these fastening problems, however, there are thousands of balsa-cored hulls in daily use with complete success.

The decks of fiberglass yachts are commonly built with balsa-core sandwich construction to give a more solid feel to a person walking on deck. Balsa core also stops ceiling condensation in the cabin by adding a layer of insulation. Unfortunately, because of marginal construction practices and careless owners who—without thinking—drill holes to mount tracks and blocks and a dozen things more, a whole mini-industry now repairs saturated balsa-core decks on sailing and power yachts. Unlike cored hulls, decks are easier to repair because they are essentially flat and you can get at both sides (well, almost).

Sandwich construction is also good for one-off hulls that are made over male molds (erected upside down for ease in working). In one building scheme, sheets of core material are bent, fitted, and fastened to the mold. Then the outer fiberglass is applied and faired. Next the hull is turned over, the male mold is removed, and glass, frames, and bulkheads are added to the inside of the new hull. The keel area is usually strengthened by laying up solid FRP. This all sounds slick and fast, but the downside is that it takes hundreds of hours of tedious filling and sanding and painting to achieve a finish equal to that of gelcoat sprayed into a female mold.

Note that foam-core sandwich construction isn't too far from a strip-planked wooden hull (of cedar or mahogany) with fiberglass glued (and sometimes mechanically fastened as well) to each side. During the 1994–95 BOC round-the-world race, Australian David Adams sailed a high-powered 50-footer (with an 82' mast) based on a strip-planked hull of light cedar with Kevlar and E-glass on each side. The hull proved to be remarkably stiff and well able to cope with the high loads of the lofty rig.[14]

Still another way to build over a male mold is to use C-Flex, a patented material that uses long, thin glass rods within a fiberglass fabric. The C-Flex "planks" come in long rolls and can be bent in two directions to follow compound curves. Again, this technique is somewhat analogous to strip-plank construction in wood.[15]

The latest buzzword in the fiberglass industry is the Seemann Composites Resin Infusion Molding Process, or SCRIMP. This program attempts to combine easy layup with vacuum bagging and results in a high-strength fiber content of 50 percent or more, plus a much-improved environment for boatyard people, who can work without masks, throwaway clothing, and breathing terrible chemicals all day long.[16]

SCRIMP begins with a female mold and the usual spraying of gelcoat. Then workers fit in all the precut fiberglass materials for the outer laminate, layer after layer, *but without any resin* (except for a little local adhesive to hold things in place). Next the core material, if any, is laid in place *with no resin*. Finally, the inner laminate fiberglass, *still dry*, is arranged layer by layer over the core.

Perforated resin-infusion tubes are now placed over the work and their delivery lines are led to drums of resin. Release fabric, breather material, and heavy plastic material are laid over the entire dry laminate and resin delivery lines and are sealed around the edges. Vacuum hoses are connected to the plastic bag and the pump is turned on. As the vacuum increases, an operator opens the resin delivery valves.

Freshly catalyzed resin flows into the dry laminate until it is saturated. The excess resin runs off into channels along the edges of the mold.

This all sounds like a fabricator's nightmare, and it is, but once working, the results are remarkable: a tightly compressed cored or solid high-strength lamination with neither air pockets nor excess resin, plus approval from government air-quality experts concerned with worker safety. The core material needs a special coating that allows a good bond but prevents the resin from filling the core. In addition, SCRIMP requires a proprietary compound to ensure the flow of resin to all parts of the layup to prevent any dry areas.*

Large numbers of fiberglass yachts were built in the 1960s and 1970s. By the 1980s and 1990s these yachts were 20 years old. Many (not all) of these vessels began to be affected with underwater blisters, particularly as the protective gelcoat was knocked or broken or sanded through in places. The blisters appeared regardless of the make of the vessel but were more likely to occur in warmer waters. The experience of the builder seemed to make no difference. Expensive Hinckleys and Swans were not exempt.

The quick fix was to grind out the blisters, dry the area with heat lamps, then slap on an underwater epoxy (Marine-Tex, for example) and switch on the heat lamps again. The final step was to grind the area smooth and roll on bottom paint.

But what makes blisters in the first place? Why not treat the cause instead of the symptom? Blisters may result from beginning the layup of fiberglass too soon after spraying the gelcoat into a female mold. This may cause tiny bubbles of gas released from the drying gelcoat to be trapped between the gelcoat and the fiberglass laminate. Later in the hull's life, someone may sand the gelcoat and open many of these tiny bubbles. If the gelcoat is then painted with an impervious polyurethane or epoxy, each bubble may become a small blister. Thus arose one explanation of this complicated problem.[17] This was not the whole answer, however, because blisters developed in yachts that were built without any gelcoat at all.

A 1990 *Practical Sailor* magazine survey concluded that one boat in four would experience blisters in her lifetime. Blisters became such a serious industry-wide problem (worsened by rumors and false solutions) that desperate builders sought help from universities and research agencies. Even the Rhode Island state government got involved.

---

*Predictions are risky and crystal balls often shatter, but the next step after SCRIMP might be to use fiberglass materials that are pre-impregnated with resin, kept cool, and set off by heat. The material could be laid up dry, forced together by vacuum bagging, and the mold could be wheeled into a giant oven. This would eliminate 80 or 90 percent of resin handling, infusion pipes, mixing, and a lot of complication. Maybe a vacuum bag could have built-in heating wires to combine heat and pressure.

In time, investigators learned that polyester resin is very slightly porous. After a number of years of immersion, water can penetrate the outer layers of a fiberglass laminate. The problem then is not merely blisters, but potential destructive damage to the entire laminate.

"Blisters occur when water that has penetrated the laminate dissolves water soluble materials within the laminate and accumulates in voids or cavities below the gelcoat layer," says a recent West System study. "The solution of water and water soluble materials, through the process of osmosis, attracts more water to the cavities to try to dilute the solution. The pressure of the accumulating water enlarges the cavities to form gelcoat blisters."[18]

The liquid in blisters is an acidic fluid that can attack polyester resin throughout the laminate. Not only does the acid work to sever the chemical bonds that hold the resin matrix together, but it attacks the resin-to-fiber bonds. This process is called hydrolysis and can be disastrous to fiberglass if left unchecked. The researchers also found that water in the bilge and high humidity in the bilge area can cause water penetration of the laminate and blisters *from the inside out.* "It is important to keep the bilge as dry as possible," said the scientists. "We strongly recommend active ventilation in bilge areas with powered vents, especially on boats that have previously blistered."[19]

A discussion of blister and hydrolysis repair is beyond the scope of this book. Nevertheless, here are a few remarks on how experts would proceed.

The first step is to inspect the laminate by grinding several 5-inch-diameter patches through the gelcoat and looking for signs of hydrolysis (whitish fibers and laminate damage). If there are problem signs, then additional inspection patches are necessary. If widespread damage is apparent (I've seen 2 × 3' sheets of fiberglass delaminating on a Swan), the entire gelcoat must come off.

This can be done by grinding, but it takes considerable skill and may leave the hull uneven and bumpy. Blister cavities will need filling and fairing, and this can be a big undertaking. A second way to remove the gelcoat is by sandblasting. A third scheme is to remove the gelcoat by peeling. This is a professional process in which an electric or hydraulic head shaves the gelcoat. The peeler follows the contour of the hull and works something like a milling machine as the cutting head goes up and down the hull. The procedure is expensive, but it's often cost-effective because it leaves the hull smooth and fair.

After the gelcoat is removed, the hull should be sounded with a small hammer and visually inspected to locate voids and problem areas.

If the hull is damp or wet—as measured with a moisture meter—it needs to be thoroughly dried out. This is best done by putting the yacht in a shed, covering her with plastic sheets that extend to the floor, using infrared space heaters and dehumidifiers. This generally takes about two weeks, but the time can vary. As some yachts dry out, the soaked laminates produce astonishing amounts of water in the dehumidifiers, which often need to be emptied daily. In a warm, summery climate the vessel can simply be left outdoors. This is cheaper, but the drying process may take months. From time to time the hull will need to be washed to remove salts and chemicals that come to the surface.

Next the blister hollows, small and large voids, and hydrolysis damage will need to be dealt with. This is mostly routine filling, fiberglass patching, injecting epoxy into small areas with a syringe, and fairing. The hull should now be smooth and in excellent condition. Finally, a waterproof barrier coat is rolled over the entire bottom. This can be epoxy resin, vinylester resin, or a special two-part paint. These compounds often include proprietary additives to promote watertightness and durability. One company recommends five coats or more of overlapping layers so that the yacht ends up with a single tough waterproof blanket about 20 mils ($\frac{1}{2}$ mm) thick.

A full-blown osmosis job is a big deal and is best done by recommended yards that have special tooling and experts who will guarantee their work in writing for long periods. If you need such work, talk to a number of yards, ask for references, and *call the references*. Avoid fly-by-night operators who promise the moon at cut-rate prices.

When Margaret and I bought our present *Whisper* as a used boat in 1993, she had had at least one bottom job. Yet she sported a remarkable set of blisters. I learned that on the U.S. East Coast the yard with the best reputation for bottom work was Jamestown Boat Works in Jamestown, Rhode Island. In 1994 I took my problem to its manager, Jono Billings. In two months, Jono and his experts peeled off the gelcoat, dried out the hull, and put on layers of vinylester resin followed by fairing compound with more vinylester. When I got the yacht back, her bottom was as smooth as a glass bottle and fairer than when she was new. Jono warranted his work for five years. The cost was $7,875 ($225 a foot × 35 feet). So far (after nine years in the water) I have had no problems.

In the early 1990s, many builders began to use vinylester resin for new hull construction. Other boat makers roll on epoxy coatings after the hulls are built. Why not ensure watertightness by doing both? The time to take these steps is when the yacht is built, not years later when water has seeped into the laminate and remedial procedures are incredibly difficult and expensive. If you're buying a new boat and epoxy coatings are an optional extra at the factory, by all means have them put on.

Many new yachts are now sold with 10-year bottom warranties. With competition for sales, waterproof bottom materials will probably become standard and force a general upgrading of hull construction. I hope the problems of hydrolysis, blisters, and hull delamination belong to the past.

Years ago the Valiant Company of Seattle built yachts with fire-retardant resins. It was the only boatbuilder to do so, and advertised with much ballyhoo that you were safer in a Valiant 40 than other companies' boats. Unfortunately the additives used in the resin to restrict fire caused delamination problems. Disgruntled owners sued Valiant and eventually the company had to pay. Valiant was later sold to a builder in Texas who now makes excellent yachts with conventional materials and chemicals. The point of this story is that although fiberglass technology seems simple and direct, any deviation from the basic process—things that work well—is risky. Perhaps it's better for a buyer to stick to something that's been made for a few years.

Another consideration is the ballast arrangement. In my judgment the best ballast system by far is an external one-piece lead molding that's substantially bolted to a massive FRP layup or to heavy floors that are well glassed to the hull. If you go aground with such an exterior keel, the mass of lead takes much of the punishment. Inserting the lead *inside* the hull is simple, cheap, and quick, but much less satisfactory to the captain who sails the yacht in difficult places and may go aground occasionally.

The resistance of FRP to abrasion is poor, particularly if you put the full weight of the yacht on a small area of fiberglass. If you go aground with a fiberglass keel and are unfortunate enough to pound for a few hours, rocks will chew right through the fiberglass and reduce it to a useless hash. Such damage is tedious to repair when the yacht is hauled out because it's difficult to raise the keel high enough in the air to work on it easily. And if a place is hard to work on—no matter who does it—the repairs are liable to be marginal in an area that should be as strong and fair as possible. Nobody likes to grind copper paint and fiberglass above his head.

A grounded yacht is always in a chancy position; yet vessels with exterior lead or iron keels have escaped with only superficial dents and gouges. The sailor with a fiberglass hull with the ballast inside the keel molding is less fortunate.

If the ballast is inside the fiberglass molding, the builders should encapsulate and partition off this area from the rest of the yacht. This will ensure that if you knock a hole in the bottom of the fiberglass keel, the yacht will not fill with water. Interior lead blocks are usually cemented in place with a mixture of resin and sawdust or fibers of some kind to fill the entire cavity. However, the semiskilled workers who usually do this job sometimes leave large voids open to the bilge area. Then even a small hole or crack in the bottom area of the keel molding will allow water to run directly into the bilge and the interior, and the yacht will fill. The top of the keel molding should be closed off from the bilge area with heavy layers of glass. Since this area is largely out of sight and is soon covered by floor timbers and the cabin sole during construction, it tends to be forgotten and neglected.

Occasionally builders use lead shot or small bits of lead for ballast. I have heard of an unfortunate Englishman who punched a hole in the keel area of his vessel and lost his entire ballast, which ran out like watery soup. As I said earlier, builders use encapsulated ballast for only one reason: it's cheaper. There is much talk about keel bolts leaking, but substantial Monel or stainless steel bolts (you need fewer than a dozen) fastened through stout floors, heavy FRP, or both will not leak a drop if properly caulked at building time.

A second reason for favoring an external bolted-on keel is that the lead can help take the shocks and strains of haulouts. In some places, haulout cradles are rickety and ill-fitting. A block of lead 3 or 4 feet long gives a helpful margin for error if the yacht comes out of the water with the cradle in the wrong place.

In remote Pichidangui, Chile, the man in charge of the boatyard sent down a diver to check that the car on the marine railway was set correctly. Unfortunately it was not, and when the yacht, our first *Whisper*, came out of the water, the entire weight of the vessel rested on the edge of a thin steel brace that ran athwartships across the end of the marine railway car. Part of the fiberglass keel was crushed and cracked. It took a long time to dry the damaged area before I could grind out the broken fiberglass and lay up new material.

A third reason for preferring an exterior keel and keel bolts is that it's easy to fit one or two lifting eyes to the tops of several keel bolts. You can lead a stout cable from the eyebolts vertically through a skylight or overhead ventilator to the lifting hook of a crane. In many places a 25-ton (or more) crane is available that can easily lift a yacht for bottom painting. If copper paint is sprayed or rolled over a smooth, well-sanded bottom, it's possible to get a perfect job on the sides and the entire keel in one pass without having to move blocks and so on.

Such a lifting arrangement is ideal because no paint-gouging straps or cables go around the hull, and you dispense entirely with cumbersome marine railways. When we were in Callao, Peru, for example, there were several 50-ton cranes at the naval shipyard; no other haulout arrangement was available. In Buenos Aires the Argentine yachtsmen use this system to perfection and routinely haul their vessels for a two-hour scrub. I have seen yachts lifted similarly in Japan. Sometimes it is possible to get a friendly cargo ship captain to lift you on board in a perfectly calm harbor if the ship has no pressing business. The advantages for shipping a yacht are obvious.

These two chapters on boat construction have been long and tedious. We've seen that wood rots and steel rusts. That electricity can be fatal to aluminum, that ferrocement building is labor-intensive and mostly unsatisfactory, and that each year fiberglass construction gets more complicated and costly.

Which is best? You can make good and bad arguments for each building material. Just remember one thing: it's not the yacht, but what you do with your pride and joy that counts.

On one of our Atlantic crossings, the 131-foot Polish sail train-
ing ship Dar Pomorza *glided past us with 25 sails set. Everybody*
waved. It was like opening a window on a forgotten world.

Consider buying a secondhand boat. Many yachts last forty or fifty years, but in truth are used very little and may be ideal for a new owner who wants to go on long or short trips. Purchasing a secondhand boat may allow an owner to go sailing years earlier. Unlike automobiles, whose designs change each year primarily for sales reasons, yachts have had few meaningful design changes during the last half century; often new yachts are constructed from plans drawn long ago.

4
TO FIND A YACHT

I f we all had lots of money we'd go to a prominent naval architect and have him or her design us a magic ship that would include all of our preferences and dreams. Then we would hurry to one of the top builders and have him or her put together a gorgeous new hull with a gently curving sheerline and sparkling topsides. We could have the interior made of solid cherry, butternut, or teak, built by master craftsmen and varnished to perfection. We could have a carbon-fiber mast, the best of sails, lots of big winches, and the finest of everything. Unfortunately, most of us don't have deep pockets, but we still want to sail. What to do? Even if we have some money, we can't spend it all on the yacht. We need to save a little for the grand voyage. And in the real world, we may have other obligations.

Why not save big money by buying a used boat? Remember, yachts last a long time. Most spend 90 percent (or more) of their lives sitting quietly in marinas. Sometimes the engine and sails may need replacing, but paint and varnish are cheap. Often you get a substantial inventory (radios, spinnaker gear, extra sails, big winches, autopilots, and joinery upgrades) thrown in for nothing.

Let's look at the used market.

Before we start, however, you need to decide a few things.

1. the size of boat you're after
2. whether you have the skills to handle a vessel this big
3. who will be traveling with you
4. the percentage of your budget that you'll spend on the yacht
5. the amount of work you're willing to do

1. What Size Boat?

If you're thinking of local or regional cruising for a few weeks in the summer, a yacht 25 or 30 feet long may be large enough. For more ambitious cruising, however, a bigger vessel will be more comfortable and provide better sleeping and stowage space and luxury devices. Remember, as you go up in length, the costs rise quickly because they're based on increasing tonnage, which means more materials and labor. A 50-footer can easily cost twice as much as a 40-footer, which in turn can cost twice as much as a 30-footer. In dollar terms, a fancy new 50-footer may cost $500,000 (or more) compared with $250,000 for a 40-footer and $125,000 for a 30-footer. Used prices may be only half as much or less.

Or said another way, if you go into a marina or boatyard with a 50-footer after sailing a 30-footer, brace yourself when the manager hands you the bill.

Margaret and I have had good luck with a 35-foot length. This gives us a boat with reasonable sailing qualities and adequate room for living aboard that we can both afford and maintain to a high standard. In 1965, the average cruising yacht was between 30 and 35 feet. Recall the 30-foot Tahiti ketch designed by John Hanna and the 30-foot *Wanderer III* of Eric Hiscock, both famous cruising vessels of thirty-five years ago.

Today, however, because of the increasing affluence among people involved with sailing, the average length has crept upward. The 1999 roster of the Seven Seas Cruising Association listed 653 members, whose sailing yachts ranged from 26 to 78 feet and averaged 41 feet in length. For the same year, the 362 members of Great Britain's wide-ranging Royal Cruising Club owned boats from 26 to 130 feet. These boats averaged 38 feet in length. The increase of a few feet may seem trifling, but as the length increases, the displacement tonnage climbs rapidly. For example, two recent designs by Niels Jepperson for X-yachts of Denmark have the following numbers:

X-332 (33.8') has a displacement of 9,590 pounds
X-382 (37.7') has a displacement of 14,333 pounds

Note that there's a difference of less than 4 feet between the lengths of the two yachts. However the longer boat has a displacement of 4,743 more pounds. The extra weight means higher upkeep costs but adds comfort, speed, and enlarged carrying capacity. This translates to increased tankage, engine size, stores, sails, luxuries, and personal gear.

When you look at cruising yachts, there are many things to examine. Number one on my list is sleeping arrangements at sea, an area of design that seems studiously avoided by naval architects, most of whom apparently never go to sea. Perhaps the sales departments think that TV viewing centers are more important. In my experience, however, each member of the crew needs a snug, comfortable place to sleep. Out on the ocean a sailor should have his own narrow sea berth with his own shelf or drawer and his own light. Then he can arrange his sheets and blan-

August Night *is a Valiant 42, an updated design by Robert Perry that's been in production (as the Valiant 40) for an amazing thirty years. She's a well-known, nicely designed cutter with a modest fin keel and a skeg-hung rudder. Her mast height towers above the water 1 inch short of 58 feet. The yacht's most distinctive features are a boxy coachroof and a gracefully rounded stern. The design has an external lead keel (9,600 lb.) that's bolted to the hull with seventeen ³/₄-inch-diameter stainless steel J-bolts. With her heavy displacement (24,600 lb.), she can power her way through seas that would stop smaller creampuffs. Well-known as a ma-and-pa boat, the Valiants have competed with honor in a whole series of races, and continue to do well on long world cruises. Once built in the state of Washington, these yachts are now constructed in Texas on a semi-custom basis. They're expensive but come with a substantial inventory and are a real liveaboard proposition. Many older Valiants are out there and worth a look.*

kets and lee cloth so that he's able to rest or sleep in a dry, familiar, secure place. See the photograph of a lee cloth design that I've found good at sea on page 261.

If possible, try to avoid sharing berths. Hot-bunking is a scheme of berth rotation that's often practiced in competition boats during long races, but it's a wretched arrangement. The much-advertised double berths, which may have a place in port, are useless at sea unless there's a high board or divider down the middle and a lee cloth arrangement to keep the sleeper from rolling around or being thrown out and possibly injured. If the sailing is a two-person operation, there should be two sea berths. For a crew of three, there should be two settee or pilot berths plus a dry quarter berth, and so on.

At boat shows I've noticed that bulky bags of sails are always absent so the number of berths can be emphasized. Yet at sea you may lose a berth or two because of stowage demands.

Forepeak berths are generally untenable at sea because of the motion. Additionally, in the real world, the forepeak becomes the catchall stowage area. Anything you don't know what to do with gets heaved up forward. This generally means that spare oars, wind-vane blades, a solar panel, and rolls of charts are placed along the outsides of the V-berth. Right up forward are big plastic boxes with toilet paper and paper towels, the mainsail cover, the big harbor awning, and the hatch screens. Then a stack of extra blankets and pillows and a side bin with scarves, gloves, hats, and caps. The other side bin is filled with bags of dried fruit and packaged pasta dishes. Farthest aft are boxes of fresh vegetables and open-mesh string bags with oranges and other fruit. There may even be a sailbag or two stuffed in there somewhere. In other words, from the midship head compartment forward, it's generally a full house.

This translates to Rule 1: In the real world of cruising, forget the forepeak for sleeping.

The larger a yacht, the faster she can sail from A to B, and being good-sized means that she can carry plenty of supplies. It's ironic that because a smaller yacht goes more slowly, she will be at sea longer and need to carry more food and water.

All yachts—big or small—require a clutch of anchors, a dinghy, plenty of food stores, anchor warps, clothing, tools, medical supplies—a hundred things more. The 25-footer, which may displace as much as $4\frac{1}{2}$ tons, must carry all these items (albeit smaller) just like a 40-footer, which may displace 12 tons. The cruising equipment (say, 1 ton) for a long voyage amounts to 22 percent of the smaller yacht's weight and takes up a great deal of her room, while the figure for a larger yacht is only 8 percent (or maybe 10 percent because of heavier gear). Also, a ton of stuff—not so much, really—easily disappears into the roomier shelves and lockers and bilges of the larger vessel.

What I'm saying is that you can make a strong argument for buying an older, larger yacht instead of a smaller, new vessel if you're going to make an ocean passage.

Before you go off on any big trips, by all means make a series of trial sails with the crew you're going to take. Check out your people and the yacht for a few days on a local cruise. Pick somewhere that's harder than you usually try so you have to stretch a little. If you have problems, come back, fix things, and try again. In other words, expand your nautical horizon little by little. Don't overdo it. If you get into trouble, turn around. Smart sailors are never too proud to head back.

2. What Size Yacht Can You Handle?

The larger the yacht, the more skill and muscle you need to deal with her. She may have bigger winches, but they will be harder to crank. Hoisting or furling a 500- to 600-square-foot mainsail on a 50-footer is easy to joke about in a yacht broker's office, but can be a surprising handful for you to deal with in a breeze at night. Just because a yacht has a powerful engine doesn't mean she will be easy to manage in a windy docking situation.

I think all experienced world cruisers will agree that learning how to enter and leave tight spots under sail is a skill you should have in your pocket. Unfortunately this is completely alien to present-day U.S. marina-type sailing, in which a person motors out from a dock, puts up the sails, goes out for a few hours, and does the same routine in the opposite order when she returns.

You may scoff at this, but if you're in distant waters and there are problems (engine not working, a line around the propeller, dead batteries), you will be very glad to know how to work yourself in and out of restricted waters.

Suppose you want to take fuel and water from a dock against which a fresh breeze is blowing. Do you know how to drop an anchor when you're going into the dock so that you can pull yourself off when you're ready to leave? If you're anchored near a rocky shore and the wind shifts and begins to blow toward the land, do you know how to sail out the anchor without winding up on the rocks? These techniques are not hard to master, but it's smart to practice them regularly. It may be useful to learn these maneuvers in a small sailboat and then work up in size because of the considerable weight and the restricted turning ability of a bigger boat. Mistakes are unthinkable and can cost thousands of dollars.

Don't consider close-order maneuvering under sail a troublesome thing to learn. It's challenging and great fun to sail in and out of tight corners. Half the time it's just a matter of turning the yacht to head downwind, paying attention to any tidal stream or river current, carefully checking for traffic, and hoisting a jib. Then you let go the stern lines or haul up a stern anchor, and you're away. Once you have a little sea room, you can hoist the mainsail.

The other half of the time, it requires more study, care, and practice. One person must be in absolute control. You need to figure out exactly what you're going to do, have every bit of your gear ready, have an alternate plan if possible, and carefully explain what's in your head to each person involved. Often you need to use lines to warp the vessel around to another dock or to turn her so that the wind is more suitable. Again, you must check the tidal stream and current if they're factors.

A way of practicing these maneuvers without embarrassment is to go to a safe, shallow, deserted anchorage. Drop a fender on a light anchor for a mark and use it as a practice target for sailing out the anchor and other procedures.

The staysail schooner Sauvage *was built in France to the designs of the celebrated naval architect Dominique Presles. Her aluminum hull is quite fair and no fillers of any kind were used. The owner and his wife wanted a low-maintenance yacht, so—like many French aluminum yachts—the topsides are unpainted. The bottom is coated with an arsenic base paint. With the exception of the stainless steel propeller shaft, all underwater parts—including the propeller—are made of the same aluminum alloy to reduce possible galvanic action. Her electrical system uses a two-wire ungrounded scheme. Measurements: 47'11" ¥ 40'4" ¥ 13'1" ¥ 6'5". Displacement: 13 tons (14 tons loaded). Sauvage's rig is of particular interest. With five sails flying (the fisherman has just been lowered as she is shown here entering St. George's Harbour, Bermuda, after an ocean passage), Sauvage has plenty of power in light airs. With more wind, the fisherman and jib are handed. This leaves three sails, all on self-tacking booms. If the wind continues to rise, these sails can be individually reefed. In all, the rig can be reduced from five sails to one (the reefed main staysail) in seven easy steps. Possible criticisms are that the rig is complicated and costly and poor on downwind courses in light airs.*

3. WHO WILL BE WITH YOU ON YOUR TRIP?

Your wife? Husband? Children? A close friend? Pals from the office? Do they know anything about sailing, or is it all bluster and bravado? Do they have the skills to really help? Are they going to come or will they back out at the last minute? Will they be able to stand watches at night? Are steering vanes and autopilots going to be essential?

Rule 2: Try out the crew on shorter trips and easier goals while you work up to the big departure.

To find out how people work together on a yacht, you might volunteer to crew on a boat sailing to some distant place. In short order you'll see how others deal with cooking, standing watches, navigating, and mixing with strangers in small spaces. You may not agree with your captain on all things, but he's in charge, and you'll certainly learn what works and what doesn't.

Another suggestion is to hire a sailing instructor or charter captain to conduct a little dress rehearsal with you and your crew. You can ask him (or her) to take you on an overnight trip to the next harbor or to a nearby island or anchorage to try different sails, the anchor, cooking on the go, and sailing at night. This way you can see how the people in the crew interact with one another and fit (or don't fit) into a sailing routine. A good thing about hiring an expert and having him on board is that you can fire questions at him all day long.

I think of Dr. Claud Worth's famous story about learning from authority:

"One hand, if he happens to be a sailor himself, will take an interest in teaching a keen but ignorant owner.

"But two men," said Dr. Worth, "will form a society against you and always find excuses not to do what you want."[20]

4. HOW MUCH OF YOUR BUDGET SHOULD YOU SPEND ON THE YACHT?

As I've mentioned, when you go up in size, boat costs rise quickly. Do you have enough cash to handle the yacht you want? Remember that it's much easier to bargain with a seller from a position of strength. Don't forget possible associated costs: a survey, repairs, a marina slip, a haulout, painting, and new equipment.

Al Petersen, one of my sailing heroes, once told me that it usually costs as much to install a piece of equipment as to buy it in the first place. Initially I scoffed at this, but over the years I've learned that Al was right. Suppose you purchase a new front hatch ($425). First you remove the old hatch and molded-in deck coamings. You rent a power saw with a special blade to enlarge the opening. Next you (or a carpenter) make long, curved teak coaming pieces to adapt the flat hatch to the curved coachroof. Then you hunt up sixteen stainless bolts and drill the holes. Finally you disassemble the parts, vacuum up the shavings, and bed everything with 3M 5200 compound. A messy job. The last step is to go inside the cabin, cut off the extra bolt lengths, and deal with the overhead trim. Now add up your time (including the hours spent chasing parts and people) and what you paid for the carpenter and saw rental. You may be surprised.

It's the same with a new radio (antenna and ground problems); a windlass (strengthen the deck, deal with the navel pipe, the bow roller); or a mainsail traveler (decide on the position, arrange the mounting, beef up the coachroof, make backing plates, find the bolts, and put it all together). But wait! There's a winch in the way. This means removing it, plugging the holes, slapping on some fiberglass underneath, sanding, painting, and mounting the winch somewhere else. And oh dear, the winch project wasn't even on the list!

Be realistic about how much you can spend on the yacht. Beware of financial entanglements that have sunk many a South Seas dream. If you're short of money, maybe it would be better to crew for someone else. To settle for a less expensive yacht. To go in partners with a friend. Or to postpone your trip for a year. Certainly you can't spend everything on the yacht. You must reserve some money for outfitting and equipping. For a long trip, you can easily spend $2,000 on charts. Plus light lists, Pilot books, cruising guides, safety equipment, medical supplies, boltcutters, spare rigging wire, bottom paint, and on and on. Should you hang onto the old patched-up inflatable dinghy or buy a new one? Should you keep the old loran set or chuck it in favor of a GPS unit? Do you need an electric anchor windlass or can you get by with the old hand-crank job that's already on the foredeck? Don't forget to allow something for emergencies in case you get sick or injured.

Rule 3: Costs don't stop when you finally purchase the yacht of your dreams. That's the moment the costs begin!

5. Do You Have the Patience and Skills to Purchase an Old Boat and Bring Her Back Up?

Some people love to do boat work; others hate it. Whichever type you are, dealing with old boats requires a plan. The work may take six weeks or it may take two years. Suppose you purchase a 1974 Alberg 37 for $40,000. Buying a boat that's more than 25 years old is not as crazy as it sounds. Sailing yachts are not like automobiles that run daily and wear out quickly. Many boats are used perhaps two or three times a month and may spend fall, winter, and spring hauled out and stored on land.

Are you going to restore the Alberg to museum-quality condition? Most people don't, and it may not be necessary. Let's run through a quick list to suggest the variety of jobs you may encounter:

1. Look into the watertight integrity of the fiberglass hull. How much water is in the bilge? Can you see where it has come from?

How many drips are coming out of the stuffing box? When the boat is out of the water, check all the through-hulls, the hoses, and the tightness of the double hose clamps. (If there's only one hose clamp, add a second.) Try wiggling the cutlass bearing, and check for underwater blisters. Hit the hull-to-deck joint with a powerful stream from a hose while someone in the cabin hunts for leaks.

2. The rig: check the mast and all the running and standing rigging. This may require several hours up the mast. Has the standing rigging of this 30-year-old yacht ever been replaced? Try cranking each winch. Can you afford to update the winches with self-tailers? What's the condition of the blocks and the running rigging? Don't just glance at things. Take down the main halyard, for instance, and run your fingers over the line to check for wear and frayed places. A new main halyard can cost $80.

3. Look at every part of the steering system. If it breaks down, is there an alternative tiller arrangement? Try it out. Does it work? Is it practical?

4. The galley. Run a hand over every inch of the hose from the gas bottle to the stove. Turn on the gas pressure and test the stove burners and the gas shut-off valve with soapy water. See that the galley pumps work and that there's a spare.

5. Check that the head works easily. A little lubricant often does wonders. If the smell is bad, dump in a little Clorox.

6. For a real learning experience, put a freshwater hose in the bilge and use the ship's bilge pumps to see if you can stay ahead of the incoming water for fifteen minutes. Take off the inspection plates on one of the water tanks and peer inside with a flashlight. Musty-smelling, unused tanks generally need wiping out with clean cloths plus multiple flushings with lots of freshwater and perhaps a half teaspoon of Clorox.

7. Run the engine until it's warm, and change the lubricating oil and the oil filter. Change all the diesel oil filters and screens. If there is no off-engine diesel filter, install a supplementary filter. (I recommend the Racor 500 FG.)

8. Throw away the old batteries and buy new ones.

9. Take the sails to a sailmaker. He will check them over and give you a figure for repairs. (Old sails always need repairs, particularly the leech of the mainsail, which rots first.) The sailmaker may condemn your sails and suggest new ones. Listen to him. He's an

expert. If you doubt what he says, try a second sail loft, where you'll probably hear the same story.

If you feel nervous about any of these areas, hire an expert. Pay him his professional fee. Learn by watching him and asking lots of questions.

OK, what do we have if we've done everything on this quick list? We have a hull, rig, steering system, galley, head, bilge pumps, engine, batteries, and sails. Suppose seven of the nine areas check out perfectly, but two categories require repairs or replacement. Maybe you need a new marine head and a new stove. Toss out the old and install new units.

Finally, if you and the experts are satisfied with these nine areas, at least the yacht is operational. The paint and varnish and fine stuff can come later. The main thing is to go out sailing, which is the whole point.

Here's how an expert deals with the jib on a double-headsail rig with a bowsprit. Al Petersen stands on footropes with his knees securely around the bowsprit. Note how Al has tied off the staysail boom to keep it out of mischief while he is nearby. This is the bow of Stornoway, *the 33-foot cutter that Al sailed around the world.*

THE SEARCH CONTINUES

There are three sources of moderately priced cruising yachts:

- ex-racing boats
- ex-charter boats
- secondhand cruising yachts

The first category is yacht racing, the game of trying to outsail a group of similar vessels around a set of buoys or competing with other boats from one point on a coastline to another, usually for an afternoon or for a day or two. Racing can be great fun. It's challenging and a good way to learn about strategy and tactics, sail trimming, steering, boat speed, how to sail in light airs, the importance of a clean hull, and so forth. Yacht racing is responsible for enormous improvements in sails, winches, foul-weather clothing, and the general streamlining of boats above and below the water. Yet I don't believe the artificial standards of racing yachts are a logical way to find the best vessels for the sea.

Racing boat designs have long been based on faddish racing rules that produce groups of similar yachts designed to compete with one another like horses on a track or greyhounds on a racing oval. The important things for racing boats are speed and a low rating. If it's a one-design class, the emphasis is on sailing tactics and yacht gear. Hovering on the edges of all this are the naval architects and boatbuilders, who have a direct financial stake in winning yachts. A winner sells best.

What have been the guidelines of racing in past years?

When the racing criterion was *waterline length*, the bow and stern overhangs became excessively long and unseaworthy. The overhangs meant that when the yacht was heeled in a breeze, her immersed waterline was longer and she sailed faster. Yet her rating was based on her waterline length when measured sitting upright at a dock.

When the racing criterion was *fixed sail area*, the naval architects drew plans for high and efficient sailing rigs on light hulls with heavy keels to give stability to the tall rigs. Since the sail area was critical, the designers read the rules with the intensity of Supreme Court justices and took advantage of every loophole in the rules, particularly with regard to unmeasured sail area.

When the racing criterion was *displacement*, the builders produced lightweight, fragile hulls that would go fast in light to medium airs. In strong winds the yachts stayed home. If they attempted heavier weather, they sailed at risk and broke apart, as have recent entries in the America's Cup competition.

When the racing criterion is based on *overall length*, the designs feature ugly-looking plumb bows and sterns to maximize waterline length. When this is combined with no restrictions on beam and only lip service to self-righting regulations, the results seem good at first but end up being dreadful. The current yachts in the Around Alone and Vendée Globe single-handed races are extremely beamy and use the weight of water ballast tanks, canting ballast keels, or both to balance an enormous amount of sail that powers the boats to incredible speeds. Unfortunately, these ocean racers are not self-righting and float nicely upside down, a deplorable trend that's caused half a dozen widely publicized sailing disasters. Personally, I think the designers and race organizers should be put in jail. It seems to me that the first responsibility of a naval architect and a race sponsor is to get the crew home alive. All else is secondary. Even some of the leading French sailors who have campaigned these yachts in the past have backed off.

Various regulations (the International Offshore Rule, the International Measurement System, the Channel Handicap, and others) have been adopted by racing organizations to encourage competition and to allow different kinds of yachts to compete evenly with one another by establishing handicaps or ratings. What happens in practice is that a designer finds a way to exploit a rule in some manner. All at once his yachts begin to win the races. This causes a lot of design copying and general grumbling until a new set of rules is worked out. Eventually, most of the regulations become so complex that they defy understanding by anyone except mathematical specialists with arcane computer software.

The result of all this competitive sailing is that yacht brokers have plenty of ex-racing boats that have been out-maneuvered by the rules. Yet these boats are available and perfectly good for less intensive, non-rule-oriented sailing. And they're much cheaper than a new yacht that's specially designed and built for long-distance voyaging.

An aging thoroughbred can still make reasonable time around a track, but just as a veterinarian checks a horse, a tough surveyor should evaluate a used yacht, no matter what her history and her seller's claims.

This photograph was made from a distant video picture shot from an airplane by the Chilean navy. It shows Groupe LG, *a 60-foot entrant in the 1996–97 Vendée Globe round-the-world race. The vessel is upside down and floating nicely with the ballast keel and twin rudders intact. The picture demonstrates that excessive beam can be a lethal factor in a capsize situation. These superwide vessels (with a beam of 18' or more) are apparently more stable upside down than right side up, particularly with the mast and sails hanging down in the water.* Groupe LG *capsized in a violent storm in the central Pacific at 55° S on January 7, 1997. During the next six months, the upside-down vessel drifted almost 2,000 miles east and a little north to a position about 280 miles west of the Chilean coast at 50° S, where she was reported by a Panamanian ship. A Chilean military plane photographed the wreck on July 18 and made the picture we see here. A few weeks later, the hulk drifted ashore in a remote area and broke up. Her unfortunate French captain, Gerry Roufs, apparently perished months earlier.*

Unlike a used car, the mechanical aspects of a yacht account for only a small part of its value. The hull, deck structure, keel, rudder, and rig will last for decades—unless they're terribly abused and neglected—particularly since 90 percent of present-day boats are constructed of fiberglass and have aluminum spars. The engine, sails, head, and electronics may need attention, but these things can function at three-quarters throttle for years. If the electric wind-direction indicator doesn't work, it's not the end of the world. Like me, you can always put a meter-long red ribbon on a pivot at the top of the VHF antenna at the masthead.

Racing yachts tend to be lightly built, and the cockpits—sized for a big crew—may be large and able to hold too great a weight of water for ideal safety at sea. The accommodations, galleys, and chart tables of racing boats are often poor to marginal in order to save weight. Because of minimal joinerwork, the stowage spaces are undeveloped for all the supplies and spare parts that cruising vessels carry. You may need to build in drawers, cupboards, and lockers, but these can be added gradually.

Since a used racing boat represents a smaller amount of material and labor and was built under rules that may be going out of style, her price is lower. In August 2003, I could buy a 35-foot fiberglass racing yacht 5 years old for $99,000 (new cost: $150,000–$160,000). If I chose a 1985 model—18 years old—I could spend as little as $55,000, according to one magazine.

A second source for a less expensive cruising yacht is a charter company. Old charter boats are cheaper because they've been heavily used by a succession of short-time customers who hired the yacht for one or two weeks at a time. Charter boats come from the factory generally lightly equipped except for (1) upgrades in anchor windlasses, (2) increased freshwater tank capacity, (3) engine-driven refrigeration systems with stainless steel holding plates, and (4) more durable cabin soles and companionway steps to take the wear and tear of many people.

In a single year the engine, sails, winches, head, galley stove, and seat cushions get plenty of use. Often a charter company serves as the agent for a private party who owns the yacht and leases it back to the charter company, which pays the owner a negotiated fee based on usage. The charter company takes care of all maintenance and berthing and makes the vessel available to the owner for 5 to 6 weeks a year (sometimes up to 14 weeks).

A typical bareboat yacht is chartered for 27 to 30 weeks a year for $5\frac{1}{2}$ years, after which she is sold. During much of this time the charterers push the vessel hard because they want to go to as many places as possible. Perhaps some six hundred people will have lived on the yacht for short periods. It's just the opposite with private owners, who use a vessel much less intensely.

After a few seasons of chartering, the boat tends to lose her luster; the gelcoat on the hull becomes chipped from banging into docks and other yachts. The paint and varnish look grungy; the white sails become gray and baggy. Compare a taxicab with your own automobile. Which would you rather own?

Another problem is that it's hard for bareboat charter companies to check on the sailing skills of their customers. Charter managers and rescue captains know all about groundings, collisions, sinkings, and mishaps with rocks and reefs caused by inexperienced customers. "Yet accidents are surprisingly infrequent," says Terry Axley Jr. of Sunsail. "Most people underestimate their abilities and go easy for a few days until they get the hang of things."

When a yacht's money-earning ability drops—either from increased maintenance or because the competition has newer boats—a charter company sells the boat in question. As I said earlier, this usually takes place after five or six years. Or it may be because of her size (yachts are getting larger), new equipment options (electric winches; furling mainsails), or styling changes (a raised center cockpit; twin steering wheels).

Certainly an ex-charter yacht needs to be surveyed. If the inspector finds a problem, it may be smart to get another opinion from a second surveyor or a boatyard manager. The hull should be checked at close range, from a distance, and from all angles. A 4-foot flexible batten can be run up and down the outside of the hull to spot old wounds. There's nothing wrong with a repaired hull if the problem has been dealt with properly. However, hull repairs should be thoroughly looked at inside and out—even if the surveyor has to take some ceiling or joinerwork apart.

What's available? Start telephoning the charter companies. Check their websites. Be prepared to fly out at once to inspect their offerings. If you're handy with tools and a paintbrush, the prices of retired charter boats can be attractive because used boats change hands for about half the new price.

A new 35-foot Beneteau with tax and a few extras costs about $130,000. The price of a five- to six-year-old Beneteau from a private owner in the open market is about $95,000. However, you can purchase a five- to six-year-old Beneteau from a charter company for $65,000. This is $30,000 or roughly 30 percent down from the open market and a 50 percent discount from the new cost.

If you find something you like, fly in your own surveyor (not the charter company's). Often when a company decides to sell, they want to do it quickly and without fuss. Time and cash offers are generally the buzzwords, and you'll have to take her away from the company dock in a few days. This works against many purchasers, who like to poke around and think about a purchase for months and are not used to flying to distant locations and doing business quickly and for cash.

The buyer of a small charter boat should put aside $13,500 for the following:

- survey ($500)
- engine overhaul ($2,000)

- new galley stove ($1,000)
- replacing some or all of the standing rigging ($3,000)
- new sails ($5,000)
- painting and miscellaneous ($1,000)
- haulout and bottom painting ($1,000)

* * *

Yachts that are damaged by hurricanes or other causes and sold by insurance companies are in this same category. Often an underwriter will sell a severely damaged vessel cheaply because of the cost of getting her to a boatyard and making difficult repairs that an owner may challenge. Such sales are usually on an "as is, where is" basis.

Sometimes this gives a person who is a hard driver an opportunity.

Some years back, the renowned sailor and author Don Street anchored his 44-foot wooden yawl *Iolaire* in Lindbergh Bay on the south shore of St. Thomas in the Virgin Islands. Don thought the bay was sheltered, but a 30-knot weather system blew up from the east. An associated southeast swell hooked around nearby Water Island and swept into the bay.[21]

Don learned that his vessel had been driven ashore. He rushed to the bay and found *Iolaire* on her side near the beach in three feet of water. Initially she was OK, but attempts to pull her into deeper water failed. She was soon holed and filled with water.

Iolaire's port side was a mess; there was a hole "large enough to crawl through" that measured 8 feet long and 3 feet from top to bottom. Attempts to jack her upright would have destroyed the hull. A simple grounding had turned into a disaster.

The insurance adjuster took one look and declared the yacht a total loss. At the same time the manager of the hotel in Lindbergh Bay demanded that the wreck be removed from the beach at once. The insurance company wanted closure, so Don bought the vessel "as is, where is" for $100, with the responsibility for her removal.

Don borrowed two ship jacks from a boatyard and rounded up a collection of wooden blocks and short 2 × 4s and 4 × 4s plus a number of large wooden wedges. Then together with friends, he stripped out the interior joinery of the yacht and quickly knocked together several stout athwartship X-frames in the interior to keep the hull from collapsing. Using wooden supports, jacks, and wedges (driven with a 10 lb. sledge), and pushing against the outside planking where it was supported by the X-frames, Don and his helpers gradually raised the hull from 50 degrees to a vertical position.

Fortunately, the weather remained calm.

To patch the hole, the men used ordinary 3-inch-wide, $\frac{3}{8}$-inch-thick tongue-and-groove boards placed horizontally. The workers painted the edges of the hole with roofing tar, slapped on a tongue-and-groove board, and nailed it in place. As each new board was added, the edges were smeared with roofing tar. After the hole was closed, Don covered the patched area with canvas soaked in tar.

"The hull was weak in the area of the patch," Don recalled when I interviewed him. "However, there was little load on it because of the X-frames we'd put in place in the interior. The yacht was not sailing so there were no rigging loads on the hull. The only function of the patch was to keep the water out."

Meanwhile Don hired a big crane from the West India Company for one day ($425). In a series of lifts, the crane maneuvered the yacht into deeper water. The temporary patch held nicely, and the wooden yawl was whisked off to a nearby boatyard. Three carpenters plus their helpers put in 11 new planks, 22 frames, a stout bilge stringer, plus a rudder and a new interior.

Iolaire was soon sailing again. With grit, determination, round-the-clock vigilance to deter looters, and a little luck, Don had outwitted both the insurance company and the chorus of doomsayers on the beach.*

I saw the same trick pulled off in 1970 in Monterey, California. A sailor and his crew left San Francisco and headed south in a new Porpoise, a 42-foot Bill Garden design. She was a pretty bermudian ketch built of wood, with a bowsprit and an exquisite sheerline. Once clear of the Golden Gate, the captain headed south along the coast.

Unfortunately, fog rolled in from the west. Suddenly the yacht was enveloped in a thick, blinding blanket of white. The crew was inexperienced. Instead of following a strict compass course and heading a little offshore—the captain had the entire Pacific Ocean to starboard—he steered toward a fog signal that he heard off to port. It wasn't long before he piled up on the rocks beneath the Monterey lighthouse. The yacht was holed and suddenly full of cold water. The people on board, who had lost all interest in further sailing, hurried ashore and turned the ship over to the insurance company, which declared the yacht a total loss.[22]

A local man—let's call him Mr. Smith—now appeared on the scene and bought the wreck from the insurance company, which was glad to sell it before the coast guard labeled the boat a menace to navigation and demanded removal. Smith immediately hired a local contractor, who trucked a heavy Caterpillar tractor to the nearest beach. While the Caterpillar tractor was coming, Smith and a couple of helpers emptied the water tanks and removed as much weight from the boat as possible. Since the wreck lay over on her side, Smith took out both masts by disconnecting the rigging and running lines ashore. When the Caterpillar tractor arrived, it pulled the masts from the inclined wreck and dragged them up on the beach.

---

*Afterward, Don discovered that his anchor was dug in perfectly and that his chain was OK. The shackle that attached the chain to the anchor had exploded into a dozen pieces that Don found in the sand next to the anchor. "I should have put out two anchors," he said.

A broken spade rudder on an Islander 37. This rudder came with a new yacht made by a supposedly reputable company. In spite of naval architect Bill Tripp's careful drawings that showed a heavy-walled stainless steel pipe the full length of the rudder, the builder substituted an appalling iron weldment. Externally, the rudder looked perfect, with the required rudderstock disappearing into a carefully streamlined fiberglass-covered foam section. Just below the surface, however, there was no strength at all against the stresses of sailing, and the first time owner John Warren took his new yacht Beyond *into the ocean, the rudder folded up like a piece of cardboard. Warren hired an attorney but was mollified by the company, which supplied a new rudder and an excuse that a subcontractor was responsible. How to check the spade rudder on a new or used vessel? When you're hauled out, drop the rudder and have it X-rayed (not a big deal), or do some careful cutting, probing, and patching.*

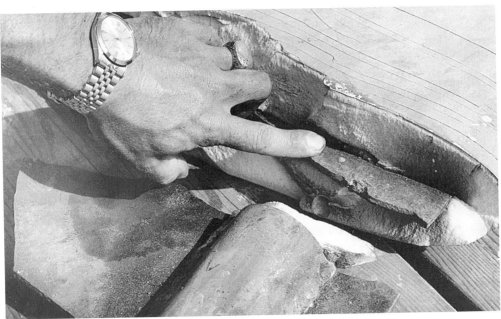

A closer look at the Islander 37 rudder shows no proper rudderstock at all. Instead there is a piece of flat iron totally lacking in athwartship bending strength. No engineer ever approved this! The fabricator who ignored the naval architect's plans and constructed this cheapened rudder certainly never went to sea.

The weather remained calm.

Smith ringed the hull with stout ropes and ran the lines to the beach. The big Caterpillar began to inch the wreck toward the shore. It took two days of maneuvering, rock moving, line adjusting, skid placing, and great effort, but by noon of the second day, the battered wreck was on the beach. Smith hired a crane to lift the yacht onto a big flatbed truck. The dripping, angled load was then taken to a local boatyard, where she was blocked up and began to look like a proper vessel again. The waterlogged engine was lifted out for overhaul. The wooden masts were put alongside on sawhorses.

The costs to Smith? He bought the wreck cheaply. The costs for the tractor, crane, and flatbed truck were reckoned in hundreds of dollars, as were the charges for the heavy, long ropes and the hired laborers. The engine overhaul and the repairs to the hull and the wet interior were a few thousand dollars. The yacht was valued at $40,000. All these figures are from 1970 and should be multiplied by five in the year 2003, but you get the idea.

In salvage cases, the chances of loss of equipment from a yacht are very real. The wrecks must be guarded every second to keep looters from taking compasses, sails, winches, tools, clothing, stoves—anything of value. Even a piece of wood ripped from the deck is somehow considered a worthwhile souvenir.

Stealing from a wreck is illegal, but the popular conception that *anything taken is free* is a constant danger. Ordinary people turn into raging thieves and will strip a momentarily deserted wreck like vultures ripping into roadkill. For the owner, it's time for brute force and lines drawn in the sand. It's the moment to hire big, brawny, nasty-looking uniformed security guards with snarling German shepherd guard dogs (one on the wreck, one on the beach) and to wave around empty shotguns. Local police are usually hesitant and useless in salvage situations. While they dither and vacillate, the goodies disappear.

I have noted these two salvage incidents to illustrate what a determined person can do. Both stories are true and show that it's possible to acquire a valuable yacht for a small sum. But in each case the chances of failure were considerable. The purchase of an old charter boat, a wreck from an insurance company, or a seized drug boat may sound romantic and exciting, but for most people it's too risky and difficult. I don't recommend it.

Banks and loan companies often finance yacht purchases. Occasionally the owner defaults on his note and the yacht is seized and sold. Usually the bank officers know little about the vessel they suddenly own except that they want to collect on the outstanding note and end a problem loan. This means you can make small cash offers (you can always go up, but not down). Try 10 cents on the dollar and see what happens. The trick is finding out about the default in time to make an offer.

I believe the smallest size yacht that's practical for long-distance sailing is this snappy-looking Vertue-class pocket cruiser. She's a heavy-displacement (9,447 lb.) 25$\frac{1}{2}$-foot sloop designed by Laurent Giles. With an expert and determined skipper at the helm, she can go almost anywhere. Indeed, at least three owners—Ed Boden, Bill Nance, and John Struchinsky—have completed single-handed trips around the world. Others have made dozens of ocean crossings and hundreds of notable cruises. Several skippers have reported 24-hour runs of 150 miles or more in ideal conditions—astonishing times for a yacht only 21 feet, 6 inches on the waterline. Most owners campaign the yacht without an engine. Her narrow beam—7 feet, 2 inches—and generally small size restrict her to two people for any extended adventures. Enduring bad weather in such a small vessel can be a daunting experience. The basic problem of such a yacht is her lack of space to carry all the food, water, sails, anchors, tools, books, charts, and personal items needed for life at sea. In this photograph, American sailor Ed Boden is about to leave Avatiu Harbour on the north shore of Rarotonga in the Cook Islands in the South Pacific. "Making this trip was the greatest adventure of my life," Ed said.

* * *

The third category for a less expensive yacht is a used cruising boat. A yacht just back from a long voyage. One owned by someone who is too busy to use his boat. Sometimes the owner's wife may have grown tired of sailing. Or sometimes you'll hear the eternal refrain: "I want something bigger."

The August 2003 issue of *Soundings* magazine listed eighty-one 35-foot sailing yachts for sale. The average price was $80,841 and the average age of the listed boats was eighteen years. Since actual selling prices are usually a little lower, this suggests that you can buy a 35-footer that's eighteen to twenty years old for $70,000 to $75,000, depending on her pedigree and equipment. A Hinckley or a Swan is a deluxe, premium-priced vessel and will cost perhaps twice as much as a Catalina or a Jeanneau. Nevertheless, all four will take you across the Atlantic, just as you can drive an economy Ford ($14,000) or a new Lexus ($34,000) from New York to San Francisco.

Before you head off to Hawaii, however, the used yacht will need a careful survey. The odds are that the engine of a 1985 yacht will have had far more attention than her standing rigging. This is why you need a surveyor to inspect all the 1×19 wire fittings with dye penetrant and a high-powered eyeglass. The inspector should unroll each sail and comment on its condition. He should check the compression of each engine cylinder. If the underwater part of the hull is plagued with blisters, there's a potential for a big repair charge. Fortunately, experts can do quite a bit of work on the bottom for $4,000 or so, which should go into your cost considerations.

Here's a ragtag budget for a 1985 yacht preparing for ocean sailing:

survey	$500
engine overhaul	$2,000
new galley stove	$1,000
replacing standing rigging	$3,000
new sails	$5,000
painting and miscellaneous	$1,000
haulout and osmosis work	$4,000
Total	**$16,500**

We have established that you can buy a 1985 middle-of-the-road yacht for about $75,000. My estimate for repairs and upgrades is $12,500 plus an allowance of $4,000 for bottom work. This totals $91,500. From the same used-boat list mentioned above, you could choose a 1995 Freedom ($149,000), a 1998 Tartan ($162,000), or a 1975 Halberg-Rassy ($51,000).

The only way that I know how to find a suitable yacht is to inspect lots of them. Walk up and down the marina docks. Climb in a dinghy and row past the moorings in the summer. Look around the freezing boat sheds during the winter. Try to size up all the yachts that appeal to you. Fat ones, skinny ones, beat-up old woodies, steel streaked with rust. Cast-off aluminum racers. Tired-looking fiberglass boats. The lot. Take a couple of photographs of each one you like. Talk to the owners. Find out where the boats have gone.

Some of the yachts will appeal to you aesthetically and grab your heart. Perhaps it's the canoe stern, a yawl rig, or the angle of a jaunty coachroof. Maybe it's the way the early sunlight falls across the mast and boom. Perhaps it's all these things . . . or none of them.

If you're a serious looker, buy yourself a bound notebook and use two facing pages to keep a record of each yacht you inspect. When you're comfortably seated aboard the boat, start writing. Begin with the date and location. Then the yacht's name. Her overall length, waterline length, beam, and draft. (If you need a measurement, you can whip out your tape measure.)

Note the rig. The age of the boat. Hull material. Mast material. Sails (number and type). Radios. Engine (how many hours?). Steering vane or autopilot? Boarding ladder? Dinghy? Is there a place to stow the dinghy on board? Is the price open to negotiation or a trade? How long has the vessel been on the market? Is the owner anxious? Look over the yacht for her general condition, and grade her on a scale of 1 (a wreck) to 10 (too good to believe).

Write down your contact. Is there a "For Sale" sign on board? If you're there because of an advertisement, jot down the owner's name and telephone number. If you saw the boat with a broker, note his name and number.

Look at the condition of the berth and seat cushions (check underneath for dampness and mildew). Stretch out on the bunks and see whether they're comfortable and OK for your body size. Try to visualize sailing in the vessel. Does she seem pleasant or is she too far gone? How many anchors does the boat have? What sizes? Is there an anchor windlass? Does it work, or have rust and corrosion sealed it forever? Write down both the good and the bad. Be specific. If you have questions (Capacity of the water tanks? Number of hours on the engine? Extra mainsail?), list them in your notebook. Take a couple of color photographs of the yacht. These don't have to be artistic wonders, but something to help you recall the yacht. When you get the prints, staple them to the appropriate page.

What often happens is that after a few weeks of looking, you try to recall a certain yacht. But was it in Mattapoisett or Marion? Portland or Bass Harbor? Annapolis or Oxford? When we hear a lot of numbers, we tend to mix up prices, ages, and yacht names. Sometimes after a few days, you want to take a second look. Just where did you see that Cal 40?

After you look at twenty or thirty different boats, you'll find that you like a certain design. Or maybe two kinds. If you're unsure about making an offer, try to arrange a sail. I would have no hesitation about offering the owner and his wife a nice lunch or the payment of $75 or $100 for them to take me out for a couple of hours, particularly if I do all the string pulling. This little fee may put you next to information (good or bad) that you never thought about. For example: Can one person sail the yacht or does the distance from behind the wheel to the sheet winches mean that you need two people in the cockpit? Must you walk up to the mast to adjust the topping lift? The reefing arrangements for the mainsail may seem impossibly complicated. And what about that terrible vibration when the owner put the engine in gear?

So far we've considered ex-racing boats, ex-charter boats, and ordinary used boats. Each category has good and bad points. What about buying a new yacht?

A deluxe new 35-foot yacht designed specially for cruising may cost $200,000 or more. But she's all new and pristine. No nicks in the gelcoat. No grubby spots or tears on the cushions. A brand-new engine with a warranty. Gloriously white sails. A new mast and rigging. Wow! It's convenient and tempting to buy various factory options for special equipment, but the costs are high because you pay the full ticket for both the item and its custom installation. The blandishments of the dealer may be hard to withstand. Also, some of the goodies (suede fabric for cushions, a two-color deck, a larger engine) may be of doubtful value. In any case, together with taxes, preparation, commissioning, and delivery, the tab can easily climb another 20 percent. With storm sails, a spinnaker, a dinghy, mast steps, extra anchors and warps, and an anchor windlass, a new, high-line 35-foot production yacht can easily cost $237,500 or more.*

The gloomy reality is that if you get tangled up with installment payments and finance charges, you may never get away. This means that from a dollar-and-cents point of view, *buying a used yacht may allow you to go sailing years earlier.*

To summarize my investigation of yacht prices in the 35-foot range, the figures look like this:

1. An ex-racing boat from 1998 (5 years old) will cost $99,000. A 1985 (18 years old) model is $55,000. She will sail particularly well and have many sails but may not be entirely suitable because she is set up for a large crew. Her interior will be rudimentary. If you add joinerwork and cruising equipment (water tanks, anchors, chain, extra sails, etc.), you will increase her displacement and degrade her performance. Vessels of her type tend to lose value faster because of obsolescence. Her price may be open to negotiation. Offer half and see what happens.

*Sometimes it's possible to avoid paying taxes completely. Policies are different from state to state, and the enforcement mechanisms vary. I am not suggesting doing anything illegal, but you may be able to save significant sums by taking delivery in another state or in a state that doesn't levy sales taxes (New Hampshire, Delaware, or Oregon). North Carolina has a fixed fee of $300 on yacht sales. Canada, Mexico, and Great Britain's Channel Islands are worth studying, particularly if you plan to sail outside the United States for several years. Another problem is the VAT (value-added tax) if you sail in the European Community. Americans have had particular trouble with this in France. Yachts built before 1985 are exempt.

2. An ex-charter yacht five to six years old will cost $65,000, perhaps less depending on her condition. Typically she will need $13,500 worth of equipment renewal, painting, and sails. Charter yachts tend to be of average quality. If you're after a deluxe yacht (Alden or Cherubini), you'll have to look in the used market.

3. A boat five to six years old will cost from $99,000 to $185,000 depending on the original price. A 1985 yacht will cost about $59,000. I estimate repairs, equipment, and sails will be $16,500, which will bring the total to $75,500. A Hinckley, Crealock, or Tartan is more expensive than a Catalina, Beneteau, or Jeanneau, mainly because of more deluxe equipment and better finishing details. Are the more costly boats safer? Do they sail better? Not necessarily. Remember, most of the designs are roughly similar. You will probably be replacing the sails so they become a standard item. Many of the masts and rigging come from the same sources.

Try to satisfy yourself that the hull, deck, rig, rudder, and steering are well built and have worked for others. You don't need such things as television viewing centers, complex electrical systems, satellite radios, watermakers, fancy metalwork, turbocharged engines, exterior varnished trim, and so on aboard a small cruising sailboat. I've found that my life is simpler, more satisfying, and easier without these things.

What fun to see this delightful carving going to sea! Some anonymous woodworker with the soul of an artist has turned the forward end of this taffrail into a thing of pleasure and beauty. Any clod could have screwed a piece of wood between the upper and lower rails, but only an inspired man could have fashioned this frolicking figure for all the world to see and admire.

6

THREE SAILING YACHTS

The hull of our first *Whisper* was built in October 1965. We took delivery of the completed vessel early the next year and sailed her across the oceans of the world for the next twenty years. In the beginning, we were a little nervous about taking a fiberglass hull to sea and were frequently warned that we were foolish. Certainly our cockleshell would founder and lead to our deaths.

In 1966, fiberglass was new and untested in large hulls. The skeptics said that the hull would crack and fall to pieces after a year or two. Certainly the sun would react with the material and destroy it. Fiberglass was said to be dangerous and unproven. Rumors and an active whispering campaign said that it was bad stuff. Why take the risk? "Stick to wood," said the naysayers. "It's traditional and well proven."

This is the original Whisper, *which we sailed for 20 years. She was designed by Canadian naval architect John Brandlmayr, built of fiberglass by Phil Hantke in Vancouver, British Columbia, and was number 29 of a series production called the Spencer 35. We always liked her pleasant sheer and graceful overhangs. We grossly overloaded her with cruising gear, but she never failed us in a dozen far corners of the world.*

L. Francis Herreshoff, then the high priest of naval architecture, ridiculed fiberglass and called it "frozen snot."

We disagreed. We thought that *Whisper*'s hull was magnificent. We had no trouble. Yet a number of bright people confidently predicted that a large fiberglass hull would last only 1 year. After the first year passed, we were told that our hull would fall to pieces after 5 years. But when the 5 years passed (which I noticed while we were at sea) and nothing happened, the criticisms changed to 10 years and gradually faded away. Now 38 years later, the yacht is still sailing. Most of those early critics are long gone.

Our *Whisper* was a pretty yacht with a gently curving sheerline and a graceful bow and stern. The hull was gleaming black with a gold cove stripe, and her spruce mast and boom glistened with varnish. Appearance aside, however, how did she work out as a practical liveaboard long-distance cruising yacht for two people?

Whisper was one of a class of sloops called a Spencer 35 that was designed by the Canadian naval architect John Brandlmayr. The hull was of medium displacement (6½ tons) with a beam of 9 feet, 6 inches. The bow had a moderate overhang with rounded V-shaped sections, and the hull ended in a counter of medium length.

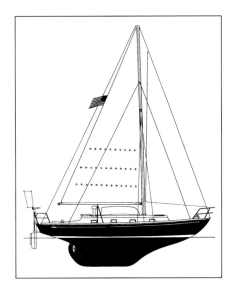

Our first Whisper *was typical of the yachts built under the old CCA rule that encouraged overhangs at the bow and stern. We thought her hull had grace and beauty, and we always tried to keep her looking smart.*

Her stern and midship sections were quite hard, and she carried 4,200 pounds of lead ballast at the bottom of her keel, which had a designed draft of 5 feet, 3 inches. She had a small doghouse (with four large portlights) raised above a low coachroof that extended from the cockpit to 5 feet forward of the mast. The cockpit was 8 feet, 6 inches long. The boat had a single-spreader masthead rig.

Much of the bilge area was partitioned off into tanks: 35 gallons for diesel oil and 39 gallons for freshwater. The designer gave *Whisper* an 8-foot flat-bottomed keel that was horizontal in profile and continued forward into a slightly concave forefoot. The rudder was hinged to the after end of the keel in the traditional manner.

Although details differed, our little vessel resembled a Nicholson 35, Alberg 35, Ericson 35, a Pearson Vanguard, and various Allied, Cal, and Columbia yachts of the time. This was the era of long-keeled yachts—just before the general adoption of separate keels and skeg-hung or spade rudders in pursuit of less wetted area and a little more speed. All these vessels had a waterline length of about 25 feet, a bow overhang of 4 feet, and a stern counter of 6 feet or so.

With a short waterline and a beam of $9\frac{1}{2}$ feet, the Spencer's interior volume was a good deal less than today's 35-footers, which have a beam of 11 or 12 feet. We had no room for double berths, private cabins, or giant cockpit lockers in the aft part of the yacht. However, *Whisper*'s moderate beam gave her excellent steering balance in both strong and light winds on all points of sail, and she had a well-designed layout down below in her cabin.

The Spencer yachts were built in an industrial suburb of Vancouver, British Columbia.

I bought a mainsail, three jibs, and a trysail, all nicely made, from Rolly Tasker in Hong Kong. We fitted the boat with a Taylors two-burner kerosene cooking stove whose pressure tank was made of brass that was (incredibly) riveted together. We acquired a sextant, sight reduction tables, an almanac, a pile of charts, and a compass. We also ordered a couple of spools of $\frac{1}{2}$-inch-diameter three-strand Dacron line for running rigging, two sets of oilskins, an 8-foot Davidson fiberglass dinghy, a self-steering gear, spare parts for the engine, and an electric depthsounder with a noisy 12-inch revolving neon light on its readout dial. We had no radios (except for a shortwave Zenith portable set for time signals), no life raft, and no satellite navigation (satnav) or GPS unit (which hadn't been invented yet). *Whisper* had a 15-horsepower 2-cylinder saltwater-cooled Volvo Penta MD diesel auxiliary for her first 13 years of life. We put an extra freshwater tank underneath the forepeak area, which gave us a total of 78 gallons.

When I signed the contract for *Whisper* in 1965, she cost $16,000. Margaret and I spent another $4,000 outfitting the yacht and preparing her for sea. In year 2003 dollars, $20,000 is equivalent to $113,000.[23] This figure suggests that boats were a better buy in 1965 because new 35-footers can now cost more than $200,000. At that time, however, labor rates in western Canada were low, and the builder, Phil Hantke, controlled his costs by making almost everything himself. One of his joiners constructed the mast, spreaders, and boom in a few days. Another man cut out and polished all the metal fittings. A nearby foundry poured the bronze for the stem piece and boom hardware. A welder from across the way fabricated the pulpits from pieces of scrap stainless steel tubing. And so on.

Speaking generally, our new vessel was adequate and had everything she needed but was simpler than the yachts of today.

With her traditional hull form—a long keel and attached rudder—*Whisper* sailed and steered well. Her only fault was that she was almost impossible to back up with the engine, particularly in a crosswind; we learned to warp her around with lines. In the 1960s a fin keel and a separate rudder attached to a skeg were OK for round-the-buoys racing but untested and considered dangerous for offshore sailing. At least that's what all the books and magazine articles of the time said.

On long passages at sea, we found that we could average 110–120 miles in 24 hours. Our best ever was 155 miles (with a little help from current). Of course, we tried to pick routes with fair winds and no gales, but no matter how clever you think you are, you get hit with bad weather from time to time. Margaret and I learned that we could bash along and log 95 or 100 miles a day under shortened sail even in hard going. If the weather turned really bad, we simply stopped and hove to under short canvas. This generally meant taking down a large hanked jib, stuffing it into a sailbag, hoisting a small jib or staysail, and balancing it with the reefed mainsail. (See chapters 16–19.)

Our single biggest problem with *Whisper* was hull-to-deck leaks. Sailing to weather in a rough sea meant that salt water and spray pummeled the hull-to-deck joint; some of the water leaked below. Soon our bedding, clothes, and spirits were soaked; our cameras, charts, and books were ruined. We tried every kind of caulking, but the leaks continued. It was impossible to deal with this problem from inside the cabin because bulkheads and woodwork were in the way.

After two crossings of the Pacific, I tore into the problem. I removed 75 feet of bolted-on teak toerail and dug out all the bedding compound. I soon found out why the boat leaked.

The hull and deck moldings were bonded together on the inside with a 6- to 8-inch-wide buildup of glass mat $\frac{1}{4}$ to $\frac{5}{16}$ of an inch thick, quite a stout bond really. This joint along the outer edge of the deck and transom—not glassed on the outside—was then pierced 150 times (every 6") for bolts to hold on a teak toerail. What happened during hard sailing was that the hull worked slightly and allowed water to run beneath the toerail, even though it was well bedded and fastened with $\frac{1}{4}$-inch-diameter bolts. The water ran along the hull-to-deck crack and came out inside the hull by way of a bolt hole or at the chainplates, which, though strong, were fabricated in such a way that water could trickle inside from the hull-to-deck outer crack beneath the toerail.

Why is it that yachts must have hundreds of holes drilled through the deck? With a little planning, half the holes—and half the potential leaks—can be eliminated. After a good deal of thought, Margaret and I cleaned out and filled the 150 bolt holes with thickened polyester resin. We then forced a mixture of sawdust and resin into the hull-to-deck crack. (It's impossible to match two large moldings.) Next I took a disk grinder and—using a plywood template—cut a $\frac{1}{2}$-inch radius along the top outside corner of the hull molding to make a softer edge for a fiberglass overlay.

After roughing up the hull-to-deck joint area with the grinder, we laid a strip of 10-ounce fiberglass cloth, $\frac{1}{2}$ inch wide, over the joint. We followed this with a second strip 1 inch wide, then 2 inches, 4 inches, and so on up to 8 inches. We used

Bulwark detail.

many gallons of resin. The six to eight strips we put over the entire hull-to-deck joint (70' plus 5' for the transom) added about $\frac{1}{4}$ inch of fiberglass material. This sealed and strengthened the hull-to-deck joint on the outside and gave us a total thickness of $\frac{1}{2}$ inch with no holes and no cracks. In the chainplate area, I added extra fiberglass on the inside. From there on we had only a cosmetic problem. A friend who was an expert with a high-speed grinder smoothed off and tapered the outside glasswork, and we filled and painted the area.

The result? The hull-to-deck joint was much stronger and the annoying leaks stopped immediately. After painting, we could see no trace of the work except for a slight flare at deck level.

In place of the toerails along the outside of the deck, we added a 1-by-4-inch teak bulwark 34 feet long set $\frac{3}{4}$ of an inch above the deck. The bulwarks were fastened every 6 feet to vertically placed fore-and-aft Everdur plates ($\frac{5}{32} \times 3\frac{1}{4} \times 3\frac{1}{4}$") that I had welded on the outside of each bronze stanchion base (see photograph). The bulwark was a complete success because it was higher and because the $\frac{3}{4}$-inch space underneath allowed any water that landed on deck to run off at once. The decks were much drier than previously. The space under the bulwarks appears to have reduced some of the force of boarding waves that might otherwise have smashed the wooden strips.

Apparently *Whisper*'s hull-to-deck leaks were not unusual because many owners of other fiberglass yachts asked me for details of my modifications.

In French Polynesia, Edward Alcard, the famous English single-handed sailor, came to dinner aboard *Whisper* one night. "I like your yacht except for two things," he said during the evening. "The portlights are big and vulnerable, and the cockpit is too large."

We were aware of both problems. During storms we had filled *Whisper*'s big cockpit many times. In conditions when the top of a wave fell into the cockpit, much of the water was thrown out on the next roll of the boat. Even so, it took fifteen minutes for the 1$\frac{1}{2}$-inch drains (we started out with 1$\frac{1}{4}$") to empty the cockpit. I calculated that if we filled the 8$\frac{1}{2}$-foot cockpit up to the tops of the coamings, it held more than two tons of water.

The danger was that the weight of the water could depress the stern and overcome the buoyancy of the after part of the hull. The yacht could then be swept by succeeding waves whose weight and battering force might fracture the main hatch, vulnerable portlights, or the coachroof itself. Such waves could sweep crew members into the sea. If the force of the water broke into the cabin, the yacht could fill and sink.

We had always carried storm shutters for the portlights, but I worried about the ¼-inch Plexiglas. During a storm off the Oregon coast, a fair-sized wave broke on board and swept the compass off its mounts. I felt lucky not to have had the portlights stove in.

The big cockpit had to be changed.

I took *Whisper* back to the Spencer yard. I wanted to extend the cabin 3 feet aft and eliminate the raised doghouse entirely. By reducing the height of the doghouse area 4 inches and building a new top on the cutaway portion, I would have an unbroken line for the full length of the coachroof. This would give us stowage room for a dinghy up to 9½ feet long, and we could store poles, oars, and awning battens along the unbroken coachroof. The new cockpit would be 5½ feet long, still a sizable well. A worker picked up a saber saw with a long blade and began to cut . . .

The Spencer people built the new coachroof over a wooden male mold. They constructed a sandwich of ½-inch Airex foam core and glassed three mats and two rovings to each side of the core.

I thought the appearance of the yacht was improved; surely she was stronger and safer (see the photograph on page 78). In the process, we had lost 4 inches of headroom—from 74 to 70 inches—but we considered that trifling. Below in the cabin, Spencer's expert Scottish joiners enlarged the galley and put in new drawers and stowage areas. A carpenter built an athwartship chart table with a seat, made the quarter berth more usable, and found space for an oilskin locker. The engine was now in the cabin instead of under the cockpit and more accessible. We covered it with a large teak box that made a nice seat for the cook.

These changes made life aboard more pleasant.

Later I cut out the floor of the cockpit, reversed its slope so that it drained aft, and installed 2-inch-diameter direct-exit pipes to the transom. Now the smaller cockpit drained quickly.

The yacht's mast was deck-stepped and a good installation, with no deck leaks at all. As the years passed, however, I found that varnishing the mast was tedious and never-ending. We had already replaced the original wooden mast because of an alarming S-curve in the lower part. We finally swapped the wooden mast and boom for aluminum spars. They weighed a little less and we were able to run the halyards and reefing pendants inside the metal extrusions. Best of all, the anodized aluminum needed no paint or varnish.

World cruisers must carry a thousand things on their long voyages. The summer clothes are not a problem; it's the heavy stuff: the anchors, the windlass, and

Whisper's cabin arrangement was built around a substantial permanent table to star-board with settee berths port and starboard that we used as berths at sea (with lee cloths). We also had a quarter berth to port. Sometimes in harbors we slept in the fore-peak berths, but this area was generally piled high with food stores and miscellaneous gear. The chart table is to port with the galley opposite.

the chain for dealing with coral; the cans of bottom paint that won't be available during haulouts in faraway places; the spare mainsail; a shelf of big naviga-tion books; the boxes of steel tools; jugs of diesel and kerosene and emergency water; canned foods; the sack of rice; extra storage batteries that are so hard to lift aboard.

When you're off for a year or more, the list is long and the weights are signifi-cant. Margaret and I have always tried to be conscientious and prudent, but the real-ity is that long-distance sailors play the game of the disappearing waterline. Yachts of 30–45 feet are typically down 6 inches. *Whisper*'s draft increased from 5 feet, 3 inches to 5 feet, 9 or 10 inches. As I've said elsewhere, this makes a strong argument for buying a larger used yacht rather than a new smaller vessel.

In 1979, in an effort to reduce weight and still have reasonable engine performance, I changed to a 1-cylinder 12-horsepower German Farymann engine (see chapter 22) that was 100 pounds lighter than the Volvo. I mounted the engine at a slight angle so the drive shaft was angled to port 5 degrees and came out just above and behind the trailing edge of the rudder. I built a new rudder, closed up the aperture, faired everything nicely, and fitted a two-bladed folding propeller whose torque I hoped would just equal the shaft offset (see pages 332–33). This change made a big improvement in sailing in light airs. The performance under power seemed almost equal to the heavier 15-horsepower Volvo and with the helm neutral, she steered straight ahead. Perhaps it was because the propeller worked in less obstructed water. A few years later, when we motored through the flat desert expanse of the Suez Canal where no sailing was possible and managed to keep up a steady 5 knots, I felt quite proud of my work.

After three or four years, the topsides of a yacht become faded, scratched, and shabby-looking, particularly if the vessel is sailed a lot. The paint protection continues to be perfectly good, but fussy owners (me) compare their topsides with new yachts at boat shows. It's impractical to spray new gelcoat on an old hull because the material is neither self-leveling nor glossy. It must be sanded and polished, and the amount of time and labor for this is excessive. Owners often elect to paint a beat-up hull with two-part polyurethane coatings (such as AWLGRIP, IMRON, or Sterling) applied professionally at great expense. This is usually done in special buildings, which requires the mast(s) to be unstepped and the boat to be masked with sheets of paper or plastic.

Yet marine alkyd enamel paint is very satisfactory if applied carefully. And it often can be done outside during a normal haulout. Over the years, my wife and I repeatedly painted the topsides of our first *Whisper* with ordinary one-part polyurethane—which is merely a urethane-modified alkyd enamel—with superb results. We used black, which most painters agree is the most difficult color.

After many hours of filling, sanding, and dusting (and more hours of filling, sanding, and dusting), I would roll on (with vertical strokes) slightly thinned, strained paint with a new foam roller. Margaret followed me with a wide foam brush to smooth (tip in) the paint. We had scaffolding or barrels all set up and worked fast (20–25 minutes a side for the 35-footer) to keep a wet edge. We tried to paint very early in the morning (if it was dry) before the workforce and automobiles appeared and stirred up dust.

We let the paint dry for a day. Then we sanded very lightly with grade 220-grit paper and rolled on a second coat. We hired a sign painter to put the name on the transom in gold paint and to do the gold cove stripes along the sides. *Whisper* looked very smart.

In 1985 in Roadtown in the British Virgin Islands, we were almost threatened with bodily harm by the local AWLGRIP licensee who inspected our work. He was furious and was certain that we had sprayed AWLGRIP at night! What a compliment!

The six keys to perfection were preparation; reasonable scaffolding (or barrels and planks) so that we didn't have to stop and could keep a wet edge; 15 percent thinned, strained paint; new rollers and brushes; no dust; and luck with the weather.

Expert friends tell me that you can apply two-part polyurethane paint in the same way—that is, with roller and brush. In this case, use the recommended proprietary thinner and add it in small amounts. Too little thinner and the brush strokes won't disappear; too much and the paint will run or sag. Test the mixed paint on a piece of window glass before you put it on the boat.

We campaigned *Whisper* from 1966 to 1986. She was a good yacht, and we had her accommodation and gear well worked out. We could have continued our voyages, but I got the urge to try single-handing, that is, to sail by myself. I entered a round-the-world race called the BOC Challenge (now titled Around Alone) in 1986–87 and again in 1990–91. I liked the races and would have gone a third time in 1994–95, but I couldn't raise enough money.

I've told the stories of my participation in these two events in *Chasing the Long Rainbow* (Norton, 1990) and *Chasing the Wind* (Sheridan House, 1994). Most people think that big companies would line up to sponsor a well-known sailor in a prominent event. The truth is that in the United States, the sport of offshore racing is unknown, unappreciated, and not visual enough for corporate satisfaction. Stick to golf, tennis, baseball, basketball, and football if you want sponsors.

The race rules called for yachts between 40 and 60 feet. Unfortunately, *Whisper* was too small for the event, so I sold her. (It's so easy to write those three words, but my heart fairly breaks when I think of the yacht and what we went through together during all those years.)

After a long search, which included trips to England and France, I settled on a big Cali-

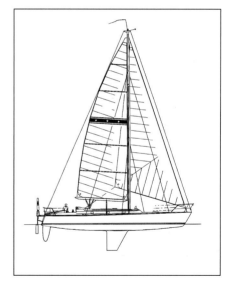

American Flag *was a first-class yacht that was long, slim, and always exciting to sail. It was a wonderful experience to take this fine vessel across the Atlantic and back, and then twice around the world. The whole episode was a sort of college education in the art of sail and self-sufficiency.*

American Flag, *sailing in front of Table Mountain in Cape Town, South Africa, in November 1986. Here I'm about to start out for Australia via the Southern Ocean on the second leg of the BOC round-the-world race. I have one reef in the mainsail, and I'm hand-steering with the long tiller. The yacht performed splendidly, but sometimes when it breezed up, she was a handful.*

fornia sloop called a Santa Cruz 50, designed and built by Bill Lee. *American Flag*, as I named her, opened a whole new world for me. She was long and sleek and measured 50 by 46½ by 12 by 8 feet. Her mast was 65 feet high. She weighed only 19,000 pounds and was called a ULDB, which stands for ultralight displacement boat.

In 1986, as far as I knew, no one had ever dared take such a yacht across the Southern Ocean, that cold and stormy sea that encircles the globe at the bottom of the world. I was told that the mighty storms of Cape Horn and the Roaring Forties would destroy such a flimsy vessel, that I was crazy for even thinking about it, and that I would need an experienced crew of seven or eight husky men to make such a voyage.

However, on her very first sail, Margaret and I took *American Flag* from Florida across the Atlantic to the Azores. We found that she was docile and easy to manage. She had no bad habits that I could find except that her sails and winches were larger than I was used to. I certainly needed all my muscles. Bill Lee knew where the yacht was headed and had constructed a first-class yacht.

American Flag's hull form was wonderful, and it was exhilarating to sail a fast boat and log 240-mile days. In light winds she glided through the ocean with the greatest of ease and scarcely left a track behind her on the sea. When it breezed up, her acceleration was remarkable; above 10 knots, the hull made a wonderful roaring sound. In heavy going with severely reduced sail, she never faltered. Her narrow hull form was magnificent, and she was so easy to steer that I used a tiller instead of a wheel. Her only problem was that she heeled a lot going to weather in strong winds. I later installed water ballast tanks to keep her more upright and to increase her power.

I completed the races handily, but I didn't win them. In the first race, I had a good chance to win, but I didn't drive the vessel hard enough. I should have used spinnakers much more. In the second race I was very well prepared, but North Sails made a dreadful mistake and sent me off with faulty sail hardware. Later in the competition, I had severe rigging problems. (Full disclosure: the French designers, sailors, and financing completely outclassed me and the sailors from other countries.)

When she was built, I had *American Flag* fitted with a 3-cylinder Yanmar engine of 24 horsepower and a Martec folding propeller. During the races I took off the propeller, strut, and shaft and used the engine as a generator. The yacht had six berths, lots of drawers and lockers for stowage, a big chart table, and an excellent galley with centerline sinks that drained on both tacks.

Margaret and I lived aboard *American Flag* for four years between the races and sailed up and down the east coast of the United States many times. We were told that her 8-foot draft would be a problem, but with moderate care, we didn't

The business end of American Flag. *Here we're far out at sea and hurrying along with a fair wind over the port quarter. The port running backstay is set up, and the mainsheet is well eased. With a lot of complicated running rigging, I try to keep the lines tidied up in bags or reels or coiled and hung from cleats. The entrance to* American Flag's *cabin required a big step, but it kept the water out. I made the storm door in two parts: The bottom half was for a moderate storm. For the unthinkable, I closed both halves. With a 50-foot overall length, it's possible to build a permanent dodger arrangement the height of the coachroof that's strong enough to take winches and still have enough clearance for easy passage to the cabin.*

find it a handicap. We even made a winter cruise in the Chesapeake and ran aground only once.

Because of her size, it took care to handle the vessel around docks. In the beginning she was bigger than I was used to, and maneuvering 54 feet (including the steering vane gear and anchor) in and out of marinas gave me a few thrills until I got the hang of it. A big advantage of the design, however, was that with her spade rudder I could back her under power with complete control.

One thing we noticed during our sailing years in *American Flag* was that it was a bit harder to make friends. The size of the yacht tended to put people off. There's a social group in the 30- to 45-foot size that moves less easily with people in the 50- to 60-foot-plus class. I suppose it's the same reason that there are more Chevrolet owners than Mercedes people. Owners of the 30-foot boats considered us wealthy and out of reach, which certainly wasn't true. We found that people on land (the nonsailors) can identify more easily with a smaller sailboat because it's a size they might buy someday.

In the end I suppose what turned us off the 50-footer was that she was too expensive for what we received in return. A smaller boat was easier to sail and had ample room and everything we needed.

Haulouts with the Santa Cruz were a big deal because the long hull had to be supported by a number of jackstands, and each one needed to be carefully positioned against a bulkhead or an internal frame. This meant a specialist yard. The balsa-cored hull was OK, but it was a more delicate proposition and simply couldn't take the knocks and bangs that a solid FRP hull could. Certainly there was no drying out between tides alongside a marginal dock or dragging the boat up an ill-fitting marine railway to slap on bottom paint.

The sails were larger and heavier, and the loads on the rig and sails required substantially bigger gear in every department. Marina fees and insurance were more. The windage of her tall mast and rigging wires was considerable, and with wind of any significance she needed a 75-pound anchor and a long length of chain in an anchorage. Yet heavy ground tackle defeated her basic lightweight design.

We bought our third yacht in 1993. We were back to 35 feet again, a length we liked, and a successor to our original *Whisper*. After some intense shopping, we decided on a fiberglass sloop called a Pretorien 35, built in 1984 and designed along moderate racing lines by the English naval architects Holman and Pye. Again we named her *Whisper*.

The boat came from Lille, France, and was superbly constructed by a builder named Henri Wauquiez (pronounced *VAW-kee-ay*). She looks something like a Swan, Baltic, or Sweden yacht and shares their lineage of comfortable accommodations and first-class interior woodwork. The standing headroom of 6 feet, 3 inches in the saloon gives a nice feel of roominess, and we like the large chart table and the small aft cabin, a surprise in a small yacht.

Our boat is number 143 of a series production, and her measurements in feet are 35.3 by 29 by 11.9 by 6.2. The hull is well built throughout and has six full-length longitudinal stiffeners. The bulkheads are bonded to the hull and deck and are reinforced by drilling holes through the bulkheads underneath the edge taping and connecting the fiberglass on the forward side of each bulkhead to the glass on the after side. The yacht has a Volvo Penta 2003 diesel engine with a conventional shaft, strut, and folding propeller. (For remarks on her displacement and rig, see page 156.)

I particularly wanted a vessel with an external ballast keel and a 30-foot water-

The most obvious thing about the Pretorien is her tall rig—some 53 feet above the water.

line. Our new *Whisper* has 6,490 pounds of external lead fastened to the hull with seven large bolts. With her increased beam and volume, our cruising gear deepened her draft by only 2 or 3 inches. However, this extended her waterline length to about 30 feet.

The first change we made was to junk the large steering wheel and put on a tiller. The wheel took up too much room and acted as an iron curtain between the helmsman and the sheet winches. In addition, it's easier to hook up a steering vane to a tiller. The mainsheet arrangement on the bridge deck at the front of the cockpit was cumbersome and terribly in the way. It was a big improvement when I installed a Harken mainsheet traveler immediately forward of the main hatch. To help with

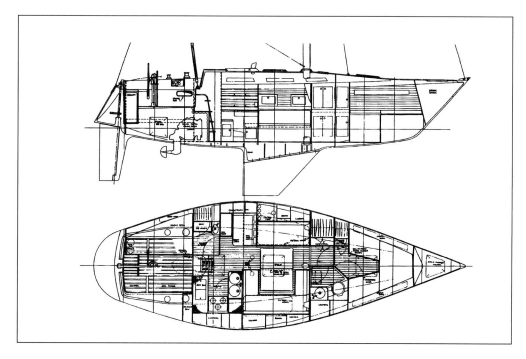

Our new Whisper *has a fin keel, a rudder hung on a narrow skeg, and fairly rounded sections. These underwater appendages seem to cause no more or no less rolling than we had on our long-keeled old* Whisper. *The biggest differences are in the higher aspect ratio sail plan and in the greater beam (9'6" vs. 11'9"). With 25 percent more beam we have much greater internal volume and room for a more luxurious interior and plenty of lockers, which makes stowage easier. Also the boat is stiffer when sailing because of the beamier hull. However there's more boat to force through the water so in the end I think it's a tossup. What I particularly like about the new* Whisper *is the external lead keel, which is strong and more damage resistant if we go aground. This drawing shows an inboard engine with a sail drive unit. However, we have a conventional transmission, shaft, stuffing box, strut, and propeller.*

stowage we had an expert carpenter build eight drawers and three bookcases into the joinerwork in the main cabin. I mounted a small hand windlass on the foredeck to deal with the anchor chain.

The yacht is rigged as a masthead sloop with a tall, skinny sail plan and an area of 640 square feet. The top of the mast is 53 feet above the water (compared with a 42' mast and almost the same sail area in our earlier 35-footer). With her longer waterline and taller mast, our daily runs are 20 miles more than the former boat—say, 135 miles rather than 115. This, of course, is a subjective thing. Margaret and I may be better (?) sailors than we were in the past, and today's sails may have improved. Certainly with four full-length battens, our current mainsail has a better airfoil shape.

Perhaps it's only a trick that I've learned recently, but our new *Whisper* is particularly good at slipping into windward anchorages. One example: In the Aegean Sea during the summer a strong wind called the *meltemi* blows hard from the north and is sometimes boosted by squalls brutal enough to blow olives off the trees. Once near an anchorage, I roll up the headsail and continue tacking to windward with, say, two reefs in the mainsail. Without a jib we sail very slowly, say at 2 knots, but we are under full control while we look around and decide what to avoid and where to anchor. The yacht *always comes about*—slowly to be sure—and we go back and forth until we move into smooth water near the shore and drop the anchor.

The downside of *Whisper*? Her sheerline is a little flat and the transom seems enormous. I like her tall rig, but even with two sets of spreaders and 10 rigging wires, the upper part of the mast is a little nervous in a lumpy seaway and needs the support of a running backstay. She's quite good with a spinnaker in light following winds, and with suitable sails goes well to weather in winds up to 25 knots or so, depending on the sea conditions.

With beam winds of 20 knots or more across her deck, she's a bit frisky in her steering. I suspect this is because of the considerable width of her hull. In these situations I've learned to change course a little or take down her mainsail entirely. This improves her steering and she goes just as fast.

So far we've made three voyages in the Pretorien. From Chesapeake Bay in the United States across the Atlantic to Gibraltar and thence to the northwest coast of Turkey and back to our starting point. Then two trips from the Chesapeake to Newfoundland and Labrador and back. With satellite navigation and an excellent windvane gear, the trips seemed easier and more enjoyable than ever.

Some of our experiences have been incredible. This Japanese farmer lived on a small island in the Inland Sea north of Shikoku. He couldn't believe we had sailed all the way from America in our little boat. He thought we must be joking. While we attempted to talk to him using our phrase book, he kept smiling. Meanwhile, his wife continued working. In fact, his wife appeared to do all the work while the farmer stood around smiling. We all had a good laugh.

THE RIG

In recent years, small-boat sailors have circled the globe under every conceivable arrangement of masts, spars, and sails. There are devotees of the sloop, cutter, ketch, yawl, and schooner—each of whom will fill your ears with reasons why his (or her) sail plan is superior.

Gipsy Moth V was designed by Robert Clark, built in Ireland, and sailed by the late Sir Francis Chichester during his 1971 attempt to log 4,000 miles in 20 days between two fixed points in the Atlantic. She measured 57 ¥ 42 ¥ 12 ¥ 8½ feet and displaced 38,000 pounds. Her sleek hull was built of three layers of cold-molded wood. The staysail ketch rig is of particular interest. The mizzen, mizzen staysail, and main staysail are small (less than 270 sq. ft. each) and boomed to make tacking easy. The addition of the main topsail (370 sq. ft.) and the first jib (510 sq. ft.) bring the total to a powerful 1,630 square feet. Yet each sail is small enough to be easily handled, and the mast height is modest. Today the first jib and perhaps the main topsail would be handled with roller-furling gears, which would make the sail handling even easier. This sail plan is particularly good for reaching and close-reaching courses and less efficient downwind, where the lack of a spinnaker is a handicap. The photograph was taken in Bermuda in 1976 when the yacht was being campaigned with a set of well-patched sails. The vessel—in other hands—was lost in Australian waters in 1982.

Most of these yachts have lofty masts and tall, skinny, triangular sails that are derived from racing designs. It's a reasonably straightforward arrangement: you erect a pole, support it with wires, and hang the sails from it. What could be simpler? The tooling exists, and there's been a long period of practice and use.

Ask a child to draw a sailboat and he or she will invariably come up with a curved hull and a triangular sail on each side of a single mast. Such sail plans are called bermudian or Marconi rigs. (Marconi because they resemble the lofty antennas and wires the radio pioneer used for his wireless telegraphy.)

There's also the gaff rig, a traditional sail plan that employs a four-sided, trapezoidal mainsail set behind the mast. The top (head) of the sail is laced to a gaff boom that's angled up 30–50 degrees above the horizontal. A triangular jib goes on the forward side of the mast. This means that for the same sail area, you can get by with a shorter mast. The advantage of a gaff rig is that the mast is stumpy, solid, well stayed, and will be standing when all the tall bermudian masts have long been leveled. In addition, the gaff rig has a lower center of effort, which means that the yacht heels less. Gaff-rigged boats perform well off the wind.

New yachts come and go, but John Hanna's gaff-rigged Tahiti ketches and Colin Archer's famous gaff cutters continue to do a good job of crossing the oceans when the wind is at the side or a little behind. Since most cruising is off the wind and world-cruising sailors go to fantastic lengths to find fair winds, I suppose you can make an argument for a gaff rig, especially with a short gaff boom, perhaps even made of aluminum, although I think the idea of a light-alloy gaff would make the traditionalists gag.

The trouble with the gaff rig is that its performance to windward is poor because the top of the mainsail sags off heavily to leeward. In addition, the leading edge of the jib is short, and the solid masts and booms are heavy. We all respect tradition, but the gaff rig is a little behind in the 21st century.

But back to our tall (bermudian) sail plan, the mainstay of today's voyaging. A sloop with triangular sails is an efficient, simple rig with only two sails. As long as the sail area suits the wind strength and the wind is ahead or on the side, the performance is excellent. When the wind increases, you reef the mainsail and change to a smaller headsail.

If the wind is behind the yacht, you ease the mainsheet, and the mainsail goes on one side or the other. The jib is now useless because the mainsail blankets it. The effective sail area has been halved, and the boat speed drops. To maintain good performance, you have three options:

- Roll up or drop the jib and set a spinnaker.
- Sail wing and wing by using a spinnaker pole or a whisker pole to hold out the clew of the jib on the side opposite the mainsail. This

makes the full area of the jib essentially a flat plate before the wind.

- If the wind is strong and from behind, you may be able to run with just the mainsail or even a reefed mainsail. Margaret and I do this a good deal and it's easy and effective. The rig is snug, and no one has to go on the foredeck at all. We have run at hull speed before strong winds for days at a time.

To gain any significant drive from a jib when running with the mainsail, *you must use a pole of some kind*, particularly if there's any swell or wave action. Without a pole you can try adjusting the jib with the windward sheet. It's possible to get the sail to pull nicely for a few minutes, but when the boat rolls, the wind will be knocked out of the sail and it starts to bang around uselessly and chafe on everything in sight.

So for following winds, you need a rigid pole, even if it's just a long piece of bamboo or a series of two or three telescoping aluminum tubes. The pole—placed horizontally—goes between the clew of the jib and the mast and should be in line with the mainsail boom. When the wind changes or you select a different course and you adjust the mainsheet, you should ease or trim the jib sheet so the pole stays in line with the main boom and is at a right angle to the apparent wind. (For details, see chapter 9.)

If you use a sloop rig to cross an ocean in the high latitudes, you're sure to get a physical workout. During an eastward passage that Margaret and I made from Atka in the Aleutian Islands to southeast Alaska, for example, we reefed and unreefed the mainsail and changed headsails 61 times during a 19-day passage, or about 3 times a day.

It was on that trip that I decided to break up *Whisper*'s single headsail into two sails for easier handling. I wanted to make changes without physically taking sails on and off the foredeck. Hanked-on headsails allow three possible sail combinations. With a roller-furling jib, there are four:

- In light winds we carry a jib on the headstay and a staysail on the forestay.
- When it breezes up, we drop the staysail and sail with the jib.
- With more wind, we put four rolls in the jib (which necessitates sliding the sheet block forward).
- When the wind freshens still more, we drop or roll up the jib and raise the staysail.

The staysail should set properly and be the largest possible staysail for the rig. I have learned to avoid ill-fitting, awkwardly sheeted, overly small, storm-jib-type sails made of ridiculously heavy material. We have the option to take three reefs in the mainsail, and by the time we hunker down to, say, two reefs in the main and are flying just the staysail, we have a fairly bulletproof rig for stormy weather. And all without unhanking, bagging, dragging around, and stowing wet sails either belowdecks or in a cockpit locker. In terms of physical effort and simplicity, this sail-handling scheme works well, and when the weather turns around and the wind eases, it's easy to put up more sail.

I always find it astonishing how well a yacht sails with winds forward of the beam when a small headsail is set properly and its area is suited to the wind strength.

Recently a few sailmakers have begun to speak of a double headsail rig as if they had invented it. Captain John Illingworth was winning ocean races with the *Myth of Malham*, a masthead bermudian cutter, more than fifty years ago. English gaff cutters (with topmasts and bowsprits of incredible length) go back hundreds of years.

The distinction between a cutter and a sloop, however, is a bit hazy. There's often talk about a sloop having one headsail and a cutter requiring two sails forward. By definition, the mast of a cutter is located 40 percent of the waterline length behind the forward end of the waterline. Naval architects sometimes draw a sail plan with a large foretriangle that fits the definition of a cutter and call their creations a sloop. However, the name is not important; it's the concept of two headsails instead of one that I've found helpful.

The forestay for our present 35-footer parallels the headstay at the front of the yacht but is 5 feet farther aft. The wire is shorter and terminates at the second spreaders, where there's little fore-and-aft mast support. This means that when I use a staysail, the rig needs the support of a running backstay to balance the pull of the forestay.

I like the forestay in combination with a running backstay because the extra rigging nicely stabilizes the mast when the yacht is banging about in an ocean swell. This extra bit of rigging gives me a feeling of confidence. Another advantage is that if I were unfortunate and lost the headstay, the standing backstay, or a topmast shroud, the running backstay and forestay might keep the mast up until I could set up alternate rigging. At worst, these two lengths of rigging ought to save three-quarters of the mast, not a small consideration on an unfrequented ocean.

The downside is that the forestay interferes with tacking because there's less room to pull the clew of the jib from one side to the other; nevertheless, the sail will usually blow through. Once in a while the sail gets hung up and someone has to go forward to help the sail around, but this is infrequent. It's possible to disconnect the forestay and tie it out of the way when there's a lot of tacking, but this means more hardware and complication. Depending on the wind, it's possible to have the jib rolled up and to tack to weather with just the staysail. I can tell you, however, that all this sounds much worse in words than in practice.

For running backstays on my 35-footer (and on my former 50-footer) I use a sin-

A good running backstay arrangement. The line comes in from up the mast (see arrow), goes around a strong block, through a line jammer, and to a winch.

gle piece of ½-inch-diameter standard braided Dacron line. At the cockpit end I lead the backstay through a block (angled inboard 10°), a line stopper, and to a dedicated winch (see photograph). I particularly like the polyester line instead of wire because the line is much easier to handle and there's less chafe on the mainsail. Unlike the metal levers that I've used in the past, I can crank up the line to whatever tension I want. I've used this line arrangement for the last seventeen years and recommend it highly. Designers often show a four-part tackle to tension running backstays, but such an arrangement is so awkward that I can't believe they have ever tried it themselves.

I like to keep unused runners under control; I do not want them flopping around. When I'm not using a running backstay, I immediately tie it off at the mast where it is stowed vertically downward on the after side of the spreaders. To do this I unreeve the line from the cockpit block, carry the end of the line forward and run it through a small deck block outboard of the mast. I then walk back to the cockpit with the end of the line, haul it tight, and belay it to a cleat at the front of the cockpit. To walk forward and deal with this line takes about thirty seconds or maybe a little longer.

It's possible to rig a small purchase to do this from the cockpit, but it adds another complication; I find it simpler to walk forward and secure a single line. In reply to the argument that runners are too much trouble, I can only say that I am quite unimpressed by sailors who readily crank enormous headsail sheet winches yet complain about setting a running backstay, which is easy. In light weather it's unnecessary to set up the runners. In fact, I use them only half the time, I suppose, but when I need extra mast support, they're on call. Note that when it's stormy and you have a reef or two in the mainsail, you can often leave one or both runners set up and still tack or gybe.

In addition to the double headsail rig that I've described, there are $^7/_8$ or $^3/_4$ jib-headed rigs, in which the mast is set farther forward and supports a large mainsail (with a high percentage of the sail area) and a small jib (that may or may not be changed). Certainly cruising sailors ought to like this arrangement because main-sails are quick and easy to reef and unreef, while changing jibs is a tedious business.

Another scheme of running downwind is to furl the mainsail and use twin jibs poled out on opposite sides, with their sheets running to the tiller or wheel for self-steering. In some of the old books there's a lot of talk about twin headsails or trade-wind rigs. The captain is depicted as a pipe smoker sitting on a soft cushion in the cockpit while he reads Gibbon's *Decline and Fall of the Roman Empire*. Mean-while the yacht steers herself toward Samoa or the Philippine Islands. This all sounds vaguely romantic. Is it something one should try?

I say yes to Samoa, but no to twin headsails. I have found that a mainsail, a poled-out headsail, and a wind-vane steering gear are superior in all ways. The points against twins:

- Without the mainsail up, the boat rolls heavily from side to side.
- The necessity for two sets of twins, for winds above and below 12 knots of true wind. In light airs, with the mainsail down, you will need large, lightweight sails to keep moving.
- Twins give you free and reliable self-steering, but you're limited to courses that are almost dead downwind. It may be possible to angle the course a little by adjusting the sheets and poles.
- You need two poles, two lifts, and a way to secure the sheets to the tiller or wheel, a tricky job for one person in a fresh breeze. Be aware that some yachts, depending on their underwater design, may go downwind steadily day after day with twin poled-out run-ning sails *without leading the sheets to the tiller. Try this first.* Also it's not necessary for the sails to be identical.
- The time required to set the twins is more than you think. Remem-ber that you need two sails, two poles, two pole lifts, and various blocks to lead the sheets (braces, really) to the tiller. This is a lot of gear.

- The time needed to change back to the fore-and-aft rig is significant. This point may seem trivial, but if you want to sail to windward quickly (man overboard or a sudden danger ahead), it's helpful to have the mainsail up and usable.

In my early sailing days, I fitted twin headstays to facilitate sail changing. The idea was to hank a different-sized sail to each of two headstays and to pull small and large sails up and down depending on the wind. At first I separated the twin stays by 2 inches; later I increased the distance to 4 inches, but I found that the luff of the headsail still chafed on the unused headstay. In addition, the idle headstay was forever catching the jib hanks of the sail on the other stay. Dozens of times I found four or five hanks open and the sail chafing on the leeward stay. Worse yet, the hanks would get around the wrong stay or both stays, which made lowering the sail difficult. I eventually got to the point of always lowering the sail and hanking it to the leeward stay. I finally junked the twin headstays, with their weight, windage, and problems, and went to a single larger wire.

Mixed up with this practice is the idea of tying an unused headsail along the upper lifeline with a number of lashings. This is another bum idea because when a wave hits the bundled-up sail, the force bends the stanchions. When you have an extra sail on the foredeck, learn to stuff it into a bag and take it to a cockpit locker or toss it below. This is more trouble but worthwhile in the long run.

We hoist our sails and use sheets and guys of $1/2$-inch-diameter double-braided polyester line, which has a strength of 7,000 pounds. I've had excellent performance from Samson LS Parallay line, the company's bottom-of-the-line product. It's soft and flexible and easy to grip. In 2003, the list price per foot was 54 cents, about the same as three-strand polyester. Various specialty lines with exotic fibers can cost up to *twenty times as much*, but I see no reason for buying such line because I can crank up whatever tension I want with the less expensive cordage. If the line stretches slightly, I crank a little more.

A basic problem with sailing vessels is chafe—things rubbing against one another to destruction—and I refer to it again and again in this book. If a piece of line rubs against a sharp metal corner, there's a good chance that the line will be ruined or cut in two in a few hours. But if protected by a piece of hose or by better routing, perhaps by way of a smooth block, a line will last for years. Veteran sailors are always looking at their rigs when under sail to check three things:

- the trim of each sail and the whole rig together
- whether the sails are suitable for the current wind strength
- what's rubbing on what

When not in use, running backstays may chafe on the mast spreaders or elsewhere. I reduce chafe by sliding a piece of plastic hose up the line and securing it with a few big stitches. This sort of chafing gear lasts for years.

To suggest what can be done, I made two circumnavigations with the same main halyard on my 50-footer. (I end-for-ended the 1/2-inch-diameter line after 30,000 miles to put a new section around the masthead sheave.) But I've also ruined new lines in a few hours because I got sloppy and inattentive.

In past years, Margaret and I fought the battle of wire halyards. We learned to hate the slow hoisting, the troublesome wire-to-rope splices, the skin-piercing broken strands (meat hooks), the wire around the mast steps, and the grooves worn in the mast. Even worse are the dangerous wire winches, which are prone to snarls and overrides, especially when you're in a hurry. Their biggest drawback, however, is that if you forget to remove the handle of a wire winch when you have a heavy load on it and release the brake accidentally or the brake slips, the handle will unwind out of control. Suddenly the winch handle becomes a lethal weapon. *This can be the single most dangerous device on board.* I have personal knowledge of four tragic accidents—including broken arms and an eye put out—from wire winch handle mishaps.

Fortunately, most sailors today use all-line halyards and ordinary barrel winches, often with self-tailing devices. This arrangement is fast and simple and can be as powerful as you want. I urge you to get rid of wire winches. Harken makes an excellent masthead sheave if you need a new fitting at the top of the mast to take an all-fiber halyard.

When you're not sailing, halyards should be tied off to prevent them from tapping or beating against masts. When you have an unused halyard, tie the end to something *away from the mast.* When I'm through sailing, I remove the main halyard from the headboard of the mainsail and tie it to a stanchion or coachroof fitting 8–10 feet back of the mast. Then I take up on the hauling part at the base of the mast. Now the halyard is tight, away from anything on which it can bang or tap. Everyone nearby can sleep, and the finish on the mast stays intact.

* * *

There's much talk about the ketch rig among cruising people, but sailors who have used this plan report that the mizzen sail is often useless. If the mizzen is close to the mainsail, the mizzen tends to blanket the main when running; when going to windward, the mainsail tends to backwind the mizzen.

In the real world, the mizzen spends a good deal of its sailing life rotting on its boom. In addition, a long mizzen boom can interfere with the mounting of a wind-vane steering gear, and downdrafts from the mizzen sail can affect the wind-vane blade itself. The mizzen is better when reaching, and a mizzen staysail or mizzen spinnaker can be set when the wind is at certain angles. I have seen an expert back a ketch out of a tight berth using only the mizzen sail when the vessel was facing into the wind.

In large yachts the ketch rig can be designed so that there is substantial separation between the mainsail and mizzen. In the round-the-world Whitbread races some years ago, Bruce Farr designed a number of high-performance 80-foot maxi

A ketch has the advantage of plenty of easily handled sail area for light airs. When it breezes up, it's simple to reef or drop individual sails to shorten down.

ketches with tall, skinny rigs. Many people considered them to be two sloop rigs on one hull.

The principal advantage of a ketch is that you can drop the mainsail and jog along with a small headsail and the mizzen when the weather is windy or you want to maneuver slowly under sail. As naval architect Frank MacLear has pointed out, however, the owners and admirers of ketches often forget the heavy price they pay for this.

The mainmast of a ketch is stepped farther forward where the beam is less, which means the athwartship staying cannot be as efficient. Because three smaller sails occupy the place of two larger sails (of a sloop, say), the ketch lacks sail area. To get around this, the ketch is often given a bowsprit, another structural complication, to enable larger headsails to be set. The combined weight of the bowsprit and the forward-stepped mast puts a lot of weight toward the bow—just where it is not wanted.

It's worth considering the experiences of Uffa Fox, the famous English naval architect:

> Forty-eight hours in a hard gale just to leeward of the Azores taught me two things about the ketch rig. We had left the northwest corner of Spain for the Azores. The night before making the land the wind increased with a very steep sea, and the two of us on deck had to reef the mainsail, which was 500 square feet in area. The other man steered, and I eased the mainsheet slightly, so that though close-hauled, the mainsail was not bung full of wind, but had just enough in it to keep it quiet and the boom steady. This enabled me to reef it fairly comfortably in spite of heavy seas sweeping over us. I put in one reef on top of the other, till the mainsail was close reefed, without undue difficulty. . . .
>
> The increasing wind and sea then forced me to stow the mainsail. We drove into the seas throughout the night, and daylight revealed the island of San Miguel ahead but slightly to windward of our course. On we drove, making leeway due to our small sail, and with the houses in plain view some four miles away we tried to tack to get under the lee of the island.
>
> All the people who argue for the ketch rig maintain that one has only to lower the mainsail and she will handle under staysail and mizzen; but though we tried some half-dozen times to get her about, we failed. As soon as we eased the wind out of her sails the windage of her spars and rigging slowed her up, and the next sea would crash

over her and knock her back on to the old tack. We set the close-reefed mainsail to try and help her, but with this on she lay right down on her beam ends with the water forcing its way in through the closed hatchway amidships. We took the main off her, and tried once more with the mizzen and the headsail, only to fail again.

We then gybed her, making the mistake of not taking the mizzen off first, for in gybing we carried away the mizzen mast. We then quickly stowed the mizzen and staysail, set the trysail, and hove to, and did not reach the island until some days later.

So besides teaching me that one man can handle 500 square feet of sail, that forty-eight hours also taught me that a ketch will not tack with only her mizzen and staysail. When the wind is so strong that she can only carry that amount of canvas, it is strong enough to slow her up as she comes into the wind through the windage in her spars and rigging. What happens is that the very next sea knocks her back on to the old tack.[24]

Writing in 2003, the expert designers at the Dutch firm of E. G. van de Stadt and Partners considered the position of the ketch to be as follows:

> Ketch rig: apart from good reaching characteristics, this rigging offers no advantages over the sloop rig. In the old days it was necessary to divide the required sail area into smaller parts because the handling had to be done manually. Nowadays, large sail areas can be managed with powerful winches. It makes more sense to take part of the money set aside for the mizzen mast, shrouds, sail, and winches and to spend it on larger halyard and sheet winches and to perfect the reefing system of a sloop rig, which is much simpler.[25]

In the end, the expense, weight, and complexity all work against the practicality of a ketch. I put the yawl in the same class except that a yawl's mizzen is even more useless; most yawl owners find that their vessels sail better with the mizzen entirely removed. Certainly life is easier in the cockpit without all the extra strings and clutter of a mizzenmast and sail.

I believe a staysail schooner rig is the best two-masted sailing plan. There is plenty of sail area with a jib, forestaysail, main staysail, and mainsail. In light weather, a fisherman staysail can be set between the masts. This sail is less difficult to handle if its luff runs up a track on the back of the foremast. For running, the eased mainsail is often balanced with an opposite poled-out headsail, though there are other choices.

In Rio de Janeiro, I spoke with Antoine Muraccioli, a French single-hander who was sailing a green 48-foot steel staysail schooner named *Om*. This intriguing yacht was a Damien II, with a $4\frac{1}{2}$-ton retracting keel, designed by the French naval architect Michel Joubert.

"I find the staysail schooner perfect for me," said the bearded rock star when I

Tom Colvin's 42-foot steel-hulled Gazelle *with her Chinese lugsail rig. Colvin, unlike British designers, prefers sails with curved leeches. These require double sheets, that is, sheets or sheetlets led to each batten on both the port and starboard sides. Otherwise the sheets get fouled by the sail when it swings across. By adjusting the sheetlets going to each batten, it's easy to alter the sail shape. The sheetlets sound like endless trouble but in fact are simple to deal with. In light airs,* Gazelle *carries 850 square feet of area in her three sails. With increasing wind, the jib is handed first, followed by reductions in the easily reefed, fully battened sails. The masts are heavy-walled ($^5/16"$) aluminum pipes. The shrouds are set up loosely—just enough to keep the masts from whipping. At least one of these yachts has sailed around the world.*

Naval architect Tom Colvin, an authority on the junk rig, adjusting the sheetlets on Gazelle's *reefed mainsail.*

talked with him. "When the wind changes, I simply put one or two sails up or down. Furling or hoisting is easy. Taking off sails is slow and too much hard work."

So far I've mentioned the popular bermudian rig in its various forms: sloop, cutter, ketch, yawl, and staysail schooner. I've touched on the gaff rig, which is used infrequently.

I've sailed on three modern yachts with Chinese lugsail rigs and found the performance much better than I anticipated. They're not racing machines to windward, but you can tack and gybe without touching a sheet, which makes the sailing easy. Reefing is incredibly simple. If you get into trouble, you just let go of the sheet and halyard and the whole rig folds up effortlessly with the fully battened sail falling neatly between lazyjacks. There are, of course, no jibs at all.

Sailing to windward with a Chinese rig requires some new thinking because the luff of the sail doesn't shake as you head up. You need to pay attention to your speed through the water, because initially it seems that you can go closer and closer to the wind (wow!). But suddenly you find that you have come to a complete stop.

The Chinese lugsail rig uses an unstayed mast that is shorter and stouter than a bermudian spar. A freestanding mast bends a bit, but unstayed masts have been used

on sailing vessels for centuries. I think the Chinese rig would profit greatly from carbon-fiber spars and battens.

Another use of carbon fiber is with the British-designed AeroRig. This is a modern sloop arrangement in which the entire sail plan—mast, main boom, jib boom, and sails—rotates as a single fixed unit on the deck. The main boom and jib boom are joined together in a straight line at the mast so that the mainsail and jib swing together on a single yard that runs from the tack of the jib all the way back to the clew of the mainsail. There is no standing rigging at all. Everything hangs on the mast, which pivots on a massive strong point built into the basic structure of the hull.

With the AeroRig, a single line, a sort of super mainsheet, partway out on the main boom, controls the long yard and both sails. In strong winds, the jib can be partially rolled up and the main slab-reefed, all still pivoting together. The makers claim better downwind performance than with a conventionally eased main and a poled-out jib. Everything can be handled from the cockpit.

In 1986, I met a man in the Azores who was sailing a large yacht with this rig. He talked nonstop about how well it worked. I have two friends, Craig and Linda McKee, who have installed the AeroRig on a new 59-footer and report that they can tack through 82 degrees true. "Downwind sailing is easy without poles and spinnakers," Linda says. "We just ease the sheet."

One drawback is the lack of light-air options; there is no provision for a genoa or an asymmetrical spinnaker. Additionally, installations on existing yachts can be difficult because the loads from the mast root structure are high and quite different from normal mast loads with traditional stays and shrouds. Finally, the rig is expensive: on a Prout 45, the AeroRig option is an extra $66,000. No doubt the cost will drop if the rig catches on.

The catboat is based on freestanding unstayed masts that are constructed of wood, fiberglass, aluminum, or more recently, carbon fiber. There are significant advantages to this scheme of sailing, and it's becoming more popular every year. In the early days the rigs were a bit chancy because the hollow spars were made of wood held together with resorcinol glue, but today's high-tech carbon-fiber masts are as strong as helicopter blades.

I like the concept of an unstayed mast because of its marvelous simplicity. Com-

The famous yacht Jester *with Blondie Hasler on board at the start of the 1964 Observer Singlehanded Transatlantic Race in Plymouth, England, an event that's held every four years. Although* Jester *is only 25.9 feet in length, she made double Atlantic crossings in 1960 and 1964. Later sailed by Michael Richey, she entered the race nine more times, a remarkable record. Engineless, and built around a wooden Folkboat hull, she is propelled by a single 237-square-foot fully battened Chinese lugsail set on a slim unstayed mast. Although* Jester's *performance to windward is poor to modest, her general performance is good and she can be handled entirely from the sheltered steering station.*

pare the smooth, uncluttered, slightly flexible wings of a modern Boeing jet with the struts and wires and clunky wings of a 1928 Ford TriMotor plane.

Today in a typical bermudian-rigged yacht we use 2 (or more) wires to keep the mast in place in a fore-and-aft direction. To support it from side to side, we add 6 (or more) additional wires. In all, at least 8 pieces of wire hold up the mast, plus at least 150 highly loaded fittings. Each part is expensive and specially made. Most are stainless steel and forged, cast, or machined from solid stock, but some are formed of bronze or aluminum. A mast 50–60 feet long typically has

20 wire end fittings	40 clevis pins
4 spreaders (2 sets)	8 running backstay parts
30 turnbuckle parts	26 mast tangs
4 spreader bases	4 chainplates
12 toggles	4 tang bolts
4 spreader endpieces	12 chainplate bolts

To repair broken wires at a swage fitting at sea, I put a short piece of 7 × 19 wire alongside the problem area and secured the wire with bulldog clamps.

Plus 60 or more cotter pins and a couple of dozen rivets. If any of the wires break, if a cotter pin somehow falls out, or if one of the special metal fittings fractures or disconnects, the spar will slip away from its restraining wires, move outside its design limits, and probably collapse.

Engineers deal with these problems at the design stage by estimating expected loads on the rig and applying appropriate safety factors—say, 2.5 for racing, 3 for inshore cruising, and 4 for offshore voyaging. Sailors and riggers are aware of these problems on the operations level and do their best to inspect every part of the standing rigging. However, the multiplicity of all these parts is a niggling worry.

Some careful sailors X-ray each part of their standing rigging and other critical parts. I recall that in 1978, Tom Watson had all the small pieces of his standing rigging X-rayed on sheets of 8-by-10-inch film by Wayfarer Marine in Camden, Maine. Every part passed except one large toggle that had an internal crack. The toggle looked perfect and had no surface cracks visible through a magnifying glass. If you struck the toggle with a small hammer, the fitting had a clear, penetrating ring. Yet this critical rigging part was faulty.

Another concern is the weight of all this hardware, especially the wire. Ten 5/16-inch-diameter wires 50 feet long weigh 111 pounds. In 1992, I weighed the entire rig (mast, all the wires, mast steps, running rigging—everything) of my Santa Cruz 50, and it came to 1,200 pounds. My point is that a conventional bermudian mast and its support hardware are much heavier than people think. This gives plenty of weight allowance for a large-diameter freestanding mast and a strongly built mast step and deck partners to hold the spar in place. There's a real opportunity to save weight aloft, which means better sailing.

Cruising boats are inextricably bound up with establishment racing rules that have long specified that "a yacht must be fitted with a bona-fide headstay." A headstay requires a backstay, which in turn demands shrouds. This conventional bermudian rigging forces sails to fit the three-sided rigging and be triangular in shape. Yet aerodynamicists have conclusively proven that sails with a curved, deeply convex leech are much more efficient.[26]

In an effort to use such a mainsail, the designer Lars Bergstrom,* long a consultant to Hunter yachts, came up with the Bergstrom-Ritter rig, which dispenses with the backstay entirely and uses 30-degree swept-back spreaders and a series of diamond shrouds to support the mast. With no backstay, a mainsail with lots of roach can be used. With the swept-back spreaders of the Bergstrom-Ritter rig, however, there are severe problems with mainsail chafe when running, and all the extra rigging is self-defeating in my view.

Are there any sailing advantages with a freestanding mast? Consider the drawing (next page) of the 30-foot catboat designed by Tom Wylie. With her single sail, angled carbon-fiber mast, mostly full-length battens, and streamlined wishbone boom to control the sail, she's obviously a descendent of the Windsurfer. However, she has some new features and they're all combined in a nice-looking package.

I've sailed one of these dainty, lightweight yachts and learned that in going to weather—say, 45 degrees off the wind—you can tack without touching a sheet or a winch. There's no need to worry about pulling around the jib *because there is no jib*. With a reaching wind you simply ease the mainsheet a little and check the speedometer to find the best sail setting. For downwind courses, you let out the sheet additionally. There's no problem with gybing because there are no shrouds for the wishbone (or main boom) to slam against. In light airs, you can easily get more draft in the sail by easing foot tension with the outhaul control led through the wishbone.

If you're running by the lee and the wind gets behind the sail, the boom and sail simply swing around to the other side. The possible downside is that a cat rig may be underpowered when running in light airs, so the rig needs plenty of sail area

*Lars Bergstrom, everyone's friend and a fountainhead of ideas and enthusiasm, was tragically killed in an airplane crash in 2000. We all miss his cheerful enthusiasm.

I like the simple, pleasant lines of this 30-foot Tom Wylie design for a high-performance catboat. When I sailed one of these boats in Annapolis, she went along nicely in light airs and we seemed to pass all the conventional 40-footers. Wylie also makes this design—which he calls a Wyliecat—in 39- and 48-foot lengths. I believe the future of sailing lies in this direction because it's so easy and uncomplicated and doesn't force a sailor to buy things he doesn't need nor particularly want in order to go sailing.

in the first place. This probably means three or four reefs for a seagoing single-sail cat rig.

When the wind strengthens and you're flying a single large sail, you need to reef promptly. Otherwise the boat will be on her ear. With a wishbone or a conventional boom properly set up, the necessary reefing is easy. Additionally, in a squall or a gust, the top of a tapered freestanding mast bends away from the wind while the upper part of the sail flutters harmlessly—a sort of automatic reefing or de-powering.

The sail area can be broken up into two roughly equal parts in a cat-ketch or cat-schooner rig. This makes each mast and sail smaller and easier to handle and for heavier vessels may be a better scheme.

In 1976, the innovative designer Garry Hoyt founded the Freedom line of yachts. Garry's idea was to produce a racing-cruising boat that was extremely easy to sail, had excellent accommodations, and featured shoal draft and a centerboard. Initially the masts were made of large-diameter aluminum tubes; later they were constructed of carbon fiber.

I was a crewman aboard Freedom 40 #1 on a trip from Antigua to St. John in the Caribbean in 1978. With two self-tending sails, the boat was incredibly simple to operate, and even with its big hull and high freeboard, surprisingly weatherly. Since then the company has gone through a series of designs and in all has built 1,300 yachts. In Canada, George Hinterhoeller has constructed 975 boats to the Nonsuch designs of Mark Ellis. (The International Nonsuch Association is the largest group of sailboat owners, with more than 600 members.) I've sailed on a Nonsuch 30, and again the vessel was a cinch to sail. A lightweight 70-foot cat-ketch charter design by Yves-Marie Tanton has crossed the Atlantic 21 times. In 1999, the American naval architect Eric Sponberg designed a 60-foot cat ketch with freestanding wing masts to compete in an international race; the resultant yacht sails spectacularly well. Until recently, a Freedom 44 held the Newport-to-Bermuda race record. And so on.

The seaworthiness of the modern freestanding mast is well established.

All these architects and businesspeople figured that recreational sailors would dump the bermudian rig and turn to freestanding masts in large numbers. Unfortunately, the builders and designers were dead wrong. They didn't realize how conservative and slow-moving small-boat sailors are. Apparently, tradition and convention are everything; boatowners are not necessarily progressive.

Although some three thousand cruising sailors have bought freestanding rigs in

This is the Freedom 40 prototype developed by Garry Hoyt, who followed up on his reasoning that a sail behind a mast on a boom controlled with a purchase is far more easily managed than a large genoa headsail. This heavy, beamy yacht has her sail area split between two freestanding masts and self-tacking sails. For off-the-wind sailing, a staysail can be set between the masts. Her bulbous appearance results from a raised-deck aftercabin and substantial bulwarks. Note the dinghy on the portside midships. During racing and in cruising with other 40-footers, the Freedom has done surprisingly well, with much less work demanded from her crew. This photograph shows double sails wrapped around the masts and joined at the leeches, which makes a smoother entry and gets rid of mast tracks and slides. This boat has no standing rigging at all. "It's safer," Hoyt says, "because you are not placing your trust in a host of potential breaking points. That's why wires were taken off airplane wings long ago." There have been many improved Freedom designs built since this early model of 1975.

the last twenty-five years, these sales have made little impact on the general market. Beneteau, for example, one of the leading yacht companies in the United States, builds and sells about five yachts a week, year after year. All have bermudian rigs.

It seems to me that the biggest problem with a catboat with a single sail, a cat ketch, or a cat schooner is *its unusualness*. We're all so accustomed to looking at the familiar bermudian rig and all those wires and spreaders that it will take a while for sailors to gain confidence in a mast without any of the usual supports. Personally, when I touch a piece of ¼-inch-diameter 1 × 19 rigging wire and consider that there are 8 or 10 such wires holding up my mast, I feel a certain amount of security. Yet the engineers tell me they build substantial safety factors into freestanding masts and that a 12- or 15-inch-diameter, 40-foot-long tapered carbon-fiber tube has fantastic strength.

Racing boats have been using carbon-fiber spade rudders for fifteen years or more, but rudders are out of sight and accepted. In the Olympics I've watched pole vaulters spring high into the air from skinny carbon-fiber poles. I play tennis with a carbon-fiber racket and it's never broken.

Another factor may be that the early cat-ketch designs looked boxy and chunky and, at least to my eye, were not pleasing. The Mark Ellis Nonsuch, which perhaps can be categorized as a second-generation design, is better looking but has a bluff bow and a single mast that sticks up vertically. In my opinion, the Tom Wylie yacht mentioned above—what I call the third generation of modern catboats—is a much prettier yacht. Although I think her daysailer cockpit is too big and the interior is rudimentary for serious voyaging, the hull and coachroof have nice lines. Her mast is angled a little aft, and she has a fin keel, spade rudder, light displacement, and plenty of sail area that combine to make her a powerful and well-performing small vessel.

I think there's a parallel in all this with the automobile. Think of the stick shift and the automatic transmission. I remember when Buick introduced automatic drive in the 1940s. It didn't work very well and was soon nicknamed "the slush-o-matic." Yet it was gradually improved, and now practically everyone drives a car with an automatic transmission. Two generations of drivers scarcely know what a clutch is. Automatic drive has been accepted because it's better. I think freestanding masts will come into wide use because they're sensible, efficient, and logical.

We saw this sleek lateen-rigged fishing boat in Bali, Indonesia, in one of the small ports on the east coast. She was one of forty or so that slipped out each morning when the weather was settled. Their bright, multihued sails were dots of moving color in the distance.

8

HOW TO MAKE
BIG SAILS SMALL

Traditionally, the mainsail of a bermudian yacht is hoisted by pulling down on a halyard fitted through a block or sheave at the masthead. The front—the luff—of the mainsail has small metal or plastic slides that run up and down a matching track fitted along the back of the mast. You pull down. The sail goes up. Simple. Foolproof.

The jib is much the same. Hanks—little loops of metal—are sewn or fastened along the luff of the sail every few feet and go up the headstay and hold the sail in

You may think you're strong, but a sailor has remarkably little bare-handed hauling power in a straight-line pulling situation. What's needed here is a multiple purchase with blocks or a simple barrel winch (with a line jammer above it to hold one halyard while you use the winch for the next). This way you can put a steady, strong tension on the jib and main halyards. Or the halyards can be led to deck blocks and the lines taken to a drum on the anchor windlass. The job is even more difficult if the sails are full of wind. This photograph shows me and a Greek friend in the Aegean in 1962. Certainly that boarding ladder hanging on the starboard running light complex would be safer if lashed down on deck.

119

place when the halyard is tight. The regular sails are designed for moderate winds, say 10–15 knots; problems develop when the wind is stronger or lighter. Another factor is whether the wind is from ahead, behind, or the side.

If the winds are too strong, you reef or reduce the mainsail in size in various clever ways that have been worked out over a long time. If the jib is too large for the existing wind, it's normally taken down, folded up, stuck in a bag, and put away. Then you drag out a smaller sail, hank it on, tie on the sheets, and hoist it. Ideally, this sail will be perfect for the new wind strength. You go through the same drill with larger sails for lighter winds, or sometimes hoist an additional sail.

Hanked sails are used by millions of small-boat sailors every year. The system is quick, reliable, inexpensive, and very satisfactory, but for the 25- to 55-foot yachts I've been discussing, the sails are often large, heavy, and difficult to handle. Changing sails at sea can be hard work and sometimes a bit hazardous; sailors have long sought easier schemes to hoist, lower, and reef sails.

Two halfway measures are foot reefs and bonnets. In the first, you have new upper cringles (and reef patches) fitted to the luff and leech at points that will reduce the sail area by 30 percent (or whatever). When you're ready for the headsail reef, you ease the halyard and change the sheets and tack connection to the upper-cringle positions. You then fold or roll up the unused bunt or foot of the sail and tie it out of the way with short lines through the reef patches. Then hoist the reefed sail and adjust the sheets.

I've tried this scheme and it works, but I've found that the furled part of the sail picks up water and tends to chafe on the leeward lifelines. Raising the sail with a short tack pendant helps. An additional small problem is that the weight of the upper metal clew cringle and reinforcing patches contributes to leech flutter. (The cringle might better be made of three- or four-strand rope worked into an eye.) As a practical matter, however, I don't think a reefable headsail is worthwhile because it's almost as quick to change the entire sail as to reef it. Remember that if a sail has three strong edges, it's sturdy and whole on all sides.

Another reefing idea for a jib, genoa, staysail, or schooner foresail is a sail with a removable bonnet or foot. I have a wonderful Melbourne Smith drawing of *Swift of Norfolk*, a 19th century pilot schooner that shows bonnets on the lower parts of two sails. The problem is the connection between the bonnet and the sail. This is usually a lacing rove between eyelets dotted along each part of the two-part sail. Two generations ago, Sir Francis Chichester used bonnets on twin running sails. Each sheet was attached to the bonnet, but the bearing-out pole went directly to the original clew above. According to reports, his system worked well, but apparently it's a challenge to make a bonneted sail without a mass of wrinkles. I do not know how Chichester attached the bonnets.[27]

Larry Pardey has a chapter on bonnets in the recent Pardey book *The Cost-Con-*

scious Cruiser.[28] Larry uses a high-strength plastic zipper together with snapshackles secured to the boltropes at the luff and leech plus leather protection patches over the metal hardware. I admire Larry's efforts, but when I asked my local sailmaker about this scheme, his eyes went all glassy. Carol Hasse, who owns a large sail loft in Port Townsend, Washington, and specializes in bulletproof cruising sails, reports that bonneted sails work OK. "However, they're very labor-intensive because you have to make a three-cornered sail plus a four-cornered sail and then work out the connections between them."

I don't use foot reefs or bonnets on my headsails because the schemes seem too complicated for what you get out of them.

In this chapter, I discuss a number of mechanical schemes for shortening sails. However, I want to say at the beginning that hanked-on sails will always have a secure place on sailing vessels. No matter what slick systems you may have on board for managing sails, it's a good idea to have at least one sturdy working jib, large staysail, or small genoa with hanks and a way of hoisting it. Then if a sail is torn or a furling system is damaged (a headstay extrusion smashed by an errant spinnaker pole, corrosion problems, escaped bearing balls, and so forth), you can at least get operational with an effective sail. Without a proper headsail, the performance of a yacht may be severely limited, and she may not be able to sail out of danger.

Today there's a lot of emphasis on roller-furling headsails and mainsails that disappear into the mast or main boom. You pull a couple of strings and—zip—the big sails magically become small sails and then disappear entirely. There's no need to leave the cockpit, no fumbling with sail hanks, and no stuffing of sails into bags and dragging them along the deck. You dispense with sail covers entirely. It's all wonderful, but of course nothing is free. The tradeoffs are weight, complexity, expense, and decreased reliability.

In the case of in-the-mast mainsail furling, the efficiency of the sail is less because of sail shape, particularly when the sail gets old. If a sail rolls up on a vertical axis, it's not possible to fit effective horizontal battens. Sailmakers have tried various designs of vertical battens, but no one has found any that really work. And without battens, there's flutter and vibration along the back—the leech—of the sail. To deal with this, sailmakers cut the sail without the usual convex curve (roach). They may even undercut and hollow out the leech a little. The result is a loss of about 15 percent of the sail area.

The reduced sail area and a hooked leech mean poorer performance.

In-the-mast furling arrangements (or add-on systems that fit behind the mast) require a long and heavy vertical rod or wire the entire height of the mast. This generally means a bigger mast section with more weight and drag. In addition, in-the-mast rigs need a special main boom, various swivels and bearings, and a geared crank, ratchet, or spool system to turn the rod or wire to pull the sail in and out. The cost of one such system (by Seldén) for a mast and boom for a 38- to 42-foot sloop including rigging, turnbuckles, halyards, a new mainsail, and installation was $22,500 in 2003. A similar-sized complete new rig for a conventional mainsail (hoisted by a halyard and slab-reefed) was $16,000.

Engineers have worked long and hard to perfect these mainsail furling and reefing systems, but I've talked to people who have had problems at sea, and the repairs can be a nasty business. With the add-on wire systems behind the mast, you can at least get at the deck-level components. Some in-the-mast systems, however, have their vitals cleverly hidden away inside the mast.

If you decide on in-the-mast furling, you can make a good argument for adding a separate trysail track to the outside of the spar. Then if the furling system fails, God forbid, you can still hoist a trysail, which in an end-of-the-world scenario can be a blessing.

Where in-the-mast sail handling shines brilliantly is with reefing because the sail can be made smaller and smaller with ease and safety. The clew block on the special boom follows the clew of the sail so the shape of the reefed sail is automatically adjusted as the sail is cranked into the mast.

Another way to handle mainsail furling and reefing is to fit a roller-furling *boom*. This is a scheme in which the horizontal main boom revolves on what is essentially a horizontal pin mounted on the mast. As you turn the boom and adjust the halyard, the mainsail rolls up and down like a window shade. With boom furling, the mainsail can carry some extra roach to increase its area, and employ either short or full-length battens to help maintain good sail shape. Since both the revolving boom and battens are horizontal, you roll up the battens with the sail. Generally you need an end-of-the-boom mainsheet arrangement.

A roller-furling boom is an old idea that seems logical and simple. The problem has always been to get the forward end of the sail to roll up evenly. This is difficult because the reinforced luff has to roll up on top of itself, and as it does, it makes more bulk. Most of today's systems use a boltrope or jack line that runs up and down a vertical aluminum or plastic extrusion that's secured to the back of the mast or held a few inches behind the mast with special fasteners. In one scheme, the sail track is mounted 5 inches behind the mast on small horizontal fittings that can double as steps for climbing the mast.

In the past, I've seen systems that use an adjustable light line that zigzags between mast-track slides and corresponding grommets along the lower part of the luff of the sail. This helps deal with the problem of the sail rolling up unevenly and thus putting heavy strains on the fabric. Another plan employs battens of wood that are inserted or fastened along the middle part of the boom to increase its diameter

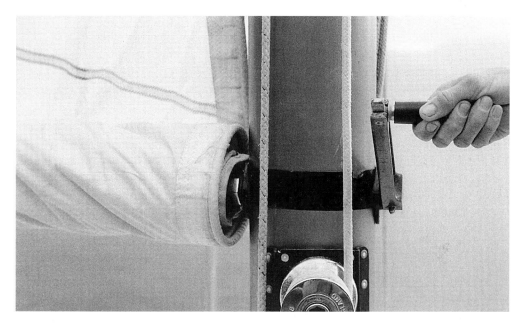

This roller-reefing boom on a Contessa 32 works like a roll-up window shade. The setup is simple and easy to use on a small mainsail, but with larger sails, the buildup of the luff tape/boltrope can be a problem. The through-the-mast crank needs a foolproof holding arrangement to keep the sail from unrolling when the sail is reefed. Note that there is no sliding gooseneck at all. Some people (me) worry about drilling a substantial hole through the mast. Nevertheless, many owners report complete success with this scheme, and these yachts have sailed all over the world for many years. The horizontal black line on the mast is from tape used for sail measurement purposes.

so that when the boom is revolved, it rolls up more of the middle part of the sail.

With roller-boom systems, it's important that the roller axle is at right angles to the mast; otherwise, when the axle goes around, the sail will roll up cockeyed and askew. Most of the current commercial systems specify a boom-mast angle of 88 degrees and mandate that a support (boom vang) be installed underneath the boom to maintain this angle. Unfortunately, rigid boom vangs are anathema to most cruising sailors because they interfere with dinghy and other stowage on deck.

I recently looked at a through-the-mast roller-reefing setup on a British-built Contessa 32. The main boom has no vertical sliding gooseneck at the mast at all, being held in a fixed position by a large horizontal stainless steel pin that goes right through the mast in a fore-and-aft direction. The pin is connected to the boom with a double pivot so that the after end of the boom is free to move up or down or to swing from side to side. The forward end of the pin has a convenient handle at the front of the mast, which, when turned, rotates the entire boom like an axle or a mandrel. The mainsail requires no setback at the bottom of the luff and rolls up on the boom like paper towels around a cardboard tube. The entire sail can be rolled up if desired, certainly a marvelous idea for furling. When I tried it, the mainsail rolled up fairly well, with only a few creases. However, the sail area is modest—less than 200 square feet.

This scheme is an advance over old types of worm-gear roller reefing because you apply the turning motion to the boom from a convenient position forward of the mast, and with a long handle, you have plenty of power. The reefing handle can be permanently attached and is arranged to lock so it can't turn. Designs vary; one setup for boats of 40 feet or more has internal gearing and a standard socket to take a detachable winch handle. I'm told that this system has been used on 65-foot ocean racers, but I wonder whether a mainsail of 500–600 square feet will roll up smoothly enough to make it practical. I'm certainly not excited about drilling a big hole through the mast. However, the spar people say it's OK.

There are half a dozen boom-furling gears available (with a custom boom and all the hardware and mast parts) whose manufacturers claim great things. Before buying, however, be aware that you will probably need a new mainsail with special construction along the luff and leech to help the sail roll up evenly. With these systems, the amount of halyard and outhaul adjustment is limited; in addition the boom and axle arrangements are fairly heavy and increase the problems from an accidental gybe. Boom-furling gears tend to be difficult to reef off the wind, and the luff tapes need frequent renewal. The theory of boom furling is wonderful; in practice it's somewhat less grand.

For a 35-foot yacht, in-the-boom reefing-furling gears from four companies averaged about $7,500 at the time of writing. For a 42-footer, the cost was $10,000, and for a 50-footer, the bill was $13,000. Before you think of buying one of these systems, ask for sailing demonstrations on several private yachts so that you can see how the gear actually works and hear what the owners have to say.

Years ago I had a fancy bronze roller-reefing gear that seemed to work OK. However, I discovered that as soon as I cranked in a reef and turned my back, the boom unrolled itself. I finally learned that it was necessary to *tie the handle in place* to maintain a setting. How nice it would have been to have known more about that quirky gear before I bought it.

Equipment manufacturers offer furling schemes with powerful electrical or hydraulic motors, particularly for larger yachts. You flick a switch or open a valve and—zip!—the sails go in and out. As long as everything works, these powered systems are spectacular. But the forces involved are considerable, and if something goes wrong there can be a major problem (a stripped gear; a twisted rod; a pool of hydraulic fluid on deck; a ruined sail). Of course, limit switches and various controls can be built into electrical furling systems, and bypass or pressure relief valves can be incorporated into the plumbing of hydraulic units.

But you don't want all this in a simple sailing yacht! When a cruising yacht begins to resemble a small jet aircraft in complexity, it's time to back off.

At least when you have trouble trying to turn the handle of a hand-cranked winch, you get a signal that there's a problem somewhere. You stop and begin to look around. Maybe it's merely a loop in a furling line that's jammed in a block. A hydraulic winch may rip the block out of the deck. With a hand-operated system, however, you stop, untwist the line with two fingers, and continue. Again and again in small boats *simplicity is best*.

Most people reduce the sail area of mainsails with tied or jiffy reefs. This is a popular arrangement in which the bottom panels of the sail are taken out of use by pulling the sail progressively downward and using new and higher tack and clew cringles that were built into the sail when it was made. The bottom 40 to 60 percent of the sail is divided into two or three roughly rectangular panels. The lowest panel is known as the first reef and generally reduces the sail area by 20 percent. The second reef takes out another 20 percent. If the mainsail is tall and narrow or the vessel is headed for stormy places, the sailmaker may put in a third reef, which results in a 60 percent reduction. The clew cringles for the reefs are made a little higher than the tack cringles so that the boom will be angled up slightly to keep the boom end away from crew heads and the water in case the sheet is eased and the ocean is rough. Since mainsail reefs sometimes have to be pulled down in heavy weather and left in place for long periods, the reefing pendants, blocks, and line jammers are usually substantial. Most sailors like tied reefs because the sail shape is better than with any other system of mainsail reefing, particularly with full-length battens. (See chapter 10 for more details.)

Roller-furling gear on the headstay to control a headsail is well developed, and most cruising sailors use one of a dozen systems on the market. They're all roughly similar, quite reliable and strong, and competitively priced.

The units are sized according to the length and sail area of a vessel and generally utilize a small teardrop-sectioned plastic or anodized aluminum extrusion on the order of $1\frac{1}{2}$ by $\frac{3}{4}$ inches that fits loosely around the headstay wire. The extrusions come in lengths of about 6 feet (2 m).

Each extrusion has a small slot along its length. You thread six or eight of these skinny extrusions on the headstay wire one after another and join each to the next with a sleeve and pins or screws. This results in a single, long, streamlined extrusion with a slot at the back that runs the length of the headstay. This slot takes a special boltrope that's sewed along the luff of the sail.

To hoist the sail, you feed the boltrope into the slot while someone hauls away

Thank heavens for the creative spirit and for a little fun! The builder of this Italian yacht could easily have fitted a turnbuckle at the stem. Instead he welded this playful snake to the stem fitting and employed a deadeye and lashings to set up tension on the headstay. Could this be Cleopatra's asp spitting at the waves?

on the jib halyard. When it's all in place, the luff of the sail is supported along its entire length by the extrusion. The entry of the sail into the wind is now smooth, streamlined, and slick as a bird's wing.

Bearings are fitted to the top and bottom of this long extrusion, which rotates freely on the headstay. Near the bottom bearing is a drum with a line that goes to the cockpit. When a length of line is wound on the drum equal to the clew-to-luff distance on the sail and you pull the string, the sail rolls up around the extrusion (and headstay wire) just like the window shade I spoke about earlier.

If you sew a strip of 18-inch-wide sun-resistant fabric along the leech and foot of the sail and roll up the sail, it will be entirely covered with protection against the sun.

Since these furling units are located at the front of a vessel and are continually blasted with salt water, all the manufacturers except one use high-quality corrosion-proof plastic bearings. The ProFurl design has steel bearings that are sealed against salt water. The furling drums themselves are made of anodized aluminum or stainless steel.

A potential problem with roller-furling gears is that the extrusions fitted over the headstay wire hide the wire and make it difficult to check for broken strands or deterioration. It's a lot of trouble to lower the extrusions and wire for an inspection, and the job tends to be ignored and put out of mind. Nevertheless, the headstay wire needs to be checked on a regular basis and replaced if necessary.

In my experience, the main operational problem with jib-furling gears is chafe on the furling line, a piece of cordage that—after the main halyard—has become the most important piece of running rigging on a yacht. The furling line is generally a piece of $^5/_{16}$- or $^3/_8$-inch-diameter braided Dacron line 60 to 80 feet long. The line goes through a series of small blocks that guide it from the furling drum at the bow all the way back to the cockpit. Sometimes the furling line is tight and moves slightly back and forth, especially when the yacht is sailing to windward and the bow is rising and falling on swells or waves.

If this line is exposed to anything rough or sharp, the back-and-forth rubbing motion will saw the line in two. Nicked screw heads on the forward end of a spinnaker pole stowed on deck, a bumpy weld on the bow pulpit, rough corners on anchors, and a hard edge on a windlass are especially lethal.

During a squall or sharply rising wind, it may be necessary to run off before the wind, reduce sail quickly, or both. A parted furling line means that you can't roll up the sail. To keep this from happening, I glance at the line and the row of small blocks along the lifeline stanchions (or deck) once in a while. These little blocks tend to get knocked out of position, so occasionally I get down on my hands and knees and follow the line both visually and by feel from the bow to the cockpit. I align the blocks with regard to height and adjust them so the furling line runs on the middle of each sheave and not along the hard metal edges.

The most important block is the first one aft of the furling drum. This should be carefully aligned vertically and adjusted sideways so the furling line doesn't rub on the drum or anything else. The pull should be in a straight line. I have found it worthwhile to fit a special horizontal crossbar (see photograph next page) from one side of the bow pulpit to the other side a little aft of the furling drum to hold the block.

When you're sailing and have the entire headsail set, it's a good plan to ease the furling line slightly. A little slack will eliminate chafe problems. In addition, it's useful to have a spare furling line made up to the right length with the ends whipped and ready to use. But on a dark night when you're on the wind and busy with navigation, when water is flying around, and you need a reef is not the time to have to reeve a new furling line. The difficulty is not in slipping the line into place, but in putting enough turns on the drum to deal with reefing and furling.

It's possible to replace the furling line with thin (say, $^3/_{16}"$ dia.) 7 × 19 stainless steel flexible wire. Unfortunately, wire is hard on the hands and is a problem to deal with in the cockpit. A rope tail on the wire or the use of a special wire winch doesn't seem practical.

I apologize for beating the subject of furling lines to death, but this small control line tends to be neglected and forgotten until it chafes through and breaks. Once set up properly, however, it will last for years.

Much of the appeal of a roller-furling headsail is based on its reefing potential. It's possible to reef a roller-furling headsail a little or a lot by rolling the luff of the sail

A good mounting place for the first lead block for the roller-furling line (see arrow) is on an athwartships crossbar on the bow pulpit. This position will assist in reducing chafe on the roller-furling gear control line and will help keep the line in order. In addition, the crossbar greatly strengthens the bow pulpit and is a good place to sit when you're at the bow. Early on I made the crossbar from a piece of wood. It worked so well that I replaced it with a piece of stainless steel tubing that I had welded in place.

around the revolving extrusion fitted over the headstay wire. In theory, it would seem that with such a window-shade arrangement, one sail would cover all wind strengths. You could buy a very large sail, perhaps 150 percent of the foretriangle. This would work well in light airs. Then as more wind came up, you could crank in a few rolls. With still more wind, you'd roll up the sail until you had the genoa down to the size of a storm jib.

Unfortunately, headsail roller reefing doesn't work well beyond five or six rolls because of the draft or fullness built into a sail. The headsail is roughly a triangle with its apex at the head and a substantial foot dimension (roughly half the hoist). This means that as you roll up the sail, more cloth is taken up at the bottom (foot) and less in the middle. This makes the sail inefficient in the center and upper portions: your beautiful sail has become a useless bag.

Another point: Should the sail be made of light cloth for when the full sail is used? Or heavy cloth when it's substantially reefed? Whatever the choice, it will be right only half the time.

When reefing, it helps to move the sheet block forward to maintain equal tension on the leech and foot parts of the sail. If you hear flapping and noise, the sheet block is not properly positioned. You may need to adjust the leech and foot lines on the sail as well.

It's a useful step to fill about 80 percent of the center part of the luff with a few strips of $\frac{1}{4}$-inch-thick foam sewed and centered along the front of the sail. Or you can use a skinny bundle of old short pieces of $\frac{1}{2}$-inch-diameter line (or whatever is handy) placed parallel to the luff and stitched in place. This extra bulk takes up more of the belly of the sail as it's rolled up. Complicated, eh?

It's definitely worthwhile to have your sailmaker put a row of small metal eyelets in the tabling along the luff of every headsail that's set with a luff tape—say, at 18-inch intervals. During a long passage in the Atlantic in 1986, I had a headsail furling system completely fail. While at sea, I managed to remove the gear and set up a wire headstay. I didn't have enough spare hanks for an entire sail, so I used adjustable nylon cable clamps (for bundling electrical wires) as emergency links between the eyelets and the headstay. The nylon loops worked surprisingly well and lasted until I reached Cape Town a week later. (I had considered loops of light line or wire.)

Of course, someone is going to ask: "If you've had a furling system fail, why continue with such devices? Why not go back to hanked sails, which are simpler and more reliable? Why not eliminate the weight and windage of the extrusions altogether?"

My reply is that I believe a roller-furling headsail for a cruising yacht is a good idea and allows sailors to operate their vessels more efficiently and with less effort. Furling gears are universally popular, and 90 percent of today's cruising yachts employ them. I think the figure is 100 percent for charter yachts. A century ago, gaff-rigged yachts and fishing boats were often fitted with the Wykeham Martin furling gear, a crude forerunner of today's improved devices, so the notion of windup sails is nothing new.

However, let's be clear. A big genoa cannot be rolled to storm-jib size and give reasonable performance. You need to take other action if the weather gets nasty. You have five choices:

1. Depending on the wind and where you're going, you can simply roll up the big headsail and continue with the full or reefed main-sail. This is easy, simple, and often a good plan, but it's limited to downwind or reaching goals. It's surprising what you can do if you can arrange your course to keep the wind behind you.

2. The customary move, and one well endorsed by tradition and experience, is to roll up the big headsail completely and to set a staysail on the forestay.

3. If the forestay is not available, it's possible to set a staysail or storm staysail *flying*, that is, hoisted without setting the luff on a permanent stay. Another idea is to set a small sail on a second per-manent headstay wire set ahead (in front!) of the regular headstay (on which the big sail is now furled) as a sort of reserve headstay. This of course takes a good deal of preplanning; additionally, two headstays introduce some wire tensioning problems.

4. Take down the big headsail and put up a smaller one. This can be hazardous with a roller-furling gear. The change will be easier if you can back the sail or at least run off downwind or across the wind. Try to make the change during daylight if possible and with two people, with one *slowly easing and controlling the halyard* (keep a turn around a winch barrel) while the second person puts ties around the bulk of the sail to throttle it. The second per-son should have plenty of 4-foot-long ties handy.

The ATN Gale Sail.

5. A Fort Lauderdale sailmaker named Etienne Giroire (whose company is called ATN, a takeoff on his first name) markets a storm jib called a Gale Sail. This is a storm jib whose entire luff fits *around* the sausage-shaped mass of a large roller-furled head-sail (see photograph). The luff of the storm jib is secured back on itself with eight (or more) Wichard hanks. The sail is hoisted with a spare halyard, and its luff slides up over the big roller-furled jib or genoa to a position well above the deck on a long tack pendant. The sheets are led in the usual way to blocks along the decks or coachroof. In a strong wind, the storm-jib luff attachments can help keep the furled genoa under con-trol. Etienne's sail is a clever idea.

What can be nicer than to have six winsome young ladies sitting in the cockpit and singing for you? Here in Apia, Samoa, these laughing and smiling women are enjoying themselves almost as much as I did when I took the photograph.

9

SPINNAKERS, LIGHT-WEATHER SAILS, AND MORE ON SAIL HANDLING

There's a longstanding myth that a yacht headed for deep water should have a small rig because of possible heavy weather out there. I think this is a bum idea and is based more on nervousness and uncertainty of the captain than on reality. In my experience in both the high and low latitudes, 50 percent of the time, the wind strength is 15 knots or less. Often the wind conditions are light to moderate

Here I am on the Santa Cruz 50 during the 1990–91 round-the-world solo race. I have one reef in the mainsail, and we're hurrying along with a reaching spinnaker, or gennaker, pulling hard. I handled this sail with a furling sock that is shown bunched up at the masthead. The black square on the coachroof is four solar panels. I called the yacht Sebago *during the race.*

because small-boat people try hard to pick fair winds and summery conditions. Normally we try to stay away from gale-swept waters and don't try to cross the Bay of Biscay during the winter.

The ideal sailing vessel needs clouds of sails to keep moving in light airs. Yet the rig should be set up so the crew can reduce sail quickly and efficiently when the wind increases. Then even in stormy conditions, you will be able to move along smartly without being pressed, hopefully toward your destination. Progress at the light end of the sailing scale is more chancy because if you don't put up lots of sails to keep her moving, you'll never get anywhere.

I remember a 37-foot ketch named *Snoris* that was owned by a pleasant young Swiss couple named Robert and Claire Haymoz. The yacht was a heavily built wooden Bristol Channel pilot cutter. Robert and Claire were in the Pacific and had left the Galápagos Islands for the Marquesas, a 3,000-mile run westward along the equator. Partway to their goal, the wind died. Their sturdy ketch with her modest rig was becalmed. There was no possibility of going back because the South Equatorial Current was pushing the yacht slowly westward.

Snoris was becalmed for three weeks. To pass the time, the Haymozes sanded and painted the entire interior of their vessel. Finally, the wind returned and they made a landfall in the Marquesas. They had run out of food a day or two before and were glad to reach the lush islands, where there was plenty of fruit, vegetables, and meat. If *Snoris* had had a higher rig and light-weather sails, she might have made port a week or more earlier.

When you sail in feather-strength winds and zephyrs that barely caress the water, you need big, tall, light sails. Whether they're called genoas, ghosters, spinnakers, drifters, asymmetricals, gennakers, star-cuts, or water sails is not important. Old, half-rotten sails work almost as well as new sails because you don't blow out sails in light winds. Put up your largest and hoist them as high as possible. Some people prefer to split up their extra sail area into small, more easy-to-handle parcels, and a ketch or staysail schooner may have some advantages. Whatever plan you elect for light weather, you need to show plenty of cloth to the wind to generate enough horsepower to move.

Ease the outhaul and halyard of the mainsail to give it a deeper airfoil shape. Try different positions of the mainsheet traveler. Slack the halyards and sheets of headsails to make a slightly wrinkled luff and a fuller belly. Move the sheet leads forward. Experiment with significantly less backstay tension. If you're running and have a jib poled out for a fair wind, you may be able to set a second jib "flying" (by the tack, clew, and head) to leeward of the first.

Sometimes it's worthwhile to bear off or head up a little from your goal if you can sail faster. If you have a headwind and can't aim directly for your target, calculate which tack is better. Pay attention to weather reports and which way the wind is likely to go. In some places, there's a regular diurnal wind shift.

A few years ago Margaret and I were in the Mediterranean, sailing west-south-west from the Pelopónnisos in Greece. As we approached our destination in southern Tunisia, we paralleled the coast of Libya to the south. Every day the blistering summer sun beat down on the Sahara—out of sight on our port hand—and made the air rise over the desert. This hot air sucked the wind from the cooler area in the sea around us; our early-afternoon sea breeze was as predictable as the calm that followed at night.

Whenever there's a land mass next to a body of water and the land mass is heated and cooled by the sun, land and sea breezes spring up. Generally, the land breeze is localized, is close to the shore ("within a pistol shot of the beach," say the accounts of two hundred years ago), and occurs at night when the land has cooled and the air circulates toward the water. The sea breeze springs up in the late morning or the early afternoon and is often more vigorous and widespread. The land breeze may not be as useful since it occurs at night and is close to shore (where it's hard to see the rocks in the darkness). Land and sea breezes are often pronounced along rivers. Patient sailors can sometimes combine these upriver and downriver winds with tidal streams and make remarkable progress under sail. Of course, if you hit it wrong, you're dead in the water, and about all you can do is anchor or tie up somewhere and wait.

Is there any tidal stream or ocean current where you are? If so, how will these water movements affect you? By all means, use the wonderful tool of GPS, and plot a series of two-hour positions occasionally to see whether the water is pushing the ship one way or another. *I can tell you that water movements far out at sea and occasionally along a coastline are sometimes astonishing, completely unexpected, and usually undetected.* The erratic movements of the Gulf Stream in the North Atlantic are well known, but significant rivers far out in the ocean occur in a thousand other places all over the globe. No wonder there have been so many wrecks.

Some years ago I was sailing west-northwest in the Southern Ocean toward Cape Town when I was becalmed off the Cape of Good Hope, one of the great landmarks of the world. "The east-setting Southern Ocean current and the north-setting Benguela Current come together here," I wrote at the time. "However their meeting ground is not a simple black and white line, but a lazy battleground where a thousand micro-currents push one way and then another. We go 100 yards north and come to a stop. Then we're set south 200 yards. Now we slowly pirouette and stop. Then a turn to the right. . . . Finally a few puffs of wind come from the WNW and we slowly creep northward."[29]

At that time I could see Cape Point and keep track of my position visually. Today, however, most people have satellite navigation receivers that are inexpensive and widely available. It's simple to determine your exact position when out of sight of land and to learn if the water is pushing you one way or another.

I have to be honest and admit that it took me years of sailing before I got up enough courage to walk the plank and use a spinnaker. But once I took the plunge and learned something about these balloonlike running sails, I found they could do wonders in light and moderate airs.

In truth, I taught myself. I tried to find out about parachute spinnakers by sailing as part of a crew on a racing boat, but there was so much shouting, really nasty swearing, recriminations, dirty looks, and belittling and snarling contempt of anyone who was slow or who made a mistake that I lost interest. In fact, this and the utter disregard of the rules while rounding marks cooled me off round-the-buoys racing.

Before discussing the care and feeding of spinnakers, I need to mention spinnaker poles (and their lightweight cousins known as whisker poles) and their place in long-distance sailing.

It's foolish to consider coastal or ocean cruising without bearing-out poles of some kind for downwind sailing, especially if there's any swell or waves running and the boat is rolling and knocking the wind out of the sails. There's no substitute for a pole to hold out the weather clew of a spinnaker, genoa, or jib when the wind is aft of the beam. Any kind of a pole will do. The wind does not distinguish between a carbon-fiber tube with titanium endfittings and a length of $2\frac{1}{2}$-inch-diameter bamboo with string ties on each end. Adjusting the sheet will not do it. Most spinnaker poles are based on racing rules and are usually the length of the base of the foretriangle (the J measurement) and are beefy enough to deal with a spinnaker in a breeze. A whisker pole is lighter, more liable to break, and is sometimes as long as 135 percent of J.

Depending on the wind strength, a jib, a genoa, or an asymmetrical spinnaker works well with beam winds or thereabouts. When the wind moves farther aft, it's time to switch from the fore-and-aft rig to the running rig. You can delay this by changing course a little, but if the wind continues to move aft, you need to either pole out the headsail or put up a conventional spinnaker. Of course, you can tack downwind and forget about spinnaker poles, but for most cruising-boat skippers on long downwind passages, it's not practical in spite of the nifty tacking tables that sailing mathematicians are always waving around.

How can one person or a shorthanded crew safely deal with an unwieldy spinnaker pole? While you're busy with one end, the other end is often out of control. Just when you're fastening the aft part to the mast, the front end may fall into the water, angle down, and collapse like a soda straw. The cursed thing may even get away from you, slip over the side, and disappear.

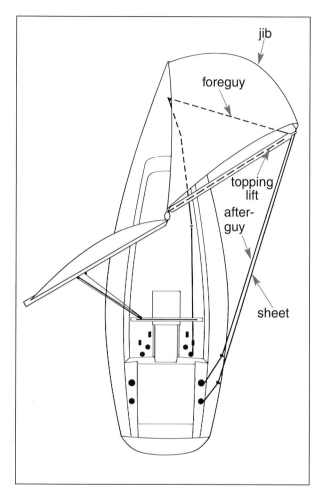

A poled-out jib set to weather wing and wing is an efficient way to run before the breeze. Note the redundancy—and shorthanded security—gained by a sheet and dedicated afterguy.

During the long trips aboard my 50-footer, I set up and took down the 21-foot, 50-pound aluminum poles hundreds of times and worked out what I believe is a foolproof scheme for safe pole handling. And because most yachts are less than 50 feet, the poles are usually shorter and lighter. On our current 35-footer, each spinnaker pole is 15 feet long and weighs 34 pounds.

I call my system The Loose Tie. It's cheap and simple and you need nothing new or extra.

Let's say we have 10–12 knots of apparent wind from the starboard quarter. The main is well eased to port. The jib is rolled up, and I've belayed the jib sheets on the forward mooring cleats to keep them out of trouble.

I'm ready to put up the starboard pole, so I walk forward to the mast and loosen the spinnaker-pole topping lift from its cleat. I then take a couple of steps forward, kneel down, and untie the other end, which I keep at the base of the baby stay. I carry this end forward to the pulpit, kneel down, and tie it to the front end of the spinnaker pole. Now I have the pole tied to the yacht. No matter what happens, I cannot lose the pole.

I unclip the front end of the pole and slide it forward a little to release the pole from its rear chock (or whatever). I then lift the forward end of the pole and lay it on top of the pulpit. *This is easy because I'm lifting only one end of the pole.* I put a short loose tie (3–4' of ⅜" dia. line) around the pole and pulpit and tie a square knot. The front of the pole is now safely secured to the pulpit by the loose tie and cannot slip over the side. The only line to the pole is the slack topping lift.

I walk back to the aft end of the spinnaker pole, pick it up, shove it forward a little, and connect it to its mating fitting on the mast. I jiggle the pole to make sure the latch has caught. Still at the mast, I take a strain on the spinnaker pole topping lift (which pulls slightly against the loose tie) and belay the line.

Now the pole is in place and ready for use with either an ordinary jib or genoa or a spinnaker. Note that since I have a baby stay and a forestay, I cannot swing a spinnaker pole from one side to the other. I carry two spinnaker poles, one for port and one for starboard.

It takes five lines to control a spinnaker. If you handle the sail with a furling sock (see page 140), you need a sixth line to raise and lower the sock. In an ideal world, you'd have a different color for each of the six lines, but somehow this never seems to happen. But even having two or three colors helps sort things out.

1. *The halyard* goes from the base of the mast to a pivoting block generally mounted at the top extremity of the spar, above the headstay. This block should be clear of everything. The halyard then runs to the head of the spinnaker, where there

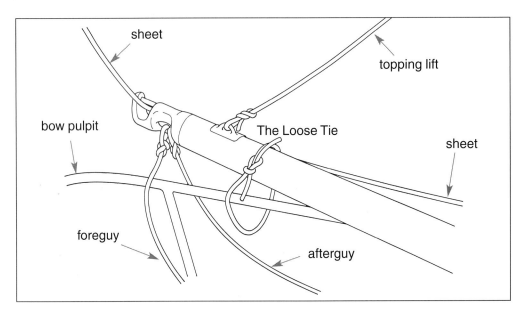

When rigging the pole prior to hoisting, my secret for shorthanded sailing is a loose tie. This secures the pole to the pulpit and permits the crew to work without fear that the front end of the pole will slip over the side and be bent and broken by the forward movement of the yacht.

should be a swivel to get rid of twists. Sometimes after a day or two of running, there's a chafe problem where the halyard passes through the masthead block. You can check this from the deck with binoculars. It may help to ease the halyard 3 or 4 inches to freshen the nip on the sheave where the line changes direction 90 degrees. Or you can sew leather around the line or slip a snug piece of engine-cooling-water hose on the top 2 feet of the halyard, making sure beforehand that the leather or hose will feed into the sheave. It's worthwhile to have a big, deluxe, oversize block at the masthead.

2. *The spinnaker sheet* goes from a cockpit winch through a turning block on the aft lee quarter directly to the clew of the sail. The block should be mounted as far aft as possible.

3. *The afterguy* (also called the *guy*) is on the windward side and runs from a cockpit winch through a block on the rail (at maximum beam) to the spinnaker pole. It passes through the jaw at the forward end of the pole and is tied or snapped onto the windward spinnaker clew (sometimes called the *tack* to further confuse things). If you ease the afterguy, the pole and the windward clew move forward and to leeward. Trimming the afterguy pulls the forward pole end and the sail back and to windward. Chafe on the afterguy where it passes through the outer pole end can be helped with snug-fitting thick-walled hose. The outer pole end should be super-smooth; check it with a finger from time to time. If necessary, smooth the area with various files and strips of fine emery paper or crocus cloth.

4. *The spinnaker-pole topping lift* runs from the base of the mast to a block mounted partway up the front of the mast and then to the outer end of the spinnaker pole. This line controls the height of the outer end of the pole. As I said earlier, when you're setting up the pole, it's important to take up on this line at once to keep the forward end of the pole from falling in the water. Since only one pole is generally used at a time, a single topping lift will serve either the port or the starboard side. I find it convenient to deal with this line at the mast.

5. *The foreguy* goes from a cockpit winch to a block at the base of the first stanchion just forward of the cockpit, then along the inside of the lifeline stanchions (via small stanchion blocks) to the foredeck, thence to a substantial block shackled to a pad eye on the foredeck, and finally to the forward end of the pole. I get by with one foreguy for either the port or starboard pole. Look out for the forward lifelines when routing the foreguy so the line has a clear run and doesn't chafe against the metal lifelines when the pole swings to the side. The foreguy can be run in many ways. Just make sure it's clear of chafe. Fit a substantial foreguy block to something strong because the foreguy and the block take big loads in squalls.

OK, let's sum up the spinnaker pole and its lines. The inner end of the pole is clipped to the mast. Three lines control the outer end: The topping lift holds up the end of the pole. The foreguy keeps the pole end down, that is, from rising above its usual horizontal position. The afterguy deals with the fore-and-aft movement of the outer end.

Furling socks not only make the use of light sails quicker and easier but help protect them from damage. I hoist my large running or reaching sails (generally made of 1½ oz. nylon) with furling socks variously called a *snuffer, choker,* or *squeezer.* They're all roughly the same—a tapered cylindrical tube of light cloth 10–18 inches in diameter and just slightly less than the hoist length of the sail. When the furling sock is extended, it encapsulates and safely holds the entire sail and makes a sausage about 50 feet long. When the sock is retracted, it goes to the head of the sail, where it's pulled into a squashed-up bundle about 2 feet long.

I don't even consider a spinnaker unless the weather is reasonably settled and we have plenty of untroubled room so that we can fly the sail for many hours or days. A spinnaker for a typical bermudian rig is about twice the sail area of the normal rig, so if you take down a jib (half the normal sail plan) and put up a spinnaker, you increase the total area by 250 percent. No wonder performance improves! However, if you look behind the yacht and see low, dark clouds (particularly with

The outer end of the port spinnaker pole. The bottom line is the foreguy, which keeps the pole from rising. The upper line is the topping lift, which supports the pole. The line coming from the lower left is the guy, which goes through the end of the pole and is secured to the port clew of the spinnaker. I tie bowlines for everything. Note that the jaw end of the pole must be very smooth; otherwise, the end of the guy will chafe through. If there's a problem here, I fit a short length of hose to protect the line.

ragged bottoms) beginning to chase the vessel, *forget the spinnaker*. Pole out a jib instead.

Let's assume we still have the steady wind from the starboard quarter. We're ready to use a spinnaker flown from a sock. I drag the spinnaker bag to the foredeck and pull out the sock with the sail inside. I connect the deck-level control lines. I already have the starboard spinnaker pole set up with the topping lift (as described earlier). Now I tie the foreguy (paying attention to the lead through or above the lifelines) to the forward end of the pole. The sheet from the port cockpit winch goes through the turning block on the rail and then forward to the port spinnaker clew sticking out from the bottom of the furling sock. (I lead this line outside of everything and tie it to the clew of the sail above the port lifelines.)

Are you still with me? I pull the starboard clew (sometimes called the tack) of the spinnaker around *in front of the headstay*. I take the afterguy, coming from the starboard cockpit winch via the turning block on the aft rail, and put it through the outer end jaw fitting of the pole. I then tie the afterguy end to the starboard spinnaker clew. I use bowlines for everything.

I tie the halyard to the swivel at the top of the sock. Remember that since I'm hoisting the spinnaker behind the mainsail on the port side in my run-through example, both the sheet and the fall of the halyard will be to port. The pole is on the starboard side.

I take a few seconds and glance around to see that the lines make sense. The spinnaker pole is to starboard. The afterguy (coming forward on the starboard side outside of everything) goes through the pole end and then to the starboard clew of the sail just peeking around (and in front of) the headstay. The port clew is tied above the lifelines to the sheet coming forward along the port side. Visualize the whole spinnaker blowing forward from the halyard, the port sheet, and the guy at the end of the pole. Three lines.

Now at the mast I raise *the inner end* of the spinnaker pole to a point above my head. (The outer end of the pole is still fastened to the top of the pulpit with the loose tie.) I go back to the cockpit and crank the slack out of the sheet and guy. I have these two lines and the foreguy (with a little slack) on three separate winches, each with a handle in place.

Now things go fast. I walk forward to the pulpit and remove the loose tie. I go to the mast and heave down on the topping lift to raise the end of the pole to a horizontal position. I belay the line. I grab the spinnaker halyard and haul away. The spinnaker sausage unwinds from its pile on the port side of the foredeck and climbs to the masthead. I belay the halyard. The long sail sausage now hangs down from the spinnaker block at the masthead to the deck in the lee of the mainsail. Is it clear all the way up? Yes!

I haul away on the line that runs from the bottom of the furling sock to a small block at the top of the sock. As I pull down and the bottom of the sock goes up, it begins to collapse on itself and the sail starts to open. Usually about a third of the way up, the wind takes over and the sock flies to the top, where it stays. I then belay or clip the sock control line to the mast and hurry back to the cockpit to adjust the control lines.

Under no circumstances should you let go of the sock control line, because it will blow to leeward and be out of reach. If this happens, you can usually catch it with a boat hook (as the boat rolls) but try to keep the loop of the control line untwisted and fastened somewhere handy. A nonrevolving snapshackle at the base of the mast works well, or you can belay it anywhere that's convenient.

The only problem I've had has been the control line getting wrapped around the sock. The sock made by ATN cleverly deals with this by running the control line up the outside of the sock in a pocket that's stitched along the full length of the sock. The pocket is made in a contrasting color (helpful when working with a flashlight at night) to help spot any twists or problems.

Hooray! The spinnaker is finally up and pulling and the boat is creaming along. Back in the cockpit, I control everything with three winches and fiddle with the sheet, afterguy, and foreguy. With these last two lines I can adjust the pole to move in an arc anywhere between the headstay and the shrouds. The basic idea is to have the spinnaker pole and main boom adjusted so that they're in line and at right angles to the apparent wind. The spinnaker pole should be horizontal and its outer end held immobile by three lines.

I ease the sheet until the luff of the spinnaker (the part above the end of the pole) is on the point of collapsing ("a little curl") and then trim it back slightly. If the sheet is pulled in too much, part of the drive of the spinnaker will be diverted to heeling and side forces and wasted.

On high-powered racing boats, there's a constant dialogue between the helmsman, the sheet trimmer, and the person adjusting the afterguy. I'm sure this triumvirate achieves much better results than I do because the yachts I'm on are generally steered with an autopilot (in a very light following wind) or a wind-vane gear (with more wind). I adjust the spinnaker and let her rip because I'm busy figuring out where I'm going, what's for dinner, and other things. I'm probably wrong, but I think constant spinnaker trimming is somewhat overrated and perhaps a psychological game. I adjust the lines from time to time (the heel of the yacht and the sound of the sail are factors) and achieve maybe 80 percent efficiency. Fortunately, modern triradial spinnakers are efficient and forgiving.

If you have a chute up and the wind begins to increase, at some point you will decide to take it down. With a sock it's easy. Pull in the sheet and ease the guy so that the forward end of the spinnaker pole goes to or near the headstay. This will position the spinnaker behind and in the lee of the mainsail. Then pull down the sock to throttle the sail.

Or you can simply let go of both the sheet and the guy. (Both lines should have figure-eight knots tied in their ends so they can't escape from their blocks.) The sail, held by the halyard at the top, will blow out to leeward behind the mainsail. This sounds impossibly dangerous, but it works. I quickly pull the sock down over the sail, which throttles it, and lower the sausage to the deck. Then I deal with the spinnaker pole. First, I lower the pole at the mast. Next, without moving, I ease the pole topping lift and swing the outer pole end down and safely *inside* the pulpit.

Now it's clearing-up time. I stuff the spinnaker sausage into a sailbag and stow it away. I put the spinnaker pole on deck, secure it in place, and tie the forward ends of the sheet and guy to the pulpit, where they stay permanently. I secure the end of the foreguy to a deck fitting, and the pole lift to the bottom of the baby stay. I go to the mast end of the pole topping lift, pull it tight, belay it, coil up the line, and tuck it away. Then back to the cockpit, where I pull in the slack of the sheet, guy, and foreguy, belay them on cleats, and coil up the line ends so that nothing gets over the side. Finis.

Can one person deal with a 2,000-square-foot spinnaker? In a true wind up to 15 to 20 knots or so, I would say yes. Here's a photograph I took from the top of the mast on the Santa Cruz 50 more than 1,000 miles from land to show what things looked like. My left shoe shows at the top.

You can handle a parachute spinnaker without a sock, but it's less convenient. You prepare or "stop" the chute beforehand by stretching out the sail (in sections) from top to bottom (head to the clews) in the cabin. You start at the head and tie a single loop of light thread (or put a rubber band) around the squashed-up bulk of the sail at 18-inch intervals. If you use an 8- or 10-inch-diameter piece of cheap plastic pipe about a foot long and pull the spinnaker through the pipe, starting with the head, you can slide on a rubber band at intervals as the sail goes through the pipe. (Before you start, loop a big handful of rubber bands around the outside of the pipe.) You need about 30–35 rubber bands or thread ties to stop a spinnaker.

The idea is to compress the sail into a tall, skinny bundle. You then hoist this delicately compressed sausage to the masthead with all the rigging lines in place as I've discussed. Then you go back to the cockpit and yank on the sheet and guy. This breaks the threads (or rubber bands) at the bottom of the sail, which begins to open. This action breaks the next thread up, and so on, as the nylon billows out. If the thread is too heavy, the sail won't open; if too light, the sail opens before it's fully hoisted. You will have to experiment to find the right strength rubber bands or cotton thread (one turn at the head, perhaps five or six at the clew end).

Before the sock was invented and its details perfected, most spinnakers were set stopped. Small ones were sometimes set directly from a deck bag or turtle. Many racing yachts still use stopped spinnakers.

The stopping method emulates the sock in a slightly more cumbersome manner.

To take down a spinnaker (or gennaker) without a sock, ease the pole near or against the headstay and pull in the sheet. This will put the big sail in the lee of the mainsail. The idea is to get the sail close enough so that you can seize a handful of the foot material near the clew. Grab it *over the lifelines*. Then ease the halyard and begin pulling in the sail. In a perfect world, I would have two people pulling in the sail and another person on the halyard. But you can do it with two people or even one if he or she is nimble and quick.

Ease the halyard as you pull the sail in on deck. If you ease the halyard too quickly or lose control of it, the sail will fall in the water, which you want to avoid. I've found that if I keep a half turn of the halyard on a cleat and let out, say, 10–12 feet of the halyard and then stand on the halyard, I can pull in three or four big handfuls of the sail. Then more halyard and more sail, and so on until the entire sail is on deck. Be sure to have a figure-eight knot at the end of the halyard and a line jammer or bull's-eye fitting on the mast within easy reach to hold the end of the halyard in case it gets away from you. Sometimes during sail handling you need a third arm; I keep about twenty $\frac{3}{8}$-inch-diameter ties 4 feet long of soft line dotted around the lifelines in the mast and foredeck areas so that I can grab one and tie it around part of the sail or whatever. Like many sailors, I often clamp a couple of ties between my teeth.

Some of these suggestions may sound difficult or even hazardous. Remember that we're talking about light-weather sails and modest winds. By the time 20-knot winds begin to overtake the yacht, you should have the featherweight sails bagged and tucked away.

If when the spinnaker is up, the wind drops, the yacht is rolling a little, and the sail is gently swishing, there's a slight chance that it will wrap around the headstay one or more times. This may sound impossible, but believe me, it happens. Spinnaker wraps are a curse, particularly at night. The only thing you can do is try to unwrap the sail. Unfortunately, these efforts may begin a new wrap in the opposite direction. It can help to remove the sheet, use a boat hook aloft, or release the halyard. If you can slide the whole mess down to deck level, at least you can get at it.

My friend Ed Boden suggests the following: "Simply gybe, and the chute miraculously unwraps. Before you gybe back, be sure to trim the sheet. This scheme unwinds the sail in about four out of five times for me."

Some sailors hoist a special triangular net made of widely spaced flat webbing to form a barrier against spinnaker wraps, but it's one more thing to do. Since most yachts have a roller-furling headsail on the headstay, it's possible to unroll a few turns of the sail and secure the sheet as high as possible on the mast. This erects a sort of barrier against wraps. Most people ignore the problem and take down the spinnaker when the wind stops.

When I'm through with a spinnaker, I find that it's best to put the sail, pole, and lines completely away rather than to leave the pole and sail partially in place in the hope that the wind will change back to earlier conditions. This never seems to happen, and if the weather deteriorates with the spinnaker and pole on the foredeck, it's more trouble to deal with them. By putting everything away at once, I'm ready to go through the setting procedure from scratch when I need to.

Most of the foregoing has been about symmetrical parachute spinnakers. These are good for points of sail from the beam to dead aft, say with apparent wind angles of 90 to 180 degrees. As we've seen, these require a pole. There are also asymmetrical spinnakers (often called gennakers) that are a cross between a genoa and a symmetrical spinnaker. These usually have less area, do not need a pole, and are cut for reaching courses, say wind angles from 60 to 120 degrees. They often have luff tapes made of low-stretch Spectra. It's best not to use a gennaker at its extreme limits because, while it may look good and seem impressive, the sail may be developing more side force than forward drive. In addition, its wind ranges should not be exceeded. Most should be handed and put in the bag at 15 knots apparent or so. These sails are usually made of 1$\frac{1}{2}$-ounce nylon, which is available in a dozen bright or pastel colors. The sails can be set with a sock and give excellent performance in light airs.

Poling out a jib or genoa for downwind sailing is much easier than dealing with a spinnaker. The sails are smaller, and the luff is already attached to the headstay, either with hanks or to the headstay extrusion of a roller-furling gear. The spinnaker pole (or whisker pole) is set up the same as before (see pages 136–38), with the back of the pole connected to the mast and the front of the pole resting on top of the pulpit and held with a loose tie. I have tied the end of the spinnaker-pole topping lift (line 1) to the end of the pole and taken a slight strain on the topping lift so the pole pulls lightly against the loose tie. (Remember, this ensures that the pole doesn't fall over the side.) At this moment there is no other rigging on the pole.

Let's assume I'm going to set the pole and headsail (now rolled up) to starboard. I walk forward and pull open the spring-loaded jaw at the outer end of the spin-

Fix, fix, fix! The French sailor Lisa Pittoors stitches sails with her faithful Read's hand-crank sewing machine aboard Sauvage.

naker pole. I drop the starboard sheet from the clew of the jib (coming down from the sail above me to the left) under the pin of the jaw and let it snap shut. I follow the sheet aft to the cockpit, where I untie the figure-eight knot at the other end of the line. Next I take a couple of steps forward and pull the sheet clear of the jib sheet block on the deck. Now the jib sheet is clear all the way to the spinnaker pole up forward. I put the aft end of the line outside the lifelines and lead it under them and through a block on the rail and to a winch, not forgetting to tie another figure-eight knot in the end of the line.

The sheet (line 2) is now unobstructed from the clew of the headsail through the pole end to the rail block to a winch.

Now I take the guy, which I keep stored along the deck outside the lifelines. This line runs from the bow pulpit (where it's tied when not in use) all the way aft to a block on the rail and then to a cleat in the cockpit. To hook it up, I put some slack in the line and tie the forward end to the front of the spinnaker pole. This guy (line 3) controls the fore-and-aft movement of the pole.

Finally, I deal with the foreguy. This line runs from a cockpit winch (or cleat) and along the deck or coachroof to a foredeck block and is tied to the front of the spinnaker pole. The foreguy (line 4) keeps the outer end of the pole from rising above the horizontal. The foreguy and the foreguy block must be positioned so that the foreguy is clear of the pulpit and lifelines (so there's no chafe) when the pole is raised and swung out to starboard.

Let's review. I have the jib rolled up. I have laid the pole on top of the pulpit and secured it in place with a loose tie. I have also done the following;

1. tied on the topping lift to raise the forward end of the pole and put a slight strain on the line
2. led the sheet from the cockpit through a rail block and outside the lifelines all the way forward and through the jaw of the spinnaker pole to the clew of the jib
3. run the afterguy from the cockpit (outside the lifelines) all the way forward and tied it to the end of the pole
4. tied on the foreguy to hold down the pole end to keep it from rising above a horizontal position

Now things go quickly. I raise the mast end of the pole to a height above my head. Then I step forward, cast off the loose tie, and return to the mast, where I haul on the topping lift to raise the outer end of the pole to a horizontal position. I belay this line.

From now on, I handle everything from the cockpit, where all the control lines are on winches or cleats. I cast off the furling line on the roller-furling gear and start cranking on the starboard jib winch. As the sheet tightens, the clew of the sail pulls against the forward end of the spinnaker pole and it moves aft. To match this, I ease the foreguy. I crank away on the sheet until the pole is at right angles to the apparent wind. By now the sail is extended, is full of wind, and the speed of the yacht has picked up a lot.

I pull the slack out of the afterguy and belay it. This line gives me complete control of the spinnaker pole. If there's a chafe problem at the jaw of the pole, I can take up a little on the afterguy to change the nip on the line. If a squall comes, I can roll up the jib and forget about the pole, which will be firmly held by three lines (up, down, and sideways). If I need to reef the sail, I can easily roll in a few or many turns.

When I want to put the pole down, I ease the afterguy and take up on the foreguy until the pole is only a few inches from the headstay. Then I can go forward and ease the topping lift. This will drop the outer pole end neatly inside the pulpit, where I can secure it with a tie until I put it away (now or later).

Note that the afterguy is not essential. I can do the whole poling-out routine with just the sheet running through the end of the pole. However, being able to control the end of the pole with certainty gives a shorthanded sailor an edge and allows some of the subtleties mentioned above.

If the jib is mounted on hanks, it's quite possible to do all of the above. Instead of rolling up the sail, you let the halyard go and drop the sail on deck. You can do these various maneuvers with the sail up and drawing, but with winds from astern, the sail tends to flap around and sometimes slap you in the face while you're setting up the pole. I've lost many a cap or hat doing this. If the wind strength changes and you decide to set a different hanked jib, you can leave the pole up because the lift, foreguy, and afterguy will hold it nicely.

If you don't have a furling sock or it's torn or out of commission, it's still possible to use light nylon sails. The setting and recovery is more complicated, but well within the compass of one or two people. Experts have written entire books about spinnakers, and videos show foredeck experts aloft in bosun's chairs whizzing around like bats while they disconnect pole fittings.

Dip-pole gybes, end-for-ending the pole, and other spinnaker maneuvers are all very well for yachts with large crews but are difficult or impossible for shorthanded vessels at sea where there may be a substantial swell. Also, most cruising yachts have forestays or other inboard rigging that precludes swinging a spinnaker pole from one side to the other. When I gybe a spinnaker, I take down the pole on one side, secure it on deck, and set up the pole on the other side. This is twice the work, but most of these steps take longer to write about than to do. Don't forget that we're at sea and presumably on long runs. We're not going around buoys on a ten-mile closed course.

Some sailors stow a single spinnaker pole up the mast, raise the outer end with a lifting line, and can swing the pole (often angled) either to port or starboard, depending on what rigging is ahead of the mast. I prefer to keep my poles on deck because although there are two poles, the weight of the poles is lower, and the stowage is more secure (I don't like the top of a vertically stowed pole rattling around). In addition there's less wind resistance, and in an end-of-the-world scenario, I can set up an A-frame jury rig if the mast goes over the side.

What about night sailing? Small boats run on a 24-hour schedule; otherwise they'd never get anywhere. The exception is entering strange ports at night, which we never do. The drill at night is mostly the same as daytime sailing because at sea, the wind pays little attention to time. Poles go up and come down in a sequential, orderly fashion. We reef and unreef sails and press onward. If it's pitch-black, I often carry a small penlight (see page 378) that I clamp between my teeth when my hands are busy. I have a deck light that shines down from the mast, but I find that the reflected glow from a headsail lighted by the steaming light is often better. If the moon or a partial moon is up, the light from it may be enough, especially after you've been in the dark for a while. I keep no lights in the cockpit except for the compass, whose light I have damped down to a deep red. If I want to study a chart or look at a dial, I switch on my penlight.

What about sails that fall in the water? When dealing with large, light sails, sooner or later a line may chafe through, a corner of a sail will rip out, or perhaps an inadequate foreguy block will explode, as two have for me. You may even hear the terrible sound of fabric ripping (a voice you don't want to listen to).

A sail over the side is essentially a big sea anchor; the most direct first aid for recovery is to slow or stop the way of the yacht through the water by heading into the wind or taking down the mainsail. *Don't even think about running the engine and engaging the propeller, which surely will wrap itself in fabric and lines.*

The best recovery plan that I know of is to put one corner of an overboard sail (or a line leading to it) underneath the lifelines in the cockpit area and lead it to the biggest sheet winch. Crank up as much slack as you can. Then let go of the other two corners of the sail so that it will stream out alongside the yacht. Then drag the sail back on board little by little. If you pull two corners, you will be trying to lift a bag of water and will surely destroy the sail. You can also try this game with the anchor windlass. Patience can save you thousands of dollars. If it's nighttime, try to wait for daylight so you can see what you're doing.

A boom vang is an adjustable tensioning device that keeps the main boom from rising, especially when running with a fair wind, and helps control the shape of the mainsail. A vang is usually mounted between the base of the mast (at the back) and a point at the bottom of the main boom—perhaps one-quarter of its length from the mast. The boom position and the length of the vang depend on the size of the yacht, the length of the boom, and its height above the deck. The vang generally makes an angle of 30–45 degrees above the horizontal.

A rigid vang will support the boom and can replace the topping lift. However, if the vang is rigid, it puts heavy loads on the connections at either end and is usually the culprit when a boom breaks in an uncontrolled gybe or a spinnaker broach in strong winds. Even extrathick metal fittings at the ends usually show signs of strain and severe wear. (You can see this if you walk around a marina and look at the big racing boats.) To introduce limited flexibility in rigid vangs, some builders install large metal springs or a gas cylinder. You can make a good argument for connecting one end of a rigid vang to a small block of rubber (say, $1 \times 1 \times 1^{1}/2$") that will take tension and compression but will break before the boom. There are also excellent hydraulic systems; unfortunately, they sometimes leak, make a terrible mess, and are impossible to service in distant places. The smell of hydraulic oil does not go well with a queasy stomach.

Usually a vang is simply a four- or six-part tackle with the hauling part led back to the cockpit, where it can be put on a winch. A vang works in connection with the topping lift. The vang keeps the boom down; the topping lift supports the boom and keeps it from falling into the cockpit. When the mainsail is eased forward for a fair wind, the boom rises and the wind pushes the sail hard against the lee shrouds and spreaders.

When you crank away on the hauling part of a vang tackle, it pulls the raised boom to a horizontal position. This improves the shape of the sail by removing excessive twist in the upper part of the mainsail. This also forces the sail slightly away from the rigging and lessens the chafe of the sail against the mast and spreaders.

A basic problem with boom vangs on cruising yachts is that the space under the mast is essential for dinghy stowage and other uses. There's no room for the vangs that I've described.

Sailors have worked out alternative arrangements. When running with a fair wind with the boom way out, they rig a vertical tackle from the boom directly down to the toerail or to a headsail-sheet-block track that runs along the deck. Years ago a common item for sale in chandlery catalogs was a wide, heavy-duty Dacron strap with metal rings that you slipped around a wooden boom and connected to a tackle.

In 1986, Margaret and I crossed the Atlantic from Florida to the Azores in our Santa Cruz 50. We started out with a fancy metal boom vang made with telescoping aluminum tubes held apart with a large metal spring. I was assured that it was the ultimate in design, but on our first day at sea we found that every time the boat rolled, the vang made a horrible scraping noise. Sleep was impossible, and the rasping and grating threatened to ruin the trip. In desperation, I disconnected the device. The silence was wonderful; life aboard improved greatly.

In the Azores I met Mark Schrader, who suggested that I use the system he employed aboard his Valiant 47. Mark had two four-part tackles—one to port and one to starboard—that ran from heavy through-bolted pad eyes on the middle of each side deck to the midpoint on the main boom. By easing the tackle (sailors pronounce the word *TAY-cul*) on one side and taking up on the other, the boom could be kept under complete control. The hauling parts ran to the cockpit. Usually you could deal with them by hand. If there were bigger loads, you could put the hauling part on a winch.

I set off across the Atlantic and found that the two tackles worked to perfection. Even better, they were silent and I was able to sleep. The loads on the pad eyes mounted on the balsa-cored fiberglass decks were considerable, however, and soon both pad eyes were leaking. I moved the bottom anchor points from the pad eyes outboard to the heavy aluminum through-bolted toerail and removed the pad eyes. To reduce the shock loads on the tackles, I rerigged them with ⅜-inch-diameter three-strand nylon line that has a bit of resilience and stretch.

As I sailed onward, I discovered other advantages of the two boom tackles:

- When becalmed or in light airs, I could set up both tackles firmly to keep the boom quiet and in whatever position I wanted.
- I found that if I moved the tackle toerail position a little forward of the maximum eased-boom position, I could use them as preventers to stop accidental gybes. In other words, I moved the bottom fiddle blocks of the tackles so that when the boom was all the way out for running, the tackles pulled slightly forward. No longer did I have to rig an awkward line from the end of the main boom to the stem.
- The tackles—with a couple of turns of the hauling part around a winch—were perfect for controlling the boom when gybing. Later in the Southern Ocean, I repeatedly gybed the rig in heavy gales and storm-force winds with complete control. This is an excellent sailing tool that has made my life easier and safer.
- I was able to do all these things without leaving the cockpit.
- The tackles cost much less than a manufactured device.

Initially I thought the tackle lines were troublesome and in the way when I went forward. Now many years later and with thousands of miles on the system, I am an enthusiastic advocate of using two tackles to control the boom. Instead of being obstacles, I find them welcome handholds when I go up and down the decks.

I'm aware that there is a possibility of breaking the main boom with the tackles that I have described. This might be a problem with a narrow boat and a long boom. However, the present design trend is for beamy boats and short booms.

Unless you use a rigid vang, you will need a topping lift to support the main boom. This is an important line and keeps the boom from falling on your head. For my present 35-footer, I use a piece of ⅜-inch-diameter braided line that runs from the end of the boom to the masthead and to the foot of the mast, then along the coachroof and back to the cockpit to a dedicated cleat. For a larger yacht, a simple tackle will add power without complication (see page 383). The hauling part of the topping lift needs to go to the cockpit because it's a line that requires frequent adjustment to minimize chafe as the mainsail is trimmed or eased.

When the mainsail is up, the topping lift should be set so that it is snug, but not tight. You don't want the line loose and swinging around. Remember that when you reef and ease the main halyard, the topping lift will have to support the boom. If the lift is loose, the boom will come crashing down. When running or reaching, the topping lift should be on the windward side of the sail. I find I can loosen the topping lift and flick it around the headboard to the other side if necessary. I do not like wire because of the chafe potential and the difficulty of dealing with the hauling part.

I do not use lazyjacks to guide the mainsail down for furling on the boom because of the potential for chafe on the sail. To me, furling the mainsail is just one of the routine chores of sailing. I have enough lines and complications already.

Again and again, Margaret and I have made small changes to make sail handling safer, quicker, and easier. (The Loose Tie and the boom tackles are two examples.) When the wind changes, we want to be able to handle our gear efficiently so that we can continue to press on in a seamanlike manner. I hope you don't think that we have heavy, slow boats that are sailed in an ultraconservative fashion. We like to keep our rig well tuned and to crack on all the canvas we can. Our best run for one week has been 1,003 miles, not world-beating certainly, but reasonably good for a 35-footer at sea. We like to make smart passages, but not push to the danger point. After all, we're sailing for pleasure, not to prove anything.

Let's see now . . .

10
ONE MAN'S SAIL INVENTORY

A fter trying many sails and lots of sail-handling schemes, I have learned which sails to buy and how to use them quickly and efficiently. I've discovered nothing new or startling, but my wife and I have been able to make our sailing easier and keep the yacht going better by the use of slab reefs, roller furling, deck bags, and furling socks.

I've tried to sort all this into a reasonable progression—a sort of master plan—so that in the normal wind range (say 0–30 knots), our transition from one sail to another is reasonable and orderly. We want to make the maximum use of each sail for its wind range and to avoid overlaps. We consider the weight of all the sails, their cost, and the room they take up when stored. We know that the seven sails in our inventory (plus two spares for a world-ranging yacht) include some compromises but ensure the following:

What sails do I need?

- Good performance in strong and light airs, both on and off the wind.
- Ease in dealing with and changing sails, with a minimum of hazardous foredeck work. In particular, there's no changing down from a large genoa rigged on a forestay furling system when it breezes up.
- Reasonable spares in case of damage.

We are learning all the time, and when we find something that's better, we switch to it. Our golden rule is *the simpler the better*.

Our yacht *Whisper* is a 35-foot masthead sloop. She has a sail area of 640 square feet, which includes a 100 percent foretriangle of 359 square feet. Like many International Offshore Rule (IOR) boats designed twenty years ago, the boat has a tall and skinny high-aspect mainsail (of 281 sq. ft. for us). The top of her mast is 53 feet above the water. Her designed displacement is 14,184 pounds. My guess is that with all her cruising gear on board (anchors, tools, fastenings, sails, clothing, charts, books, dinghies, spare parts, food, liquids, etc.), she would hit the bathroom scales at a real-world weight of 18,000 pounds.

Whisper's sail inventory consists of seven sails, plus two spares.

THE MAINSAIL

The mainsail is 281 square feet or 45 percent of the total sail area. The sail, made of 8.3-ounce Dacron, has three reefs, is triple-stitched throughout, and has four full-length flat battens. Each reef reduces the area by about 20 percent and is quick and easy to tie. The mainsail is up all the time we're sailing, and much of the time it is in direct sunlight.

We have found that after five or six years (or half a circumnavigation or the equivalent), the material generally becomes rotten and worthless. The middle and upper leech go first. One day when furling the sail, you will suddenly hear a dreadful ripping sound (surprise!) and see that you've put your hand through the leech. When you try to sew on a patch, you will find that the stitches tear out of the rotten fabric. About all you can do at sea is to slap on some 3-inch-wide white sticky-back sail-mending tape on both sides of the damage.* Then treat the sail gently until you can find a sailmaker, who will shake his head and sew on a big patch. Some sailors carry a sewing machine with them, but we don't have room for one.

When you hear a person boast, "My mainsail is fifteen years old and in perfect condition," it means that the owner hasn't sailed much.

THE JIB

We have a medium-sized roller-furling jib of 6.6-ounce Dacron. This sail is 378 square feet (110 percent of the foretriangle area) and goes on the headstay. I do not

---

*If the torn sail is wet, try wiping the area with a rag soaked in acetone.

change it. I estimate that 70 percent of all sailing is done with the mainsail and this sail. I generally use the full area, although I can roll up a reef. I do not have a foam luff insert because I try not to roll in deep reefs. I have a Harken roller-furling gear that works well.

THE STAYSAIL

We set the staysail on the forestay. This sail is 138 square feet (40 percent of the foretriangle area), made of 7.5-ounce Dacron, has hanks, and I keep it and its sheets in a sailbag at the base of the forestay. Since the sail is small and already hanked in place, it's easy to use. I see no reason to put it on a roller-furling gear with the resulting windage, weight, and complication. I always set up a running backstay when I use this sail because of the forward load on the mast from the inner forestay. When the weather is poor, the winds are gusty, and I'm uncertain what sails to use, I find that the mainsail with one or two reefs and the staysail are a handy combination. It's easy to tack with this sail because the sheets are a cinch to pull in with the big winches.

STORM JIB

The storm jib is only 78 square feet (23 percent of the foretriangle area) and goes in place of the staysail. It's a hanked sail, simple to handle because of its small size, and is made of 7-ounce Dacron with all-around tapes. We fold this sail carefully, and it makes a small bundle that we store in the forepeak. We seldom use this sail.

TRYSAIL

When the wind is too strong for the deeply reefed mainsail, we take it down and replace it with a storm trysail. This small, elongated triangular sail is 85 square feet (hoist 12'; foot 14') and is made of 8.5-ounce Dacron with triple-stitched seams and all-around taping. The trysail is fixed to the mast with nylon slides; the three grouped at the head are sewn on with stainless steel wire. Along the luff we have a row of worked eyelets, so if the mast track is unusable for any reason, we can lace the trysail to the mast and hoist the sail as high as the spreaders.

In area, the trysail corresponds to $5\frac{1}{2}$ reefs in the mainsail. This seems drastic. Yet, when we're far out on the ocean in a violent storm and big seas are running, the trysail and the storm jib make a helpful combination that keeps the yacht on her way, steadies the boat, and eases the terrible rolling.

The biggest problem with a trysail is the work of setting it in storm conditions. The drill is as follows:

1. Drop the mainsail and secure it to the boom.
2. Remove the mainsail slides from the mast track.
3. Find the trysail and feed its slides into the mast track.
4. Switch the halyard from the mainsail, secure the tack pendant, arrange the sheet, and hoist the sail.

When water is flying around, the yacht is rolling madly, and you are spending half your energy holding on, setting this sail can be an exhausting job. At night, the job is harder because you can't see as well. A safety harness slows you even more. It can easily take one person one hour to set a trysail in gale- or storm-force winds. But it's not the time that's important; it's the energy you spend. In practice, this means that you tend to delay putting up the trysail until the wind is quite strong. This makes the job even harder—particularly if you are not feeling too well.

Margaret and I learned all this ages ago and decided that our trysail handling needed a number of improvements. We installed a separate stainless steel track that runs up the mast alongside the mainsail track. The trysail track extends from the top of the coachroof to above the spreaders and is fastened every 3 inches. We keep the trysail permanently bent on and stow it, the sheet, and the tack pendant in a small sailbag at the foot of the back of the mast.

To speed up handling, we have the upper end of the tack pendant (in our case, 8 feet long) eyespliced to the tack cringle of the sail. At the lower end of the pendant is a snapshackle that clips on to the mast collar at deck level. During normal sailing we forget about the bag (which has drainage holes in the bottom). When we want to use the trysail, which is infrequently, all we do is untie the front of the bag and pull it off the sail. Then we attach the halyard, deal with the sheet (premarked for position), and haul away. The system is quick, and there is no fumbling with slides or hammering on corroded trysail transfer tracks. This arrangement makes it easy to get the trysail down and out of the way when the wind drops and we want to hoist the mainsail again. The trysail lives on deck permanently. We have found that a single piece of $1/2$-inch-diameter line led to one of the aft mooring cleats is adequate for the trysail sheet, which is a control line that is seldom adjusted.

GENNAKER

This is a light-weather sail of $1\frac{1}{2}$-ounce nylon—an asymmetrical spinnaker of 1,100 square feet—that I set and douse with a furling sock. The luff rope is made of Spectra, which I tighten as much as possible with the halyard winch on the mast. Since the sail is set flying from the tack and head, however, the luff sags off to leeward as soon as the sail is full of wind. We use it for reaching and close reaching, with no pole. In prolonged light airs in the tropics, this sail can be a savior because it keeps the yacht moving when all else fails. I suggest nothing lighter than $1\frac{1}{2}$ ounces, and you can make an argument for heavier cloth ($3/4$-ounce material is less resistant to sun and the abuse that all sails receive).

SPINNAKER

Our downwind hope in light airs is a triradial spinnaker of 1,240 square feet. We set this sail with a spinnaker pole and deal with the sail handling with a furling sock. The spinnaker is made of $1\frac{1}{2}$-ounce nylon with reinforced corners. This is a wonderful sail

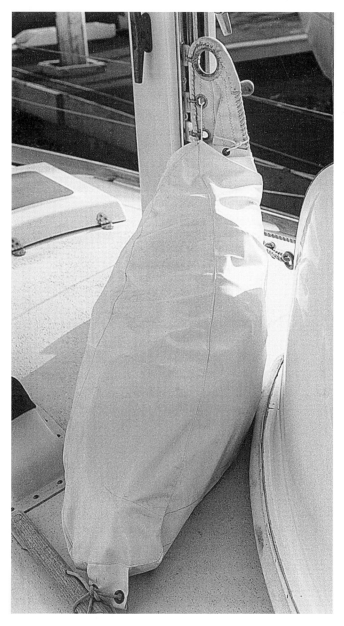

We keep our storm trysail permanently attached to a separate track that runs up the mast alongside the mainsail track. The tack pendant (in our case, 8' long) is already secured in place and kept in the bag. To use the sail, we merely untie the bag, attach the halyard, secure the single part sheet (also kept ready in the bag) to a stern mooring cleat, and hoist. The bag needs half a dozen holes (grommets) in the bottom so that water can drain out.

in light airs and keeps the yacht going hour after hour. Because it spends most of its life away from the sun in a bag that I store in a locker, this sail lasts a long time.

SPARES

I carry an old mainsail (with short battens) and an old jib for emergencies. I consider an extra mainsail to be the most important spare part on a voyaging yacht. (See page 399.)

SLAB REEFING

I like to tie in mainsail reefs because it's a simple and positive scheme that's been used by sailors for centuries. Tying reefs gives the mainsail excellent sail shape and frees us from a lot of heavy, complicated, and expensive gadgetry that I don't need or want.

Let's run through the system in detail. First, let's arrange the reefing lines.

When I install reefing pendants, I tie the end of each line around the boom with a bowline or clove hitch. These lines and knots are sometimes subject to violent shaking when reefing in a strong wind so I always put a racking seizing on the knot ends for safety. Since the foot of our mainsail has a boltrope that slides along the boom, the only way to get the line around the boom is to cut a small hole through the sail at the foot where the leech reefing cringles are supposed to land. This is no problem because there are many thicknesses of Dacron at the foot of the sail, and the hole helps keep the pendant located in a fore-and-aft direction so it pulls down the sail at the right place. If you use slides at the foot of the mainsail (which cause less chafe) or if it's loose-footed, you don't need holes because you can pass the pendant underneath the sail and tie it around the boom. Alternatively, each pendant can go to a suitably placed pad eye screwed or bolted to the boom or to a Spectra webbing strap sewed around the boom.

The general lead of a reefing line is from a fixed position near the after end of the boom up to the leech cringle, through the cringle, and down to the end of the boom. (Up on one side of the sail and down on the other.) Then inside through the hollow boom to the forward end of the boom. Finally, vertically down past a line jammer, and out the bottom of the boom to the reefing winch at the back of the mast. Since most cruising sloops use three reefs, there are three reefing lines, each a different length. This arrangement requires three sheaves at the aft end of the boom plus an outhaul line or a mechanical setup of some kind to tension the foot of the mainsail.

If possible, make each reefing line a different color, say, red, white, and blue for reefs 1, 2, and 3. I use $^3/_8$- or $^7/_{16}$-inch-diameter ordinary Samson braid. The number 3 reefing pendant on *Whisper* is 50 feet long.

I always sail with the reefing lines worked out and in place. Trying to reeve these lines at sea with the mainsail down and the boat rolling around is not the way to do it. Spend an afternoon at anchor or alongside a quiet dock. Try each reefing procedure until you're satisfied.

When you have a reef down, mark the pendant at the winch with a piece of colored yarn sewed through the line. This will make reefing quicker next time. After you have each line worked out, measure its length and write the figures in the ship's book (see page 381). This will be a big help when you need to replace the line.

When I decide on a reef, I ease the mainsheet and any tension on the main boom from the vang tackles. Then I walk forward to the mast. I take the main halyard off its cleat on the mast and hold the line in one hand beneath the barrel winch, which has three turns of the halyard on it. With my other hand, I release the sheet stopper above the winch. I begin to ease the halyard, and the mainsail starts to come down. I keep easing the halyard with one hand while I pull down the sail with the other. When the luff reefing cringle is down to the boom, I reach over and throw the sheet stopper to hold the halyard.

Depending on the wind direction and strength, the sail may now be flapping and noisy. Pay no attention to this.

Next I take a piece of $5/16$- or $3/8$-inch-diameter line about 3 feet long and push it through the metal luff cringle. I reach under the boom and sail, grab the end of the tie, and pull it down and around the forward end of the boom (at the gooseneck), where the diameter is small. Then I run the tie back up to the cringle a second time and down around the gooseneck. Both ends of the tie now face me. I shake the line tight and tie a square knot. The new tack of the sail is now down and forward and firmly in place. Then I crank up the main halyard until the luff of the mainsail is tight and belay the line.

I turn to the winch at the back of the mast below the boom and put three wraps of the correct leech reefing pendant (remember, there are three, each a different color) on the winch drum. Meanwhile with my other hand, I've switched the winch handle from the halyard winch to the reefing winch. As I crank away on the leech pendant, the back of the sail (still unreefed) begins to come down to the end of the boom. (This is why I eased the mainsheet earlier.) The noise and flapping stop.

I crank the winch until the reefing pendant is very tight. Then holding the line on the winch with one hand, I reach underneath the boom with my other hand, press the reefing line jammer, and let go of the pendant. The jammer grips the line. I put the winch handle in its plastic holster and tidy up the main halyard. The reefing job is done. Time to complete the process: maybe three minutes.

The second and third reefs are like the first. I tie in the second after the first and the third after the second. When I shake out the reefs, I do the same thing in reverse, although as a practical matter when a strong wind is over, it's usually finished and we're back to the full sail.

Note that I *tie* the sail down at the tack. I find this faster and more positive than hooks or other arrangements if one person is dealing with reefing. (A hook can shake out when you turn your back.) In the past, I put ties or a lacing through four or five reefing patches along the new foot of a reefed sail to hold up the unused part of the sail. In the BOC races, I learned that none of the competitors did this because it's unnecessary. I soon picked up the habit and now let the unused part of the sail simply hang down. If you choose to tie up the bunt of the sail, try to use colored ties through the reefing patches to remind you to untie them before you release the luff and leech cringles. Otherwise, you risk tearing the sail.

Problems? Sometimes when we're running with a hard wind and need a reef or two, the wind jams the mainsail against the mast and rigging and makes it impossible to pull the sail down to reef it. It helps to haul in the mainsheet and pull the traveler to windward. If I still can't get the sail down, I take one step up the mast or hop up on the main boom and tie a light line to the highest luff reefing cringle that I can reach. Then I jump down, put the light line on the main halyard winch and crank away. (Be sure the main halyard is slack and you don't have the line jammer closed.) If we're sailing in a hard-weather area, I sometimes leave a pull-down luff line in place as I've described, but I prefer not to because it's one more line to get into trouble.

Other problems? Occasionally when reefing, the unused reefed part of the sail bunches up at the clew. This doesn't hurt anything because sails are always reinforced in this area. To avoid this, however, pull the unused part of the sail on one side of the boom or the other, generally on the leeward side, before you start tightening the leech pendant.

If the reefing pendants are not set up tightly, there will be chafe where the line goes through the leech cringle. One way to deal with this is to take a couple of turns through the leech cringle and around the main boom with a piece of $^3/8$- or $^1/2$-inch-diameter line 4 feet long and tie a square knot. Old, hard, braided, or three-strand line works well. Then go back to the reefing winch behind the mast (or wherever), crank the pendant tight enough to release the jammer, and ease the line a little so that the extra tie mentioned above takes the load. Some people do this routinely, but it's an extra step, and I normally don't do it unless the weather is abysmal and I think I'll need the reef for a long time. In any case, keep an eye on the pendant where it passes through the cringle. The Antal company makes a clever block (no. 994.065) to alleviate this problem.

To check whether this chafe difficulty is something new, I looked at a few old sailing books. Sure enough, Conor O'Brien, in *The Small Ocean-Going Yacht*

(Oxford, 1931), writes: "The pendant should only be regarded as a means of getting the reef down till the lashing is put on, for it is bound to slack up more or less when it will chafe the sail, and itself" (page 64). Of course, O'Brien used natural-fiber lines, not the low-stretch synthetic braid that we have today.

I don't mean to overemphasize reefing and sail changing, but they're all part of the game. Even during summer weather, the wind goes up and down, and it's necessary to be able to reef promptly and easily, although days or weeks may go by without the need to reduce sail area.

How often do you reef the mainsail, anyway? To find out, I looked in my old logbooks.

I saw that our last west-to-east Atlantic crossing was between Chesapeake Bay and Gibraltar. It was a leisurely passage of 3,843 nautical miles in 34 days in light summer weather. During that trip, Margaret and I reefed the mainsail as follows: first reef, seven times; second reef, six times; third reef, one time.

This works out to be a mainsail reef about every 2½ days.

This contrasts with a stormy winter passage from Ushuaia, Argentina, in the Beagle Channel to Mar del Plata, Argentina, 1,215 miles to the north. During 12 days of mostly westerly gales, we were obliged to take down the reefed mainsail seven times and hoist a storm trysail five times. Every day we made two or three sail changes. Once we ran before a southwest gale for six hours under bare pole when the wind was too much for the trysail.

During a 16-day summer run in the Mediterranean between Gibraltar and Kusadasi, Turkey (1,653 miles), we shortened the mainsail as follows: first reef, seven times; second reef, seven times; third reef, one time; or about once a day on average.

In June 2000, on a seven-day passage between Cape May, New Jersey, and Cape Breton Island, Nova Scotia, we logged 781 miles. During that trip, we put one reef in the mainsail twice and a second reef once, or roughly one reef every two days.

Reading back, I see that I've spent pages describing tied reefs, but I can assure you that once the sail and boom and lines are worked out, the arrangement is simple and quick. Tens of thousands of yachts use this system, or a close variation, with complete success.

Naval architect Garry Hoyt has designed and patented a clever system of tied reefs using a single line that's easily adapted to cockpit control. The main halyard (taken to the cockpit via a turning block at the foot of the mast) is eased. The single reefing line in the cockpit is put on a winch and trimmed until the reef is in place. This arrangement is repeated for the second reef and the third. The details are in the Harken catalog.

This all works very well, and can be handled from the safety of the cockpit, but for a three-reef mainsail, you must run the three lines, plus the main halyard, to the cockpit. These four lines make still more clutter in the yacht's main workplace. I admire Garry's idea, but I prefer to deal with the reefs at the mast, which is only six or seven steps from the cockpit.

I'll end this chapter with one more idea to save a little reefing labor if you use tied or jiffy reefs. After you hoist the mainsail and are neatly coiling up the halyard, leave 10 feet or so of slack between the cleat and the halyard coil. Then you can tie in (and shake out) the first reef without upsetting the halyard coil.

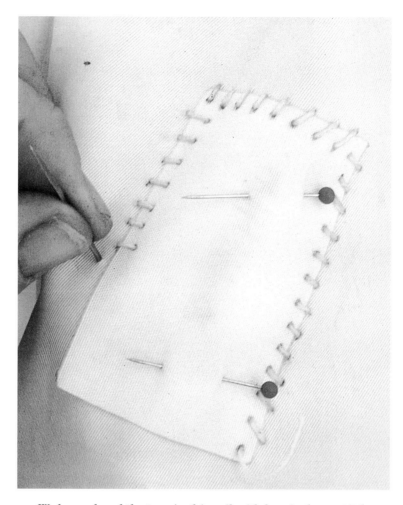

We have closed the tear in this sail with herringbone stitching. The little patch covers the repair. The needle looks too large and the thread is much heavier than necessary, but you get the idea. Another way is to slap a piece of sticky-back Dacron tape over the tear and a second matching piece on the other side of the sail. Then put in widely spaced stitches to keep the two pieces of tape from peeling off.

11

PLANNING THE TRIP

The sternest test of a small vessel is to encounter a severe storm at sea. In prolonged winds of 60 or 70 knots, a yacht will be lucky to survive. Even if she weathers the seas the wind kicks up and has enough room to run off, she may suffer severe damage. Her crew may be injured and terrified, and her passage will be slow and unpleasant.

Fortunately, good planning can help keep you away from storms and nasty weather and aim you toward light or moderate winds, which in turn mean light or moderate seas.

We know that the habits of hurricanes, typhoons, tropical storms, and severe gales have been studied and charted for hundreds of years. With care in the planning of an ocean crossing, the chances are excellent that you can avoid bad weather or at least diminish the risk of unexpected meetings. Of course if you continue to sail on the oceans of the world, sooner or later you will get a blast of heavy weather. But careful planning can minimize a severe drubbing by winds and big seas.

Preparing the charts for a major sailing trip is a big undertaking.

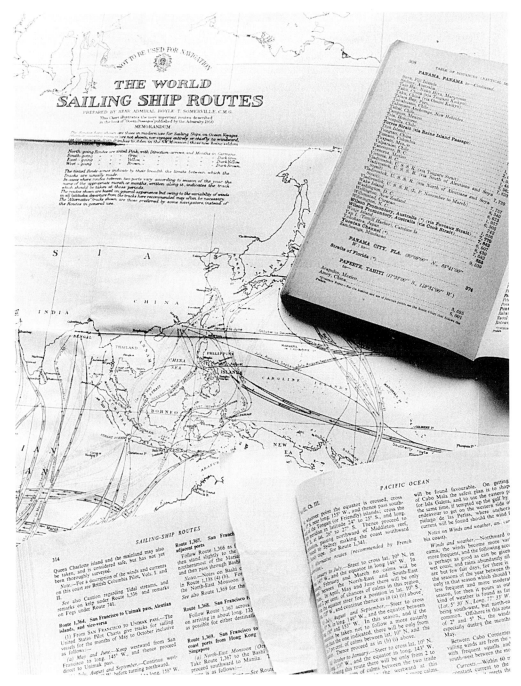

Realistic planning takes time, reading, access to sailing books and charts.

Management of a vessel in hard going is an important part of seamanship. A smarter and more basic approach, however, is to try to avoid storms in the first place.

We have three kinds of guides to help us.

The first is a big book called *Ocean Passages for the World*. This is a British Admiralty publication that makes hundreds of recommendations for long voyages and is a basic source of planning and scheduling information. My edition is dated 1973. The book is written in telegraphic style, and a spartan text tells about routes, courses, dangers, special problems, and likely winds and weather. The text is somewhat general, however, and is more a telephone directory of routes than a reading book of ocean highway information. My edition has 27 pages on wind and weather, 190 pages on steamship routes, 18 pages on sailing ship routes, and 30 pages of general notes and cautions.

The appendix of *Ocean Passages* has eight foldout charts that show climates, currents, and sailing and steamship routes. No potential voyaging sailor will fail to be enthralled by Chart 7 (Admiralty Chart 5308), *The World-Sailing Ship Routes*, a sketch map on which pink, gray, yellow, and brown bands flow arterylike across the oceans of the world to suggest routes in various directions for certain times of the year. It's worthwhile buying this chart separately and tacking it above your desk.

These colorful tracks are based on the experiences of thousands of large commercial sailing vessels over a century or more. Some of the routes have limited suitability for yachts. Not many small vessels, for example, run down their easting in the gale-swept Southern Ocean. Nevertheless, *Ocean Passages* is a good place to start, and the book's warnings are worth strict attention. Instead of buying this bulky and expensive (£45 or $64.42) book, however, it's easier to borrow a copy, have a look, and type out or photocopy the few pages you want. You may be able to have your local library borrow the book through interlibrary loan facilities.

Another useful planning guide is *World Cruising Routes*, by Jimmy Cornell (International Marine, 2002, $49.95). This book, now in its fifth edition, describes hundreds of routes in the Atlantic, Pacific, Indian Ocean, Red Sea, and Mediterranean in terms of small-boat transits. If your heart is truly in distant places, I suggest that you look at *Ocean Passages*, and at Admiralty Chart 5308 (which you can buy separately) for the big picture, then focus on the Cornell book for a closer look. But don't slavishly follow others—do your own thing. Just be aware of routes and seasons that have been successful for others.

Pilot charts are the second type of planning guide. These are inexpensive general ocean charts with details of winds, calms, fog, severe storms, wave heights, gales, sea and air temperatures, magnetic variation, currents, ice, barometric pressure, big-ship tracks, and a weather summary.

These special charts are road maps of the sea and, with their neat wind roses and curved lines of different colors, are fascinating documents. They are based on the pioneering work of Matthew Fontaine Maury, a U.S. Navy officer who was appalled at the miserable times that both military and commercial sailing ships made from port to port in the 1840s. Maury collected hundreds of logbooks and trip reports. He analyzed the routes and each captain's experiences and made suggestions based on prevailing winds, seasonal patterns, gale frequencies, and so on. He sorted out the trade winds, the westerlies, the variables, and the doldrums on a month-to-month basis. He put all this information into tabular form with clever symbols and compiled sets of easy-to-read charts. It was Maury's genius to turn a hodgepodge of largely useless private information into a scientific methodology of routes and winds.

Maury proved to captains that longer routes in fairer winds were often much faster. Ships' officers were quick to follow Maury's suggestions because it made their passages easier on themselves, the crew, and the ship. The owners of the shipping lines embraced these new ideas because they made more money for the company. Even today's enormous, full-powered container ships and immense oil tankers benefit from not bashing into extreme headwinds and blockbuster seas (they call this *routing*). Maury remains a hero to sailors.

The U.S. pilot charts of today are based on thousands of ship observations taken by generations of seamen. These charts aren't infallible, and it's possible to encounter conditions other than the stated figures, which are averages, not certainties. Yet the numbers are on our side, and these charts are marvelous planning aids.

I have the 37-page *Atlas of Pilot Charts, North Atlantic Ocean* in front of me. It measures 20 by 29 inches and has a chart for each month for the North Atlantic, the Arctic Atlantic, and the Caribbean Sea and Gulf of Mexico. If I look at my area of interest on several charts, it's easy to follow seasonal weather patterns. For example, checking the gale frequency off the southeast coast of Newfoundland, I see that in January, there are ten storms of force 8 or more. In June there is one; in July, none.

In my judgment the best pilot charts are published by the U.S. government. Five atlases cover all the oceans. In 2002, the prices varied from $16 to $39. Since the information is based on data collected over a long period, updating is not important.

The third planning guide is a class of books called Sailing Directions or Pilots. In these you will find information about coastlines, ports, hazards, buoyage, regional weather, pilotage, and local regulations. Sometimes there are aerial photographs or sketches of a coastline. Although many countries publish Sailing Directions for their own waters in their national language, the main Pilots are from the United States and Great Britain, and these volumes tell about every part of the world. There are 42 volumes of U.S. Pilots and 74 volumes of Admiralty Pilots, all in English. Of course, you need books only for the part of the world you plan to visit—generally 1 or 2 volumes.

These are of inestimable value to mariners, and you should purchase new volumes—together with the latest supplements—to cover your itinerary. Although there is almost universal interchangeability, U.S. Pilots are written with U.S. charts in mind; Admiralty Pilots have many U.K. chart references. If there's any choice, try to buy Pilots and charts from the same country. I recommend Admiralty Pilots.

Both the U.K. and U.S. Pilots are big hardbound books with text, sketch maps, photographs, and drawings; storage can be a problem. The U.S. Pilots measure $8\frac{1}{2}$ by 11 inches (each comes with a CD-ROM of the contents) and cost from $20 to $45 in 2002; most were in the $20 range. The Admiralty Pilots measure $8\frac{3}{8}$ by 12 inches and cost £37 ($52.39) in England. Supplements are issued from time to time, and every few years, each volume is reprinted.

Though the Pilots are prepared for all mariners, the emphasis is on commercial vessels; in recent years, the tendency has been to put less emphasis on smaller places and to deal more with major ports. Nevertheless, these books are helpful to small-boat sailors and are definitely worth having on board. For example, I have recently been sailing along the coasts of Newfoundland and Labrador. The Canadian government publishes four soft-cover inexpensive Pilot booklets to cover these waters, which constitute the only up-to-date, reliable guides. Without them, I would never have been aware of several excellent small harbors in strategic but unexpected places.

Among my books I have the Admiralty publication *Africa Pilot*, volume 1, 13th edition. The 1st edition was published in 1849, so the book comes from a long line of sources. Like their U.S. counterparts, the Admiralty books are packed with information about a particular area and always include a chapter on regional weather. The writing is clear and pithy but decidedly pessimistic and negative, as such books must be that describe every treacherous current and hidden rock.

Charts and nautical publications are big business. In 2001 in England, 159,033 Admiralty Pilots were sold for more than $8.4 million. A surprising thing about these volumes is that the writing staff is the same size as it was in 1907—just 3 naval assistants and 1 clerk, helped by 18 retired naval officers who work at home as revisers. "The terse, clipped, informative style of these volumes is familiar to yachtsmen," noted an article in *Yachting Monthly* magazine. "Verbiage and time-wasting and wooly conceptions are rigidly excluded."[30]

Many are the navigators—including me—who have constructed a crude harbor chart based on the sentences in Admiralty Pilots when a vital large-scale chart has suddenly been found to be missing.

A special kind of Pilot or Sailing Directions that's often available is a yachtsman's guide prepared by a sailing group, a knowledgeable author, or local authorities. For example, the Clyde Cruising Club publishes an excellent, up-to-date Pilot for Scottish waters. *A Cruising Guide to Nova Scotia*, by Peter Loveridge, is help-ful. There are six or eight useful yachtsman's Pilots for the West Indies. In the Galá-pagos Islands, a local charter boat captain has written a handy little guide. The vari-ous Pilots for the Mediterranean by Rod Heikell have a fine reputation.

All these books and others need to be used with caution depending on the publication date, the author, and his or her sailing style and experience. These small-boat guides are usually worth buying *even if you pick up only a single use-ful point*. You don't acquire these guides for writing style and beautiful pho-tographs. You read them for information.

Note that I am speaking of guides prepared by experienced navigators, not publicity handouts put out by tourist bureaus or hokum written by pompous boat-owners or others whose main purpose is to steer you to advertisers. *The best guides carry no advertising.*

Most successful Pilots are constantly being revised, so be sure to inquire about the latest printing before you buy. Ask for the latest supplements, which are usually free.

To explain the use of these books and charts, let me tell about a Pacific trip that Mar-garet and I made a few years ago. Our goal was an extended voyage around the major part of the Pacific basin. When we studied the planning guides, we discovered that we faced three main problems: the South Pacific hurricane season, typhoons off the coast of Japan, and a high gale and fog frequency in the Aleutian Islands. The chal-lenge was to juggle dates so that we would minimize our exposure to these hazards. In addition, we hoped to stay in the belts of running and reaching winds, to sail with favorable currents, and to maintain a reasonable schedule.

We pulled a figure of 18 months out of the air and started sticking pins with date flags into a general Pacific chart.

Reading *Ocean Passages* and various Pacific Pilots and studying the pilot charts along with accounts of other voyages told us that we should sail north from Samoa by November to miss the South Pacific hurricane season. Similar reading about the east coast of Japan suggested that we should be away to the north and east before July. In the Aleutians, we had no season of severe storms to worry about, but there was a winter gale frequency of up to 20 percent (a force 8 or higher storm every six days on the average). We changed dates, moved the schedule backward and for-ward, and decided to leave Japan in midsummer so that we would be in the North Pacific when the gale frequency was not so severe. As expected, we encountered some fog, but the August gale frequency in the Aleutians varied from 1 to 7 per-cent, suggesting that summer was the time for a visit.

In other words, we tried to play the averages to have as storm-free a trip as pos-sible. This could have meant staying in a protected harbor during a bad season or hurrying to cross a dangerous area to minimize exposure to severe hazards. We also

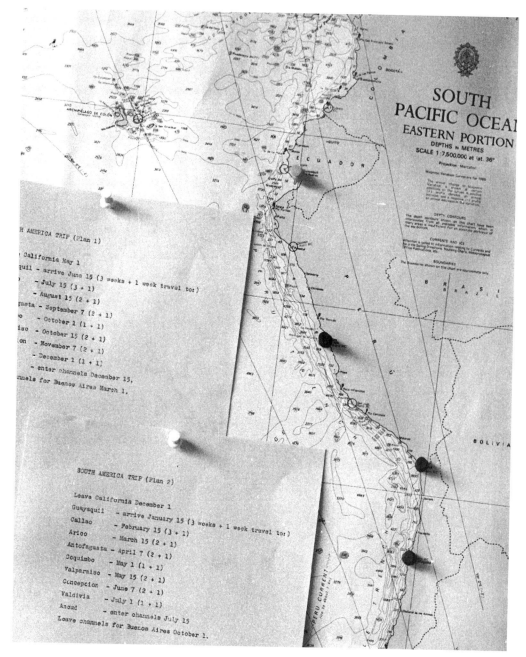

We made provisional outlines and stuck colored pins into a large-scale chart as we worked toward a reasonable sailing schedule. We learned not to try for too much, nor to plan too optimistically.

talked with several friends—merchant ship officers—who made useful suggestions about routes and places. We have found that big-ship people are often fascinated with small sailing vessels and will go out of their way to help you. The captain and mates will sometimes give you extra charts and pass on all sorts of good ideas and advice. If it seems convenient for them, Margaret and I always try to pay courtesy calls to the captains of nearby big ships when we are in foreign ports. We have made some wonderful friends.

To sum up: To learn about sailing conditions for a long route, we study *Ocean Passages*. We look at Pilot charts for more detailed information. Pilot books tell us about destinations and the next port. All these guides help us avoid severe storms and find fair or reaching winds.

The long way around is often shorter if the detour takes you away from strong headwinds and adverse currents. For example, we know a yacht owner who repeatedly tried to go northeastward into the Caribbean toward Venezuela from Cartagena, Colombia. The month was April and the trades blew strongly; according to the Pilot chart, the prevailing wind was force 6 from the northeast plus 28 miles of adverse current per day. Though the captain was determined and the big ketch was powerful, she could make no easting until the owner abandoned his head-on approach. He finally made his easting via long reaching legs to the north where the wind and current were less unfavorable.

Ocean Passages does not recommend the direct route between Hawaii and San Francisco because a sailing vessel would be thrashing to windward for hundreds of miles and beating back and forth trying to make mileage to the northeast—directly into the trade wind and contrary current. The suggested route is roughly northward or a little west of north, close-hauled or almost close-hauled on the starboard tack, until you pass above the northeast trades into the westerlies, whose latitude varies somewhat with the month, depending on the location of the North Pacific high-pressure area.

In time, you learn a few other wrinkles. For example:

- If you're going to sail through an island group, it's helpful to arrive at the windward end so you will have a free wind from island to island.
- In the Tuamotus, there are often extensive underwater reefs running far out from the south and southeast sides of the atolls. I am told that the coral grows toward its nutrients, which flow from the southeast trade wind. A mariner is advised to sail around the north rather than the south side of an atoll. By all means, purchase French charts for the islands and atolls of French Polynesia. Details can be found at www.shom.fr/.

- You may wish to delay a passage through a hazardous area until you have a full moon to help you see at night.
- In going northward from Rio de Janeiro against the Brazil Current, it may be wise to wait until the northeast monsoon (so called locally) has eased. A week in port may be a week gained.
- The weather systems around Vancouver Island come from the northwest or southeast. Depending on your direction of sailing, it will pay you to wait for a fair wind.
- When sailing in the South Atlantic and heading to Cape Town from the north, work well south of the city before you head east. The prevailing winds are from the southeast and often blow very hard ("a black southeaster"), making it almost impossible to work to weather. But if you stay 40–50 miles south before you aim for the coast, you will have a fair wind.

And so on.

A sound investment for safety and peace of mind is a great stack of up-to-date charts purchased before you set out on a long trip. If you are in doubt about a certain chart, buy it. You need small-scale charts for planning and navigational use, medium-scale for the approaches to islands and coastlines, and large-scale detailed drawings to guide you into harbors and through intricate passages. Not only should a prudent mariner have adequate information about intended ports, but he ought to have limited coverage of contingency stops. If you have a problem along the way and decide to run off to a convenient port to leeward, you will need the chart. If you haven't room for all the charts when you set out, or are unsure whether you will continue after the first long jump, arrange to have a batch of charts sent to you at a convenient port.

Unfortunately, the cost of charts has risen astronomically. It's hard to believe, but years ago, I used to have a half-dozen U.S. charts of the Chilean channels with officially stamped prices of $0.15, $0.25, $1.00, $2.60, and $3.50 in the lower margins. All the old prices (except the last) had been crossed out. In 2002, the official U.S. price for new charts of the same places in Chile was $17.00 each. For an extensive trip requiring fifty or seventy-five charts, the charges can be heavy.

World-cruising sailors crossing paths and going in different directions often trade charts. Yachts in Suva, for example, will swap plans of the Society Islands for Vanuatu charts. Sometimes when a family has completed a big trip, it will give away or sell a great pile of charts for a low figure. Often big-ship officers pass along slightly outdated charts to small-boat sailors.

In the Pacific, Margaret and I met the Norwegian yacht *Preciosa*, whose crew was given a set of charts for almost the entire world by a friendly shipping company. I have heard of small-boat sailors buying old charts from large chart agents that periodically replace the charts of big ships.

While I am not a fan of outdated charts, which can be dangerous to use, an old chart is certainly better than no chart. Furthermore, old charts can be brought up to date by consulting Notices to Mariners, which are available on the Internet and easy to download. Occasionally you can borrow donated charts from cruising associations and sailing clubs. In the eastern Caroline Islands, I salvaged an enormous roll of southeast Asia plans from a wrecked tuna boat.

A few years ago in Monastir, Tunisia, I borrowed a dozen German charts of the Italian coast from a German yacht next to us. The captain told me how to find a nearby copying place. I walked into town to an office where a local entrepreneur had a giant Xerox machine and a sizeable business copying charts. The cost was $2 each. I noticed that the young woman in the office also dealt with Canadian and British charts, which are copyrighted and are not supposed to be duplicated. Not only did the Monastir clerk copy the German charts that I had brought in, but she quietly made a negative of each plan to add to her stock for future sales to others.

U.S. charts are not copyrighted and can be duplicated by anyone. Another scheme is Chart-Kits, which are privately printed chart selections for a given U.S. area that are bound into convenient portfolios. Unfortunately, the charts are reduced in size and are hard to read because of loran lines. Occasionally, parts of charts are omitted because they don't conveniently fit into the abridged form. Don't assume that these folios include everything, but look with your own eyes to see that all places that you're thinking of visiting have been included. In the Chart-Kit that includes Maine, for example, the upstream portion of the Kennebec River, a legitimate waterway and a beautiful area for sailing, has been omitted.

It's best to purchase British charts and Pilots directly from England because they're cheaper and are more likely to include new printings. You can telephone or fax an order (using a credit card) from abroad; the order is usually airmailed the same day. For example, from the United States, I have telephoned an order to Kelvin-Hughes (001-44-20-8500-1020) in Ilford and had the mailing tube with the charts in my hand forty-eight hours later in Maryland.

In 2002, the cost of an Admiralty chart in England was £16 or $23.00 (a U.S. dealer charges $36.50, or about 58 percent more). A Pilot book in England costs £37 or $52.39 (a U.S. dealer charges $92.50 for a single volume, a markup of 75 percent at retail). There is no customs duty on books or charts. You have to reckon in postage costs, of course, but if you share an order with a sailing friend, the postal costs can be halved.

To find out what's available on a worldwide basis, you need the big *Catalogue of Admiralty Charts* (NP-131), which costs £18 or about $26 and is good to have on hand for purchases, for general planning, and for use as a world atlas. I keep mine at the bottom of the chart table. It's a great help.

Admiralty charts fold to a consistent size, while U.S. charts come in a collection of sizes that are less handy to fold and store. Admiralty charts arrive corrected to the date of purchase. U.S. charts are corrected up to the time of printing and must be corrected from Notices to Mariners by the purchaser. This is not a small matter.

What about digitized charts on CD-ROMs or other types of digital cartridges or memory cards? At first glance, this scheme seems to have wonderful advantages. Fifty or a hundred charts can be put on a digital disc or other storage device and viewed on various onboard screens. At a stroke, the stowage problems of paper charts are solved because you don't have any.

Not only can tide and current information be visually integrated with the image on the screen, but the ship's GPS position can be shown on the digital chart. This advantage alone is significant because using dividers to plot the position of a mark on a paper chart and entering the coordinates in a GPS device are steps prone to error. Most cruising sailors use GPS devices and have a second battery-powered GPS for a backup.

But what if the electricity fails? Or if there are a few drips from your oilskins or a splash of salt water on the chart table that leads to problems with the reading device? "Laptops are notoriously water-sensitive, and can be ruined in one regrettable wet moment," says the West Marine catalog, which features a big advertising section on digital charts. Suppose you have trouble seeing a clear image on the screen. Of course you can send the machine to the manufacturer for repairs, but I can tell you with certainty that in many foreign places, the problems with delivery services and customs agents are not only disheartening but often insurmountable.

The makers of digital charts recommend that you carry "adequate" paper charts (whatever that means), just in case. In addition, it's disappointing to often read the legend "Not for navigation" on these devices.

Another factor with digitized charts—at least for me—is that I'm in the habit of spreading out paper charts and examining them to get a feel for an area. I am used to drawing lines on charts, showing charts to people, and thinking about the pros and cons of this route or that while I make up my mind. Usually when I sail into a port, I have a large-scale, folded chart in one hand and the tiller in the other. I like the size, clarity, and mass of detail on a paper chart.

To equal this I would have to take my laptop or a viewing screen into the cockpit. How long, I wonder, would these devices work with salt spray flying around?

On a viewing device, I tend to lose perspective, orientation, and a sense of exactly where I am. It's not a question of magnifying a part of a digital chart, but of looking at the large and familiar expanse of a paper chart. I suppose in time I could learn to work around these subjective considerations, but they're important to me.

At the moment there are a number of digitized charts for popular sailing areas, but few for remote places. In addition, the reading devices and digitized charts are expensive; updating the charts is another cost. It would be easy to spend thousands of dollars to get ready for a long trip and have this jeopardized by a change in technology. I suspect that in a few years, when competition between software vendors increases and the weak players drop out, the prices of digitized charts and reading devices will plunge. By then the mapping should include more areas, and the viewing devices may be better. I suspect the way this technology will develop will be for governments to put their paper charts on CDs and for the private sector to perfect the viewing devices.

I plan to watch the development of digitized charts and their use, but for the present I am definitely sticking to paper charts.

At the moment we have about 150 paper charts on *Whisper*, plus 6 volumes of Pilots, *Ocean Passages*, a slim atlas of Pilot charts, 3 cruising guides, and a Reed's Nautical Almanac. We have about 35 charts in current use. I carefully fold each chart exactly in half (with the printing outside so I can see what it is) and then stow it flat in the chart table. We store the other charts away in three or four big rolls (kept dry in black plastic garbage bags) in the forepeak.

Margaret keeps a list that shows all the charts on board by number, title, and geographical area. Borrowed charts (if any) are on a separate list.

Half our charts are from the United States, but as I've indicated, we often buy Admiralty charts directly from a British agent. I find the Admiralty small-scale charts are especially good for planning purposes, and in general I prefer the English plans because of more detailed information, better draftsmanship, and the uniform paper size. If possible, we try to use the charts of the country through which we plan to travel (Canadian charts for Canada, New Zealand for the Cook Islands, Chilean for its channels and long coastline, etc.).

When you sail to foreign places, it's hard to decide where to go. Venice and Rome are famous and you want to see them. Tahiti and Mooréa are easy choices, but should you go to Kapingamarangi or Pingelap? To Suvorov or Rakahanga? To La Digue or Raroia? To Funchal or Lanzarote? You make some stops because of your reading or recommendations of friends, because of protected anchorages, because you are tired and want to rest, or simply because you are intrigued with the name. Margaret and I prefer to make fewer stops but to stay at new ports for longer times.

Another planning consideration—at least in the areas of the world with low and dangerous islands—is a clear and uncluttered route. It's best to go out of your way to avoid unlighted islands at night. Not only will your passage be simpler in deep water, where the currents may not be so variable, but you can relax and enjoy the passage instead of dying a thousand navigational deaths. Commercial shipping lanes mean constant vigilance and worry; if you can arrange to cross shipping lanes at right angles in daylight and to leave them far behind, all the better.

Ocean cruising isn't the only kind of sailing that needs careful planning. Coastal passages and lake trips are easier, more satisfying, and safer if you check the prevailing winds, storm patterns, tidal action, land breezes, and so forth. While genuine local knowledge is helpful, waterfront gossip sometimes has little value; the loudest talkers may never have left the harbor. You may be surprised at what a little study of books and charts will reveal.

A voyaging sailor's schedule shouldn't be too detailed and structured. In the first place, you are almost never on time. You are behind schedule because of maintenance on the yacht (the parts didn't come) or because you have found a delightful new place (great scenery; nice walks on the beaches). Perhaps in ports along the way you have met new people or old friends. Or best of all, the sailing may be so pleasant you would like it to last forever.

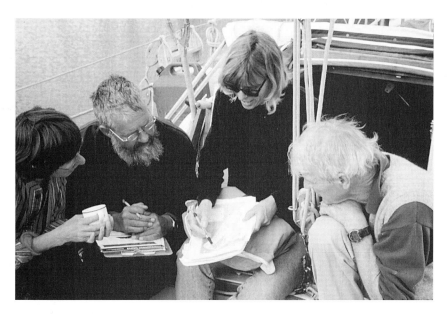

Some of the best ideas for the next stop come from friends you make along the way. Here foreign voyagers Corri and Willem Stein (at left) from the 39-foot yacht Terra Nova *of Hilversum, Holland, get information from the American sailors Nancy and Tom Zydler about sailing along the coast of Georgia in the southeastern United States.*

12

THE ANCHOR GAME

When we last visited California, we tied up *Whisper* at a friend's dock in beautiful Newport Beach. Next to us was a sleek new 46-foot New Zealand–built cutter that belonged to Ed Carpenter, who was busy completing the interior. Ed often stopped to look at *Whisper*'s 45-pound CQR plow anchor hanging on the stemhead, the windlass, and the $3/8$-inch chain that disappeared inside. One day Ed asked me about an anchor.

"Say, Hal," he said. "If you were fitting out *Matangi*, what kind of ground tackle would you choose? I mean if you were going anywhere. My boat displaces about 12 tons."

"Since *Matangi* is twice the weight of *Whisper*, I would buy a 60-pound plow, 45 fathoms of $7/16$-inch chain, and a suitable windlass to handle both," I answered after some thought.

My answer so upset Ed that he went around in a daze for days.

Sometime later, Ed asked the same question of Al Liggett, who had recently returned from a sailing trip around the world.

The CQR anchor was invented by Geoffrey Taylor in 1932. It's a fiendishly clever design and is used on thousands of yachts. I send the 4-foot fluke line overboard with the anchor. When stowed, I use the line to pull the plow or fluke to one side. I then lash the end of the line tightly to the bow pulpit to keep the anchor quiet.

181

"What anchor would you pick?" Ed asked.

Al tugged at his beard, eyeballed the long blue hull, and replied, "Well, if she were mine, I'd find me a 75-pound plow or a nice hefty Danforth anchor and a big hunk of chain to quiet her down. If it gets to blowing some awful night, you don't want to worry."

Again Ed shook his head in disbelief. When he put the question to a third world-cruising sailor and got essentially the same answer, he scratched his head.

"I think you fellows are trying to tell me something," he said. "I had no idea you needed such heavy anchors and chain. In southern California, we use 15- or 20-pound anchors and nylon, but then we tie up mostly in marinas or use moorings. I guess when you're in a distant land somewhere, your gear needs to be beefy and beyond doubt even if it weighs a quarter of a ton."

Ed's figure of a quarter of a ton wasn't far wrong. Only he forgot to count the other anchors and warps. On *Whisper*, our ground tackle is as follows.

1	CQR anchor	45 lb.
	30 fathoms $\frac{3}{8}$" dia. (9 mm) chain	295
	Windlass (S-L 555)	50
2	CQR anchor (spare)	45
	1 fathom $\frac{1}{2}$" chain	14
	45 fathoms $\frac{5}{8}$" dia. nylon	31
3	Fisherman anchor (Herreshoff)	65
	1 fathom $\frac{1}{2}$" chain	14
	30 fathoms $\frac{5}{8}$" dia. 3-strand nylon	21
4	Danforth anchor	35
	17 fathoms $\frac{1}{2}$" dia. 3-strand nylon	14
5	Danforth anchor (spare)	35
	1 fathom $\frac{1}{2}$" chain	14
	40 fathoms $\frac{3}{4}$" dia. 3-strand nylon	35
	50 fathoms $\frac{5}{8}$" polypropylene line	22
	1 anchor line weight (for use on all)	25
	Total	760 lb.

This equipment gives us five sets of anchors and cables. I carry spare anchors in case of loss because it's impossible to replace them in remote places. We reckon we can use all chain and anchor in 6 fathoms of water or less with a fair amount of safety. In deeper water, we use chain and nylon or chain and polypropylene. My choice of anchors and cables is worked out on the premise of stout gear to handle the worst conditions; yet I need to deal with the ground tackle quickly and with a minimum of fuss and wasted energy.

Handling the Main Anchor

Our CQR anchor runs over a substantial bow roller that allows the shank of the anchor to go out or come in over the roller so the anchor can be dropped or weighed without touching it. All Margaret or I need to do to recover the anchor is to work the windlass lever back and forth while standing at full height in a comfortable position. The chain falls below—fathom by fathom—until the shank of the anchor starts up the bow roller. If the anchor has been raised with the fluke (plow) upward or at the side, the weight of the fluke rolls the anchor over so that the fluke hangs downward in its proper stowing position. A few more cranks pull the shank of the anchor aft until the widened part of the shank (near the pivot pin) is jammed between the bow roller and a U-shaped metal piece fitted over the roller to keep the chain from jumping off (see photograph).

To stop the fluke of the CQR from banging around, I have a 4-foot piece of ⅜-inch-diameter line permanently tied to the crossbar between the ears of the fluke. This fluke lashing goes overboard with the anchor. When the anchor is recovered, I take this small line to the starboard side of the pulpit, pull it as tightly as possible, and secure it with three round turns and a couple of half hitches. This jams the fluke of the anchor against the metal stem piece and keeps everything quiet, yet I can quickly cast off the fluke lashing and the anchor is ready to drop.

Not only does this anchor-handling scheme obviate lifting an awkward and heavy weight over the lifelines and pulpit, knocking the paint, and getting the anchor person covered with whatever may be on

One arrangement of anchor handling. The anchor is always ready to use and is self-stowing and quiet while under way if the fluke line is pulled tight. Note how the bow roller fitting is reinforced with heavy stainless steel angles. This fitting takes terrible abuse from the chain when the yacht is swinging around in gusty winds and should be ten times stronger than you think necessary. The one failing of the arrangement shown here is that the anchor rollers are too small. Ideally, they should be 6 inches in diameter to reduce friction during anchor recovery.

the seabed (often gluey black mud), but the anchor is in position, ready to be let go again. During the entire operation, I have touched neither the anchor nor the chain. And my back is not wrenched from lifting a big weight at a bad angle. If the cable is muddy, it's a good idea to pull it up slowly and to stop now and then to give the sea a few minutes to flush off the mud. If necessary, we use a brush and buckets of seawater to complete the scrub. Don't stow muddy chain or line below; clean it as it comes on board. If this takes an extra fifteen minutes, so be it.

If the chain locker is tall and narrow, the chain will be self-stowing and require no attention. If the chain locker is wide and flat and open to the cabin below, a crew member will have to go down to knock down the mound of chain as it builds up. Failure to keep the chain orderly can result in tangles. Ideally, because of the weight, the chain locker should be midships around the mast area, but this is hard to arrange and means that the chain has to be led along the deck—one more complication.

Chain lasts for a long time, but when wear has knocked off much of the galvanizing and you begin to see rust, it's time to end-for-end it. In the past we had our chain hot-dip galvanized every five years or so, which made it like new. It's hard to believe, but galvanizing costs have become so high in the United States that it's a tossup whether to buy new chain or to treat the old. If the costs are close, buy new chain because galvanizing is troublesome since you have to transport the chain to and from the plating works. Sometimes the chain comes back with many of the links stuck together with zinc. Outside the United States, galvanizing costs are less and often include pickup and delivery.

To keep track of how much chain is out, we tie three 1-inch-wide, 12- or 15-inch-long strips of red cloth at 5 fathoms, white strips at 10 fathoms, and blue strips at 15 fathoms. I then repeat and put red at 20 fathoms, and white at 25 fathoms. The sequence of red, white, and blue is simple to remember. The strips of cloth are easy to see (and to renew occasionally) when they fly past the windlass gypsy as the chain rumbles out. At night, the strips are quite visible with a flashlight. I find using the cloth strips easier than painting marks on the chain.

The anchoring system that I have described has worked perfectly for many years and thousands of anchoring episodes. Margaret and I find the recovery of the chain and anchor is not difficult at all. Normally it takes about ten minutes to crank up 20 or 30 fathoms of chain. When we're ready to go and have a lot of chain out, I generally crank in half of it and then stop and coil up a few lines or look at the chart. This gives me a breather and allows the sea to wash some or all of the mud from the chain.

People are forever telling me how hard the chain is to recover and how tired I must be. Obviously my observers have never used a good manual windlass. I am perfectly satisfied with my anchoring technique and see no reason to complicate it with an electric or hydraulic device.

If the chain locker is open to the interior of the yacht and you're going to sea or anticipate a long slog to windward, it's a good idea to plug the navel pipe—the deck opening. Otherwise, an astonishing amount of water can find its way below. One idea is to disconnect the chain, and tie its end to a short piece of light line that hangs down from a tapered (greased) wooden plug that seals the navel pipe. The weight of the chain holds the plug in place. Never drop the end of the chain into the chain locker without tying a rag or something on the end; otherwise, it will be very hard to find. If you don't want to disconnect the chain, try tamping oily rags around the chain or nylon line in the navel pipe.

NYLON

Nylon line is a wonderful material for anchor cable. Its natural stretch evens out shocks and jerks, it doesn't rot or rust, and its strength is unbelievable. It works silently, is easy to recover, and generally comes aboard clean. The line is not heavy and does not cause a weight problem in the ends of a vessel. It is, however, extremely subject to chafe, which makes it hazardous to use in tropical waters, where razor-sharp coral can gnaw through the line insidiously and steadily until the yarns and fibers silently part.

Nylon is not self-stowing, as is chain, and is hard to haul by hand because it's slippery and sometimes can severely cut your hands without you knowing it. Another disadvantage is that in gusty winds, a yacht may sheer from side to side when anchored with nylon. Chain is much heavier, hangs in a catenary, and will help hold a nervous ship steady because the chain resists back-and-forth dragging on the seabed. In waters where coral is not a problem, you can use a long piece of chain together with nylon to gain some of the advantages of each. A short length of chain leading up from the anchor will reduce the chafe of the nylon against the seabed. If the bottom is rough, however, you need to think of chafe at the chain-nylon connection. Veteran sailor Bob Griffith suggests a small sunken float to lift the splice area, plus the use of polypropylene floating line (instead of nylon) up to the yacht.

Where a fiber line—of whatever material—comes aboard the yacht, it must be carefully protected with chafing gear. Although some sailors wrap canvas around the line where it passes over a roller or through a chock, it's difficult to keep the canvas in place even if it's carefully tied or sewn.

I have had better results leading the line through a piece of old rubber engine-cooling-water hose 3 or 4 feet long whose inside diameter ($5/8$ or $3/4''$) is a snug fit for the cable. The thick-walled hose is easy to lash to fittings and protects the fibers, yet it is quite resistant to chafe. You can keep the hose in place with pieces of small stuff tied around the line (use constrictor knots) above and below the chafing gear. Metal hose clamps also work well. But no matter what sort of chafing gear you decide on, it must be inspected every several hours during a storm because hundreds or perhaps thousands of pounds of pressure are concentrated on one or two tiny points. And if the chafing gear goes, the anchor line is next. You need to move the line and chafing gear only a few inches to find a new place to start over again.

For the hard usage that anchor warps receive, braided line seems superior to three-strand construction, which is sometimes weakened by hockling, an annoying back-twisting in which one or more strands get a reverse twist and stick out laterally from the main body of the line. These unwanted twists ruin the strength of the line and make it hard to handle or run through blocks.

A principal advantage of nylon is its marvelous elasticity; we must not lose this property by using a diameter that is too large. For vessels of 25 to 55 feet—the concern of this book—nylon of 1-inch diameter is too big; ³/₄- or ⁵/₈-inch-diameter nylon is ample; even ¹/₂-inch-diameter nylon is adequate. The late Captain Irving Johnson anchored his 40-ton ketch *Yankee* for years in European and Mediterranean waters with ¹/₂-inch nylon (and no chain) with excellent results. The smaller line is also cheaper, lighter, and much easier to store. Half-inch line seems absurdly small for a 40-ton vessel, but it works well.

I have had great success with this simple anchor arrangement at the stern of the yacht. I keep a Danforth anchor permanently stowed in this position, where it is always ready to go. All I have to do is untie three knots and heave the anchor over the lifelines. Note the lead of the line from the bucket, and that the line is simply pushed or faked (not coiled) into the bucket. This anchor is an old 35-pound Danforth, but others will do as well. I have a short tie between the pulpit and the bucket handle to hold the bucket when the boat heels.

"I feel certain that you should not use too large a diameter of nylon because if you do, it spoils the chance of getting some elasticity," Captain Johnson told me. "You will never break a ¹/₂-inch nylon unless it chafes, and if you get chafe you can break a 2-inch nylon." [31]

In the Mediterranean it's usual for yachts and fishing boats to tie their bows to a quay or dock and to put out a stern anchor so the vessels lie at 90 degrees to the wharf. This allows at least three times as many boats to use a given dock frontage, a scheme that Americans have yet to appreciate.

On a recent trip in the Mediterranean, I put out a stern anchor in 95 separate anchorages with complete success. I keep this stern anchor ready for use at all times by tying it to the cockpit lifelines (see photograph). I lead the $\frac{1}{2}$-inch anchor line over the lifelines from a mooring cleat, and stuff (not coil) 100 feet of nylon into a small plastic bucket (with drain holes punched in the bottom) that I store at the back of the cockpit. No chain. Not only is this anchor handy and quick to use, but it makes a great emergency brake if I need to stop the boat in shallow water.

To use the anchor, I untie shoestring knots on three small ties and toss the anchor over the side. As the warp pays out from the plastic bucket, I can take a turn or two around a winch for control. I'm the first to admit that $\frac{1}{2}$-inch line seems ridiculously small, but it works to perfection if you keep it away from sharp corners and anything abrasive. If you can't stomach the idea of line this small, try $\frac{5}{8}$-inch-diameter line.

The main difficulty with long fiber warps is stowage. It seems that no matter how carefully you coil lines and tie them off, as soon as you turn your back, they get into snarls. A small warp can be stored in a plastic bucket as I mentioned above. Another stowage scheme is to coil the nylon or polypropylene in a large circle (with, say, a 60" diameter or so) and tie the line every couple of feet with a piece of small stuff. (Twenty-four inches is a good length for short ties; I always keep a dozen in my pocket.) Then if half the coil is turned over, you get a figure eight, one coil of which can be pushed over on top of the other to make a smaller unit. When you want to use the warp, you reverse the process. No matter how you stow lines, however, it's troublesome to get them ready to let go, particularly if you need long lengths, the vessel is rolling, and you're in a hurry.

After fighting the battle of warp stowage for many years, I designed a stainless steel frame and drum (with plywood sides) to hold 300 feet of $\frac{5}{8}$-inch-diameter line. We mounted the drum on the port side of the afterdeck on our first *Whisper*. We kept a fathom of $\frac{1}{2}$-inch chain and an anchor shackled to the warp. The anchor was at the stern and always ready to drop. In practice, the warp drum worked to perfection, and I liked the ease and speed of both letting go of and recovering the line. The surprising thing is how small 300 feet

Small drums to hold anchor lines, sheets, and halyards are incredibly handy because the line can be used immediately without tangles. Additionally, the line takes up much less space. It's more seamanlike to have lines orderly and neat instead of thrown into odd corners where they get all mixed up.

I have used small drums for mainsheets with complete success.

of line is when it's coiled tightly. The warp drum was only $14\frac{1}{2}$ inches in diameter and 12 inches long and showed that the trick of good line stowage is a simple system of even coiling on a readily accessible drum. To recover the line, I turned the drum with the flat of my hand and a back-and-forth motion. Cranks did not work. Unfortunately, I have no afterdeck to hold the warp drum on my current vessel. The stainless steel drum and frame were troublesome to make. I think a better and lighter drum and frame might be devised from a plastic garden-hose windup reel, sold in hardware stores for a few dollars.

Polypropylene line is useful in anchoring maneuvers. It has a specific gravity of 0.91, doesn't absorb water, and will float indefinitely, which means it will stay clear of the seafloor. It has half the stretch of nylon and is only two-thirds as strong, but it costs half as much, which is why practically all the fishing boats in the world use it for everything, including dock lines and net warps. Today, most polypropylene fibers are stabilized to provide resistance to the sun's ultraviolet rays.

In addition to floating clear of the bottom when used with an anchor, polypropylene makes a mooring line that stays on the surface and is easy to pick up. As a towline, it doesn't get mixed up with rudders or propellers. A length of polypropylene can be dragged behind for swimmers or tossed to a person overboard. If you take out an anchor in a dinghy, a polypropylene line will tow easily behind on the water, and finally, if you lose a coil of polypropylene line over the side, it won't sink.

A fault with polypropylene is that, unlike nylon, it floats on the surface, particularly in a calm, and can be a trap just waiting for a passing propeller. Small weights will sink the line slightly.

THE DIFFERENT TYPES OF ANCHORS

The big four anchors are the CQR, the Danforth, the Bruce, and the fisherman. The first three are burying anchors, while the fisherman is a surface anchor. It's useful to keep these distinctions in mind, because each class of anchor works in a different manner and is better suited to certain conditions.

The CQR (the name is a sort of acronym for *secure*), or plow, was invented by Geoffrey Taylor in 1932 and was engineered for British flying boats. Today this design is in wide use among cruising yachts. The anchor is made of drop-forged steel and consists of a V-shaped plowshare connected to a long H-sectioned shank by a massive pin (see photograph page 180). The plow, or fluke, is free to pivot from side to side over a prescribed limit. There is no stock. The anchor is extremely difficult to bend.

In use the CQR falls to the seabed, the tension on the cable straightens out the anchor, turns it on one side or the other, and the plow begins to dig in. In suitable holding ground, the fluke goes deeper and deeper as tension on the cable increases. Often the entire anchor becomes buried. If the yacht swings with the tide, the cable will not foul the anchor (as with a fisherman). A pull from a different direction merely resets the CQR in a new alignment. The CQR is difficult to foul unless you have the bad luck to pick up a tin can with the point of the plow.

The genuine CQR anchor is made by Simpson-Lawrence of Glasgow, Scotland, and is widely distributed. Besides the design, the main feature of the Simpson-Lawrence CQR is that both the H-section shank and the pin and horn (which carries the plow) are made from solid, one-piece drop-forged steel. The plow is stamped from heavy plate steel and is welded to the horn. The anchor is then hot-dip galvanized. Unfortunately, there are bad copies of the CQR, none of which I recommend. In particular, I have knowledge of a German imitation (which I hope has been improved or withdrawn) that doesn't hold at all and is worse than useless because the bad copy gives false confidence.

The Danforth anchor is well known and consists of a shank loosely slipped over the midpoint of the stock to make a strong T-shaped fitting (see photograph on page 186). Two paddle-shaped flukes are then welded to the stock, one on each side of the shank. To control the shank-fluke angle, two small pieces of metal are welded to the fluke-stock assembly so that the digging angle of the flukes—the fishhook angle—remains at 32 degrees no matter which way the anchor falls to the seabed.

If the Danforth initially hits on its side on the seafloor, the protruding stock makes the anchor fall over to its proper position for digging in. Tension on the anchor cable causes the flukes to open until they are held at the proper angle by the small pieces of metal at the crown, and the pointed steel flukes are forced into the seabed. The harder the pull of the cable, the more the anchor digs in. The Danforth cannot be fouled once it is dug in a little. As with the CQR, a pull from a different direction merely resets the anchor.

One fault with the Danforth is that it is possible to get chain or line between the flukes and the shank (sometimes wrapped around and around). This rarely happens unless the anchor and slack cable are thrown haphazardly into the sea. If cable does get between the flukes and the shank, the anchor is, of course, fouled and will not hold at all. You will know at once because the anchor will drag. If a Danforth is let go slowly with a slight tension on the cable, the anchor will not foul this way. If you hold your hand on the cable while the yacht moves slowly, you can feel the anchor bump along the bottom and suddenly grab as it digs in.

The pivoting flukes of a Danforth can also be jammed open with a small rock or clam shell. When the anchor turns over, the frozen blades will not fall down but instead will skid merrily along the bottom. This is an unusual occurrence but possible. Again, you will know because the anchor will drag. These anchors have a hard life on a rocky bottom where their thin metal pieces can sometimes be twisted and bent.

Danforths have been manufactured in all sizes from $2^1/2$ pounds (for dinghies) to 10,000 pounds (for battleships). During World War II, tens of thousands of them were made, mostly of ordinary steel, usually galvanized, but many were fabricated of bronze (nonmagnetic for minesweepers) or stainless steel. Various manufacturing techniques have been used—stamping, forging, casting, riveting, and welding. Often you can buy Danforths at commission sales outlets; years ago I bought an excellent 33-pound Danforth with curved flukes from a stack of two hundred at a war surplus warehouse on the San Francisco waterfront. The anchor cost $10, and I used it for years.

The stowage of a Danforth is easy because the anchor lies flat. Recently, some models have been made with very skinny shanks. In tension these shanks have plenty of strength, but in the twisting and bending situations that all anchors go through in their hard lives on sea bottoms, I fear the skinny shank will turn into a pretzel. Fortunately, there are plenty of regular-shanked Danforths in the marketplace.

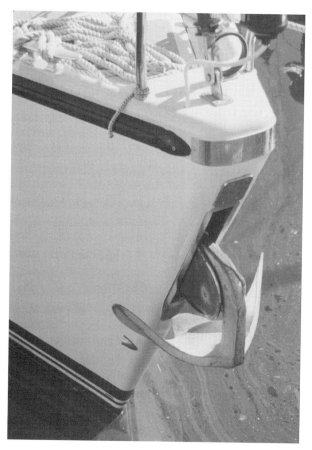

The clever designers of the German Dehler 41 use this self-stowing anchor arrangement to run a Bruce anchor in and out over a large roller. The windlass is located in a self-draining locker below the foredeck, which leaves the deck clear and uncluttered. When not in use, the tension on the chain keeps the anchor pulled in tightly against the bow roller. Note the wide fluke area of the Bruce anchor.

*   *   *

The third type of burying anchor is the Bruce, a recent entry in the stable of ground tackle for cruising yachts. The Bruce was developed to hold huge offshore oil platforms in place and is made in weights up to 15,000 pounds. Such anchors are transported on railroad flatcars and on enormous 20-wheeler trucks. The yacht and workboat versions are in the 20- to 150-pound class.

The Bruce is a one-piece casting of heat-treated steel. It has no stock and looks something like a CQR except that the plow part is flattened and the sides broadened out into what I would call "winglets" that serve as the stock to roll the anchor over so that it can begin to dig in. The shape of the anchor is impossible to describe in words; certainly in the world of the future, the Bruce will make many an archae-ologist scratch his head.

Two of my cruising friends with heavy-displacement yachts use Bruce anchors. Willem Stein has a 110-pound Bruce for his 39-foot Joshua steel ketch. Herb Weiss uses a 75-pound Bruce to keep his Hallberg-Rassy 42 in place. As we've seen, how-ever, all anchors have pluses and minuses. A few years ago in St. Barthélemy, a friend named Bill Goodloe, who was anchored next to me in his yacht *Black Dragon*, suddenly began to drag out to sea. Bill dropped another anchor and pulled up his Bruce. He found that the fluke of the anchor had picked up a piece of coral the size of a head of cabbage. This fouled the anchor and made it useless.

It's not that the Bruce is bad—it's an excellent anchor. But all anchors are imperfect in one area or other, and sailors need to be wary. I believe the most important use of an auxiliary engine is to try to drag the yacht astern at full throttle to check that the holding ground, anchor, shackles, chain, line, bow roller, anchor spring, and windlass are doing their job.

The fisherman is the age-old traditional anchor of the sea and is the pattern often tattooed on the backs of sailors' hands or forearms. I have seen fisherman anchors in many parts of the world—Japan, Chile, Greece, and Yemen. Though details dif-fer, the design is always the same: two arms fastened to one end of a long shank to make a T-shaped contrivance. The arms are curved slightly toward the opposite end of the shank, and the ends of the arms usually have widened points or flukes to grip the seabed better by pro-viding more resistance.

The most familiar anchor (and difficult to handle) is the age-old fisherman with its wide flukes and heavy weight.

A long stock (sometimes of wood and usually removable so the anchor can be lashed flat on deck when not in use) is led through the shank at the opposite end from the arms of the anchor. The stock is positioned so that if you view the anchor from either end of the shank, the stock and the arms are always at right angles to each other. This is done so that if the stock hits the seabed, it makes the anchor unstable and it falls over and posi-tions the flukes so they can dig in.

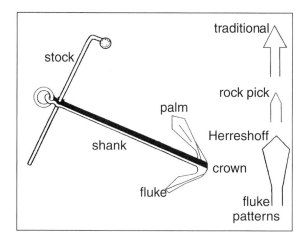

The fisherman anchor is the traditional and best known of all anchors and is recognizable on everything from tattoos to postage stamps. Note that when viewed from the end, the alignment of the stock is always at 90 degrees to a line drawn from one fluke to the other. This is done so that when the anchor drops to the seabed, it is unstable and falls over. Then with the stock parallel to the seabed, the lower fluke is in position to dig into the holding ground. This downstanding fluke plows its way into the sand or whatever, and generally forces the palm deeply into the holding ground. Unfortunately, this leaves the upper fluke sticking straight up. When the vessel swings with the tide or in a calm, the chain or line tends to hook underneath this upper fluke, particularly if it is the equilateral triangle design of the traditional anchor. In 1865, Charles Frederic Herreshoff made a fluke design in which the lower part descended toward the crown in a long sloping taper that is much less likely to snag the cable. The chisel-shaped Herreshoff fluke is considered to be the best because of its increased area and nonfouling properties. The third type of fluke, the rock pick, often used by fishing boats, is useful on a rocky bottom, particularly on short scope with a heavy anchor.

Once a fluke is set on the floor of the sea, the harder the pull on the chain or anchor line, the more the fluke digs in until it is buried up to the crown. However, the basic drawback to the fisherman anchor is that the other fluke sticks vertically upright. This means that if the yacht swings with the tide or drifts in a calm, it's possible for the anchor line to catch or get around the upstanding fluke and to foul the anchor. This problem may require a second anchor, a line ashore, or some close attention.

The fisherman is a surface anchor and is restricted by its design from digging deeper than the depth of one arm (the distance from the crown to the tip of a fluke). The anchor, therefore, relies on considerable weight and an initial grab of the seabed. In soft mud or loose sand, a fisherman may drag; once the anchor lets go and begins to scrape a furrow across the ocean floor, its holding power is gone. In spite of these disadvantages, however, the fisherman is excellent at times. Its flukes are heavy and dig in quickly and hard. On a rocky bottom, a CQR and Danforth—burying types—may not work at all, while a fisherman will hold well, particularly on short scope. In sand or shells with a hard crust and in weeds, a fisherman is often the only hope.

On the common fisherman, the palm of its fluke is spade-shaped (see the illustration above). As I mentioned, when the yacht swings or drifts in a calm, the anchor line may catch on the fluke that sticks up and become fouled. On the Herreshoff pattern, the palm is diamond-shaped and tapers gradually toward both the tip of the fluke and the crown. An anchor line will usually (not always) slip up the arm past the palm and not foul the anchor.

You sometimes see fisherman anchors with no palms at all—the arm merely runs out to the fluke in a long tapered point. These anchors are rock picks and are used mostly in halibut boats for fishing purposes and have no place on yachts. A halibut anchor will pull right through most types of holding ground because with no palms, there is scarcely any resistance.

When you're pulling up a fisherman anchor from the bottom, it can be recovered without trouble until it's clear of the water. Then because sharp iron points stick out on all sides, the anchor becomes a monster that threatens not only to tear off the topside paint but to rip through the hull itself, particularly if the vessel is rolling and pitching as she gets under way.

I've found that it's helpful to have a line around the crown of the anchor. Then I bend the line to a jib halyard, and put the hauling part of the halyard on a winch. This will recover the anchor upside down and bring it to the rail or the deck without trouble. But how do you work a line around the crown of the anchor when it's in the water? You don't. You fit a short line beforehand.

The line around the crown can be an anchor buoy line or a short piece of ½-inch-diameter polypropylene line. I eyesplice one end of the line to the crown or arm just inboard of the right-hand fluke; the other end is eyespliced inboard of the left-hand fluke. This U-shaped line is about 10 feet long and goes overboard with the anchor. When you're recovering the anchor and it breaks the surface, you can pick up the floating line with a boat hook or with a chain hook tied to the end of a halyard.

You can minimize damage from the ends of the stocks of fisherman and Danforth anchors by putting rubber crutch tips over the ends of the stock.

I have talked about four well-known types of anchors. Which is best? My answer is that, as many world-cruising people do, we carry three of the four because each is good for different conditions. I use a CQR for a basic anchor; the Danforth is ideal for a kedge or a second anchor, and the fisherman is unsurpassed in difficult holding ground.

I have found the CQR excellent in 80 percent of the anchorages we have visited. Yet I can easily recall four places—Caleta Morning in Canal Beagle on Isla Hoste on the south side of Tierra del Fuego; a beach anchorage on Isla Española in the Galápagos; a palm-shaded paradise near the western end of the lagoon of Rangiroa atoll in the Tuamotus; and a sheltered bay near Linaria on the Greek island of Skíros in the Aegean—that were special problems. The first three sites had a sand or shell bottom with a hard crust that the CQR would not penetrate even when the anchor was dropped time after time. In two of these places, the flukes of a Danforth—kept sharply pointed with a little hand filing from time to time (especially before regalvanizing)—dug in quickly. At the third place, the Danforth skated across the seabed like the CQR, and we tossed over a fisherman, whose heavy flukes penetrated the crust at once. On Skíros, the problem was thick grass, and again the fisherman helped us. You need a variety of anchors.

Paul Luke of East Boothbay, Maine, manufactures the best fisherman anchors in the United States. The Luke anchors (in weights of 25, 40, 60, 75, 100, 150, and 200 lb.) are close to the original Herreshoff patterns and are made in three pieces for ease of stowage. These anchors are heavy and solid and expensive, but with reasonable luck, one will last you a lifetime. In fact, one may extend your lifetime.

THE THREE POINTS OF ANCHORING

Although there are a number of refinements—none to be neglected—the three main requirements of successful anchoring are an anchor of ample weight, plenty of scope, and suitable holding ground.

Weight

The first rule of anchoring is to consider the weight of the odd-shaped piece of iron that ties you to the earth. The weight means a lot. A 25-pound anchor will often skid over a veneer of weed or grass on the seafloor, while a 40- or 60-pound anchor will dig through to sand or shells below. There is no substitute for a heavy, properly dug in anchor. A novice may boast that an 8-pound Danforth held his yacht in a storm. This may be perfectly true if the anchor was well dug in. The problem is that the 8- or 15-pound anchor may not dig in at all in many types of bottom.

It's for this reason that I recommend that a 25-foot yacht carry at least one 30-pound burying-type anchor, a weight most adults can handle by hand.

I know that many people will accuse me of overkill and extra expense. The anchor people with their 8-pound anchors and their crafty little tables will say that my advice is bizarre. Nevertheless, after anchoring thousands of times in all kinds of bottoms, I have no hesitation in making this recommendation.

Concerning the general weights of anchors, a handy rule for cruising yachts is $1\frac{1}{4}$ pounds of anchor for each foot of length. This is for burying-type anchors. For fisherman anchors, I believe you should have 2 pounds for every foot of length. For areas where anchoring is difficult, you may well increase the weights.

Note that all the anchors I've discussed are made of iron or steel and are hot-dip galvanized. Because of the weight issue, general strength, and a tendency to bend, I do not endorse aluminum anchors.

Holding power can be improved by sliding a weight partway down the cable. If you hang a 20- or 30-pound pig of lead (or anything handy) on a large bow shackle and ease it down the cable on a light line, the weight will increase the curve, or catenary, of the chain or line. When the vessel pulls on the cable, the tension will have to lift the weight and straighten out the cable before there is any significant pull on the anchor.

Such a weight is handy if you are anchored in a shallow harbor with power-boats running back and forth. The weight will pull the cable away from the surface and hopefully keep it clear of thrashing propellers.

Although a fathom or two of chain is usually employed with an anchor, some very experienced sailors have had good luck using a heavier anchor and bending a nylon line directly to the shank of the anchor. These skippers feel that the heavier anchor is of more benefit than the chain plus an anchor. For example, a 20-pound Danforth and 2 fathoms of ⅜-inch chain weigh about 38 pounds. If seabed chafe is not a problem, you might be better off using a 38-pound anchor without chain. Most sailors, however, use a little chain because of the chafe potential and because the heavy chain helps ensure a pull closer to the horizontal.

Some people space two anchors along the same cable and claim good results when both anchors have dug in. I feel it's better to employ two separate cables, each of which can hold the vessel in case a line, shackle, or chain parts.

Scope

The second rule of anchoring is plenty of scope (the ratio of cable to depth), which decreases the angle between the cable and the seabed. The shallower the angle, the more the anchor will dig in. Ideally, the pull on the anchor should be horizontal. A scope of 5:1 should be regular practice. If the anchor drags when it is first dropped and you have let out cable to five times the depth, try veering additional cable and see if the anchor grabs the bottom. Likewise, if the holding ground is poor, if there are spring tides, or if the wind is strong, you may have to veer more cable. Conversely, if the anchor sinks in right away, someone is on board and alert to the vessel's situation, and the weather and water are quiet, less scope is possible.

Certainly if you are up a quiet, shallow creek in settled weather, the anchoring requirements are minimal. This, however, is an exception, and for ordinary anchor work a scope of 5:1 should be regular practice. Who can tell when the weather will change? It may switch from calm to stormy while you're asleep or ashore. I have seen more yachts in trouble from insufficient scope than for any other reason.

A scope of 5:1 means you will need to veer 20 fathoms of cable in a depth of 4 fathoms. If the water is deeper, say 10 fathoms, you must have 50 fathoms of chain, or part chain and part nylon or polypropylene, to get sufficient scope. Normally, you anchor in 5 fathoms or less, which means that 25 fathoms of chain or nylon is adequate. It's only rarely that you need longer lines. I recall that Margaret and I bent two warps together to make an 80-fathom length when we anchored in the Society Islands in the lagoon at Bora Bora, which is 16 fathoms deep. In the Chilean channels in Cahuelmó fjord, we lay to a 110-fathom nylon warp in a depth of 22 fathoms during a violent three-day storm. Again, in remote Puerto Molyneux in the south of Chile, we anchored in 17 fathoms with 100 fathoms of line. Such a long line is wonderfully elastic and smoothly stretches and shortens as the yacht reacts to blasts of wind. However, anchoring in such depths is unusual and best avoided if possible.

In tropical waters with coral, you must be extremely cautious when you have a lot of chain or line out. The use of several cork or plastic floats will help raise a nylon line off the bottom. A stern line to the shore or a stern anchor can keep some tension on the main anchor to keep its line out of mischief. A polypropylene line that floats may help. I advise frequent swimming inspections with a face mask or the use of a look box from a dinghy. If possible, go to a shallower anchorage and use all chain.

It's painful to write that every year a dozen or more yachts are wrecked because the owners fail to use all chain in waters where coral grows. Writer after writer has chronicled these misfortunes. Yet some new sailors think that they can ignore the warnings of experience. Fiber line in coral waters means trouble.

Typical was the unfortunate experience of David Boyce and Tim Noot in *Amazing Grace* in the Marquesas a few years ago. The two men anchored with 30 feet of chain attached to their anchor. Nylon line led up to the yacht from the chain. In the beginning there was enough wind to keep a little tension on the cable, which held it above the coral heads growing upward from the seabed. But in time the wind changed. The chain wrapped around and around the coral until the line was pulled down to the level of the razorlike stone growths, which soon sliced through the nylon. Meanwhile, the surface of the anchorage was smooth and untroubled. . . .

Just because you use all chain in coral waters doesn't excuse you from vigilance. It's possible for slack chain to wrap around a coral head as a changing wind or the tidal stream moves a yacht back and forth. The gradually shortened chain silently pulls the yacht closer and closer to the coral until the yacht is directly above the danger, with tight chain leading vertically downward. Then if a swell lifts the yacht, the taut chain may snap a link. Worse yet, if the coral head is close to the surface, the yacht may be slowly worked up to the hazard with disastrous results.

In his book *An Island to Myself* (Holt, Rinehart & Winston, 1966), Tom Neale detailed the loss of Ed Vessey's *Tiburon* at Suvarov Island in the northern Cook group in the Pacific. One night it was "blowing like hell." Ed had just turned in when he felt the anchor chain snap. He immediately jumped up and started the engine, but couldn't see where to steer because the water and nearby shore were impossibly dark. The 40-footer struck a coral head, knocked a big hole in the hull, and sank instantly. Ed and his wife and daughter barely managed to jump in their dinghy and row ashore. With hindsight, which is always unfair, Ed might have been better to have skipped the engine and tossed over another anchor.

I always thought that chain was totally resistant to chafe until I read an account of *Thelma*, an English yacht that anchored in Chatham Bay at Isla del Coco on the Pacific side of Costa Rica in Central America. While the crew was ashore hunting for buried treasure, the anchor chain sawed back and forth on a coral head until the chain parted.

"At low water *Thelma* was almost high and dry and I was able to discover the cause of the wreck," the captain wrote later. "Trailing from her bow were many fathoms of anchor chain but no anchor. One of the links had been sawn clean through as if with a file. It was the work of the mushroom coral. So sharp was the edge of it that in five days it had cut through a heavy link as the vessel swung gently to her hawse. I should never have believed that coral could cut through solid iron so efficiently. . . . Some time after the wreck we found the anchor still firmly embedded in the sand and it took four of us to weigh it from the lifeboat."[32]

One way to prevent chain wrapping around coral or to prevent chain from sawing back and forth on coral is to anchor near the shore. Then take a line to a tree, or run an anchor to the beach. Another scheme is to simply anchor in a clear patch of water with both bow and stern anchors to keep the yacht from swinging over coral heads. Whether this is possible depends on the individual anchorage, the depths, and what the wind is doing. If you anchor with bow and stern anchors, and the wind moves to one side or the other, you put heavy side loads on the yacht and the vessel will heel a lot. This may cause the anchors to drag.

You can improve on this arrangement by linking the bow and stern cables together and leading both to the bow. This will allow the yacht to swing easily with the wind. (You may have to tie the stern anchor line to the bow anchor line and then ease a little line at the bow and slack off the stern line so the join is below the level of the keel.) This is called a Bahamian moor. In a few days the chain, lines, or both will become twisted around one another, but it's not a hard job to untie one line and deal with the turns.

A problem with a Bahamian moor is that if another yacht or fishing vessel anchors close to you with a single anchor, the other boat may swing into you because you will be more or less stationary. As a practical matter, Bahamian moorings are best in isolated anchorages. (See my remarks under Mooring in the next chapter.)

Holding Ground

The third rule of anchoring is to place your iron hope in suitable holding ground. But what is the nature of the bottom? You can find this out by consulting the chart, which may indicate sand, mud, ooze, clay, gravel, shingle, pebbles, stone, rock, shells, oysters, weed, grass, or kelp. Often, however, there is no notation on the chart. You should then investigate the bottom yourself by putting a little grease or tallow on the base of the lead on the lead line (arming the lead) and sampling the bottom. The tallow will pick up a little sand and small shells or mud and gravel. Or if you bounce the lead along the bottom, you will feel separate rocks or hardness or softness.

Smooth rock is the poorest holding ground of all, because on it an anchor is nothing more than a large fishing sinker. *Broken rock* is all or nothing, depending on whether a fluke of the anchor catches on an embedded rock. A heavy fisherman anchor is best; a burying-type anchor may be useless. Sometimes a fluke jams between two rocks or gets stuck in a crack and becomes hopelessly fouled. At other times the anchor may find a crevice and hold well with a pull from one direction; a wind shift, however—even days later—will change the angle of pull and the anchor may drag.

Pebbles and shingle (coarse gravel) are unpredictable and may jam the flukes of a Danforth anchor. The grip of an anchor may suddenly give way in a seabed of small stones. Certainly you should lay out maximum scope. *Gravel* is better, especially for a burying-type anchor. *Mud* is difficult to discuss unless you have some idea of its viscosity, which can vary from a thin and useless ooze to the beginnings of clay. Certainly a burying-type anchor is best, because it can work its way down to where the mud may be stiffer. *Weed and grass* are troublesome and require an anchor with enough weight to force its way beneath the growth. *Kelp* is particularly nasty because of its toughness and slippery nature.

Sand, clay, hard mud, shells, broken shells, and various combinations offer an excellent grip for anchors. The majority of traditional anchorage sites have bottoms of these substances. In considering various bottoms, pay particular attention to any references in a Pilot book or cruising guide that speak of poor holding ground or to such statements as "rock thinly covered with sand" or "a layer of mud over rock." You can be sure that no mention of bad holding ground is made unless some poor mariner has had trouble.

Unfortunately, the charts that you buy these days tend to omit bottom identification in useful terms and to substitute instead the misleading words *soft, hard,* and *sticky*—words that mean little to sailors or to anyone else. The accuracy of the old days is gone because soundings are taken with electronic depth sounders rather than a hand-sounding lead armed with a bit of tallow to pick up a sample of the bottom. Where are the supermen of yesterday?

Each part of the anchor gear must be strong and up to the standards of the rest. You need a single, unbroken unit of uniform strength. Take the galvanized shackle that joins the chain to the anchor. The shackle must be stout, of proper test, and the pin should be secured with two or three wraps of thin galvanized wire tied so that any untwisting motion will pull against the wraps of the safety wire.

If you are using nylon and chain, their strengths should be comparable. For example, it's ridiculous to use $^5/_{16}$-inch chain with $^3/_4$-inch-diameter nylon. The chain has a proof load test of 2,618 pounds, while the nylon has strength more than 5 tons. A length of $^1/_2$- or $^9/_{16}$-inch chain is more suitable. Do you really need $^3/_4$-inch nylon?

The bow roller ought to be 6 inches in diameter (but seldom is). If the roller is to be used for chain alone, a groove around the middle of the roller slightly wider than the diameter of the chain (say $^7/_{16}$" for $^3/_8$" chain) should be machined around the circumference. This step will allow the face of every other link to seat itself on the roller. This reduces friction enormously and will make it easier to recover the anchor and chain.

If the roller is to be used for line alone, it should be smooth with well-rounded edges. Whether for chain or nylon, the sides of the roller housing should be built up so that a pin or a heavy metal strip can be put across above the cable so it can't jump out of position. Chocks or fairleads should be deep, with carefully rounded edges and preferably of closed construction.

If there is no windlass on board, fit a chain pawl at the stem. A chain pawl is a pivoting piece of metal that allows chain to come in when pulled but jams in a link when the chain tries to go out. Save your back by avoiding hard pulling at a bad angle. If necessary, take a nylon line (the anchor warp itself or a short piece of line clapped onto the chain) along the deck to a cockpit winch. It's useful to have a snatch block for $^3/_4$-inch-diameter line. Nicro and others make handy trunnion snatch blocks that can be secured around the deck as necessary. The trunnion arrangement allows the blocks to pivot on two axes to accommodate loads that a single shackle can't handle, and are well worth buying.

If the anchor cable goes to a bollard or a windlass, the hold-down fittings of the unit should be through-bolted with backup plates underneath. (Have you inspected the bolts recently? I hope they're not red brass.) If the pawl that keeps the wildcat on the windlass from turning looks suspect, fit a sturdy chain stopper ahead of the windlass to hold the cable. An eyesplice in nylon should have half a dozen neat tucks before tapering and should be fitted over smooth, large-diameter metal (not plastic) thimbles that, in turn, are held with shackles of generous size whose pins are wired. In short, go over each part of your ground tackle and eliminate the weak and the marginal. Arrange your systems so that each part suits the next and everything is uniformly strong.

You can use duct tape to hold your oilskins together. You can get by with unvarnished oars or a spinnaker with a dozen patches. You can skip cockpit cushions entirely. But when it comes to anchors and cables, you want the best.

A fisherman's anchor in northern Brazil. I've seen similar anchors all over the world. This one is clever in that it uses no metal fastenings. The design is really a rock pick because the flukes are narrow and have limited holding area. Because of its design, however, when there is tension on the anchor line, two flukes are always dragging against the bottom. I would like to see the flukes a little wider to compensate for the weakening hole bored through each fluke. This would give each fluke more resistance in the mud, sand, or whatever. Note the simplicity of the anchoring arrangement: a clove hitch around a Samson post and no iron at all.

13

THE PRACTICE OF ANCHORING

An important part of seamanship is the ability to handle a second anchor. A storm may come up when you're in an anchorage. You may need a stern anchor or kedge (noun) to keep from swinging near another vessel. You may have to pull or kedge (verb) the boat away from a dock or other problem if a sudden onshore wind descends in the night. You may go aground and urgently need an anchor to pull you off. A light kedge can keep the yacht at right angles to incoming swells in a rolly anchorage and make the difference between comfort and a night of misery. And as we saw in the last chapter, a second anchor can keep the slack chain of the main anchor from winding around a coral head.

Anchor gear is only as strong as each connecting part. We use stout tested shackles and seize the pins in place with galvanized wire wrapped round and round, aircraft fashion, to prevent the pins from opening. The twisted wire ends can be poked into the eye of a shackle pin to keep the sharp points away from fingers and sails. There are neater arrangements, but they may not be as strong and reliable.

Nothing else can equal the peace of mind a second anchor gives the captain.

The easiest way to put out a kedge is to load it and a long piece of line in a dinghy and secure the end of the warp to the yacht. Then row or motor the dinghy to where you want the anchor, and drop it in the water. There are a few subtleties that I'll talk about in a minute, but that's the general idea.

I prefer to carry out a kedge anchor with a hard dinghy and oars because it's easy to maneuver, and I can use the little boat in a few inches of water. An inflatable dinghy rows poorly and in any wind of consequence may be impossible to row at all. An inflatable is much better with an outboard, but this requires deeper water, and it takes some expertise to back up slowly with one hand while paying out the anchor warp with the other.

Here's my procedure:

1. I decide which way I want the warp to run. If I'm concerned about bad weather, I generally put the second anchor at 45 degrees to the first so that each anchor takes half the load. For my rowing target, I try to find a tree, a building, a prominent hill, an anchored ship, a distant light, or the moon. If someone on the yacht is going to direct me, we work out visual signals in advance because it's impossible to shout to windward in bad weather. Remember that half the time, you will be doing this at night.

2. Next, I pull out the entire warp on deck so I don't have to fight tangles when I'm in the dinghy. If the yacht is in a depth of, say, 30 feet, I use a warp 150 feet long. It's better to be too long than too short. I don't attempt to coil the line. I let it fall free on deck. If there are tangles or twists it may be necessary to overhaul the line, but this can be done quickly. I belay the end of the warp to a mooring cleat after leading it outside the lifelines and through a deck fairlead. If it's night, I stick a small flashlight in my pocket.

3. I jump into the dinghy, which is tied alongside the yacht. I reach up to the deck, pick up the anchor, and put it in the rear of the dinghy. Then beginning with the end shackled to the anchor or chain, I pull the entire warp into the after part of the dinghy over the anchor. I don't try to coil the line in any way but let it fall into the dinghy a couple of feet at a time, stacking it over itself so it will run out smoothly when the pull goes the other way. I double-check that the warp is not fouled with the lifelines on the yacht and that the line runs from the dinghy straight to the deck

fairlead and thence to the mooring cleat. If there are any problems, now is the time to fix them because the dinghy is still tied to the yacht and I can use both hands.

4. I get the oars ready, untie the dinghy, and push off, rowing smartly toward my target. Often the wind is dead against me and the rowing is hard. As I pull away from the yacht, the line pays out through the sculling notch in the transom of the dinghy until I reach the end. I row as hard as I can to stretch the warp to its maximum length. I reach aft (I do not stand up) and toss the anchor into the sea.

5. One problem with this procedure in deeper water is that I lose some of the length of the warp by the time the anchor hits the bottom, turns over, begins to dig in, and someone on board hauls in the slack. I generally extend the length of the warp by bending on an additional light line 50 or 60 feet long before I lay out the kedge. Then by the time the anchor is set, I have hauled the light line back on board. This dodge—which I always use except in shallow water—gives me the full length of the kedge warp.

The foregoing applies to nylon or polypropylene warps. It's not possible to lay out chain from a hard dinghy in the normal way because the weight of the chain and anchor may swamp a small tender. The only way of doing it is as follows: (1) Run out a kedge anchor well beyond where the main anchor is to be dropped. (2) Load the chain into the dinghy and balance it by lashing the main anchor from the stem of the dinghy. (3) Pull the dinghy out along the kedge warp, paying out the chain as you go. (4) When the chain is all out, cut the lashing. Note: the person in the dinghy should definitely wear a life jacket. It may be easier to lay out chain with an inflatable dinghy with a hard floor and an outboard. Even better: try to deal with long lengths of chain by moving the yacht (if possible) instead of using a dinghy.

When you are in faraway places by yourself, prompt anchor work can mean the difference between routine seamanship and big trouble. One summer, for instance, along the west coast of Vancouver Island in British Columbia, we sought refuge in Clayoquot Sound during an afternoon when the wind began to blow hard from the south. Once inside the large sound, we sailed to Flores Island and anchored in 5 fathoms in Matilda Inlet, a narrow finger of water whose entrance faced north. We were well protected and put out all our chain and lay with the cable taut while the wind whistled across the steep hills and through the tall firs near us. Though the tide was near maximum height, we thought we would have adequate swinging room when the tide fell.

Late that night the wind dropped while we were asleep, and we swung ashore at low water. A sudden lurch announced our new status. In a few minutes, *Whisper* was tilted to 50 degrees and high and dry on rocks near the shore. If we had done nothing, the incoming tide would have lifted us higher on the rocks. We launched the dinghy and carried out two anchors—both aimed toward deep water—and winched the cables as tight as banjo strings. I passed the night by changing the propeller zinc and scrubbing the bottom with a brush. Finally at 0415 the flood tide began to lift us, and as the yacht rose, the taut cables eased us into deeper water.

We had had a night of hard work. My mistakes were not allowing enough swinging room and not putting out a second anchor. I should have checked the swinging room by rowing around the yacht in the dinghy and sounding with the lead line.

Eventually this grounding situation happens to every captain. You must be prepared to put out a second anchor quickly and without fuss.

MY ANCHORING TECHNIQUE

I try to anchor when the yacht is heading slowly downwind or down tide. With headway of 1 or 2 knots (no more), I drop the anchor at a selected place and rapidly pay out scope. When enough chain is out, I snub it. The chain will begin to tighten, the anchor will dig in hard, and the vessel will stop and quickly turn around and head to wind or tide. If there is a problem with the holding ground, you will know it at once. Notice that I let the anchor go *while the vessel is moving*; this keeps the chain from piling up on the bottom.

One difficulty with this scheme is that the chain going aft along the hull may scratch off some topside and bottom paint. If you initially limit the scope of the chain to three times the depth of the water and don't have her going too fast, the chance of paint damage is lessened because the chain will make an angle from the vertical that will not exceed 71 degrees.[33] Also, as soon as the chain begins to tighten, I give the yacht full opposite rudder to sheer her away from the chain. On *Whisper* the chain runs out on the starboard side, so to sheer the yacht away from the chain, I shove the tiller hard to port, which gives right rudder and turns the starboard side of the yacht away from the chain. Of course, if you are using all nylon or nylon and chain, there is no problem. After the vessel has swung, I veer more cable to five times the depth.

If at first the anchor drags, I let out more cable to help the anchor set. The yacht should be moving, but not going more than a knot or maybe a little more. What you want is a gentle first bite, followed by a steady pull to set the anchor. If you steam around an anchorage at 5 or 6 knots, you tend to pluck out the anchor just as it begins to dig in. This scenario is not fantasy because you can see all this

Woe is me! Florence Robinson ashore on the Shambu River in southeast Panama. Sooner or later, all voyaging sailors run aground. Light groundings are routine and usually involve nothing more than carrying out an anchor in a dinghy and pulling the boat into deeper water. Severe groundings are a challenge because you may be in a remote place and any remedial action is up to you. This can mean patches, pumps, lines, multiple anchors, hydraulic jacks, wedges, timbers, local assistance, and heavy prayers along with much stroking of a rabbit's foot. In this photograph, the yacht—a 32-foot ketch—was run ashore by a confused river pilot during a colossal rainfall along a grossly swollen river. When the rain stopped and the river went down, the boat was high and dry among the trees of the jungle. It took the crew and a group of hired helpers three weeks to cut away trees, level the boat, patch the holes in her hull, and move her to the water, where she continued on her travels. During such episodes, the biggest obstacles may be despair and the cries of those who say it can't be done. Often, it can be done.

happen if you jump in the water with a face mask and watch other captains anchor.

I think it's a good plan not to anchor on the first pass when you're in new waters. Sail slowly through an anchorage on a scouting pass to check the depths, other vessels, mooring buoys, fish traps, wreckage, and God knows what else. If possible, have a lookout at the bow or up the mast. On the second pass, you'll have a better notion of the place.

Pay attention to how other vessels are anchored. Usually boats lie to a single anchor. If they have bow and stern anchors out (perhaps there's a tidal problem, the anchorage is small, or there's a shoal or a sunken boat), then you should anchor the same way; otherwise, you will swing into a previously anchored boat. By custom and common sense, the first boat in a harbor anchors as he pleases. The second boat anchors in the same manner as the first boat and keeps clear of number one. And so on.

If there's a choice, you should anchor so that the vessel is between her anchor and a danger. This may seem obvious, but if you anchor in a calm or in a contrary breeze or around other vessels that are headed in another direction, it is easy to set your anchor at right angles to a shoal or to aim the fluke away from a danger. Then if the yacht darts about at anchor and sheers because of the wind, the tide, or her rudder position, the vessel may drag onto the danger before the anchor has reset itself. In a strong wind, of course, there is no choice.

The system I have described works well for us eighteen times out of twenty. However, as I said in the last chapter, if there's any doubt about the anchor holding, I use the engine to drag the vessel astern. Many times we have sailed into complicated anchorages without using the engine and then have fired up the diesel to pull the yacht hard astern to see if the anchor was really holding. Initially I use low power. When I feel the anchor bite into the seabed, I slowly increase to full power. To check whether we are moving, we look shoreward at near and far points (say, two trees, one almost behind the other) to see if the relative bearings change. In fog you can use the trick of lowering the lead line vertically over the side until it just touches the bottom. If you drag astern, you can feel the lead bouncing along the bottom.

If you get into a mess while anchoring—and everyone does occasionally, including me—it may be best to pull up everything and start afresh. Swearing and shouting at others does not help. If time is not a problem, sail around a little, get your breath, decide what went wrong, and plan your next move. Review in your mind exactly what you are going to do. Explain your plans to the crew. Get everything ready for your next attempt. If you are in a difficult or dangerous situation, don't hesitate to ask for advice or help from the biggest yacht in the harbor. Anchoring is a great spectator sport, and some very experienced people with local knowledge may be just waiting to assist you. Nevertheless, you must evaluate advice from strangers carefully.

Be sure to allow a previously anchored vessel sufficient swinging room. If you anchor too close to someone already at anchor, it's your responsibility to move, even if the task is difficult and unpleasant. If a crew member on a previously anchored vessel questions your closeness and asks you to move, don't snap his head off with a string of oaths. He may be right. Perhaps you should move. It's better to move at once than to risk damage or to be disturbed at 0200. Besides, it's impossible to rest properly if you're worried about banging into another vessel.

If there are others nearby, don't pay out a ridiculous amount of scope. Think of your neighbors. In normal weather, a scope of 5:1 is adequate. Even this means a swinging circle of 370 feet for a 35-foot vessel in 5 fathoms. I recall a big fishing boat from Manta, Ecuador, that was anchored at San Cristóbal in the Galápagos with an inordinate amount of manila line while the crew was having a run ashore. The swinging room of the fishing boat seemed to take up the whole of Wreck Bay. The vessel—which had become a lethal battering ram—drove all the other fishing boats and yachts wild (Look out! Here she comes again!).

After I anchor, the next job is to take three bearings of prominent stationary points with the main compass or a hand-bearing compass and to write the bearings in the logbook. I can then easily check my position if I think the anchor is dragging. If I like the anchorage, I have the information to locate the exact spot another time (or to tell to someone else). If I should be unlucky and lose the anchor, the bearings will enable me to determine its position for recovery attempts.

You can learn a lot about anchoring by putting on a face mask and swimming out to inspect your iron hook. I was amazed when I first tried it. Once I found a pile of chain with the anchor sitting on top. Another time I discovered a nylon warp wrapped round and round the anchor. On a more pleasant occasion, I looked into the water to see chain disappearing into sand where the anchor had dug in and vanished.

TIDAL CONSIDERATIONS

In an anchorage with wind against the tide, a vessel that's on a mooring or at anchor may either face the wind or head into the tide. This depends on the windage of the craft, her underbody, whether she is on chain or nylon, and whether she is on long or short scope. A stranger seeking a place to anchor may have to sail through the anchorage a few times to find space that won't be obstructed by a vessel that seems to be anchored over one spot but is actually at the end of her cable elsewhere. An inviting place in a crowded anchorage may in fact be covered by two vessels, each temporarily off station in opposite directions—one pushed by wind and the other by tide. Pay attention to the direction of anchor or mooring cables leading into the water from the bows of the vessels in the anchorage.

If you arrive in an area with a sizable tidal range and wish to anchor, you will have to work out the state of the tide and whether it is flooding or ebbing so you can calculate the depths at low water. If there is a choice, it's best to arrive at low water so you can see if there are any wrecks, sandbanks, or underwater obstructions that cover with the flood. Secondly, if you should be unfortunate and run aground, the rising water will float you off. With tide tables and accurate large-scale charts of a harbor, you can make precise calculations of the water depths at low water so you won't

This is what a fisherman anchor looks like underneath the water. One fluke has dug in to the depth of the shank. The chain leads lazily away across a sandy bottom and up to the yacht. We are in a depth of 3 fathoms in the Abaco islands in the Bahamas.

go aground. The English are particularly expert at this, and their East Coast sailors can tell within a few inches how much water will be over a certain bar or shoal.

Unfortunately, different countries use various datum levels on their charts; the terminology describing the tidal heights is sometimes confusing. Just follow the directions in whatever tide tables you have on board. Don't forget about daylight saving time.

As a practical matter, you often don't have pertinent tidal tables or large-scale harbor charts when you're away from home. You may have a small-scale chart with a few soundings, and tidal calculations based on a port or river many miles away. A persistent wind sometimes makes substantial differences in predicted tidal heights. In these cases, I sail in cautiously, in daylight, noting the depths with a depth sounder or lead line and comparing what I find with the charted soundings. I try to tell from the tidal stream in narrow places whether the stream is ebbing or flooding, and from the shoreline (or snowline) whether the tide is high or low. I look to see where other vessels are anchored and try to anchor with a fathom or two or three beneath my keel at low water.

MOORING

Riding to a single anchor demands a fair amount of swinging room. If you have problems with coral, fish traps, salmon pens, or debris on the bottom, or if the anchorage is small or restricted, consider mooring with two or three anchors. If there's a tidal flow, one anchor should go in the direction of the ebb; the second should head toward the flood. The heavier anchor or anchors should be laid in the direction of the greater expected strain.

A 60-pound three-piece fisherman anchor with diamond-shaped flukes of the Herreshoff pattern. Made by Paul Luke of East Boothbay, Maine. Each piece can be stored separately or together. The anchor is strong and effective but sometimes it's a bear to use.

You can moor under sail by dropping the first anchor while you have way on the vessel. Or if there is a strong tide, you can hand all sail and let the tidal stream carry you along after you have dropped the first anchor. Veer twice the amount of chain—to ten times the depth—and wait until the anchor is well set. Then drop a second anchor and heave in one-half of the chain of the first anchor so that the yacht is midway between the two anchors. Secure the two cables together, let out a little more chain or line so the join is below the keel, and lead the cables to the bow. The vessel will then swing with the wind or tide over one point above the seafloor.

If such a mooring is impossible because of traffic or restricted space, it may be easier to drop the main anchor and carry out the second anchor in the dinghy (this also requires less chain heaving). Tie or shackle the kedge warp to the main cable and let out a little additional chain before it's secured.

If you're going to be moored for a long period, it may be necessary to put a heavy swivel in the chain or line below the stem to keep from twisting and kinking the cable. (A week of twisting and turning can ruin a new three-strand line.) With a long piece of unbroken chain, the swivel may be a problem if you don't have all the chain laid out.

Mooring is usually preferable to anchoring with bow and stern anchors because the yacht can swing in any direction, which reduces the load on the anchors. Life on board is more comfortable with wind (and rain or snow) coming from the bow.

BUOYING THE ANCHOR

If you suspect that an anchorage has debris (old car parts, discarded engines, sunken boats) on the bottom, the best plan is to buoy the anchor. Lead a light line (¼ or ⅜" dia.) from a float to the crown of the anchor and toss the float and line overboard when you drop the anchor. The line should be just long enough to reach the surface at high water, or perhaps a few feet more if there is a strong tidal stream. Try to keep the buoy line as short as possible because a long line can lead to many difficulties. A CQR has an eye forward of the pivot pin; on a Danforth you can thread a buoy line through or around the crown. Then if the anchor becomes fouled, you need only pick up the buoy and heave on its line. This will upset the anchor and recover it upside down. An anchor buoy is especially handy when you have two anchors out and want to pick one up.

An anchor buoy also marks the position of your anchor to other vessels. Once, however, another yacht picked up our anchor buoy and tried to lay to it as if it were a mooring. We tried to explain what the buoy was, but all we got in return was a torrent of foul language. (People seem to be particularly sensitive if you question their anchoring techniques.) We winched up our anchor, recovered our buoy, and moved elsewhere.

There are a number of problems with an anchor buoy: (1) It's one more thing to do when you are busy sailing into a strange anchorage. (2) If the buoy line is long enough to reach to the surface at high water, the line may be slack enough at low water to foul your rudder or propeller. (3) The curse of buoyed anchors is power vessels and dinghies with engines, which often buzz around anchored sailing yachts like unwanted bluebottle flies. The propeller of a passing motor vessel may sever the buoy line. If the motor vessel doesn't cut the line and instead wraps it up and fouls her propeller, the momentum of the motor vessel may pluck your anchor from the bottom. Suddenly you may be towed away by a vessel that may not wish to be a tug; her master may even get a little upset.

Sailors have used various schemes to keep an anchor buoy from fouling a propeller or rudder, but none is simple and foolproof. In any case, never use floating line. Put a small lead weight 8 or 10 feet down the line, so the buoy line will hang down vertically below the float and not drift out horizontally, waiting for a propeller to come along.

The safest anchor-buoy arrangement that I know of is to use a dan buoy, a float with a slim, 6-foot vertical pole above and below the float (a total of 12'), similar to a man-overboard pole. The bottom of the pole is held down with a lead weight, and the top of the pole can have a small flag, perhaps with the name of the yacht, the word *anchor*, or its symbol. The idea is that the anchor-buoy line will be fastened to the end of the submerged part, which should be long enough to clear any expected propellers or other problems. If a fishing boat or ferry hits the dan buoy, the force merely pushes the buoy aside. When not in use, the dan buoy can be taken apart at the float in the middle and its two halves lashed on the coachroof. Before anchoring, the buoy can be assembled and placed outside the lifelines, ready for dropping with the anchor.

One other time to buoy anchor gear is when you have to clear out of an anchorage in a hurry and have no time to recover your ground tackle. You buoy the anchor before you leave it and the cable behind. You do this by bending a light line—whose length is equal to the depth of the water at high tide—to the bitter end of the chain or warp. Tie a float or two (fenders are good) to the other end of the light line before you slip the cable. Then when the weather moderates, you can sail back, find the floats, and recover your cable and anchor. To simplify slipping the anchor, it's a good idea to fasten the bitter end of the chain to the ship with an extrastrong line that reaches the deck via the navel pipe. Then you can cut loose the anchor and cable without going below. If you buoy an anchor, try to use colored floats of some kind. The big red spherical Norwegian fishing floats are ideal. Margaret and I once had to clear out of an area in Torres Strait south of New Guinea and lost two anchors and three long warps because we couldn't find our fenders in the confusion of small breaking waves whose white crests were the same color as our floats.

FREEING FOULED ANCHORS

Occasionally when you start to recover the anchor, you'll find that it's fouled on a mooring chain or hooked under an old wire cable. If the anchor is a non-fisherman type, you may be able to slip it out by lifting the offending cable a dozen feet or so and then suddenly releasing the warp or chain on the yacht. A Danforth or CQR will tend to fly out from under the obstruction. A single-fluke anchor can sometimes be released by sailing or motoring right over it on short scope. This may cause it to turn over. If that doesn't work, try letting out all the cable (and even bending on more) and sailing in various directions.

If you have a powerful windlass on board, you may be able to lift the offending chain (or whatever) to the stemhead, where you can hold it with a second line while you extricate your anchor. The last time we anchored at the mouth of Chesapeake Bay's Bohemia River, we picked up one end of an enormous submerged log that we held with a mooring line until we unhooked our anchor.

If you're unable to lift the obstruction to the surface, try dropping a small anchor or grapnel (with a buoy line) to hook and hold the offending cable while you release and recover the main anchor. You can then slack off the line to the small anchor and recover it by hauling on its buoy line to the crown.

In all these operations, you must be careful to keep your hands, fingers, and feet away from lines and chains and cables because the forces involved can be thousands of pounds. If you have a jammed line or chain on a cleat or bollard or have an impossible override on a winch, you can often help yourself with a second line. Secure a short piece of ½-inch-diameter line to the chain or cable *ahead of the problem* with a rolling hitch. Lead the second line (sometimes via a snatch-block if the lead needs to be improved or reversed) to a winch or the windlass. When you crank on the winch, the secondary line will take the load and allow you to attack the problem without getting your fingers nipped. If this doesn't work, it may be wiser to cut away a few feet of jammed line or chain than to risk injury. If possible, wear heavy leather gloves, and treat chain and line with big loads on them like loaded guns. Be careful!

Another way to clear a fouled Danforth, CQR, or Bruce (but not a fisherman) is to pull the cable tight enough so that the chain is vertically above the anchor. Then carefully lower a separate chain loop (about 10" in diameter) down the cable on a light trip line until the loop falls to the lower end of the shank of the anchor. You can feel the chain loop passing the anchor shackle and slipping down on the metal shank. From this point, there are two variations. The first is to ease the main anchor cable so the shank falls from a vertical to a horizontal position. Then haul away smartly on the tripping line and hope that the chain loop will pull the fluke away from the obstruction. (This works best with a Bruce.) If this is unsuccessful, start all over again and drop the chain loop to the lower end of the shank as before. Then get into a dinghy with the trip line and row a long distance away while paying out more trip line. Now have someone on board the yacht ease the main anchor cable a bit. If you heave on the trip line (you will have to anchor the dinghy or do it from shore), you may be able to pull the fluke away from its impediment.

I have also had some luck in freeing fouled anchors by pulling myself down an almost taut anchor chain. I am a poor swimmer, but in desperation have put on a face mask and old gloves and hauled myself quickly down the chain and unhooked an anchor fluke from a cable on the seabed. My limit is 3 or 4 fathoms.

SAILING OUT THE ANCHOR

If your engine is dead or you have no engine and an onshore wind comes up when you're anchored near land and you want to take your anchor with you, the best thing is to sail the anchor out. You put up the sails and back a headsail (that is, physically hold the clew to windward) to get moving. Once the boat pays off, you sheet the sail in normally. The boat will sail rapidly toward the anchor while you pull in chain. Then you shift to the other tack (still hauling or winching in chain). After a few boards, you will be over the anchor and moving fast enough to snatch it out as you pass above. This maneuver leaves you sailing close-hauled into the onshore wind and away from the lee shore behind you. *Be careful to keep your fingers out from under the chain as it tightens when you change tacks.* It's easiest to sail out an anchor with two people: one to handle the tiller or wheel and the other on the foredeck. A single-hander can do it if he has a quick way of lashing the tiller.

Before starting, decide in advance exactly what you are going to do and use moderate headsail area (a staysail works nicely and is easy to back). Shorten up the anchor cable as much as possible. In tight quarters the essential thing is to keep the yacht moving ahead while you break the anchor loose from the bottom. If you don't get the anchor on board until you have a little sea room, it doesn't make any difference. The main thing is to free yourself from a dangerous lee-shore situation.

Don't save this maneuver for some terrible night when the engine's conked out and you're smothered by a big onshore wind and swell. Sail your anchor out routinely. It's both fun and satisfying, and it will give you practice so that when it's necessary, you'll know how to do it.

STORM CONDITIONS

When you are anchored, there should always be a second anchor ready to drop immediately. The bitter end of the cable should already be led over the lifelines, fed through the fairlead, and belayed to a mooring cleat. When you need an anchor, you want it at once! There's no time to go burrowing in lockers for a tangled warp, hunting under the cabin sole for an anchor that may not have been out in years, or searching for a shackle or a piece of wire to seize a shackle pin. Before you enter an anchorage you should have two anchors out and ready.

The windage of sailing yachts is considerable and escalates rapidly with increasing winds. A sleek sailing hull may appear to have little windage, but her wide and tall mast and mass of wires and lines going aloft add up to a lot of wind resistance.

Dynamic wind pressure (Q) increases as the square of the wind velocity. A useful approximation is $Q = 0.004V^2$, with Q in pounds per square foot and V in knots. In 25 knots, the calculation is $Q = 0.004(25)^2$, or 2.5 pounds per square foot. In 50 knots, $Q = 0.004(50)^2$, or 10 pounds per square foot—four times as much. In 50 knots of wind, therefore, a 50-foot-by-6-inch mast would have a wind loading of 250 pounds. The total wind pressure on all the rigging wires, running rigging, bundled sails, furling gears, hull, and deck structures can easily exceed 1,000 pounds.

These wind forces put an enormous strain on the ground tackle. In a severe storm, do everything you can to reduce windage. Take down awnings, flags, poles, furled sails, and radar reflectors. Put sailbags and loose gear below. With metal masts and internal lines, tie figure-eight knots in the ends of halyards and lifts and let all but one run up to the masthead.

When you're threatened by a hurricane, be sure to take off all the sails, particularly roller-furled headsails and the mainsail, which will be blown out of any gaskets or lines. If a roller-furled headsail opens up in a big wind, the flogging sail will certainly overload your anchors. In survival conditions, you must do everything to help your cause. Get those singing lines down! Put the dinghy in the water on a long painter and swamp it to reduce its profile and windage. Put the main boom on deck. Take down all cockpit canvas.

In addition to windage, shock loading is another factor. Gusts and squalls that rise above the level of the storm can impose severe side-to-side sheering loads. Substantial jerking strains can come from unusual swells. The combination of windage, sheering loads, and jerking strains may overpower the ground tackle and damage the anchor windlass, the bow roller, or the chain stopper, or even break the cable. If you're in a river, an unexpected current from a spring runoff in a large river plus a heavy ebb tide can cause all sorts of anchor mishaps. One study concluded that a 30- to 40-foot yacht anchored in force 12 winds could generate surge loads up to 3,000 pounds. All is not lost, however, because a 50-pound burying anchor on a very long scope in good holding ground can withstand such strains.[34]

One way to alleviate these problems and stop the terrible jerking strains is to fit a nylon anchor spring, which adds a sort of rubber band (not a coil spring) to the anchor system. I use 30 feet of ½-inch-diameter three-strand nylon. I eyesplice one end of the nylon to a chain hook (which you can buy at the local hardware store) that clips around a link of chain. I belay the other end of the nylon line to a bow mooring cleat. Then I let out chain until the nylon takes the full strain of the vessel pulling against her anchor.

In other words, we use a stretchy piece of light nylon as a rubber band between two parts of the chain to ease the snubbing. The chain is still hooked up, and if the nylon breaks or chafes through, the chain is there to hold the vessel. It's important to put the nylon through scrap pieces of old hose or other chafing gear to prevent chafe whenever the nylon is near anything, and to inspect the line from time to time to keep it from rubbing itself to destruction.

When at anchor, the yacht may swing from side to side occasionally and cause secondary anchor lines to chafe on anything in the way. I once lost a new anchor at the entrance to Barra San Juan, a small river in Uruguay. The yacht was aground and I had run out an anchor on a long length of nylon. I was attempting to pull her off and managed to turn the vessel a little by winching the nylon bar tight. Unknown to me, as she turned, the nylon warp touched a sharp edge on the bow stem fitting. Every time the line rubbed on the sharp metal corner, it severed a few yarns. In ten minutes the line was gone. From this I learned to smooth and round all sharp metal edges with files and emery cloth.

A few years ago in Honolulu, Keane

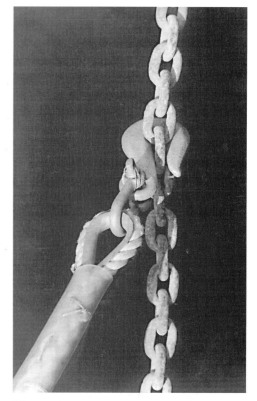

The easiest way to secure a nylon spring to the anchor chain is to use a galvanized chain hook, available at most hardware stores.

Gau told me about a different type of anchor spring that he used when he anchored his 46-foot steel ketch *Bluejacket* at Pitcairn and Easter Islands. Neither place has a suitable anchorage, but in settled weather, it's possible to put down a hook on nearby sandy patches. Keane, a superb seaman, lowered a heavy anchor with plenty of scope and led the cable to a 24-inch-diameter spherical Norwegian fishing float—cum bumper—made of plastic. Keane secured the cable to the float with a short piece of chain (nylon would have served equally well) and then veered another 100 feet of cable that led from the bow of *Bluejacket* in the usual way.

When the wind was light, the yacht merely ranged around the big red buoy, riding lightly to what was in effect a 100-foot mooring line. If the wind started to blow, the yacht tugged at the float, but before there was any substantial pull on the anchor, the buoy had to be dragged under and submerged, something the large float resisted mightily. From high on the nearby island, Keane glanced out at *Blue-*

jacket occasionally. As long as he was able to see the red buoy on the same bearing, everything was OK.

I believe this technique might be extended to storm anchoring.

With gale- or storm-force winds blowing off the land, don't overlook the advantages of lines ashore to stout trees or rocks or anything else. If you enter a bay with deep water close to the windward shore, sail up very close to the land and drop the main anchor to hold you in position. Then put the dinghy over the side and take a line from the bow of the yacht to the land. Don't let go of the yacht until you have the oars in position or the outboard engine running; otherwise, you may blow away to leeward. Before you head off to shore, toss an extralong line or two in the dinghy because you're usually farther away from the land than you think.

Once you have a line ashore and wrapped around a tree or a big rock, you can relax and perhaps run a second line to the land. If there's nothing to tie to, carry an anchor ashore and dig it into the earth. I would shut off the yacht's engine during these maneuvers because it's easy to get a line around the propeller.

Back on board, pull yourself in close and recover the bow anchor. Now the yacht is held entirely by the lines to the shore. (Remember the wind is holding you off.) Next, ease the shore lines as much as possible and drop a stern anchor over the transom to keep from swinging ashore if the wind dies. Or use the dinghy (kept safely tied to the yacht with a very long painter) to carry out a stern anchor. Finally, adjust the stern anchor warp and the shore lines to your satisfaction.

As long as the wind blows from the land, you will be quite safe. There is no possibility of dragging if you are tied ashore. Of course, if the conditions change, you will have to move. In the Chilean channels, where the depths are great and the winds are supremely violent, big and little ships alike regularly take lines ashore. Not one line, but two or three. We've also sat out some screamers in the Aegean islands and along the Turkish coast during heavy weather. A good rowing or powered dinghy is invaluable.

Years ago when Margaret and I were in the South Pacific, I talked to Andy Thomson, the famous trading schooner captain of the Cook Islands. Andy told us that he once bested a frightful hurricane in Rarotonga by putting his vessel in a narrow opening in the reef and anchoring and tying to the reef on each side *with 20 or more lines*. The ship faced the wind and seas and rose and fell as great blasts of the storm passed the island.

"We put out everything but my shoelaces," said Andy. "Warps, spare line, cargo nets, halyards, sheets, chain, cable borrowed from on shore—everything. We had the life of the ship to gain and nothing to lose by doubling and redoubling the lines. If she had been wrecked, what good would the lines have been then? After the storm, it took us days to sort everything out and to recover our anchors. It was a hell of an experience, but we saved her."

In storms it may be necessary to keep an anchor watch around the clock until conditions improve. This means that one person must be awake and dressed, alert to the yacht's position, and capable of getting the vessel under way at once. If there's a chance that other vessels may drag down on you, if the wind is strong and changeable, or if the holding ground is abysmal, a crew member must keep watch. Even if an anchorage is poor, it may be better than going to sea under some circumstances. A person may be desperately tired or sick or you may need to make critical repairs. Hang on somehow, because with care and attention, you may be able to nurse the yacht through the storm.

If you are dragging and trapped in an anchorage or on a lee shore, an engine can be extremely useful. The act of firing up the engine and putting the machinery in gear at low or medium revolutions ahead has saved many large and small ships. Meanwhile the crew members stand regular watches and hope to go nowhere. Often the winds of a severe storm change soon after their maximum velocity. Three or four hours of engine work may get you through a crisis. A lull in a storm may allow you to motor ahead or to one side enough to drop an additional anchor.

A FINAL WORD

To summarize this long discussion of anchoring, let's start from the beginning. When you anchor, look for a place sheltered from the ocean's swells. Quiet water is more important than protection from the wind, although we would hope for that too. Hunt on the chart for a bay within a bay, a hook of land that curves to form a shield from the sea, a series of close offshore islands that serve as a barrier between the ocean and the boat. Can you slip up a river a few miles? Why not go behind that big breakwater or sandbank? Will there be reasonable access to the shore? A safe place to leave the dinghy?

Pay attention to the scale of the chart. Work it out in cables (tenths of a nautical mile), which you can estimate. Sometimes a small-scale chart will have excellent coves for anchoring that are hardly visible on the tiny drawing. It may help to examine the chart with a magnifying glass.

What is the prevailing wind? Will the anchorage be safe from all winds? Will nearby canyons and mountains and deeply indented hills cause squalls to funnel down on top of you? What does the Pilot book say? If the wind shifts when you're in the anchorage, is there an alternate place of refuge, or must you clear out? What do the local fishermen advise? Go and ask them. Do their words make sense? Where do the fishermen keep their boats? If the fishermen winch their boats up a cliff or pull them up on a beach, look out.

Can you get out of the anchorage in the night if the wind shifts? If you clear out, what will the compass course be? *Write it down.* While it's daylight, work out any special strategy with regard to rocks, reefs, or a darkened shore at night. If things look chancy, but you are very tired and need rest, you have three choices:

1. head out to sea for a couple of hours, say, ten miles, and heave to on the offshore tack
2. continue sailing to a better anchorage
3. try the marginal anchorage

Choice 3 may be satisfactory, but be ready to clear out. Tie a reef in the mainsail and have a small jib ready to use. Work out the course, tidy up the lines and gear, and then sleep.

"When a Vessel comes to an Anchor," advises *Lever's Young Sea Officer's Sheet Anchor* of 1813, "it is always prudent to take three Reefs in the Topsails before they are handed, as they would be ready, should a sudden gale arise, if there be a necessity for running out to sea."

But back to the new anchorage. What's the nature of the holding ground? Is the depth moderate? Is the swinging room adequate? Does the chart indicate submarine cables, permanent moorings, commercial oyster beds, current eddies, or overfalls? If you're anchored in a river, what happens when a strong wind blows into a spring tide? I think of the many rivers that Margaret and I have visited in Europe and North and South America. All can turn into raging torrents with the wind against the tide or from an upstream cloudburst. Dinghies may be safe only at high slack water or with the flood or maybe not at all.

Will those pleasure boats with the light anchors drag down on you, or are the other vessels on substantial moorings? If you drag, where will you go? One hates to think negatively, but if you have the choice of anchoring in front of a smooth beach or a mass of rocks, the choice is obvious.

Are there traffic problems in the anchorage? Will you have to move for the evening ferryboat? Do the fishing boats go out at 0230? Will you be prey for all the bumboats on the island? Will clouds of mosquitoes and gnats descend on the ship when the onshore breeze dies? Are there glue factories or sewer outlets or cement plants to windward? Or—worse yet—military firing ranges (more common than you think!)?

These problems don't arise often, and seldom in combination, thank goodness, and dropping a single anchor is usually simplicity itself. Nevertheless, it's good to review all the contingencies. Just as the pilot of a plane scans the ground for a dozen telltale signs before he lands, so should the master of a ship look carefully before he puts his faith in an odd-shaped piece of iron that ties him to the earth.

Thinking about all the foregoing points concerning anchoring has been a long business. The task has taught me how little I really know, and that a seaman's schooling is never over. Few statements stand unchallenged, and I'm forever learning. Anchoring is 60 percent the science of hard facts, 35 percent practice and judgment, and 5 percent luck.

The dinghy is aboard. The mainsail is up. Now let's all heave together to pull in the chain, get the anchor, and off we'll go!

SELF-STEERING

When I mounted a Hasler wind-vane steering device on *Whisper*'s transom in 1966, Margaret and I were generally obliged to spend half an hour a day explaining the use and operation of the strange-looking contraption to curious people on the dock. We told how the device controlled the yacht and relieved us from the tedium of physical steering and how we were able keep a better lookout and concentrate on navigation and sail trim.

Today on many cruising yachts, we see complex frames of iron pipe, intricately curved stainless steel rods, and queer-looking aluminum castings hanging over the sterns. Above the machinery, thin blades of wood, Plexiglas, aluminum, or fabric-covered ovals of tubing swing on delicate bearings and either feather noiselessly into the wind or rock nervously from side to side. The wind blades are of all sizes and shapes and often reflect the personalities of their owners with regard to color and design. I often wonder where all the hopeful cruising yachts are headed and

Self-steering devices and arrangements vary widely but need to be conceived and used with thought and purpose. Otherwise the equipment may end up like Fritz.

whether the steering vanes were bought to go somewhere or were added for reasons of prestige and acquisitiveness.

What have I learned about steering vanes? Are they necessary, or can you get the yacht to steer herself without an expensive mechanical contraption and all that weight at the back of the boat? How does a steering vane compare with an autopilot? Do you need both?

Steering vanes need to be robust and able to take bashing about in heavy seas and nasty weather. The equipment must stand up to occasional knocks at rough commercial docks, where you sometimes tie up stern to. You should be able to operate the devices from safe and convenient locations, which means having some form of remote control. Self-steering gears need power to deal with unbalanced sail settings and weather helm. You ought to be able to make reasonable repairs at sea, and you should take along a few spare parts. And—oh yes—they have to work in light airs and not change course when the wind increases.

I've learned that enclosed bevel gears, tricky mechanisms, delicate welds, mixtures of metals, wobbly shafts, vibrating wind blades, and bearings that corrode do not do well in a saltwater world. All these mechanical troubles ought to be designed out at the drawing board stage or eliminated by trials with experimental models.

By its very nature, a vane gear is a device that responds to a wind change *after* the yacht has turned to a slightly different course. The vane gear always *follows* a change in conditions; there is no possibility that a vane gear can anticipate a change, as can a human helmsman (here comes a puff of wind; here comes a big sea).

Claims that a vane gear will never get off course more than one or two degrees are ridiculous. Out in the ocean, with from zero to forty knots of wind (or more) and corresponding seas, a small yacht gets shoved first one way and then another. A vane gear can average a certain course, but it can never steer more accurately than an alert human can. In hard going at sea, a person has to work diligently to keep within a 15-degree range of steering; on large ocean racers the helmsmen are often changed at thirty-minute intervals when the steering is difficult.

I think that if in average to strong conditions (not smooth water), a vane gear can keep the boat within 10 or 12 degrees of the course on either side, then the device is doing a good job.* The important thing is the course made good, whether steered by a person or a machine. Once these limits are recognized and accepted, the vane gear becomes a useful helper. The reason we often hear the phrase "the gear steers a better course than I can" is that many sailors—including me—are rotten helmsmen. A wind vane can be a wonderful assistant.

---

*Oversteering and dealing with problems of yaw are, I believe, separate from normal side-to-side course changes. John Letcher has an excellent chapter on this in *Self-Steering for Sailing Craft* (International Marine, 1974; chapter 7).

Years ago I wrote:

> Our vane does not complain, get tired, become bored, or require endless cups of coffee and sandwiches. The magic helmsman needs no oilskins, never flies into a rage or tantrum, and cheerfully steers at 0300 as well as at high noon. As long as the wind works, the vane will work too. It will guide you faultlessly from Newfoundland to Ireland as well as steer you straight into a granite ledge or a sandbank two miles away. No matter how good the vane is, it can never take the place of a person on watch who can think, reason, and respond.

I see no reason to change a word today.

The basic problem of self-steering in yachts is that some scheme of amplifying the power of a wind blade is necessary. In a model yacht that sails on a pond in a park, you can couple the wind blade directly to the rudder. But in a 30- or 40- or 50-foot sailing vessel, you need more muscle. A small vane gear without a power-amplifying scheme may work in strong winds, but it will not function in light breezes unless the wind blade or sail is quite large. Today there are three main systems of wind-vane gears: pendulum-servo, trim tab, and those operated by a mizzen sail. I put sheet-to-tiller self-steering systems in a fourth group. All usually need some kind of modest negative feedback to control oversteering.

BLONDIE'S GREAT IDEA

The Hasler pendulum-servo gear was invented by Blondie Hasler in 1960 and uses the action of water on a narrow submerged blade to generate steering power. An airfoil-shaped blade about 6 inches wide and 4 feet long is submerged vertically in the water with its airfoil section parallel to the fore-and-aft line of the vessel. When the yacht is moving and the blade is parallel to the centerline of the ship, no side force is produced on the blade. But when the blade is rotated slightly about its vertical axis by a linkage from the wind blade above, a powerful side force is generated. The top of the water blade is fastened to a metal framework or quadrant that pivots from side to side on the longitudinal axis of the yacht. Lines from the quadrant are led to the tiller or wheel, which then steer the yacht through the main rudder.

The narrow blade in the water (sometimes called a paddle or oar) is *not* a rudder and does *not* control the yacht directly. The blade is a lever, a power-generating device that amplifies the movements of the wind blade and gives it force.

A pendulum-servo self-steering unit is a complicated mechanism that requires a wind blade, a water blade mounted on a double pivot, and—depending on the maker—various linkages and rods and blocks and lines. In case the water blade

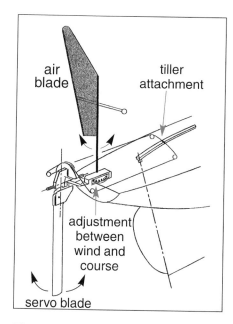

air blade

tiller attachment

adjustment between wind and course

servo blade

The Hasler wind vane gear. Movements of the air blade cause the servo blade to twist slightly to the right or left on its vertical axis. This causes the water to push on the more exposed side of the servo blade. This force swings the entire servo unit (on its horizontal axis) to the right or left. This movement is led to the tiller via lines. The scheme looks complicated, but it works extremely well and is the basis for most self-steering systems aboard yachts.

strikes anything in the water (a log, a mass of floating kelp, ice fragments) there's usually some kind of breakaway mechanism to allow the water blade to pivot up and away from the obstruction. Clever inventors and manufacturers have given their designs a high degree of reliability, as proven by the voyages of Francis Chichester and Alec Rose and several thousand single-handers in the Atlantic and round-the-world races.

A variation of the pendulum-servo design is the French Navik trim tab unit that uses a tiny air blade to turn a small tab on the *back* of the water blade. This in turn forces the larger water blade to one side or the other. The advantage is that a smaller air blade can be used, which some say is more sensitive to wind shifts. (Others claim a larger and lighter air blade is better.) The Navik unit is small and easily mounted and has a surprising amount of power.

Over the years, I've been a shipmate with four commercially built pendulum-servo units, all well made. The first, as I've mentioned, was the Hasler, which used an air blade that pivoted on a vertical axis. The Hasler gear performed admirably in all kinds of weather and on all points of sailing during a twenty-thousand-mile Pacific trip. When I returned to San Francisco, my friend Colin Darroch put the gear on his boat and headed out for further adventures.

Always searching for something better, I bought an Aries vane gear, built until recently on the Isle of Wight in England by Nick Franklin. This pendulum-servo device used a horizontally pivoting wind blade and had a clever system for remote

The Hasler vane gear in action before sizeable seas. The toothed adjustment wheel can be seen at the bottom. This design uses a vane blade that pivots on a 1-inch-diameter stainless steel vertical shaft, an arrangement that puts substantial shear loads on the shaft during storms. This is not fantasy because we snapped a shaft during a gale in the Gulf of Alaska. This design of forty years ago—still in use—seems big and clunky compared with today's vanes, but all have developed from this pioneering effort.

The Aries vane gear with its horizontally pivoting blade is robust and used by many long-distance sailors. It has a particularly good course-adjusting arrangement.

control that allowed the watchkeeper to adjust the setting from the companionway hatch. The gear was well built and designed around a massive magnesium-aluminum casting with stout bevel gears and heavy shafts that ran on plastic needle bearings. Unfortunately, my Aries vane gear never worked properly. Its action was sluggish, and it seemed to have too much friction in the various linkages and shafts. At one stage we struck some wreckage in the sea, and the breakaway device on the water blade failed to work. This bent the main shaft. Nick sent me new parts, but the patient never recovered. I sold it to another sailor, who had no better luck. I am certain the poor operation of the gear was an exception because many sailors swear by the good performance of the Aries device.

When Margaret and I sailed to Buenos Aires, I saw a French-built Atoms gear on *Lou*, a Chance 37 that belonged to Louis Brioni, a French single-hander on his way to Cape Horn. I liked the Atoms gear, which was nicely designed, and arranged to have one sent out from France. We had it on *Whisper* for many years and used it on a west-about trip around the world. The gear was small yet powerful and steered *Whisper* in both gales and light winds.

In 1986, I sold the first *Whisper* (and with her the Atoms gear) to help purchase the Santa Cruz 50 that carried me to all sorts of distant seas and oceans. I found a used Monitor gear that the makers kindly fitted on the transom of the 50-footer. Except for the bevel gears, which were bronze, the entire Monitor device was made of stainless steel. Unlike our earlier vane gears, whose water blades were wood or plastic and required antifouling paint, the water paddle of the Monitor was fashioned from sheet stainless steel formed into an airfoil shape. The paddle was hinged and could be pivoted up out of the water for an occasional scrub with a stiff brush to get rid of grass and barnacles.

The Monitor vane gear worked well and steered the Santa Cruz 50 in some frightful weather in the South Atlantic and the Southern Ocean. This self-steerer never failed me except once for a few hours when I hit some wreckage (or a whale?) at 58° S.

I was asleep at the time and didn't feel a thing. Later when I noticed that the steering was erratic, I looked over the transom and saw that the water blade shaft was twisted and bent and shoved sideways (the direction of the impact?). Somehow the breakaway coupling had not sheared. By hanging over the side, I managed to take the vane apart and repair it using large C-clamps that I left in place. Six hours later, the vane gear was steering as usual.

When I sold the Santa Cruz in 1992 and bought the current *Whisper*, I again fitted the same type of gear. In all I must have logged 100,000 miles with the Monitor vane, and with the exception noted above I have had good service. I am, however, the first to admit that pendulum-servo units are complicated devices with lots of parts thrashing around. Chafe is a problem with the steering lines, which are a nuisance in the cockpit (you learn to lift your feet and not trip over them). The complexity of the pendulum-servo units translates into high prices. To his credit, the genial Hans Bernwald, who makes the excellent Monitor vane gear in Richmond, California, offers plenty of advice and help with installation and use. He also throws in a generous bag of spare parts and tells good jokes.

RUDDER AND TRIM TAB

Another class of self-steering gears is a rudder with a trim tab on its trailing edge. This is easy to arrange on double-enders or on boats with the rudder hung on a transom stern or close underneath. The trim tab is connected to the wind blade by a vertical (or almost vertical) rod or linkage. Movement of the wind blade turns the trim tab, which can be as small as one-twentieth of the area of the rudder. If the tab turns to port, it swings the rudder to starboard with considerable force. This turns the yacht to starboard. Such an arrangement is called a Flettner rudder and is a true servo.

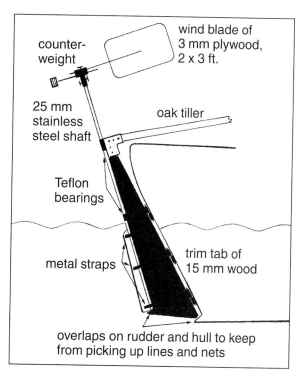

counter-weight

wind blade of 3 mm plywood, 2 x 3 ft.

25 mm stainless steel shaft

oak tiller

Teflon bearings

metal straps

trim tab of 15 mm wood

overlaps on rudder and hull to keep from picking up lines and nets

A trim tab on a transom-hung rudder is extremely powerful and has the advantage of simplicity. In addition, the air blade can be low and will work reasonably well underneath a mizzen boom on a ketch or yawl.

A trim tab device is much less complicated than a pendulum-servo unit. If a ship's main rudder is at or near the transom, the procedure is to hinge a tab along the back of the rudder and run a control rod from the trim tab upward to an air blade. With this arrangement it's important that the pivot point of the air blade be located at the convergence of the rudder and trim tab axes (see drawing). Otherwise, say the experts, the vessel will wander off course and wander from side to side (yaw).[35] This self-steering scheme was used with complete success by Bernard Moitessier on his extended ocean voyages in his steel yacht *Joshua*, which had a long keel and a transom-hung rudder.

If the rudder of a yacht is located too far forward under the counter for an easy connection to an air blade, a possible solution is to mount an auxiliary rudder and trim tab directly on or through the after part of the transom. With such an auxiliary rudder and trim tab arrangement, the main rudder is not used and is left free or lashed amidships.

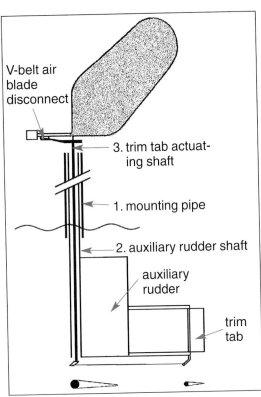

The DeRidder wind vane gear is based on a set of ingeniously engineered pipes and shafts that utilize the leverage of a trim tab to control an auxiliary rudder.

A basic advantage of an auxiliary rudder and trim tab arrangement is that you gain an extra rudder, a fair exchange for the drag of the unit. This safety feature is dear to the hearts of all cruising sailors, for few people encounter bad weather or sail to distant places without worrying about the rudder. A second advantage is that trim tab units are relatively simple, self-contained, and don't clutter up the cockpit with blocks and lines. Third, amateur builders can construct trim tab units for about one-tenth the cost of pendulum-servo gears.

I have seen excellent vanes made from scraps of material and a few days of work. Al and Beth Liggett, for example, successfully took their yacht *Bacchus* around the world with a DeRidder auxiliary trim tab gear made on the waterfront in Tahiti for the cost of a few pieces of pipe and a little welding.

The clever design of Michael DeRidder, the ingenious captain of

Magic Dragon, is simple and strong (see drawing). The auxiliary rudder and trim tab are built around a long piece of 2-inch-diameter heavy-wall iron pipe placed vertically through the center of the transom or held immediately behind the transom on strong metal frames or brackets (pipe 1). The steering vane rudder is welded to the back of the bottom part of a second, smaller pipe (2) that extends upward through the main vertical pipe (1).

To drive the auxiliary rudder, a small trim tab is placed 24 inches *behind* the auxiliary rudder on supports extending aft from the auxiliary rudder. A lightweight wind blade 6 feet above deck level directs the trim tab by means of a linkage at the bottom of a long tubular shaft (3) that runs inside pipe 2.

To disconnect the air blade from shaft 3, which is necessary when hand steering with the ship's main rudder, the air blade unit is made separately and pivots inside the upper part of shaft 3. If a sheave is secured to the top of 3, a V-belt with a simple quick-release tensioning device can be used to lock the air blade to 3.

A collar (with Teflon washers underneath) at the top of 2 carries the weight of pipes 2 and 3, the rudder, and the tab. Friction between 1 and 2 can be reduced with Teflon shims. Note that the entire auxiliary rudder assembly must be able to revolve 360 degrees so you can back under power.

The separation of the trim tab from the auxiliary rudder makes this design extremely powerful, and it can steer a yacht under almost any circumstances. On the downside, there is drag from the two units because they're permanently in the water. They are subject to marine growth and need to be coated with antifouling paint. In addition, this arrangement is somewhat vulnerable to damage, especially around docks (as are all self-steering units), because being underwater, the auxiliary rudder and tab are not normally visible. To work on the underwater parts, you generally must haul out the vessel or be able to do some dedicated breath holding.

Nevertheless, once built and adjusted, such a system will last for years. Some owners construct this device from iron pipes and sail with it for a time to get everything worked out, particularly the lever arm lengths

The wind blade for the DeRidder vane (Dacron fabric over a 3/4" dia. aluminum tubing frame) is connected to the trim tab drive shaft with a small V-belt clutch arrangement.

between shaft 3 and the trim tab. (Start with 1" at the bottom of shaft 3, and 2" at the tab.) Then at the next haulout, they take the vane to pieces and have the parts hot-dip galvanized before they paint everything and put it back together.

A clever variation of trim tab gears is Saye's Rig. This design has no quadrant at deck level and has no steering lines to the tiller. Instead, the side-to-side movement of the water blade is transmitted directly to the rudder by a long, narrow, horizontal, U-shaped piece of metal that looks like a woman's hairpin. The U of the hairpin fits around the shaft above the servo blade and goes forward to the vessel's rudder, where the sides of the hairpin are permanently fastened. As the water blade moves back and forth, the ship's main rudder moves accordingly.

When the boat gets off course a little to starboard, for example, the vertical air blade moves a few degrees to port. This movement is transmitted through a linkage to the servo blade in the water. This makes the water blade turn a little to port, which results in more water pressure on the starboard side of the blade. This shoves it sideways to port. This in turn moves the aft end of the hairpin to port; this pushes the trailing edge of the rudder to port, and the yacht returns to her proper course. Got it? Of course, instead of one gross motion, the steering forces are applied back and forth in almost constant small movements. The linkage between the air and water blades deals with negative feedback to control over-steering, as we've seen with other units. With this type of direct linkage to the rudder, it's important to put in a reliable quick-release link to the wind blade so the watchkeeper can instantly take over when he needs to steer by hand. Kelp, weed, or grass on the hairpin can be dealt with by using a boat hook at the stern.

Saye's Rig is well suited to double-enders with outboard transom rudders or for vessels with spade rudders at the end of the waterline. To me it seems pointless to hang a complex pendulum-servo unit immediately behind a stern-mounted rudder whose water flow may upset the working of the servo blade.

When Margaret and I sailed around South America, we used an RVG (Riebandt vane gear) auxiliary rudder device that steered *Whisper* with a separate small rudder actuated by a trim tab hinged at the trailing edge of the auxiliary rudder. The air blade was connected to the tab by a small linkage. Instead of a piece of flat plywood for an air blade, as the Monitor and Aries units have, the Riebandt gear used a wedge-shaped air blade (for more power) made of aluminum tubing covered with a rectangular piece of blue cloth. From the beginning, I thought the hard corners of the air blade might have been rounded a little for a better appearance.

When I acquired the unit in 1972, I complained to the builder about his mixing of bronze and aluminum parts for use in salt water and his crazy instructions that some pieces of the gear were to be coated with copper antifouling and others with tin-based antifouling. By the time that Margaret and I sailed ten thousand miles with the RVG, small pieces of the auxiliary rudder skeg were eaten away by the galvanic couple between the aluminum, bronze, and tin. When we arrived in Buenos Aires, there were sizeable holes corroded right through the aluminum. Some of the parts looked like cheese ravaged by rats. How long would the gear last before it fell apart, we wondered. In addition, there was no way of setting the gear from the cockpit. You had to climb on the transom and engage or adjust the steering gear by means of a Morse control lever that was frozen with corrosion.

The basic design of the RVG was excellent. Its material list was good; alas, the materials didn't get along with one another. It was like putting a wildcat and a snake in the same cage; something had to go. Today, the RVG would be molded of high-density polyurethane covered with fiberglass, with parts fashioned from epoxy rod, Delrin, Teflon, stainless steel, and maybe a little carbon fiber.

But by God, the RVG worked! In spite of the materials problem, the RVG steered Margaret and me around Cape Horn and through some appalling weather on a tough two-year voyage. The unit had plenty of steering power, and we always felt that the yacht was

The Riebandt vane gear is independent of the main rudder and steers with its own rudder by means of a trim tab and linkage attached to a wedge-shaped air blade. This device is extremely powerful and the strongest of any of the steering devices that I've used. It has the advantage of adding an independent rudder to the yacht. Unfortunately, the maker built the Riebandt of materials poorly suited to the sea and each other.

under perfect control on all points of sail and all wind strengths, except running winds of 6 knots or less.

In passing, I note that four of the commercially produced steering gears that I've discussed are no longer made. The marine market is small and most companies are hand-to-mouth operations that are usually undercapitalized and depend on the enthusiasm of one or two people. Often they rely on a single product, which is risky. If one of the principals gets discouraged or dies (I think of the excellent vane gear made by M. F. Gunning), it's bad news for everyone. If there's an economic downturn or a competitive product takes some of the market, the company is history.

MIRANDA

A third type of wind-vane steering gear is the Miranda configuration worked out by the late Sir Francis Chichester for his single-handed Atlantic trips in the 1960s. The Miranda gear is actually a tiny mizzen sail set on a small rotating mast. The bottom of the mast turns a large sheave or crossbar from which a single pair of crossed lines leads to the tiller. The advantage of the Miranda gear is that all the parts are on deck and easily serviceable. The unit is simple and direct and not nearly as vulnerable and unprotected as a pendulum-servo device or an auxiliary rudder and tab arrangement. There is no added drag from underwater appendages.

The Miranda-type gear is a small mizzen sail whose gaff is fastened (or goes through) a short mast that turns easily on bearings. When the wind pushes the sail, the mast pivots and directs the tiller by means of crossed lines leading from a large sheave at the bottom of the mast. In one example, a Dacron sail with about 13 square feet of area worked well on a 32-footer. This mast assembly was held by a small supporting tripod arrangement (with a Teflon bearing to allow the mast to rotate easily) that was offset slightly from the centerline of the yacht to allow the sail to clear the backstay. An improvement might be to fit a V-shaped sail to the mast to provide additional power from a smaller sail.

One drawback is that you need space for the mast and sail. This means a design with an afterdeck and a fairly clear counter with an offset or split backstay, or at least a cockpit with the steering in the forward part so you have somewhere to put the mizzen mast.

People tend to scoff at Miranda-type gears because of their size but overlook their basic design advantages. Remember that Slocum and Pidgeon used the small mizzen sails on their yawl-rigged boats for hands-off steering. The Miranda gear links a tiny mizzen sail directly to the helm; Slocum and Pidgeon carefully adjusted their mizzen sails and used them as dynamic forces for self-steering.

Margaret and I once cruised from place to place in the South Pacific with Eric Hall, a single-hander who was sailing a Nicholson 32. For his self-steering gear, Eric used a 12-foot aluminum mast $3\frac{1}{4}$ inches in diameter mounted on the transom. The bottom of the mast rested on a small ball bearing thrust bearing. The rotating mast was supported $4\frac{1}{2}$ feet from its base by struts that angled upward from the back and sides of the stern pulpit.

The steering sail (with three light battens) was shaped like an upside-down triangle and had about 16 square feet of area. The sail turned the mast by means of a short, angled 6-foot gaff at the top of the sail. Two feet of the front of the gaff stuck through the mast and provided a handy place to hang a radar reflector, which nicely balanced the weight of the sail, battens, and gaff. I think this self-steering arrangement was clever, although Eric's yacht was well balanced and did not require heavy tiller pressure.

SHEET-TO-TILLER STEERING

There's another system of self-steering that doesn't rely on mechanical devices at all. Sheet-to-tiller steering is much simpler and costs nothing, but it demands more thinking and ingenuity and a bit of tinkering to get started.

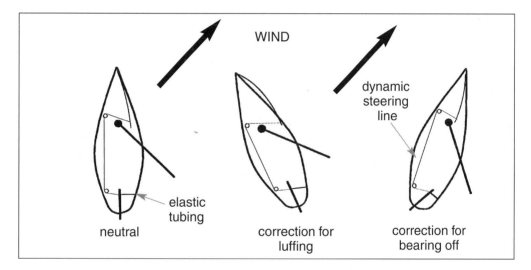

A well-proven arrangement for self-steering is to run a light line from either the main-sheet or the jib sheet to the weather side of the tiller. There is more load on this line when the sail is full of wind and less when the sail is luffing or blanketed. You balance this tiller line with opposite tension applied by a device of some kind. Shock cord or a screen door spring might seem ideal, but in practice surgical hose is better because its pull is steadier and it is less affected by sun and salt water. The sketch above shows that if the boat gets off course and heads up toward the wind, the sail begins to fill with wind. This increases the tension on the tiller line, which pulls the tiller toward the wind and makes the boat bear off and return to her proper course. Conversely, if the yacht falls off to lee-ward—away from the wind—there is less force from the sail. The elastic tubing pulls the tiller to leeward, and the boat begins to head up to her course. It takes experimenting to work out the details of this kind of steering and may require a simple purchase (a single whip) to increase or decrease the steering forces.

As a boat turns one way or the other from a desired course, the wind pressure on the sails increases or decreases. This change in wind pressure is directly related to the tension on the control lines to the sails.

If, for example, the weather sheet from a small backed staysail or storm jib is led to the weather side of the tiller (balanced on the other side with elastic), you have a form of self-steering. As the vessel—reaching along under the mainsail and jib—heads up to windward, the wind pressure on the backed staysail increases. This adds tension to the sheet, which pulls the tiller to windward, and the yacht bears off. Conversely, if the vessel falls off, there's less pressure on the staysail and the weather sheet. The elastic on the tiller pulls it to leeward, and the yacht heads up. This same scheme can be extended for use in running arrangements with fair winds.

Let's look into these sheet-to-tiller schemes a bit more. Suppose you have a beam wind. You clove-hitch a small (say, $\frac{1}{4}$" dia.) line at right angles to a headsail sheet or to one part of the mainsheet. This small line is then led outboard through a nearby block on a windward lifeline stanchion and taken aft to the windward side of the tiller, perhaps through another block hung on a lifeline stanchion.

Now you tension the leeward side of the tiller with elastic and adjust the tiller line so the pull of the tiller line just matches the elastic. The tension on the tiller line should pull the sheet (up forward) a little sideways, where the tiller line is clove-hitched to the sheet. Now as the wind pressure on the sail changes, the sheet tension changes and tends to straighten out or sag off at the clove hitch. This moves the tiller line, and the tiller goes back and forth. It's this movement that's the key to sheet-to-tiller self-steering.

When the elastic and the tiller line are balanced, the helm is neutral and the yacht goes straight ahead. If the tiller line is tensioned, the yacht bears off from the wind. If the tiller line is slackened, the elastic pulls the tiller to leeward and the vessel heads up toward its former course.

Once you understand this scheme and have it working, you can adapt it to many arrangements, both on and off the wind. The first time you try it, probably nothing will work. Keep at it, however, because instead of sitting in the cockpit and steering like a hypnotized robot, you can trick the yacht into guiding herself.

With regard to elastic to pull against the tiller, the best thing is $\frac{3}{8}$-inch-diameter surgical tubing (amber or black), sold by hospital suppliers, dive shops (for use with spear guns), and pharmacies. Six or eight feet will last for a long time, especially if you keep the tubing out of the sun when not in use. Two pieces of tubing may work better than extra tension on one piece.

Shock cord does not work as well because its stretch is irregular and it's prone to chafe and sun deterioration. Rubber bands cut from old inner tubes break in a few hours. Metal springs are mostly ferrous and rust out quickly and make a mess in the cockpit. If you have oversteering or understeering problems (often confused), at least you have the dynamics of the system going and can work on refinements.

If the pull of the sheet is too powerful, it's sometimes helpful to introduce a two- or three-part tackle used in reverse, a so-called fool's purchase. Note the difference in sheet tension between a typical sloop headsail sheet (X) and one part ($\frac{1}{4}$X) of a four-part mainsheet tackle.

Sheet-to-tiller steering is easiest with a tiller to which lines can be secured with a simple clove hitch. The tiller line should go to windward, the elastic to leeward. If a wheel system is easy to turn, it may work OK. Otherwise, the emergency tiller may be a better link.

All this information and more is detailed in John Letcher's *Self-Steering for Sailing Craft*, mentioned earlier. The book is out of print, but you may find a copy on the Internet or through your local library.

While I was working on this chapter, we met an elderly 36-foot British yacht named *Beroë* that came sailing into Maryland waters. Her owners, Simon Brown and Beverly Pilgrim, had just crossed the Atlantic and hoped to keep going indefinitely. Simon and Beverly, a cheery and outgoing couple, sail their narrow-hulled, substantially rebuilt wooden gaff cutter without an engine and are experts at working her in and out of tight corners under sail.

It's hard to believe, but *Beroë* was launched in 1889, more than a century ago. In earlier times, *Beroë* won lots of races and trophies, and with her big gaff mainsail (425 sq. ft.), she is still speedy and hard to catch. In fact, Simon and Beverly averaged 137 miles per day on their Atlantic crossing last year, which is excellent time and suggests that the old designers and builders knew a few tricks. Simon and Beverly merely smile.

The two British sailors use no mechanical self-steering devices. Instead they lead a light line from the jib sheet up near the clew of the sail to points aft as I've described. I thought that sheet-to-tiller steering was passé, but seeing *Beroë* sail so well in front of my eyes made it seem modern and contemporary.

TWIN JIBS

I have commented on twin, poled-out jibs for downwind running in chapter 7, pages 102–4. Because their steering range is so limited, I do not consider them proper self-steering devices.

AUTOPILOTS

Where steering vanes fail is when you're sailing downwind in very light airs, 6 knots of true wind or thereabouts. If you have lots of sail area up, a downwind rig is set, and the boat is going at 3 knots, then the apparent wind is only 3 knots, which is too light to overcome the friction inherent in a steering vane mechanism.

In these conditions, I use a small push-pull electric autopilot called an Auto-helm ST 4000. One end of the unit mounts on the starboard cockpit coaming, and the push-pull rod at the other end hooks on a little fitting on the tiller. A tiny 12-volt Swiss reversible motor drives a push-pull rod that moves the tiller back and forth. (There's another version for wheel-steered yachts.) A small fluxgate compass mounted below the floorboards in the cabin controls the unit, which is surprisingly powerful. At sea, we power the unit with electricity from a single large solar panel that we tie to the dinghy (capsized on the coach roof) and move around as the sun changes direction.

Initially, seawater leaked into our autopilot and ruined the motor. After repairs, I wrapped layers of self-amalgamating tape around all the joints and plastered the inlet wire with silicon sealing compound. Occasionally I lubricate the push-pull rod with a touch of Vaseline. So far, no more leaks, and the little autopilot continues to work well.

I remember a June sail in the Mediterranean from Malta to the northwest coast of Corfu in Greek waters. The distance was 335 miles. The wind was a shadowy and insubstantial 6 or 7 knots from the southwest; Margaret and I put up our largest running sails and headed northeast. The first evening we sat in the cockpit watching the sunset over the tawny hills of southeast Sicily while we drank a glass of cool white wine. It was nice.

It took us almost five days to reach Paleokastritsa. We logged only 70–75 miles a day, but the little electric box kept us right on course while *Whisper* glided across a smooth and tranquil Ionian Sea. The only sound was the soft swishing of the spinnaker.

This noisy, scrappy, madly flapping white-tailed tropicbird has come down to deck level to look us over. The bird is also called a bosun bird because its raucous call reminded early sailors of a bosun's piercing whistle when he called his crew to work.

15

CAN YOU BE SEEN AT NIGHT?

At night the greatest hazard to large and small ships is collision. All vessels carry navigation lights to call attention to one another and to define each ship's right of way. Because lights are so important, they should be bright, not blocked or masked by anything, and mounted according to international regulations. Unfortunately, the lights on many of today's small vessels are feeble and ineffective and not only are illegal but put their owners in grave danger from big ships and each other.

Inadequate lights lead to a false sense of security. Novice sailors often have the naive belief that not only will their lights (of whatever brightness) be seen by others but that the approaching vessels will take evasive action. This may be a welcome hope, but it's nonsense.

The problem areas are as follows:

- The electric bulbs are too small. Many fittings are ill-designed and flimsy. Kerosene lamps in yacht sizes are hopeless.
- The lights are badly placed and are obscured by sails, poles, pulpits, or cabin structures. The light fixtures are often mounted at

The best navigation light for a yacht less than 20 meters in length is this masthead fixture made by the German firm Aqua Signal. One bulb of 25 watts illuminates a 360-degree sector that is separated into the appropriate zones of white, red, and green. On this fixture, a separate chamber at the bottom has an all-round white anchor light.

wrong angles on bow pulpits, which makes it impossible to judge the true courses of approaching vessels.

- Battery power is limited and wire sizes are too small, resulting in a marked voltage drop at the light.
- Salt spray interferes with the lights, the wiring and fixtures, and general efficiency.
- The light loss through red and green glass or thick plastic filters can be as much as 88 percent, according to one authority.[36] At a distance of a mile or more, the colors may not be distinguishable at all.
- Boatbuilders often consider lights to be regulatory annoyances and supply minimal or substandard fixtures and wiring.

According to paragraph (a) of Rule 25 of the International Regulations for Preventing Collisions at Sea, often called COLREGs, sailing craft under way must exhibit two sidelights and a sternlight. The sector of the red sidelight goes from directly forward to 112.5 degrees to port. The sector of the green sidelight is from forward to 112.5 degrees to starboard. The sternlight covers the rear-facing area for 135 degrees (67.5° to both port and starboard). These three lights are mounted on deck or on rigging near the deck. Their sectors add up to 360 degrees and are a primary means of identifying the intentions of the vessel in question.

Paragraph (b) of Rule 25 states that if a sailing vessel is less than 20 meters (65.6') in length, the three lights can be combined in a single lantern carried at the top of the mast. This is a popular and sensible option because the elevated light is more visible. In addition, a single bulb can be used to illuminate all three sectors. With one bulb instead of three, the electricity demands drop by two-thirds.

Rule 25 allows a third option, (c): In addition to the deck lights described in paragraph (a), summarized above, a sailing vessel can show two all-around circular lights (one above the other) at the top of the mast. The uppermost light must be red and the lower, green. [These lights cannot be used with the combined lantern permitted in paragraph (b), summarized above.] The kiss of death of this option, however, is the electricity demand, and I have never seen anyone choose this arrangement. Instead of the one bulb used in (b), this lighting scheme requires two or three bulbs at deck level, plus one or two aloft.

Concerning the power of lights, Rule 22 states that the sidelights of sailing vessels less than 20 meters in length should be visible at 2 miles. For vessels less than 12 meters, the figure is 1 mile. In practice, the white sternlight is not a problem because the bulb shines through clear glass or plastic instead of the dense red or green of the sidelights.

Sailors who have experienced heavy ship traffic and are familiar with the Strait of Dover in the English Channel, for example, don't have to be told that their lights may well mean life itself. The opposite side of the world is no different. One night when my wife and I sailed south from Kobe, Japan, we counted the bright lights of 63 large and small commercial vessels heading in and out of Osaka Wan. As we watched, each coastal vessel, fishing boat, tanker, and oceangoing cargo ship maneuvered according to the rules of the road. The ship traffic flowed like automobiles on a well-ordered freeway. In such a situation, our lights were crucial. This was an exceptional situation, of course, but it shows what you can experience at night.

Yet in spite of all this salty talk about distant places, a yacht can be run down on New York harbor, San Diego Bay, or on Lake Michigan. Certainly a weekend sailor needs first-class lights because most boats are kept in marinas near cities, where there is a concentration of traffic and more chances of night collisions. To further complicate things, as soon as the skipper of a sailing yacht turns on the engine at night, the vessel becomes a powerboat, whose lighting requirements are different.

- If less than 12 meters (39.4') in length, a powered vessel must show a forward-facing 225-degree white masthead light mounted above the normal sidelights and visible at 2 miles. The sidelights must be visible for 1 mile. Although not specifically mentioned, it appears that a 360-degree white anchor light visible at 2 miles will satisfy the requirement for the masthead light and the sternlight.
- If less than 50 meters (164'), commercial ships, powered vessels, and sailing yachts under power must show a single 225-degree forward masthead light plus sidelights and a sternlight. The sidelights must be visible for 2 miles and the masthead light for 5 miles (3 miles for vessels under 20 meters).
- Ships over 50 meters (164') in length must show forward-facing 225-degree white lights on each of two masts, one forward and one aft. The forward light must be lower, the aft higher, and both lights must be visible at 6 miles. At a glance, therefore, you can always tell which way a big ship is headed. Big-ship sidelights should be visible for 3 miles.

Whether it's noon or midnight, the best way to know if your vessel and a distant ship are on a collision course is to take a compass bearing of the other boat. You can sight across your main steering compass, but it's easier to use a hand-bearing compass.* If it's a big ship, take a bearing of the aft masthead light (high and

---

*My favorite, by far, is made by Autohelm. In the United States, it's called a Raytheon Personal Electronic hand-bearing compass. It's small yet includes a memory, a stopwatch, and a gunsight aiming arrangement.

white) and write it down. Wait three minutes (depending on the distance away), then take a second bearing and write it down. Then three minutes later, take a third, and so on. Usually the bearing will change (100°, 105°, 110°) and the other vessel will pass ahead or astern. If the bearings remain constant, you and the approaching vessel are on a collision course. *You need to take immediate evasive action.* Things develop quickly because a big ship is often traveling at 10–20 knots. You will have to decide whether to turn to starboard or port. When you change course, you should make a substantial move to alert the other vessel that you're doing something significant (Rule 8).

If the other ship is closing fast, the next step is to ignite a white collision-avoidance flare and hold it as high as you can. Each flare puts out 10,000 candle-power units and has a burn time of 60 seconds. You can also use a searchlight or a bright white light. White is specifically authorized for preventing collisions (Rule 36). None of these warning lights has anything to do with distress signals, which are red.

Aboard *Whisper*, we carry three white flares in the cockpit in a halyard stowage bag, where they are instantly available. It's best to keep the collision flares handy so they can be used immediately; there's no time to go below and start burrowing in lockers.

I have never used a white collision flare, although I've held them ready in my hand many times. However, I've seen other yachts and a tug ignite flares to call attention to themselves. If there is any doubt, fire the flare. No one will chasten you for being cautious, and the flare may save your life. Note that in spite of what you read in vendors' catalogs, Rule 36 specifically outlaws "high intensity intermittent or revolving lights, such as strobe lights."

Another way to alert a ship to your presence is to call on VHF channel 13 (a one-watt bridge-to-bridge link) and tell the watchkeeper that his ship is dangerously close. A second person can do this while the helmsman is dealing with the white flare.

I believe that small oil lamps are worthless for yachts. To get reasonable light, you need a ⅝- or ¾-inch wick, which means a 16-inch kerosene lantern. Three 16-inch Davey oil lamps make excellent navigation lights but take up a great deal of space. Today, even the most diehard traditionalists use electric running lights because of convenience, size, and brightness. They can be powered from a storage battery charged by an alternator hooked to an engine, from solar panels, or by a water or wind generator.

Years ago on our first *Whisper*, our running lights were two bronze teardrops about 8 inches long that were fastened to small metal plates on the sides of the bow pulpit. Inside each teardrop was an 8-watt bulb (GE 68) whose light shined out through a substantial thickness of ruby-red or emerald-green glass. Each bulb drew 0.59 amps, or 1.77 for the two sidelights and the stern light. Close up, these lights seemed quite bright, but one dark night when Margaret and I were testing the exterior lights, I was surprised at the weakness of the sidelights when I looked at them from half a mile away.

I considered various schemes to increase the light. One idea I tried was to use silvered bulbs to collect and focus the light from a small filament. In practice, the center portion of a silvered bulb's output is high, but there's a severe falloff of light at the edges. Since each sidelight is required to be spread over 112.5 degrees, the silvered bulb idea is useless. Reflectors and mirrors behind the bulbs are also poor.

Because sailing vessels are usually heeled (and pitching as well), the use of magnifying-lens systems seems a dead end. The only hope in this direction is for someone to make a double-gimballed, dampened-motion lantern and to put a dioptric lens—the sort of light magnifier found in lighthouses—around the light source.

While I was thinking about this, I saw an ad in a sailing magazine that sent me in a new direction. I bought a tricolor fluorescent masthead fixture that was made in England. When I received it, I saw that it was a 12-inch vertically mounted tube that was split into red, green, and white sectors by a plastic housing. For a drain of only 0.8 amp, according to the manufacturer, I had a light equivalent to a 40-watt incandescent bulb. Indeed, I found the white stern sector so bright that I had to make a shield to keep the light out of my eyes when I was steering at night.

The masthead light was certainly brighter than the bronze teardrop lights on the pulpit, and my sailing friends all commented on its prominence aloft. The device drew less than half the current of the lights on deck. However, the separation from red to green to white was poor. At 2 miles I could see a blob of color but not distinct bands of vivid red and green. The word *vivid* didn't apply at all. *Murky* was better.

But murky or milky, it was an improvement, and it convinced me that the masthead is the best place for navigation signals. A light high up is unobstructed by waves or sails or anything else and is away from salt spray.

Thirty years ago, my friend Bernard Hayman, then the editor of the English magazine *Yachting World*, made a study of yacht lighting, with the following conclusions.

- Six- or 12-watt bulbs mounted behind thick glass and powered by partially discharged batteries are scarcely visible at 1 mile.
- In order to achieve proper red and green colors and to maximize light transmission, plastic or glass lenses must be carefully selected for color, density, and thickness.

- The smaller the light source, the better. A vertical-filament tungsten light bulb is far superior to the wide field of a fluorescent tube.
- In a combined port-and-starboard lantern, the width of the dividing support pillar facing forward is critical. A centerline metal divider between the red and green sectors on one commercial light caused a blind zone of 15 degrees. Bernard found that by eliminating the metal divider entirely and substituting edge-glued colored acrylic, he was able to reduce the sector of confusion from 15 degrees to 2 or 3 degrees.

A few years later, three firms were making such light fixtures (one has survived). Today the German firm Aqua Signal AG in Bremen controls most of the navigation light business for large and small vessels. The company's products are made of plastic and stainless steel and the lenses are constructed of thin, edge-glued acrylic. For yachts the cylindrical lights use vertical-filament bulbs of 10 or 25 watts, and the lamps are available in a variety of sizes for masthead, bow pulpit, or stern mountings.

I was in Buenos Aires when these lights were first made and sent to Germany for one of the masthead units. When it arrived, I was surprised at the large size of the fixture. Measured on the lantern itself, the area of each color lens was 12.25 square inches. One night on the grounds of the Yacht Club Argentino in San Fernando, Margaret and I compared the Aqua Signal lantern (using a 25 W vertical-filament bulb) with the fluorescent light at *Whisper*'s masthead. The color saturation and the brightness of the new light were outstanding; it was superior close up and plainly visible at 2 miles. The cutoff between the different colors was sharp and decisive.

With a 10-watt bulb at 1 mile, the brightness was less but acceptable. I junked the fluorescent masthead unit and since 1975, I have sailed with the German light with a 25-watt bulb. I feel that my navigation lights are a dozen times better than the toy fixtures on the bow pulpit that I once had. The current demand for the 25-watt bulb is 2.08 amperes, or 16.6 ampere-hours for an 8-hour night. The 10-watt bulb draws 0.83 ampere, or 6.6 ampere-hours for 8 hours. More recently, I purchased a tall model of an Aqua Signal masthead light that includes a separate chamber for an all-around white anchor light.

Aqua Signal AG says that the life of a 12- or 24-volt vertical-filament bulb is 1,200–1,500 hours. Unfortunately, recreational boats are usually not equipped with power stabilizers to limit voltage, and when the engine is running, the charger may supply 13.8–14.4 or 27.6–28.8 volts. This 20 percent excess voltage will reduce the life of the bulb by 80 percent. This means a reduction from 1,350 hours to 270 hours. Many electrical items on board are hit by overcharging, but lightbulb filaments suffer particularly.

While the masthead unit is excellent for sailing, it's illegal when motoring. For these times, I must carry a white light (or "steaming light") above the sidelights. In practice this means I need two sidelights and a sternlight at deck level and a white, forward-facing 225-degree light up on the mast. This is no burden, however, because it gives me spare lights in case the masthead light burns out at sea, and legal running lights if I fire up the engine. Whew! You need to be a lawyer to keep track of all this.

The collision regulations provide proper guidance, and the lamps that I've discussed are good lights. Nevertheless, many small-boat sailors with thousands of miles of ocean sailing behind them together with many big-ship captains believe that powerful *white lights* provide the most safety for small vessels. A white light has the best visibility by far and is the most efficient product for a given amperage. No ship's officer is going to ignore a bright white light at sea. Yet for it to be effective, the light should have a 3-mile range.

What do big-ship operators say?

"The distance from the bow to the bridge of a merchantman can be anywhere from 250 to 1,000 feet (a supertanker). That's a long way for the mate to see a 30-foot sailboat, especially if visibility is not 100 percent," writes Captain Paul E. Lobo of Portland, Oregon. "Remember that a one-mile sidelight looks pretty tiny from the bridge of a ship 50 feet above the water going 15 knots."[37]

His message is echoed by Captain Cornelis J. Kalkman, master of the giant oceangoing Dutch tug *Rode Zee*.

"On clear nights, most ships have only one man on the bridge. He does not normally use radar unless he is approaching land. The lights on a yacht are too close to the water to be seen from a ship, especially the red and green lights. In fact, the best red and green navigation lights on a large ship are only visible two or three miles in clear weather. Since a tugboat towing a ship needs three to five miles to turn enough to clear an object, there is a large danger to an unwary yacht.

"Yachts should always assume that a ship within a mile of them has not seen their lights," continues Captain Kalkman, "because on a ship with its bridge aft, the angle of view leaves a blind area for at least 600 yards in front of the ship."

Even worse must be the view forward from the enormous commercial ships that rush around the oceans of the world with their decks piled high with hundreds of containers stacked like chips on a craps table.

"I would show a 360° white light either at the masthead or as high in the rig-

ging as possible, where it wouldn't be blocked by the sails," Captain Kalkman con-
cludes. "Check your lights by setting them while at anchor and then leaving your
boat. If your white light is not visible at least three miles, get a brighter one."[38]

I have spent hundreds of nights on watch at sea, and there's nothing I respect
more than a solitary white light above a fishing boat. I know there are crew members asleep and I give their little ship a wide berth and quietly wish them good fishing tomorrow. According to the rules of the road, a boat that stops at sea while the
crew sleeps or makes repairs or whatever should show two all-around red lights,
one above the other, to indicate that the vessel is not under command. In the real
world, you seldom see these lights; instead, you pick up a white light, which is
much more visible.

This advice goes in two directions: either find more amperes and a bigger bulb
or keep out of the way of large vessels. For safety, I always try to pass *behind* big
ships, even if I have to slow down or make a drastic course change.

A third option might be to increase visibility through technology. I've heard
rumors of navigation lights under development that are to be powered by light-
emitting diodes (LEDs). Perhaps we'll be told to employ halogen or other types of
yet-uninvented bulbs or to use the strobe lights that we see on airplanes. But new
light bulbs belong to the future, and strobe lights are currently illegal. In the meantime, do your sleeping in the daytime so you'll be rested at night.

Show me a sailor who has never been aground and I'll show you a liar. Here you see the Golden Feather, *an early Roth yacht, on a sandbank on the Sacramento River after the captain took a clever shortcut. Margaret and I are waiting for the flood tide to lift us off the bank. I see that I had an anchor out toward deep water. I also notice that the port mast spreader needs a little adjustment.*

16

STORM MANAGEMENT 1:
HEAVING TO AND
LYING AHULL

There are far fewer storms than people think, and those that occur are over-publicized. To cover themselves, weathermen always predict the worst, the most severe, the longest lasting. What often happens is that the rain is fleeting, the strong wind is transitory, and the big gale has headed off somewhere else. But in the popular imagination, it's one tempest after another.

Journalists and authors are no better. If you read a dozen books about sailors at sea, nine or ten of them will tire you out with talk about giant waves, blown-out sails, smashed masts, exhaustion, desperation, and worse.

A favorite tactic is to recount one horror story after another. By stacking up these tales, writers try for blanket effects, perhaps thinking they're influencing juries in murder cases. On television, meteorologists turn up the sound, and show us the same storm footage over and over.

Sailors are not entirely innocent, either. When they're interviewed about their experiences, waves 15 feet high grow into 30-footers. A gale becomes a storm-force

Heading north-northwest from Guam toward Kagoshima, Japan, in late February.

wind. Unpleasantness turns into misery. Half the time, sailors laugh behind their listeners' backs as they recount the ferocity and frequency of storms. Of course there are some, but sailing is not all storms. If the conditions were like what we read about, no one would ever go to sea.

In my experience I've found more light winds and calms than gales. During my last trip around the world, I kept accurate records of weather, and when I added up the numbers, I was surprised to learn that I was becalmed 11 percent of the time. Dead calm. No wind. No seas. Nothing! And this voyage was mostly in the Southern Ocean. Of course there were a few storms, but there were also weeks of pleasant sailing in winds of 10–25 knots.

Every year thousands of small sailboats make safe, unpublicized voyages across long stretches of ocean. Only the stories of a few unfortunates find their way into the newspapers. Nevertheless, the weather gets nasty once in a while, and we need to consider how to deal with unruly seas and strong winds.

The most authoritative book on storms versus small ships is *Heavy Weather Sailing*, by Adlard Coles, a morose catalog of chilling nautical disasters and near disasters. The book is gloomy but fascinating, and as you plow through one horror story after another, you can hardly put the book down. In fact, you can scarcely see the print through your tears.

The best capsule summary of storm management I know of is the appendix to Miles Smeeton's *Because the Horn Is There*. Another useful chapter is by Erroll Bruce in his *Deep Sea Sailing* (chapter 14). My favorite is Bernard Moitessier's *The Long Way*, an absorbing study of long ocean passages, charmingly written, with a practical appendix that details many aspects of heavy going, including a lucid discussion of swell and sea conditions and how they relate to passing weather depressions.

Yet all these writers give advice with caution and readily admit to many unanswered questions.[39]

During the last thirty years, there has been a great deal of ocean cruising by small sailing vessels, and we have the benefit of many books and articles. Let's see what a careful look can tell us.

The first rule of survival for a boat in a storm is to keep away from the shore. The insurance companies that want you to stay near the land and avoid deep water have it all wrong. It's along the shore where the rocks and the shoals are, and where you get into trouble.

What you want—if you can't reach a sheltered anchorage before the storm arrives—is to find adequate sea room far from rocks, beaches, landforms of any kind, and moving water (strong tidal areas, river mouths, and strait entrances). If the shore is to the east, then you head west. If the shore is toward the west, then sail east (or northeast or southeast, whichever gives you the better slant for an offing). You must gain and maintain adequate sea room. If the wind is directly onshore, you need to get out 30 or 40 miles and continue to head away from land. This is a fundamental rule of sailing. When bad weather comes, only the foolish and inexperienced linger near a shore where there's no shelter. The other captains have gone to sea.

But how are you going to know the duration of a storm? Eric Hiscock once got into a heavy gale near Tonga in the South Pacific that lasted four days, during which he was blown to leeward 120 miles. Bad weather of this duration is unusual, however. Most storms move more rapidly and often perform to set seasonal patterns. Usually there's a major wind shift in twenty-four hours.

It's fun and good practice to sail the anchor out (see page 215) each time you leave a harbor or an anchorage. The drill is a satisfying exercise that may save you if an onshore wind blows up when the engine is not working and it's time to leave.

If you have sufficient sea room and so much wind and sea that further sailing is undesirable or impossible, you have six choices.

- heave to
- lie ahull
- run with the storm
- deploy a conical or parachute sea anchor from the bow
- slow the boat with a stern drogue
- put out oil

HEAVE TO

This maneuver is simply tacking the ship without releasing the headsail sheet. As the yacht turns through the eye of the wind, the headsail is backwinded, which pushes the vessel's head to leeward. The tiller is then lashed to leeward. (If you steer with a wheel, you turn the top of the wheel to windward or the upwind side. This moves the back of the rudder to windward.)

The backed headsail and opposing rudder tend to balance one another. Generally, by the time you decide to heave to, the wind is substantial and you have small sails up. This means there will be no trouble with the clew of a backed genoa chafing itself to death on the weather shrouds.

Because of the considerable drag of the inefficient headsail and the offset rudder, the ship almost stops, but not quite. She jogs along slowly (the term for this is *forereaching*) at perhaps $\frac{1}{2}$ knot or more in order for her rudder to have enough effect to offset the opposite push of the strong wind on her headsail or bow structures. Meanwhile, the wind shoves the yacht sideways at $1\frac{1}{2}$ to 2 knots or faster. A sailboat's behavior when hove to depends on her design. A heavy-displacement boat with a long keel may almost stop; a light-displacement vessel with a narrow fin keel and a big rig may continue to push ahead at 2 or 3 knots no matter how the captain adjusts the sails and the rudder. But regardless of the design, the hove-to yacht floats more quietly and easily because she has slowed down in relation to the opposing turmoil on the ocean.

When sailors speak of heaving to, they're referring to a range of maneuvers that slow and ease the motion of a sailing vessel. This can be as simple as tacking without releasing the headsail sheet, or it may require lowering or rolling up a headsail completely and heading into the wind with a deeply reefed mainsail or trysail and adjusting the helm to leeward. Some yachts will lie quietly; others will persist in bearing off or heading up, with the sails filling and emptying with cannonlike reports and violent shaking that's hard on both the sails and the nerves of the crew.

I have heard sailors say that to be properly hove to means that all forward motion must be stopped and that the boat is "parked." But if this is true, the vessel will not stay headed up toward the wind because her rudder will have no effect. To keep from blowing off like an abandoned barge, the boat must have a little forward movement.

"In practice," Eric Hiscock says, "the term 'heaving-to' is used rather loosely to cover varying degrees of lying-to."[40] Note that this is distinct from lying ahull, which I discuss later in this chapter.

In the past, my wife and I have occasionally hove to for celestial sights. When a position line was important, we often found that the star or sun was to windward on a spray-dashed deck, or that a sail masked the moon or Polaris. Perhaps we wanted to shoot a round of stars at dusk or dawn. It made sense to stop, and heaving to slowed us down for only a few minutes. Then we were able to shoot the heavenly bodies in any direction from a relatively smooth platform and to keep salt water away from the sextant and navigator and his timepiece.

With satellite navigation (GPS) alive and well on practically every yacht these days, the sextant is less important. Still, if you've been bashing to windward for days, it's nice to stop the vessel and let the cook operate in a galley that's not lurching up and down. (It's smart to wear oilskins when cooking if the motion is severe. The oilskins are clumsy to work in, but they're a good way to prevent burns.) When you're stopped, you can cook a meal, plot your position coordinates on a chart, perhaps improve the reef on a tied-down sail, and secure any loose gear that's been banging around on deck.

We have often hove to ten or fifteen miles away from a strange port to wait for daylight. If it's 0230, and dawn is only a few hours away, it's foolish to risk a night entry when a daylight move is much safer, more pleasant, and you can see where you're going. Always take great care not to sail too close to a new place, particularly in fog or at night, because a squall, tidal stream, or current can run you ashore before you're ready. You don't want any surprises in the middle of the night.

When a vessel is hove to, how does she lie in relation to the wind? This depends on the configuration of her keel, the windage aloft, and whether there is a mizzen. Old sailing books talk about "the grip" of a long keel on the water—that is, the ability of the boat to resist blowing off to leeward. Generally, the longer the keel, the more a small vessel will put her shoulder into the wind. The ability of a long-keeled English design like a Bristol Channel pilot cutter—which has a waterline length of about 40 feet—to head up when she is hove to is legendary.

During many voyages on our first 35-foot *Whisper* (which had a long keel with an attached rudder), we hove to quite well with a working jib (or smaller sail) and a reefed main- or trysail in winds up to 35 knots. The sails stabilized the vessel and eased the rolling. Our heading was 40–50 degrees off the wind, while the yacht made good a course of 90–100 degrees off the wind. That is, if the wind was from the north and we were hove to on the port tack, our heading was northeast and our actual course made good was east (say 90°–105°). Our speed forward was 0.5 knot; our drift to leeward was about 1.5 knots.

Our present *Whisper* (also 35 feet) has a large fin keel and a good-sized rudder and skeg and has about the same numbers except that she sails a little faster when hove to, even with a small jib.

Modern designs with minimal wetted area have much less grip and consequently do not heave to as well. *American Flag*, my ultralight-displacement Santa Cruz 50, had a narrow fin keel and a spade rudder. With her, heaving to was not entirely successful because it's hard to slow such designs, but it still proved helpful. I remember so well trying to sail the last 380 miles into Cape Town, South Africa (from the west), against a 40-knot southeaster in 1990.

The seas were large and fairly regular, but steep, rough, and nasty, perhaps from the influence of the northwest-running Benguela current along the west coast of Africa. Cape Town was almost dead to windward and I feared for the rig because the vessel was hammering dreadfully, even with three reefs in the mainsail and a deeply reefed jib on the headstay. When I hove to, however, the boat slowed from 7 knots to 3½ knots; the strains eased, and I was able to eat something and sleep. Thirty-five hours later, the wind backed to the south and began to lighten. Soon I was charging toward my target under full sail.

During the 1985–86 round-the-world Whitbread Race, a group of six 80-foot maxi yachts (with crews of up to 22) battled the same sort of southeast winds and seas near Cape Town. The hulls of two of these million-dollar superboats began to break up, a third was dismasted, and a fourth suffered major rig damage. The other two—with white-knuckled crews—finished OK.

In my judgment, these handsome big boats would have been far better off to have stopped trying to hammer their way to windward in gale-force winds and huge seas. I think it's better to lose a day or two than to arrive broken, battered, and desperate for major repairs. If the four damaged yachts had slowed down and waited for better conditions, they would have arrived intact, *and earlier than they did in the end*.

In mathematical terms, such an experience might read

$$\frac{\text{spirit \& enthusiasm}}{\text{judgment}} = \text{common sense*}$$

As the wind increases, the sails on a hove-to vessel push the ship increasingly to leeward until she begins to labor like a half-tide rock. Irregular seas and blasts of wind may upset the balance between the rudder and the backed headsail. If a sea strikes aft of the midships area and turns the bow to windward, the boat will tack and the jib will fill. This will make the yacht pay off, gybe, and then head up again.

If the wind pressure on the jib increases and overpowers the rudder, the bow will fall off to leeward. The unbalanced boat will begin a crablike course downwind until the mainsail gybes and swings her around into the wind again. All this will be accompanied by violent lurches as the boat heels first to starboard and then to port while the reefed sails slam from side to side. A little trial-and-error adjustment on the rudder offset or the headsail sheet or area often resolves these problems.

The good news is that with sufficient sea room, most yachts can deal with storms by simply heaving to. Depending on your latitude, I estimate that this step will be sufficient to get through storms 75 percent of the time. The bad news is that if the storm increases and the yacht's motion and behavior are clearly unsafe, it's time to bestir yourself to further action—just when you feel like doing nothing at all.

To Lie Ahull

To lie ahull means to let the vessel skid slowly sideways before the seas and wind without any sail up. Generally, you lash the tiller a little alee, that is, toward the downwind side, to keep the ship's head from falling off. Because of her keel, a yacht will usually assume a position at right angles to the wind, with the seas broad on the beam. This sounds dangerous, but if the wind has been blowing from a single direction for a number of hours, and there is plenty of water depth, the seas are often quite regular and the boat will ride reasonably well before the storm. If you're near a weather shore, the seas will have had no room (fetch) to build up.

What are the conditions for this storm maneuver? The answer depends on the size of the yacht, the strength of the wind, and the sea conditions, which can range from waves and swells of, say, ten feet to truly tumultuous conditions. I have used heaving to as a storm or stopping tactic in wind strengths of 20 to 35 knots. I have

*Alas, judgment multiplied by common sense does not equal spirit and enthusiasm!

employed lying ahull as a storm tactic in winds from 35 to 45 knots, but these are only vague and general guidelines.

When lying ahull, the boat appears to make a *slick*—an area of smooth water— to windward, and the seas slide past. At first the noise and motion are alarming, but as long as there are no breaking or irregular seas, you can get along tolerably well. One problem is that when you lie broadside to the sea without any sail up, the rolling can be terrible. However, some yachts don't roll at all and merely heel as the wind whistles past. It appears that the relationship between the beam and keel depth is a factor. Under these circumstances, a schooner may have an advantage because the windage of her mainmast and main boom keep her partially headed up into the storm. If there's danger to leeward, you may be able to adjust the tiller slightly to miss

If a sea breaks on board, there's both the weight of the water plus the driving force of the wave. This 37-foot Chris Craft Apache sloop got into difficulty with breaking waves off San Francisco's Golden Gate and was lucky not to have been sunk. The coachroof structure was made of a plastic sandwich without adequate fiberglass layup above and below the foam. It looks nice but has no strength. This is OK for a kitchen cabinet in a house, but not for a boat that goes to sea. Note the long cracks in the brittle filler, the missing portlights, and the crushed companionway. A vertical post inside the cabin near the hatch would have helped support the cabin structure.

any downwind targets, but this may interfere with the windward slick.

John Letcher suggests that in heaving to or lying ahull, sailors should consider the difference between the port and starboard tacks. As a storm progresses, the wind generally changes direction slightly (usually veering in the Northern Hemisphere) while the seas continue to roll in from the old direction. Unless the drift of the yacht is straight downwind, one tack or the other will send the slick off in the direction the waves are coming from and give the boat more shelter.

"When either lying ahull or heaving to," Letcher writes, "one tack will put the waves more on the bow, the other tack will put them more on your quarter. This can make a lot of difference in the motion and wetness."[41]

The danger in lying ahull with the seas broad on the beam is considerable, and you need to make this move with caution and a careful evaluation of sea conditions. If the swells are confused, the wind shifts, or the storm increases, the seas may get *out of phase* with one another. Then it's possible that a whopper may break near or on top of the vessel and overwhelm her with tons of water. The argument can also be made for seas that get *into phase* with one another and augment already existing high seas. Whatever the cause, a sea that thunders on board means trouble.

"Every cubic meter of sea water contains slightly more than one ton of mass," writes Captain William Kielhorn in *Sail* magazine. "A breaking sea wave may easily contain 500 tons or more, curling and racing downslope at speeds up to 20 or 30 knots."[42]

Even a small breaking sea is extremely dangerous. Think of a waterfall suddenly landing on top of the vessel and shoving her bodily to leeward. The impact is the same as being dropped on concrete. Damage almost always occurs on the leeward side of the boat and can mean a stove-in coachroof or collapsed portlights. The force of the water can easily carry away pulpits as well as furled sails, dinghies, and deck gear.

Breaking waves appear to be of two types:

- a spilling breaker with a quantity of foam tumbling ahead of the crest of the wave
- a plunging breaker where solid water is thrown forward in an arc or jet from the crest

"In a spilling breaker," writes Letcher, "the foam (a mixture of air and water) is clearly moving at the same speed as the wave crest. However, it is relatively light (mostly air) and compressible and so doesn't pack much of a punch, unless there's an awful lot of it.

"In a plunging breaker, the water in the jet is actually traveling faster than the wave crest, and is 'solid' water (i.e., doesn't have air mixed in it). A plunging breaker is much more threatening."[43]

It's well documented that a breaking sea can flip a ballasted monohull right over. Most boats will right themselves, but the damage may be considerable. I've always marveled at the account of Joe Byar's 39-foot yawl *Doubloon* on a supposedly easy trip along the east coast of the United States. *Doubloon*, with four men aboard, left St. Augustine, Florida, on the northeast coast of the state, on a pleasant day in May. The goal of the boat was Morehead City, North Carolina, 360 miles north, near Cape Hatteras. The barometer was high and the weather forecasts from several sources were good.

The next day an unreported force 10 northeast storm that gusted above hurricane strength slammed into the yacht. The wind blew directly against the northeast-flowing Gulf Stream, and the seas became tumultuous. During a period of 16 hours, the yacht was rolled over twice in huge breakers. In addition, four enormous waves crashed on board. *Doubloon* not only lost her entire rig and almost everything on deck, but the water's force even bent her ¾-inch bronze centerboard and partially tore off a sheet winch![44]

In our long-keeled *Whisper*, we have lain ahull a dozen times or more, certainly under far easier conditions than poor *Doubloon* faced. Sometimes *Whisper* has been in upset water, which has shoved us to leeward hard enough to put the spreaders in the water. During one storm, the sea's force ruined the bow and stern pulpits, shattered the rudder shaft head fitting, and tore away a storm jib.

From this we learned never to lash the tiller with heavy line, but to use shock cord that will stretch or break. I've mentioned elsewhere not to furl sails along the lifelines or deck but to bag the sails and carry them below or to stuff them in a locker. I've found that stout canvas bunk cloths or automotive-type seat belts will keep the crew safe.

Lockers with heavy items should be stoutly hinged along one side and have strong, bolt-type closures so that you will not be attacked by flying tools, avalanches of canned goods, or showers of glass fragments from broken bottles. Consider partitioning large stowage lockers into smaller, safer units (in which it's easier to keep track of things). Floorboards should be well screwed down. When single-hander Eric Hall was rolled over in the Roaring Forties west of Chile a few years ago, he was almost wiped out by an airborne anchor and chain he'd stored in the bilges of *Manuma*, his Nicholson 32.

I'll say it again. You must avoid lying ahull in big seas that have begun to break. Otherwise, you may get into real trouble. This has been documented repeatedly in all oceans. To take another example from many, consider the unfortunate voyage of the Contest 31 sloop *Banjo* en route from Bermuda to Long Island in the United States.

During a mid-July passage, the crew went through the usual sail reductions as the giant winds of Hurricane Blanche began to swirl around the Dutch-built vessel.

Crew member Alfred Boylen reported that in a few hours the seas had built "to fifty feet or more with big surfs." The vessel lay ahull while the captain and the two crew members were in their bunks.

"About 2000 [hours] we felt a big lift, an almost weightless drop and a sudden stop with a crash that reverberated as though we were inside a kettle drum," Boylen said. "A second later another shudder ran through the ship along with a slashing roar as the crest of the wave from which we had dropped fell on top of us while we lay in the trough. We estimated that we had dropped 50 feet on our side from a crest into a trough."

Banjo was lying ahull in a hurricane. If we assume a 60-knot wind blowing across a 100-mile sweep of ocean, the waves would have been 35 feet high. The distance between crests would have measured 390 feet and one of these monsters would have rolled past *Banjo* every 8.5 seconds (see the tables in Bowditch).

The men in *Banjo* were being speeded up, slowed down, and rotated all the time and probably had no idea of their orientation at any given moment or a proper understanding of what the waves were doing.

When the yacht fell off the wave that damaged her, the wave would have been traveling at 26 knots, or about 44 feet per second. It's unclear whether the wave broke on top of *Banjo* or the yacht fell off the top of the wave or somewhere down its face.

Banjo may have

- ridden up on a breaker that was about to plunge ("a big lift")
- been airborne on her way downward ("an almost weightless drop")
- landed in solid water with a bone-crushing thump ("a sudden stop with a crash that reverberated as though we were inside a kettle drum")

Of course each situation is different, and the precise battle encounter between a small boat and an enormous breaking wave may be impossible to chronicle. However, we know that poor *Banjo* was severely damaged. Her rudder was jammed, and water poured in from a 6-foot split in the fiberglass hull. In spite of five pumps, the crew's damage control efforts failed. Sixteen hours later, with the storm over and a big ship standing by, the three men abandoned the yacht.[45]

In a postmortem discussion, the crew blamed faulty boat construction. My feeling is that no vessel—large or small—can be expected to survive fifty-foot drops and avalanches of tons of water without significant damage, no matter what the hull material. In my judgment, the crew should have run *Banjo* off before the storm or taken more aggressive action, as I will discuss in the next chapter.

When conditions allow you to lie ahull, it's still unnerving to be in your bunk, listening to the seas hissing past hour after hour and wondering whether the weather is getting better or worse. Again and again the seas slide up and then race away with great bubbling sounds. You doze off. When you awaken and look out, you realize the rolling has lessened and the storm is moving off. The clouds are clearing. There's sunshine here and there! The storm is over. It's time to put up some sails and get moving again.

But if the storm intensifies and you hear a crash in the distance as a big wave topples into a mass of white foam, it's time to bestir yourself. The roar of a breaking wave is a signal to change your tactics before water lands on board. You must summon your reserves of energy, think clearly, and wear your safety harness.

It's time to run off.

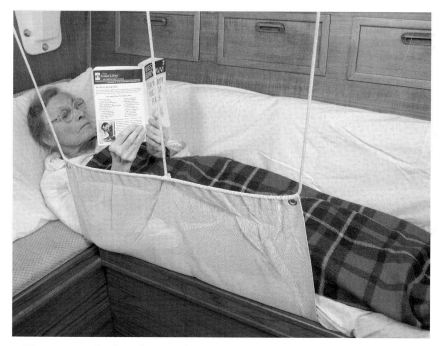

No matter whether the weather is light or heavy, it's important that all members of the crew get plenty of sleep. Tired people are grouchy and sometimes make bum decisions. Each crew member should have his or her own bunk with a lee cloth, sheets and blankets, a comfortable pillow, a shelf or drawer for personal items, and hopefully a reading light. The berth should be wide enough to be comfortable but snug enough to hold you when the boat rolls. Pay particular attention that the lee cloth is strong, high, and well fastened. Its length should reach only as far as your hips or a little more. If the lee cloth is the full length of the bunk, it is impossible to get in or out easily and quickly. With a 40-inch lee cloth, you can sit at the foot of the bunk and swing your legs in or out. I took this photograph aboard our current Whisper *in 2003.*

STORM MANAGEMENT 2: RUNNING OFF

In the last chapter, I stressed the danger of a lee shore and the importance of sea room. I then outlined six ways of dealing with storms when further sailing was undesirable or impossible. The six options were

- heave to
- lie ahull
- run with the storm
- deploy a conical or parachute sea anchor from the bow
- slow the boat with a stern drogue
- put out oil

We started out by heaving to. When the storm worsened, we lay ahull. Now the waves have grown in size and are threatening or beginning to break. Our next move is to *run with the storm*.

Running off in large seas north of the Kerguelen islands in the southern Indian Ocean at 49° S.

*   *   *

In large, chaotic seas, sailors generally choose to turn tail and flee before the storm, simply because it's the easiest thing to do. You don't need any special equipment or techniques; just steer downwind and keep the stern or one of the stern quarters dead before big overtaking waves. You need plenty of sea room, of course, since it's imperative to stay away from land because of the danger from shoaling water or, God forbid, the shore itself.

If there's a problem to leeward, you may be able to angle your course slightly to steer clear of an island or, with care, to work yourself into a sheltered bay. If you're traveling away from your goal, you will want to sail as slowly as possible. If you're trying to get somewhere, you can speed up a little.

You can run under bare poles, or maybe hoist a little of the head of a jib to help the steering. In winds strong enough to force you to run off under bare poles, the resistance of the mast, boom, rigging, and hull can easily drive your boat at 4 or 5 knots. (If not, the wind may be less strong than you think.)

There is certainly no mystery about running off before a storm. It's one of the few things you can do if the waves behind are steep and threaten to break, and you can hear them out there booming and crashing into acres of upset water. The only good thing about this dreadful scenario, at least in my experience, is that storms violent enough to make you run off are usually fast-moving and spin away in a day or so. Then it's back to normal sailing.

What about trailing lines or drogues to control speed and to hold the yacht end-on to an overtaking wave to prevent broaches and capsizes when running before a storm?

In the past, at least two very experienced captains (Vito Dumas and Bernard Moitessier) advocated keeping a boat moving at speed *without* warps. When a giant sea approached the yacht from dead astern, each of these helmsmen changed course and headed away by 20 degrees or so.[46]

This meant that the yacht took the wave a little on the quarter and that any push forward imparted a slight rolling and turning motion to the boat. Instead of burying the bow head-on, the vessel raced forward with her leeward bow sections "resting on the water like a ski."[47]

When Moitessier sailed his 39-foot steel ketch *Joshua* in a great storm in the high latitudes of the Southern Ocean in 1965, colossal breaking seas from different directions threatened to destroy his vessel. The French sailor cut loose a cluster of warps, weights, and nets that he was towing. Then under bare poles and going at 5 knots, he was able to bear off 15 to 20 degrees as the giant seas passed. He managed to skid away from "enormous breakers that looked as though they were about to smash everything to pieces."[48] This required long hours of active and alert steering by Moitessier and his wife, Françoise. This was especially difficult at night.

Hand steering in order to cope with overtaking seas is fine until the crew becomes so exhausted that errors in judgment add up to a bigger hazard than the overtaking seas. Of course, there are circumstances (short-duration storms; lee-shore conditions; a large, skilled crew) in which hand steering is in order. With a shorthanded crew, it's usually up to the boat (helped by possible sail, drogue, sea anchor, autopilot, or steering vane assistance) to deal with the storm.

Other experts (Joshua Slocum, Conor O'Brien, W. A. Robinson) have written that their main tactic is to keep large waves dead astern and to stream long warps to slow the yacht.[49]

During a violent storm, a sailboat is like a nervous cat trying to sneak down an alley patrolled by big, nasty, snarling dogs. You need to play for time; to get through a patch of rough sea; to hurry the clock ahead.

Sailing authority Eric Hiscock says that a boat moving close to hull speed causes greater turbulence and angrier-looking seas astern. Usually a slight easing of speed immediately reduces the evil-looking crests sliding up behind, he says.[50] But if you're running off under bare poles and want to slow down, how do you do it?

Sailors often drag heavy lines to slow and steady their vessels, as Joshua Slocum did in the *Spray* during a frightful gale near Cape Horn more than a century ago. (How little the sea and sailboat handling have changed over time.)

"On the morning of March 4 [1896] the wind shifted to southwest, then backed suddenly to northwest, and blew with terrific force," Slocum wrote. "The *Spray*, stripped of her sails, then bore off under bare poles. No ship in the world could have stood up against so violent a gale. . . . Anyhow, for my present safety the only course lay in keeping her before the wind. . . . She was running now with a reefed forestaysail, the sheets flat amidship. I paid out two long ropes to steady her course and to break combing seas astern, and I lashed the helm amidship. In this trim she ran before it, shipping never a sea."[51]

Tom Steele, who circumnavigated twice in *Adios*, a heavy-displacement, slightly lengthened 32-foot Tahiti ketch, wrote about his adventures with two hurricanes off the coast of Baja California. With adequate sea room and under bare poles, he dragged 300 feet of 1-inch-diameter nylon line with an anchor at the end. This drag produced an even, powerful strain at all times, and his 32-foot boat remained stern to, moving at $1\frac{1}{2}$ to 2 knots. Steele found this method superior to using a warp alone, which may skip ahead when the boat surges forward, just when more strain is needed.[52]

The English sailor Robin Knox-Johnston spent $10\frac{1}{2}$ months sailing his double-ended 32-foot *Suhaili* to victory in the 1968–69 solo round-the-world nonstop race. Knox-Johnston wrote that before the race he had always left her beam-on to the seas in gales. However, in the Southern Ocean, the seas were so big that he feared *Suhaili* would be bludgeoned to pieces.

During a force 10, 48- to 55-knot wind, Knox-Johnston streamed 720 feet of $\frac{5}{8}$-inch-diameter floating line in a U-shaped bight. Each arm of the U was 360 feet long and provided some stretch. He also set a tiny 40-square-foot storm jib that he sheeted midships.

"I got out the blue polypropylene line and put the whole coil out astern, both ends made fast to the kingpost forward and led aft," he wrote. "The bight seemed to be on the horizon, but it dragged the stern up to the wind. . . . From rolling beam on to the seas without it, and being terribly battered, we were suddenly lying very quietly stern to seas, which were occasionally breaking over the decks. We were pooped twice but not heavily."[53]

The small white ketch slowly drifted to leeward. Thanks to the rope's stretch, however, *Suhaili* was never subjected to jerking, even when riding over the steepest waves. During the latter part of the storm, Knox-Johnston was amazed to find the foredeck dry. He stressed the importance of the long floating warp to absorb shocks, as opposed to a short but heavily weighted bight that might alternatively skip and drag.

Note that Knox-Johnston's experiences with a 720-foot U-shaped floating warp and Tom Steele's use of a 100-foot warp with an anchor on the end directly conflict with the storm tactics of Bernard Moitessier and Vito Dumas. The French and Argentine sailors liked running at moderate speed and bearing off slightly at the passage of a big sea *without* dragging lines or drogues to slow their vessels.

The well-known Polish aerodynamicist C. A. Marchaj has published a paper that—in theory, at least—seems to reconcile these two different types of storm management when running before heavy weather. As we have seen, each procedure has adherents with impressive experience.

Professor Marchaj suggests that both may be correct. In the early stages of a severe storm, the waves may be very steep and may well cause broaching. However, after a high wind—say, 50 knots or more—has been blowing for a number of hours, the waves become longer and not so steep as their velocity increases. Marchaj postulates that early in the storm, the best tactic is to stream warps to stabilize the vessel directionally and to prevent broaching and dangerous surfing. Later in the storm,

This is the famous Spray *of Boston that Captain Joshua Slocum, a professional master mariner, sailed around the world from 1895 to 1898 during a voyage of 46,000 miles. Captain Slocum rebuilt the* Spray *from a derelict oyster sloop that had been abandoned in Fairhaven, Massachusetts, and the sturdy wooden yawl served him well. The photograph was taken at the Miami Boat Works in 1908, just prior to the vessel being lost at sea. She looks to be in poor condition: her gaff mainsail rig has been changed to a simple three-cornered leg-of-mutton sail. Captain Slocum, dressed in a white shirt, tie, and apron, is yarning with the man below. It's this utterly simple vessel, this man with unabated gusto for life, and his wonderful account titled* Sailing Alone Around the World *that largely initiated the world of long-distance small-boat sailing that we know today.*

Miles and Beryl Smeeton aboard Tzu Hang.

however, when the velocity of the waves is greater, the use of warps should be discontinued. The yacht should be speeded up to minimize the difference in velocity between the vessel and the overtaking seas. In other words, use warps early in the storm to control broaching; run at near hull speed later on to lessen the chance of getting overwhelmed by giant waves.[54]

In his book on heavy weather, Earl Hinz mentions that Shewman Inc. of Safety Harbor, Florida, a company that makes parachute sea anchors and drogues, tried streaming 170 feet of 2¼-inch-diameter line behind a tug at 10½ knots. The test engineers found that the total drag of the line was *less* than the 300 pounds needed to activate the tension meter from which the line was tied. The inference is that towed lines by themselves are useless.[55]

On February 14, 1957, a little after breakfast, Beryl Smeeton sat in the cockpit carefully steering *Tzu Hang*, a handsome 46-foot bermudian ketch en route from Australia to Uruguay. The boat was 50 days out from Melbourne, about 1,150 miles from Cape Horn. Her position was 51° S, 97° W.

Tzu Hang was headed to the east before a strong westerly gale with big following seas. A little earlier, the two men on board had taken down the last of the sails, and the ketch was running under bare poles. The wind was increasing, so the captain, Miles Smeeton, and the crew, John Guzzwell, let out 360 feet of heavy line from the stern to slow the yacht. Miles reckoned their speed was 4 knots. The hawser didn't make much difference because when a breaking crest overtook the boat, it carried the line with it and temporarily halved its length.

The wind continued to increase.

Beryl gave the steering all her attention as the great seas whooshed up from astern, overtook the slim white ketch with the graceful canoe stern, and roared onward as they passed. Usually there were albatrosses circling the yacht, but now they were gone.

Beryl glanced astern and saw a monstrous wave approaching. The face of the wave was extremely high and steep. "Much higher than *Tzu Hang* was long," she said later. It was a real Southern Ocean graybeard.

"This was a wall of water with a completely vertical face, down which ran white ripples of water, like a waterfall. . . . I had the stern at dead right angles to the wall. There was nothing more that I could do."

Beryl did not know how the yacht could rise above what was coming. All she could think of was the height and steepness of the giant breaking wave.

The back of the yacht was picked up until she tripped forward. Then the boat violently somersaulted, heels over head, and a little to port. In less than one minute,

Tzu Hang *9 years after her smash in the Southern Ocean. She was still a handsome ketch with a lovely sheer and an elegant canoe stern. In this picture, her hull is red and she sails without a bowsprit. The yacht—built of teak with bronze strapping—was designed by H. S. Rouse and constructed in Hong Kong in 1938. The Smeetons sailed* Tzu Hang *120,000 miles between 1951 and 1969, when she was sold to others. Later she was used in the drug trade. During a violent hurricane in 1989, the yacht was driven ashore in Puerto Rico. A man named Pedro Ramos hoped to rebuild her, but his plans didn't work out. In August 1990, 52 years after she was launched,* Tzu Hang *was broken up by a bulldozer, a wretched end for a once-proud vessel.*

Tzu Hang, before a marvel of good design, expert building, and meticulous preparation, was hurled into the sea and stripped of her masts and booms. Her strongly
built doghouse was ripped off. A waterfall of water thundered into the cabin. The
bowsprit was broken in two, and both dinghies, the cockpit coamings, skylights,
ventilators, the compass, and an anchor were torn off and carried away. Even the
tiller and rudder disappeared.[56]

The miracle of this story is that the crew of three somehow managed to bail out
the yacht, patch her openings, construct a mast and steering oar, improvise sails,
and make their way to the Chilean coast for repairs. Not only is the story of *Tzu
Hang* a triumph of the human spirit, but the sailing world learned that an 18-ton
sailing yacht can be capsized and somersaulted with disastrous results. The word
pitchpole became part of our nautical language.

This story has been discussed and argued over for forty-six years until it has
almost become a nautical cliché. The question is: Could *Tzu Hang* have made it
through the frightful overtaking sea by dragging a stern warp with a powerful
drogue at the end? Would the line, the drogue, and the fastening points on the hull
have been strong enough to have held the yacht while she was swept by the huge
wave? My answer is yes. I think it's the only possible defense.

When I sailed my Santa Cruz 50 across the Southern Ocean on my third trip around
the world in 1991, I ran off downwind before force 10 storms three times. One
depression was six hundred miles west-southwest of Bass Strait and the west coast
of Tasmania. Another was a hundred miles east of the southern tip of New Zealand's
South Island in the South Pacific. Both times I headed off about 165 degrees from
the direction of the wind, and except for a bouncy ride, I had no trouble.

I ran off from the third storm-force wind in the southeast part of the Indian
Ocean (44° S, 92° E), about thirteen hundred miles west-southwest of Perth, Australia. The date was January 11, 1991. In the beginning, the seas were quite regular,
but as the west-northwest wind increased, the waves built up to 30 to 35 feet in
height. They were long, 600–700 feet, with a period of about 11 seconds. According to a graph in Bowditch, the speed of the waves was 33 knots.[57]

The yacht was blasting along at 9–10 knots with no mainsail at all and a tiny bit
of jib. My Brookes and Gatehouse wind speed device read the apparent wind at 46
knots, which made the true wind about 55 knots. Though the barometer was rising,
I was hand steering with difficulty, and the yacht was almost out of control. Water
was flying all over the place. It was not a scene for beginners.

I could see that a secondary, smaller wave train had begun to roll in from the
southwest and was mingling with the main wave system from the west-northwest.
Occasionally, these primary and secondary wave trains mixed together and got out
of sequence. This caused a wave to gain height (45 to 50') and lose length between

crests (say, to 350'). Oceanographers tell us that when the height of a wave becomes $\frac{1}{7}$ of its length, it breaks.[58]

I knew I was in trouble when I began to see big areas of white water around me. A mile (?) off to starboard, I watched tons of water go from dark blue to white when a breaking wave turned into a cascading waterfall. As the wave tumbled, it trapped a lot of air beneath it and changed the dark sea to turquoise for a minute or two while the upset water danced and bubbled. Gradually the air escaped, the sea cleared, and the water again became dark blue. Then the same thing happened off to port. Then ahead. Now behind.

The yacht sped onward.

Running hard before big seas in the Southern Ocean southeast of Marion Island, south of the Cape of Good Hope. Most storm photographs show the wind and seas from behind. In tumultuous conditions, sailors do everything they can to avoid sailing to weather, which in any case may be impossible or extremely difficult. Pictures of yachts hove to or lying ahull need to be taken from another vessel or possibly from a helicopter. In the real world, these pictures seldom exist. Taking photographs when water is flying around is chancy. Likewise, pictures of sea anchors and drogues are difficult to take. Drawings are more practical.

"What can I do to help myself?" I wondered. The problem was not the wind, but the erratic seas from the two wave trains. Though I was steering by hand and could change course instantly, I had no way of anticipating the breaking waves that were erupting here and there. Again it was a half-mile to starboard, two miles ahead, a little behind me to port. . . . These random seas were big and mean and scary. I knew there were immense forces involved from the noise the waves made when they broke. Sometimes I could feel the yacht tremble when one exploded nearby.

The steering was hard, and I was running out of steam.

These breaking seas were like bombs in the sea. I was in a battlefield. Or to change the image, they were like two fleets of 18-wheel trucks going 70 miles an hour down a highway on a collision course.

The sea conditions were too horrendous for heaving to or lying ahull. I rejected the idea of a parachute sea anchor for reasons I will discuss in the pages ahead. I considered paying out a long line over the transom. But I was unsure what length line to use and whether I should put an anchor on the end for drag and weight. I wish that I could write that I did procedure X and was saved. The truth, however, is that while I was considering my next move, one of the giant waves erupted underneath the yacht.

Bang! There was a big explosion. Water crashed in every direction. The boat and I flew through the air as if a box of dynamite had been detonated beneath the hull. The 50-foot yacht was upside down. I was alongside in the water with the boat to my right. I was amazed to see the blue keel in the air next to me. I felt cold water running under my foul-weather gear. Was all this truly happening, or was I dreaming?

Though damaged, the Santa Cruz 50 recovered quickly. I scrambled on board (I had been tied to the cockpit with several lines) and was relieved to see that the rig was still standing. The boat hook and winch handles were whizzing around, and I could hear a great crashing below from the floorboards and the locker and galley contents when the boat rolled.

The yacht's forward motion was stopped by the capsize, and I seem to recall that the seas were less. (I was not too clearheaded at that moment.) A few hours later, my world had brightened. The wind and seas were down, and I was hoisting the mainsail.

The point of this story is to consider whether I could have prevented the capsize by employing other storm controls. If I'd used a parachute at the bow, hung on a drogue at the stern, or used oil, could I have survived the meeting with the big breaking sea? Or would the breaking wave have found the Santa Cruz 50 as it did?

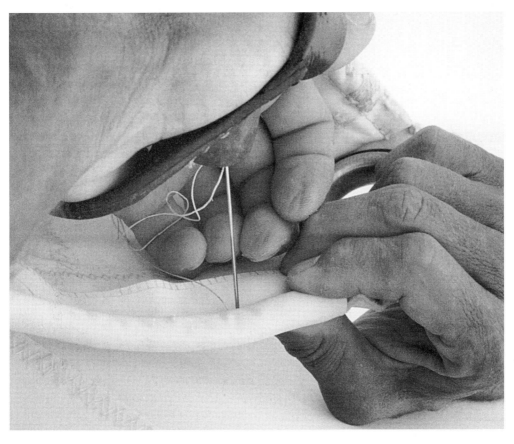

After a lot of miles, sails usually need attention. Here I'm using a sailor's palm to drive the needle through several thicknesses of Dacron material to cover a chafed place on the luff of a sail. As a practical matter, I often need a pair of pliers to force the needle through. It helps to sharpen the point of the needle on a fine abrasive stone.

18

STORM MANAGEMENT 3: DEPLOYING A SEA ANCHOR

The basic notion is simplicity itself. You drop an 8- to 25-foot-diameter nylon parachute or a big cone-shaped canvas sleeve in the water and connect it to the bow of the sailboat with a swivel and a very long nylon line. As the gale blows the yacht downwind, the parachute opens or the cone fills and becomes an almost stationary point in the sea. In theory, the yacht then turns into the wind to expose the strongest and most streamlined part of the vessel to the storm. You've anchored yourself to the sea, and the waves thunder harmlessly past.

This is a grand idea, but it's not quite that simple.

Margaret steering Whisper *northward in the Strait of Le Maire near Cape Horn. The wind is 50 to 55 knots from the southwest, and we are sailing at 4 knots under bare pole. You can tell the wind is strong by the white streaks on the water. I estimated the seas to be 25 to 30 feet, but they were upset because of overfalls caused by tidal action along the west shore of Isla de los Estados, which is off to starboard. The visibility was poor, but at times we could see dim mountains and a scary coastline. We saw nothing of Tierra del Fuego to port. Once we were through the strait and out in the South Atlantic, the sea conditions and sailing became much easier.*

The connection of sea anchors to yachts and fishing boats is largely due to a book written by Captain J. C. Voss in 1913. Voss was a professional Canadian sailor who in 1901, when he was 47, took one crewman and spent a little more than three years sailing a small boat from Victoria, British Columbia, west-about to England, about three-quarters of the way around the world.[59]

Voss's vessel was a decked-over log canoe (with slightly built-up topsides and a cabin) named *Tilikum* that was driven by a small three-masted gaff rig with a total sail area of only 230 square feet. She was 38 feet long (including the figurehead); her beam was an ultraskinny 5 feet, 6 inches, and she drew just 2 feet. *Tilikum* was hacked out of a red cedar log and stiffened with oak frames, floors, and a keelson. She was ballasted with 700 pounds of sandbags and lead.

During his trip, Voss dealt with gales by tossing out a cone-shaped canvas sea anchor from the bow of *Tilikum* and striking all sail except for a small mizzen. According to Voss's book, this kept the boat headed to within 2½ points (28°) of the wind. Meanwhile, the Canadian captain and his crewman went below to rest and smoke their pipes.

Tilikum lay successfully to her sea anchor dozens of times during the voyage. Much has been made of Voss's technique, and his name is always brought up when sea anchors are mentioned to prove how good they are. Unfortunately, this argument is passé because today's sailing yachts are completely different from the shallow, narrow, low-rigged *Tilikum* of a century ago.

Our current boats have much taller rigs that are located farther forward. The hulls drawn by present-day designers have about three times the draft of *Tilikum*, and much of the hull underbody is located farther aft. When the sails are down, the combination of the forward windage and the aft underbody turns the hull roughly abeam to the wind. Captain Voss's ninety-year-old concept for present-day monohull sailing yachts is obsolete.

W. A. Robinson, another sailor of vast experience, points out that Voss unwittingly gives innumerable arguments *against* sea anchors, which a careful analysis of the latter part of his book will reveal. "Not the least of these is the fact that after all his experience with *Tilikum*—which never met the ultimate storm—he was unable to provide a sea-anchor that would stand up when he finally did meet it years later in *Sea Queen*, a yacht of only 19 feet water-line."[60]

Eric Hiscock points out that Voss's *Tilikum* was much like a ship's lifeboat with the same draft and the same windage fore and aft. When such craft have a small riding sail set at the stern, they ride well to a sea anchor.

> But a normal [modern] yacht drawing more water aft than she does
> forward, and having greater windage forward than she has aft, will
> not lie like that. No matter how large the sea-anchor, she is bound to

make sternway; her bow, having less grip than her stern on the still, deep water, is more affected by the wind, breaking crests and surface drift, so that it falls off to leeward; the hull pivots on its heel, and eventually takes up a position more or less beam on to wind and sea, just as it will when lying a-hull. If a riding sail is set aft and sheeted flat, the position may be improved, but even then the yacht will not lie head to wind, though she may come up occasionally and fall off on the other tack, the sail flogging dreadfully at times, and the strain on the rudder caused by sternway being great.[61]

I must mention the advice of my friends Lin and Larry Pardey, who are well-known contemporary sailors and who campaign a heavy-displacement traditional English cutter, a long-keeled 28-footer that displaces 18,000 pounds. This is on the small end of world-cruising yachts, but the Pardeys are intrepid voyagers who have sailed far and wide—including a trip around Cape Horn in 2002—and have written extensively about their voyages.

The Pardeys are advocates of a sea anchor and use a technique of heaving to with a storm trysail in conjunction with a small (8' dia.) surplus nylon military parachute that is set from the bow on 250 feet of $\frac{5}{8}$-inch-diameter nylon. They rig a short line from amidships on one side of the yacht to a point on the parachute warp about 7 feet forward of the bow. They then take a strain on the short line to pull the yacht sideways (50°) to the line going to the parachute.[62]

This sideways pull keeps the wind on one side of the trysail, stops tacking, and improves the motion below. The Pardeys call their scheme heaving to, but because they use a parachute in addition to one or more stormsails, their maneuver is clearly something else. The Pardeys say that their plan eliminates backing down on the rudder; nevertheless, they recommend rudder stops and lash their tiller with shock cord.

The idea is to drift slowly downwind ($\frac{1}{2}$ kt., say the Pardeys) behind the slick made by the parachute, which tends to break up large waves heading for the yacht. Certainly if there is a lee-shore problem, this sea anchor plan is ideal.

The Pardeys write that they have had excellent results with this system for many years. Their success may be linked to the design of their boat: heavy displacement, extremely long keel, and full underbody. Several other yachts of similar design have had good results with small parachute sea anchors.[63] Most of the sailing vessels being built today, however, have a canoe underbody, a fin keel, a spade rudder, and a displacement relative to overall length of only about 60 percent as much as the Pardey vessel.

The Pardey approach fails to address the difficult problem of a large breaking sea coming from a different direction and striking the more vulnerable *sides* of the yacht. With the towline from the sea anchor parachute already angled to 50 degrees, the vessel is only 40 degrees from being broadside on to a possible breaking sea.

In a true wind of 35–40 knots, this arrangement may be satisfactory, but I should hesitate to try it in the Southern Ocean, the winter temperate zones, a northeast gale in the Gulf Stream, or similar conditions. During turbulent weather in these places, sailors may experience an occasional breaking wave that's seventy degrees or more from the general direction of the tempest.

I feel it's wise to try to keep the bow or the stern of the yacht heading into all big waves—breaking or not. Upset waves from abeam can be particularly dangerous.

PROBLEMS WITH A SEA ANCHOR

Problem 1 with a modern yacht lying to a sea anchor is that the boat doesn't head into the wind, but positions herself at roughly 70 to 110 degrees to the line going to the sea anchor. Fishing boats, motor vessels, and multihull sailing yachts that have long straight keels present much more balanced hulls to the sea. Earlier I mentioned that a modern sailboat's lateral area below the water is mostly aft. Additionally, she has lots of windage up forward because of her mast and bulky roller-furled jib at the bow, something that 95 percent of yachts carry today. The combination of the aft keel area and forward windage combine to turn the sailing yacht away from the wind. This exposes the vulnerable sides of the yacht to the force of a potential breaking wave.

"Then," writes Maurice Griffiths, the longtime editor of *Yachting Monthly*, "the merry, sparkling sea—which tops the scales at 64 lb. for each cubic foot, or 35 cu. ft. to the ton—can be about as friendly as a ton of wet concrete when it chooses to break over a small vessel."[64]

"This is exactly what happened to me during a violent Pacific storm," said New Zealand sailor Ross Norgrove when I talked with him in Tortola about his experiences with a sea anchor that he deployed from his 11-ton sailboat *White Squall*. "As soon as we streamed the sea anchor at the bow, the yawl turned sideways and I knew it was a disaster."

Sailors can help their cause by setting a small riding sail on a mizzenmast or hoisting a tiny storm jib immediately forward of the mainmast backstay to help turn the ship's head toward the wind. But if the ship's heading changes with passing seas, such a sail may flog itself to death.

Earl Hinz suggests a better idea: a wedge-shaped riding sail that will always have some sideways force no matter where the wind is. The head of this small sail can be held in place with a shackle around the backstay and hoisted with the main halyard. The tack can be secured to the main boom. The port and starboard clews can be held apart with a boat hook or a scrap of wood about 5 feet long. Two short lines from the clews downward to the aft mooring cleats complete the job.[65]

Problem 2 with a sea anchor is when the wind shifts and the storm begins to send swells and waves from a new direction. If there are leftover swells from the old direction, the vessel can be battered by two sets of waves and swells. Worse yet, the interaction of two wave trains can produce an occasional rogue wave. Although I wasn't using a parachute sea anchor, I learned about the danger of rogue waves when one caused the violent capsize of my Santa Cruz 50 that I mentioned earlier.

Problem 3 is the rudder. It's hard to think of a more appalling strain on the entire steering system than when a ship moves backward in a rough sea and the full weight of a yawing and bucking vessel slams the rudder against the water. Commander Erroll Bruce recalls that when he was in a storm in the South China Sea in a naval whaler, the rudder broke clean off while lying to a sea anchor in only 30 knots of wind. The small yacht *Nova Espero* had the same trouble during an eastward crossing of the Atlantic.[66]

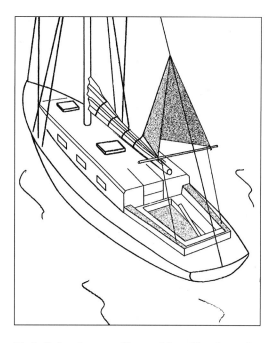

To help keep a small vessel heading into the wind either at sea or at anchor, a triangular riding sail may flog less than a reefed mizzen or a flat riding sail secured to the backstay. The triangular sail in the drawing has its head shackled to the backstay and is hoisted with the main halyard. The tack is secured to the main boom. The clews are held apart with a boat hook or an oar and secured to lines that run through snatch-blocks in the cockpit and then to cleats or winches. All the lines should be very tight, particularly the halyard, to keep the head shackle from damaging the backstay.

Problem 4 is chafe and the strain on the line leading to the drag device. The tensile loads on the warp going to a parachute sea anchor (at the bow) or to a drogue (at the stern) are much greater than most sailors realize—sometimes on the order of 15,000 pounds or more for a 40-foot yacht. Chafe problems are accelerated because of the high loads on all the fittings and attachment points.

Time after time, sailors have hauled in a suspiciously slack piece of nylon to find that the line has parted and the yacht is actually lying ahull. Even with stout lines, the loads induced by drogues and sea anchors often come close to the breaking point of the line, fittings, and attachment points, as engineering studies have shown.[67] In one case, when two sailors pulled in a 426-foot line to a parachute sea anchor after a big storm, they found that their ¾-inch-diameter nylon cable had stretched 65 feet.[68]

I have in front of me a large paperback book called *Drag Device Data Base*, written by Victor Shane and published by Para-Anchors International of Summerland, California, a company that sells sea anchors and drogues. This 1998 book is a compilation of the experiences of 120 users of these devices. The long and short accounts are broken down according to whether the drag devices were used on sailing monohulls, sailing multihulls, or power yachts. Presumably the idea of the book is for prospective purchasers of drag devices to read how these waterborne contrivances have worked for others, to learn about them, and possibly to become customers. Certainly it's useful to read about the experiences of sailors in hard going. In such a book the impartiality of the author is paramount.

The first section deals with monohulls that have used sea anchors off the bow. I plowed through all 41 cases and decided that 26 owners found sea anchors helpful. Three said no. In 3 other cases, the line to the device broke. I judged 9 accounts to be irrelevant.

According to the reports, if a large sea anchor is out ahead of a yacht on a 300- or 400-foot nylon line that is shackled to a length of chain leading from the bow, there's a good chance that the device will work. However, depending on the hull and rig configuration, the yacht may either head into the wind and seas or lie as much as 60 or 70 degrees to one side, which is not good.

I learned that sea anchors are troublesome and sometimes hazardous to set during gales and storms. There is a terrific strain on the line to the parachute, and sometimes the line breaks. The makers urge practice with a parachute in light conditions. And finally, recovering the device is usually slow and difficult. Nevertheless, when the sea conditions and anchor work together, a parachute can be extremely helpful, and in some cases has saved boats from disaster.

For example, one account tells about Stephen Edwards and Deborah Schutz, two Australians aboard *Prisana II* off the southwest coast of Australia during July 15–16, 1997. The boat was a 46-foot, 13-ton ketch with a modified fin keel and spade rudder. She was caught by a violent tornado with hurricane-force winds running against the Leeuwin current. The seas were so large (as much as 60') that the crew was forced to retreat into the cabin. According to the report, the ketch lay to an 18–foot-diameter parachute sea anchor for 59 hours. She survived the tempest handily although she suffered damage to both her rudder and to heavy stainless steel fittings at the bow where the line to the parachute was attached. The crew credited the sea anchor with saving them.[69]

An account from another book illustrates a different result.

Ardevora was a 55-foot aluminum centerboard ketch owned by Tim Traford of Plymouth, England. On September 6, 1997, after a run from Easter Island, the yacht was at 40° S and 30 miles west of the Chilean coast near the city of Valdivia. The wind was from the north and gusting up to 47 knots.

The boat was in the north-setting Humboldt Current; the wind against the current made steep, nasty seas. The yacht had been hove to under various storm sails. However, the captain decided that she was too close to the coast.

The crew put out an 18-foot-diameter Para-Tech sea anchor on 600 feet of 1-inch plaited nylon, an exhausting job that took two hours. The line was led from a closed fairlead at the bow, through a snatchblock on the starboard toerail, and then to two big cockpit winches.

The sea anchor dragged the bow of the big yacht head to wind. "The motion was appalling," the captain said. *Ardevora* was pitching up to 45 degrees above and below the horizon, rolling her gunwales under, and yawing up to 30 to 40 degrees on either side of the wind. Backing the mizzen had little effect. The crew tried to rig a starboard bridle on the sea anchor line, but it didn't work.

The load on the cockpit winch was so great that the captain feared the first winch, a big Lewmar 65, would be torn off. "No anchor winch or deck cleat could have survived the load," he said. A few hours later, it was blowing a steady 45 knots, gusting to 60, and during large breaking crests, the yacht surged astern. The captain was so worried about the rudder that he considered cutting the warp. Four hours after deployment, the line parted. "Lying to our sea-anchor was an unpleasant experience," said the captain. "The sea anchor is a tool of very last resort."[70]

Steve and Linda Dashew's book *Surviving the Storm* has a number of innovative computer drawings in which the authors attempt to show how yachts perform in various breaking-wave situations (the 700-page Dashew book is certainly an ambitious project). In it the authors tell of several sailboats that had trouble with broken warps from parachute sea anchors. One account, about the *Freya*, runs to 13 pages. Very briefly, this is what happened.[71]

In November 1998, the yacht *Freya*, a 45-foot cruising sloop with a long keel, left Tonga and headed for the Bay of Islands in New Zealand. The distance was 1,100 miles and the course was south-southwest. The vessel sailed to within 140 miles of her target when a 45-knot easterly gale overtook her. The owner put out an 18-foot-diameter Para-Tech parachute anchor from the bow and waited for the weather to improve. Though the boat sheered from side to side, the boat lay behind the parachute on 450 feet of new ¾-inch-diameter three-strand nylon. Every two hours the captain, Bruce Burman, went forward to the bow to check the line for chafe and change the nip.

Before dawn, a huge breaking wave from the south turned the yacht upside down. She recovered at once, but the inside of the vessel was a mess from food, broken glass, and drawers and lockers that had been dumped. The front hatch (whose hinges had been mounted with wood screws) broke open and let in 200 gallons of seawater. While the owner was repairing the hatch, he saw that the sea anchor was gone. When he checked the line, he discovered that it had broken 10 feet from the bow.

Burman said the line failed at the moment of impact with the big wave from the south. The rollover broke the life raft bracket; the raft inflated but was soon lost when its painter chafed through. Both the SSB (single-sideband) and the VHF radio didn't work. The Burmans turned on an EPIRB (emergency position-indicating radio beacon). In worsening weather and apparently lying ahull in breaking sea conditions, which was certainly asking for trouble, the yacht was knocked down again and the front hatch torn off. Later the yacht was capsized and dismasted. Burman, his wife, and their son were finally winched aboard a New Zealand helicopter.

The point of this story is that a breaking wave from a different direction capsized the yacht and overtaxed the sea anchor line, which parted. It's a pity Burman didn't run off after the first capsize. How unfortunate it was that the front hatch was not secured with through-bolts, which might have saved the vessel and made the rescue unnecessary.

So for some sailors, parachute sea anchors are a panacea. Others consider them hell.

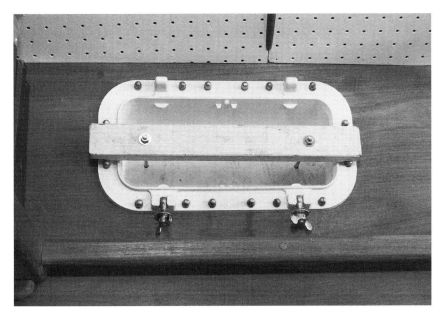

If a portlight gets broken or has a severe leak, it's helpful to have a few plywood shutters and strongbacks made up in advance and tucked away. A scrap piece of carpet or inner tube makes a suitable gasket.

19

STORM MANAGEMENT 4: DEPLOYING A STERN DROGUE

During the 1970–71 Antarctic circumnavigation of the 53-foot cutter *Awahnee*, Bob Griffith and his crew lay to a sea anchor or stern drogue time after time. *Awahnee*, however, had a strong crew of six and used a sea anchor that not many yachts would be able to produce or manage. "We hove to with the stern into the wind and swell held by a sea anchor consisting of about 300 feet of line with half a dozen car tires and a small anchor on the end," wrote crew member Pat Treston in the New Zealand magazine *Sea Spray*.

During several giant Antarctic storms ("Holding On in 90 Knots"), the crew of *Awahnee* set as many as three drogues—one of 80 feet of $7/16$-inch chain, a second of two or three car tires on 200 feet of line, and a third of 600 feet of line with an anchor and a tire on the end.

"However we had to steer all the time to try to keep the quarter to the wind and waves," Treston wrote.[72]

Broken water flew everywhere and there was some damage, but the yacht and

Running hard with a small storm jib before a gale in the Gulf of Alaska.

crew came through unharmed. I marvel at the success of the voyage and the cheerful, heroic crew, but I shudder at the work involved. Certainly a more modern drogue would have been easier.

Margaret and I have run north along the Oregon coast before a force 10 wind from the southeast in our 35-foot *Whisper*. To slow the yacht and keep her under control, we put out two 175-foot lines with tires and lead weights chained to the ends of the warps. This arrangement was helpful, but dealing with the tires, weights, and chains was awkward while the boat was rolling heavily. Sometimes the drags were picked up by waves and carried forward, which made their value doubtful.

A better scheme than towing tires is to use a Galerider drogue made by Hathaway, Reiser, and Raymond of Stamford, Connecticut. This clever device (see illustration) is a large teardrop-shaped open-mesh basket made of 2-inch nylon webbing built out from a length of heavy stainless steel wire made into a 4-foot circle. The Galerider is much easier to set, recover, and store than tires, weights, and lengths of chain.*

In the years since the capsize of my Santa Cruz 50 in the Southern Ocean, I've had plenty of time to reflect on the mishap. I believe that protection from monstrous seas translates directly into keeping the bow or the stern headed into the waves. Getting broadside on (or even close to broadside

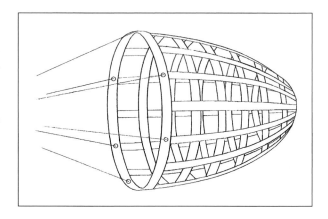

The Galerider drogue is made by the sailmakers Hathaway, Reiser, and Raymond of Stamford, Connecticut. The device is an elliptical-shaped open-mesh basket 30 to 48 inches in diameter and from 30 to 56 inches long, depending on the model. The basket is made of 2-inch nylon webbing with stoutly sewed intersections and mounted on a 3/8-inch-diameter stainless steel wire formed into a circle. Six pendants lead from the mounting wire to a swivel that is attached to a 300-foot, 5/8- or 3/4-inch-diameter double-braided nylon line that goes to the yacht. In use, the Galerider drogue is streamed from the stern of a boat and, according to the makers, is best placed so that it rides on "the second sea following your vessel." Storage of the Galerider is clever: you twist the outer metal ring into a figure eight, fold it over on itself, and slip the entire drogue into a small, flat bag that measures 2′ × 2′ × 4″.

---

*A secondary use of the Galerider basket is for hoisting. If you tie the basket to a halyard—perhaps through a block at the end of the main boom—you can use the basket to lift aboard a person from the water or to pick up heavy items from a dinghy.

on) is no good because the vessel may be rolled over or picked up and dropped on the unyielding sea. But how do we do this? Streaming a large parachute sea anchor from the bow in upset seas and winds of 40 knots and higher is a hazardous business. Even if we're successful, the result is that our modern yachts lie close to being broadside on to the waves, something we must avoid.

In 2001, I learned about the work done by Donald Jordan, a retired aeronautical engineer and former senior instructor at the Massachusetts Institute of Technology. In 1979, Jordan was appalled when he learned about the disastrous Fastnet race along the south coasts of England and Ireland. During the 605-mile competition, a severe force 10 summer storm struck the fleet. Many of the 2,700 men and women in the 303 yachts in the race suffered appalling injuries. Boats were rolled over, destroyed, and sunk in waves that were said to be as high as 50 feet. Fifteen people died.[73]

Jordan decided to use his engineering skills to try to find a way to stop such catastrophes. By 1982, he had arranged with the U.S. Coast Guard to use its test facilities, towing tanks, and powerboats to make a study of capsizes caused by breaking waves. The joint goal of Jordan and the coast guard was to increase safety at sea by preventing capsizes and damage to monohull and multihull sailing yachts going offshore. By these efforts, the coast guard hoped to save lives and reduce the number of expensive and sometimes dangerous helicopter rescues.

Most sailboat owners who venture offshore have read the works of Hiscock, Knox-Johnston, Moitessier, Slocum, and Smeeton—people who have been out there—and know all their arguments and hesitant advice about what to do in big storms.

During the last few years, we have heard much about parachute sea anchors. The problem with these devices is that the people who talk about their beneficial qualities also sell them. When, I wonder, does favorable information turn into a sales pitch? How do you separate truth from hype?

What offshore sailors need is unbiased information from scientists, engineers, naval architects, and sailors with hands-on experience, not anecdotal material from vendors and tales from the marina.

Sailing is a small sport with perhaps one million or fewer enthusiasts worldwide, depending on whom you count. The number of offshore sailors is very much less and is too insignificant to have a membership organization that can undertake technical studies. I welcome the work of the U.S. Coast Guard and qualified individuals with a concern for offshore sailing yacht safety.

Jordan began his work by investigating the nature of breaking waves and the odds of survival of small yachts from 25 feet in length (which have a high risk of capsize, he says) up to large vessels 60 feet in length (with a low risk of capsize). Jordan used computer analysis to study the performance of $^{1}/_{10}$-size model sailing

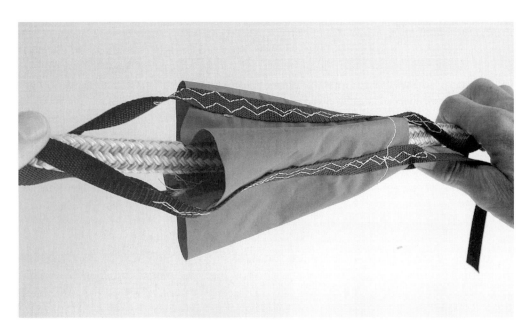

The concept of the Jordan series drogue is a series of 5-inch-long Dacron cones securely fastened to the stern warp with ¹/₂-inch-wide nylon tapes. Each cone is held in place with three tapes. One end of each tape is led through three strands of the outer braid and knotted. The tape then goes along the cone and is sewed to it with zigzag stitching. The other end goes to the line, where again it is led through three strands and knotted. This arrangement holds each cone in place so that once in the water, it will be instantly inflated and cause drag related to the speed of the cone through the water. The amount of drag in pounds equals 0.27 times the number of cones times the speed in knots squared. At 5 knots, therefore, one cone—like the one above—has a drag of 6.75 pounds. Twenty cones at 5 knots have a drag of 135 pounds. One hundred and twenty cones at 5 knots have a drag of 810 pounds. One hundred and fifty cones at 7 knots have a drag of 1,985 pounds. Obviously a Jordan series drogue is a serious device.

yachts with and without drogues (at the stern) and sea anchors (at the bow) in towing tanks and in natural waterways.

Jordan was not satisfied with the performance or strength of traditional stern drogues, so he developed what he calls a *series drogue*. This is a long, double-braided nylon line, streamed from a bridle at the stern with *one hundred or more* 5-inch sailcloth cones (see table) spaced along the length of the line and securely sewed to it. To sink the line, the Jordan series drogue is weighted at the end with a 15- to 30-pound length of chain or an anchor.

The length of line and number of cones is based on the displacement of the yacht as follows:

displacement in thousands of pounds	10	15	20	25	30	35	40	45	50
number of cones	100	107	116	124	132	139	147	156	164
length of line in feet	242	254	269	282	295	307	320	335	349
diameter of nylon braid in inches	$5/8$	$5/8$	$3/4$*	$3/4$*	$3/4$*	$3/4$*	$7/8$*	$7/8$*	$7/8$*
sinker weight in pounds	15	15	15	15	25	25	25	30	30

* the line may be tapered

When the series drogue is deployed, it hangs down behind the yacht because of the weight at the end. The cones then open and cause immediate and substantial drag. The number of cones fixed along the line is based on the yacht's displacement and is chosen to provide the correct drag. Too little, and the yacht won't be held enough to resist a possible capsize from a breaking wave. Too many cones, and the vessel will be held too rigidly and something will break. According to Jordan, *the design load should be one-half the displacement of the yacht.* This represents a once-in-a-lifetime ultimate load. In an ordinary storm, the peak load is only 10 to 15 percent of the design load.

"In general, I designed the drogue to provide a peak force of 50 to 60 percent of the displacement of the vessel when the boat is struck by a worst case breaking wave," says Jordan. "As a comparison, a large parachute sea anchor that is deployed from the bow will develop a drag more than thirty times as much as the series drogue at the same speed. In truth, a large parachute is the practical equivalent of being anchored to the bottom. Either the towline will break or the hull attachments will be torn from the boat long before such a load is reached."[74]

The length of the V-bridle streaming behind the yacht (see illustration next page) should be 2.5 times the distance between the two attachments at the upper corners of the transom. This ensures that with a straight pull, the bridle load will not exceed 52 percent of the total load. (On my current 35-footer, the transom width is 7 feet, so the V-bridle should be $17\frac{1}{2}$ feet long.) The bridle streaming behind the vessel provides a turning moment to keep the boat stern-to the wave.

In the real world this means that no steering is necessary. The crew can go below into the cabin and out of the storm, where the survivability and well-being of everyone can be 100 percent.

During the development of the Jordan series drogue, the coast guard tested the device on motor lifeboats in breaking sea conditions at the mouth of the Columbia

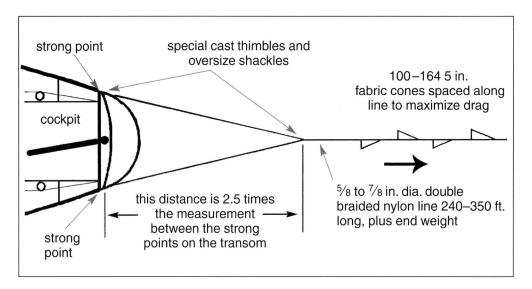

strong point   special cast thimbles and
                oversize shackles

cockpit

strong
point

100–164 5 in.
fabric cones spaced along
line to maximize drag

this distance is 2.5 times
the measurement
between the strong
points on the transom

⁵⁄₈ to ⁷⁄₈ in. dia. double
braided nylon line 240–350 ft.
long, plus end weight

Bridle arrangement for a Jordan series drogue streamed from the stern of a vessel. No steering is required, and the crew can go below.

River in Oregon, one of the most hazardous places on earth. Another test subjected a batch of the sailcloth cones to 15,000 openings and closings. After the test, all the cones were in good condition.

The Jordan engineering reports are long and complicated. Here's my take on the essential points as they apply to offshore sailors in monohull sailing yachts. Some of the conclusions are surprising.[75]

1. The number of small boats that go to sea has increased dramatically. When caught in a storm, most sailors choose to lie ahull or run off. Few sailors carry drogues.
2. A capsize by a breaking wave is rare. A sailor can go through a lifetime of ocean sailing without being involved in such a mishap.
3. Wind does not cause capsizes. The culprit is a breaking sea.
4. In tests with breaking waves, all models without a drogue capsized. When struck abeam, the models capsized violently and rolled 360 degrees. When struck on the quarter, the models sometimes turned end over end.
5. All single-element drogues will ride on the surface in a major storm and may be thrown toward the boat by a breaking wave. There are instances of a drogue being thrown ahead of the boat.

6. If a drogue is used, it should be deployed from the stern rather than the bow. With a drogue from the stern, a sailboat will lie stern to the wind and sea. With the same drogue (or sea anchor) from the bow, the bow of a modern monohull sailing yacht will turn away from the wind, often up to seventy degrees.

7. The tests clearly show that a drogue deployed from the stern can hold a boat into a breaking wave crest and prevent capsizing. Use of a drogue improves the motion of a yacht in a storm and reduces leeward drift.

8. In a great storm, the crew may be exhausted and confused. If the drogue and lines are not ready, the chance to ride through a breaking wave may be lost. Hence, the drogue should be on hand and ready, so that one person can deploy it quickly and safely, day or night.

9. Boat design changes do not affect capsizing. Models of typical sailing yachts from 1927, 1938, and 1980 showed no difference in capsize tests.

10. A boat lying ahull or sideways in nonbreaking seas moves more or less with the surface water and will not capsize. However, if a breaking wave strikes the boat, it will capsize violently.

11. Two or more storm waves may combine to form a larger wave that may become a dangerous breaking wave.

12. The drogue should be attached to the yacht with a V-bridle whose lines go to the corners of the transom, where they are shackled to stout chainplates or other special arrangements. All the drogue lines should be spliced around high-load *cast* thimbles*, not tied, for example, with bowlines. Running a bridle line through a chock and belaying it to a mooring cleat may not be adequate and can lead to fitting overload, chafe, and failure.

13. During a breaking-wave strike, a drogue puts significant loads on the hull. According to Jordan, the attachments at each corner of the transom should be built to take 70 percent of the design load. For a total drogue design load of 15,000 pounds, for example, each bridle leg and attachment should be capable of carrying 10,500 pounds, a number reached possibly once or twice during the life of the equipment.

14. When the boat is aligned to a wave, the load on each leg of the bridle is 50 percent of the total. But in a wave strike, the vessel is

*Available from Bo'sun Supplies Inc., P.O. Box 1283, Teaneck, NJ 07666, or at http://bosun supply.com/.

usually a bit to one side or the other, and much of the load is on one bridle leg. The load is not applied instantly but builds up at a finite rate. As the load increases, the boat yaws to reduce the angle. Computer analysis shows that the single drogue leg can reach 70 percent of the maximum load before the other leg kicks in and begins to take some of the load.

The yacht needs a strong cockpit (preferably small and with large-diameter, unobstructed drains) and a stout companionway and sliding hatch. The washboards and hatch must be securely fastened and have a locking arrangement because they may be swept by occasional waves. During boarding seas, however, the boat is usually accelerated up to wave speed and the velocity of the breaking crest is not high relative to the boat. Jordan says that he knows of no instances of damage to the rudder, cockpit, or companionway of a yacht with his drogue arrangement.

In 1991, Gary Danielson of St. Clair Shores, Michigan, sailed a lightweight Ericson 25-footer named *Moon Boots* from the United States to Europe and back. He had good crossings and used both a Galerider drogue and a Jordan series drogue a few times during force 8 weather. When Gary wanted to hold his position, he employed a Jordan series drogue, which worked well. His only problem was that when the boat crested a wave, the large and heavy sliding companionway hatch slid open because the inside locking hardware was broken. Each time the hatch was slammed open, 30 to 50 gallons of water poured into the cabin. This happened nine times in 36 hours. Moral: Be certain that you can lock the sliding hatch from the inside.[76]

According to Jordan, Gary's hatch was not washed open by the waves. The hatch slid forward because the drogue decelerated the boat as it passed over a crest. A latch will solve the problem.

"For small light boats, the peak load occurs when the boat is airborne from a wave strike. The drogue catches and decelerates the vessel," says Jordan. "For large heavy boats, the peak load occurs when the boat is surfing down the face of a breaker. The drogue prevents the yacht from crashing into the trough."[77]

There are no patents or proprietary fees connected with the series drogue. Jordan has no financial interest in it. Any sailmaker can make one. For information, look at U.S. Coast Guard Report CG-D-20-87, available from the National Technical Information Service, Springfield, Virginia 22161. On the Internet, visit www.sailrite.com/droguereport.htm. Another source is www.acesails.com/.

I like the concept of the Jordan series drogue because this clever drag device aligns the boat to the storm and holds the vessel from a position *off the yacht*. The series drogue keeps the stern end-on to large and small waves and prevents strains to the rudder and its fastenings. The series drogue is easier and safer to use than a parachute and aligns the boat at nearly right angles to oncoming seas.

With more development, it may be possible to use flat nylon or other high-tech tape in place of the present double-braided nylon line. This would make the drogue easier to roll in and out and store, and it might simplify the cones and their attachment. While nothing is perfect on the ocean, I believe the series drogue is the best defense against a large breaking sea.

To support the argument for the Jordan series drogue and stern drogues in general, consider the following letter from circumnavigator Ed Arnold, who wrote me after rounding Cape Horn on a single-handed voyage.

February 3, 2002

Hal,

I have used the Jordan Series Drogue many times both for safety in breaking seas and to hold position. Don Jordan estimated the forces on a boat in a breaking crest and designed the drogue to quickly establish the necessary restraining force to drag the boat through the crest. This resulted in a relatively short and stiff main line compared to many recommendations for parachute sea anchors. More or larger cones might be better if one were trying to hold position. My 20,000-lb. boat required 117 cones. I attach the bridle with shackles to tangs welded to the corners of my transom. Forces are large, and a chafe-free attachment is necessary. The drogue works well from the stern; I tried it from the bow and found it would not hold the bow closer than 70 degrees to the wind.

I have deployed it 3–4 times due to breaking seas. The first time in the N. Atlantic south of Iceland I had about F10 winds and seas of 25 feet or more. The boat was held within ±30° from the wind. Most of the sluing was in the troughs where the wave backflow reduced tension on the drogue and where the wind was momentarily less. Mary and I stayed below with periodic checks on the VHF for shipping. The cockpit would have been very wet and at times almost dangerous. Boarding seas filled the cockpit several times, but none broke directly on us. Drift was about 2.5 knots. Surface current is $\frac{1}{40}$th of the wind speed, so a knot of the drift was surface current.

I had similar results in the Gulf of Alaska and near Cape Horn during the present voyage: F9 or F10 winds with very high seas near Cape Horn. At all times I felt safe, although a full breaking sea on board might do real damage. The other 4–5 uses have been to hold position when I could no longer go upwind and I did not want to run downwind. A larger drogue would have helped. I have not had any tangles during deployment or use. I did have the bridle get under the wind vane rudder, and now use a floating line for the bridle.

Retrieving is hard work, and I would appreciate knowing an easier way. I have a retrieve line [that leads] to the head of the bridle, which I winch in. Then, with some danger to fingers, I can get the mainline around a winch during a surge of the boat. This is winched to the first cone. I take one turn on the winch and manually snub during stress and take in during a back surge. The cones survive the snubbing around the winch. With patience and effort it all comes in.

The stern and companionway of my long-keeled aluminum boat were designed to take a breaking sea. Some boats would not be strong enough.

Ed

When I visited Don Jordan at his home in Connecticut in 2003, he spoke at length about storm controls.

"Drogues like the Galerider, while they help stabilize the boat in a moderate storm, develop drag that's entirely inadequate in a breaking-wave strike," he said.

A close-up of Cape Horn, the sailors' ultimate symbol of adversity and achievement.

"Things like hawsers, tires, sails, nets, and the like are primitive and develop far too little drag.

"The series drogue has been used at sea for about 12 years," Jordan continued. "Today there are at least a thousand that I know of aboard yachts all over the world. Their use has expanded mostly by word of mouth because it's not a big commercial item. Many skippers have made their own, a tedious but not a difficult job. If you purchase a ready-made drogue from a sailmaker, it will cost about $1,000 for a 40-footer. I consider it a one-time insurance premium.

"The drogue has been deployed in many storms and in at least two hurricanes. As far as I know, the record has been flawless. No boat has suffered any damage, no crewman has been injured, and the drogues have been retrieved in like-new condition.

"When the weather gets to the point where progress is impossible, the people on board can deploy the drogue and retire to the protection of the cabin," Jordan said. "The boat rides easily with only modest yaw and with a drift rate of 1.5 knots or so. The drogue loads are low, about 15 percent of the design load, which is approached only in the rare event of a breaking-wave strike. If this happens, the drogue is designed to align the boat into the wave, decelerate the vessel, and hold it while the breaking crest crashes onward.

"With regard to Ed Arnold's letter about his Cape Horn trip, I don't recommend more or bigger cones than what is listed in my table. Too much drag is not good in a worst-case scenario because something may break. Concerning retrieval, the easiest way to pull in the series drogue is to use two helper lines about 8 feet long. Hitch the first line to the drogue at the transom and lead it to a winch. Then repeat the process with the second line, etc. Since the boat is held by the stern, she lies quietly.

"I'm an aeronautical engineer," Jordan concluded. "I view the drogue like the ejection seat on a fighter aircraft. You pull the handle and sit back until it's all over."

Earlier, in the discussion of parachute sea anchors, I mentioned the *Drag Device Data Base* book. Let's see what it says about monohull sailing yachts pulling drogues behind the boats.

In all, there are 19 accounts. Eighteen captains had excellent results by slowing their vessels with a variety of drag devices. The Galerider and Jordan series drogue were the most popular, but in a pinch the various skippers dragged anything behind them they had handy. In one case, a crew used a sunken dinghy and an Igloo icebox full of ice and soft drinks. The reports all agree that tossing a small device over the transom and letting out a line is much simpler than going to the bow and dealing with a parachute, float, shroud lines, and a cumbersome nylon warp that is sometimes as much as 600 feet long.

One user of both parachute sea anchors from the bow and the Jordan series drogue from the stern is the veteran English sailor Noel Dilly. He says that the series drogue has no give at all, "whereas with the para-anchor, it is like attaching the boat to a bungee cord that is being loaded and unloaded all the time." He adds: "The series drogue acts faster than any other device and it will align the stern to the wave direction soonest after a wave strike."[78]

SPREADING OIL

We all have heard that oil calms troubled waters, and in emergencies, big and little ships have used oil to smooth upset seas for centuries. Whether these reports are true or just folklore, I don't know. According to one account, the use of oil to calm water began during the days of whaling ships when men cutting up the whales noticed the tranquilizing effect of the whale oil that leaked overboard. Half a century ago, a hurricane swept down on W. A. Robinson, who was a thousand miles west of Valdivia, Chile, in his brigantine *Varua*. After going through the usual sail drill, Robinson finally ran off before the storm under bare poles and warps, with dripping oil bags hanging along each side deck and a crew member pumping oil through a toilet. Though reeking of fish oil, the ship survived. Robinson thought the oil helped.[79]

In 1957, the French single-hander Jean Gau was caught in the Atlantic by Hurricane Carrie about 120 miles east of Cape Hatteras, North Carolina. Gau managed to survive in his 30-foot Tahiti ketch *Atom* by lying ahull, streaming one long warp, and tying dripping oil bags to his weather rigging.[80]

Oil causes smoothing of the sea by increasing its surface tension. This is a property of liquids that makes them act as if they were covered by an elastic film. By itself, oil has less surface tension than water, but when oil spreads and its thickness decreases, its surface tension increases. "The thinner the film of oil, the better," writes oceanographer Willard Bascom. "Oil can act like an elastic membrane even when it is only a millionth of a millimeter thick. Thus, as the oil spreads away from the boat, it becomes more effective." Finally, at a distance from the boat, the wind breaks up the thinning oil film and it disperses. This is why new oil needs to be added—a few drops at a time—from the boat. Other substances in the water (ice particles or mud fragments) or things floating on it (kelp or long floating docks) also reduce wave action.[81]

To be honest, during storms at sea with the boat rolling heavily, I haven't felt like dealing with oil. On our present yacht, we carry 11 gallons of kerosene in a tank plus another 5 gallons in jugs. However, I'm told that kerosene is too light an oil to do much good. Our amount of cooking oil is insignificant. Engine lubricating oil is said to be better. We have 10 or 12 liters of lubricating oil in 1-liter cans.

During a storm, I could lash cans of engine oil to the outside of the windward lifeline stanchions and prick the cans with an ice pick. A few drops of oil might settle the seas just enough to be meaningful. I'm told that cod-liver oil is best, but I'm loath to put this ghastly, smelly substance from my childhood aboard because the storage container might leak.

I could tie a light line around a 5-liter container of oil lengthwise and sideways (with the lashing passed under the handle) before pricking the can and putting it over the windward side on a short line. Another scheme is to pump a little oil through the toilet from time to time. Since it takes a few seconds for the oil to spread, this suggests that the boat should be hove to or lying ahull, not running at speed. I've read about North Atlantic fishing boats doing this in storm-force winds, which suggests that it works because the boats came back and the accounts were printed. A crew member pumped a little oil through an aft-located head, and this eased the overtaking waves.

What small boats need is a system that is always in place and easy to use. It would be a simple matter to install a 20-gallon plastic tank in an out-of-the-way corner in the stern locker of a yacht and to run a small pipe with a gate valve through the hull. Once loaded with fish oil, it would take only a moment to open the valve slightly.

If you're a chemist and read these lines, perhaps you can suggest a superdetergent or some other magical potion with wave-calming properties—preferably one that is cheap, widely available, odorless, and noninflammable. I await your letter.

Now, briefly, I want to summarize these four chapters on storm management:

1. Try to help yourself by picking the most storm-free season (summer, not winter). If possible, check the weather over a period of days or weeks beforehand and look for a favorable trend. Tell the local meteorologists what you're doing and ask for their help. If you have to cross a stormy ocean, pick the most direct route. Don't linger on hazardous crossings.

2. If you're in a storm, *heave to*. This will almost stop the yacht and make your life much easier. Look around for traffic, mountains, and shorelines. Sit in the cockpit for a little while and watch the wind and seas. Write down the wind speed and direction. Look at the seas and judge their height ($\frac{1}{4}$ the length of the boat?), frequency (number of seconds between crests), and direction, which is sometimes different from the wind. Write the time and all the numbers on a scrap of paper that you can copy into the logbook.

3. Go below and use your GPS to find out exactly where you are. Plot the position on the chart and note the time. Turn on the echo sounder and check the depth. If you have a radar set, switch it on and look for land and traffic. If you're using traditional methods and the sky is clear, take sextant sights. Decide if you have any lee-shore problems. Can you go to a bay or harbor that is easy and safe to enter? (A large-scale chart and daylight will help.) It will almost always be safer to stay at sea.

4. Do your best to cook a simple, hot, nourishing meal. Reassure the crew. No booze. Send half the crew to sleep if possible. Put them in berths with lee cloths and lots of pillows. Insist that they try to sleep or at least lie quietly. If you are wet, change into dry clothes. Then put on oilskins followed by a safety harness. Lash down any loose gear. Put unused sails in bags and move them out of the way.

5. If the yacht becomes too hard-pressed, *reduce sail further*. If there are no breaking seas around, consider *lying ahull*. Switch on a radio for a weather report. If it's night and there is fishing or shipping traffic, turn on the anchor light or not-under-command lights (two all-around red lights, one placed vertically above the other). Have white collision flares handy.

6. *Run with the storm.* It's unlikely that you'll need to run with the storm because you can take quite a bit of wind hove to or lying ahull. Maybe you are in a squall that will be over in half an hour. Perhaps a weather front is passing. Is the barometer rising? Has there been a wind shift? If you're running and the weather grows really nasty, you can *trail a warp with one or more drogues*, but it will take some hours before the seas build up enough to require it. If there are dangers to leeward, you may have to steer a little. Sometimes you can get a wind-vane steering device or autopilot to do this.

7. *A parachute sea anchor* will work well with modest headwinds (25–35 kt.) and allow you to rest and eat. However, deploying a parachute sea anchor is heavy work. Handling three to four hundred feet of stiff, recalcitrant nylon on a rolling and pitching foredeck is not my idea of heaven, particularly at night. A drogue from the transom is simpler to deploy, but it still takes effort. Don't forget that you will have to pull in whatever you put out. If possible, try to get through the storm by heaving to. It's by far the simplest and easiest.

8. A final cheering thought is that most tempests are fast-moving in relation to the slow speed of a yacht. You need only play for time while the weather depression moves off. With luck, it will be gone in a day or so. You will be sailing in normal conditions and wondering what all the fuss was about.

CHESS PARTNERS ALWAYS WELCOME

*Life afloat is not all storms. In calm and quiet Aegean waters, this friendly yacht (*Cadoro *from Vienna) and her crew were looking for chess players.*

20
MANAGING WITHOUT REFRIGERATION

We've never had mechanical refrigeration aboard *Whisper* because it's too complicated and unreliable. In addition, my neighbors and I don't care for the noise of an engine running for an hour a day to charge the refrigeration system.

We could use an icebox, but if we can buy ice it means that we're anchored or tied up near a town or a city, where it seems more logical to shop daily for a piece of fish or a couple of pork chops than to haul ice. It may be a painful truth, but most cruising yachts spend 95 percent of their lives rocking gently on a mooring or tied to a dock in the shadow of city buildings somewhere.

"Then we have the same food as people with refrigeration," Margaret says. "Depending on the climate, we go to the store every day or two for meat and crispy vegetables—the most perishable items. For butter, cheese, and fruit, we shop every four or five days.

"Instead of frozen orange juice, we squeeze fresh oranges, which make a much tastier and more healthful drink."

Greasing very fresh eggs with Vaseline petroleum jelly to keep them in good condition without refrigeration may sound like an old wives' tale, but it has worked well for us for a long time.

So in port, we let the shopkeepers pay for the refrigeration. Once away from land or if we are sailing in a remote area, we manage without refrigeration, and we get along very well.

To the average person, refrigeration is one of the necessities of life. When we tell people that we have none on *Whisper*, the usual response is, "What on earth do you eat?" Our questioners imagine that we live on an endless diet of canned stew or corned beef hash (ugh!). This is completely untrue.

To begin with, shore people store many things in refrigerators that don't need chilling at all.

- Eggs (greased with petroleum jelly), potatoes, and onions will easily last four or five weeks—plenty of time, since most sea passages are less than a month.
- Grapefruit, oranges, limes, and lemons—especially if carefully selected and wrapped in aluminum foil—will stay fresh for a month or more. Occasionally one goes bad, but it's infrequent.
- Jam or jelly in use.
- Gouda, Tillamook, Edam, Bonbel, and various wheels of cheese keep well until the wax is broken.
- Carrots and cabbages last two or three weeks.
- Dried beans and barley for soups keep a year or more.
- TVP (textured vegetable protein) granules made from soybeans can replace ground beef in spaghetti sauce and in other recipes. TVP keeps for two years or more.
- Spaghetti and rice are good for at least a year. To defeat weevils and their eggs, soak a pad of cotton in 190-proof grain alcohol, put it on top of a full container of rice, and screw down the lid.

In general, we take a variety of basic foods that keep well and use them as foundations for meals. We add spices and herbs plus small amounts of fresh, dried, pickled, or canned foods to the basics to make them tastier and more appealing.

What follows is a week's worth of recipes for dishes that have worked well for us and are easy to prepare, plus a few notes on shipboard cooking. Some of this may seem simplistic, but sailors often have to juggle several jobs.

RECIPES

TVP Spaghetti Sauce

TVP stands for textured vegetable protein, a proprietary meat substitute made from soybeans. TVP is 55 percent protein, has no cholesterol, is an excellent source of fiber, is low in sodium, and has almost no fat. Long a staple of vegetarian cooks, the granules are loaded with amino acids, calcium, potassium, and magnesium—things that are supposed to be good for us.

You can buy TVP at a large supermarket or at a health food store. It is nonperishable and needs no refrigeration. To begin with, try a pound (about $1.50) and store it in a wide-mouthed glass jar.

Directions for two large servings of spaghetti sauce:

1. Dissolve one beef bouillon cube in $3/4$ cup boiling water. Add $3/4$ cup (3 oz.) dry TVP and the liquid from a 7-ounce (198 g) can of mushrooms. Allow to stand 10–15 minutes.

2. In a large frying pan, sauté one medium-sized chopped onion and one chopped clove of garlic in 2 tablespoons of hot cooking oil until translucent.

3. Add the TVP mixture, and stir in the mushrooms and a 6-ounce can of tomato paste. Fill the tomato paste can with water *twice* and, while stirring, slowly add the water to the pan. Add $3/4$ teaspoon marjoram, $1/4$ teaspoon pepper, and 1 tablespoon capers (optional, but it's worth buying a small bottle of capers—tiny pickled flower buds—which definitely add zip).

4. Cover and cook over low heat for 20–25 minutes, stirring occasionally. Pour the sauce over a steaming plate of spaghetti or noodles. Top with grated parmesan cheese. (Grate your own; it's better.)

Note: To cook over low heat on a kerosene pressure stove or many gas burners, you need one or two flame tamers. These are inexpensive, thin, perforated metal diffusion plates with an air space in between. You can find them at camping goods stores. Stainless steel flame tamers are best, but hard to find. Most are made of ordinary steel and rust heavily. We keep ours in a thick plastic bag. They last for years.

Eight-Inch Circle Bread

Crusty, unsliced loaves of bread are best, and even in the tropics will last a week or so before we need to trim off the edges. Then we bake fresh bread. Of course, we don't bake when the sailing conditions are rough, but when the going is light, someone is often busy sifting flour or kneading dough, and the cabin becomes filled with the delicious aroma of fresh bread.

Directions for one loaf:

1. In a large bowl, dissolve one packet active dry yeast ($1/4$ oz. or 7 g), 1 tablespoon sugar, and 2 teaspoons salt in $1^1/2$ cups lukewarm water. Let stand 5 minutes. For yeast to work, it must be warm, but not hot. It's best at 105°F to 115°F.

2. Stir in 4 cups white flour (or 2 cups white and 2 cups whole wheat flour). Knead the dough until it is spongy and elastic, about 5 minutes or a little more. It's better to knead too much than not enough.

3. Cover the bowl with a clean cloth to protect it from drafts and put it in a warm place until the dough doubles in bulk. This will take about $1^1/2$ hours or so,

Slicing an 8-inch loaf of fresh circle bread baked in a pressure cooker (without the pressure regulator on the top).

depending on the cabin temperature.

4. Grease the inside of a heavy 4-quart pressure cooker pan with margarine or shortening and sprinkle with cornmeal. Knock down the dough and put it in the pressure cooker (again covered with a cloth to protect the dough from drafts). Set it aside until the dough doubles in bulk. The second rising will take 1 hour or so, depending on the warmth.

5. Bake the bread in the cooker (with the top—including the rubber gasket—in place), but do not use the pressure device on top of the lid. This will allow the pressure cooker oven to breathe. Try a medium flame and one flame tamer for 30 minutes. Put on oven gloves and remove the pan from the heat. Take the top off, dump out the loaf, turn it upside down, and put it back in the pressure cooker (with the top on) for another 30 minutes.

Use a timer with a bell of some kind to keep track of the baking. When the bread is done properly, a sharp knife stuck in the dough will come out clean. If the bread is underdone, give it another 5 or 10 minutes. If it's burned, next time either decrease the flame (if possible on your stove) or use two flame tamers. With a little practice, the bread will turn out perfect.

This loaf needs 4 cups flour (or 1 lb.) and will last two people about three days. At this rate, bread for a month requires about 10 pounds flour, which we stow in large jars with screw lids.

We find that a stainless steel knife with an 8-inch serrated blade works best for slicing bread.

We take along a few boxes of cake mix and birthday candles for special occasions. Believe it or not, Margaret can bake a first-class cake in a pressure cooker. Of course, cake batter is lighter and more fluid than bread dough, so when the cake mixture is ready, she pours it into the pressure cooker, which has been greased with shortening and dusted with flour. She finds that a $2^1/2$-inch cake takes 45 minutes over a medium burner with one flame tamer. It's easy to check the progress by taking the top off the pressure cooker. At 30 minutes the cake will usually still be runny. At 45 minutes it will be done and a wide knife blade will slip into the dough without sticking. After cooling, it's time for the frosting. Note: Unlike the circle bread mentioned above, do not turn the cake over for additional baking.

It's worth learning to bake in one of these heavy cookers. Everything is enclosed in one pot, and the contents won't get thrown around as they can in an oven. Second, a pressure cooker is much easier to clean than an oven. However, remember that a pressure cooker is heavy, and a gimballed stove may need an extra weight on the bottom.

Don't forget that when you're baking bread or doing other serious cooking, you will run the stove for many hours. On a long trip you will need *a substantial amount of cooking fuel.* We know that no one is ever ahead of schedule, delays are usual, and shopping may not be possible. Therefore, you should load on board *at least twice* what you calculate you will require in the way of fuel, no matter what its type.

Onion Soup

Seventy-five years ago, when the famous French pilot cutter *Jolie Brise* was making long sea passages, her English owner, Commander E. C. Martin, found that his greatest triumph was onion soup. We have made *Jolie Brise* onion soup hundreds of times on *Whisper* and think highly of it. All our sailing and shore-based friends like it. The soup is quick and easy to prepare, uses ingredients common to most cruising yachts, and, best of all, is tasty and nourishing.

Here is Commander Martin speaking from the pages of *Deepwater Cruising*, published in 1928.

> Get the largest and finest onions available. . . . Peel them, for choice sitting a few points to windward of them on deck; or peel under water, or one can see to do only about three. Allow about two for each man. Cut them into quarters and put them into a large saucepan with a cover. For five men I should cut up 12 onions. Pour in enough cold water to make plenty of soup for all hands; add two full tablespoons of Bovril; about one-quarter pound of butter; a dessert spoonful of Lea and Perrins Worcester sauce; black pepper, with caution; and if there is any, a small wine glass full of sherry, or rather more white wine, when the cooking is nearly finished. It seems best not to add any salt in the cooking. Allow the mixture to boil gently, and stir occasionally until the onions have all fallen to pieces and are perfectly soft. The soup is then made. I venture to recommend the recipe because we have found this soup to be one of the very best and most wholesome forms of food which one can

have at sea. It is easy to make at any time when cooking is possible at all, and everyone seems to like it.

On *Whisper* we make a smaller amount (we are two instead of five) and substitute beef bouillon cubes for Bovril, an English product that may not be available.

Basic White Sauce

Sauces do magical things to food and either add zip to an existing taste or give a totally new flavor. Believe it or not, *The Joy of Cooking* lists 202 sauces, and an ambitious cook can spend years perfecting them. I have the space to mention only a basic white sauce.

1. Melt 2 tablespoons butter or margarine over low heat. (Butter is better.) Add and blend (with a spoon or wire whisk) $1^1/_2$ to 2 tablespoons flour. Stir for 3 to 5 minutes.

2. Slowly blend in 1 cup milk. Keep stirring over low heat. Perhaps add a small onion with a couple cloves pushed into it, and a grating of nutmeg. Continue to stir until the sauce has thickened and is perfectly smooth. Remove the onion and cloves.

We dug these large white clams along the beach at Roque Island in Maine. The long ones are razor clams. These are all deep burrowers. We used a shovel in the sand and watched for telltale jets of water along the beach at low tide (extreme low tide is better). The clams are excellent sautéed in butter or chopped and made into chowder. They generally need a couple of washings over several hours (overnight is better). Soaking with $^1/_4$ cup cornmeal to 1 quart clams in fresh seawater will whiten the shellfish and help get rid of sand and black material.

3. For a decorative touch, add a little parsley. You can vary the flavor with curry, tarragon, or oregano.

Once the basic white sauce is made, Margaret often adds a small (5 or 6 oz.) can of turkey (or chicken, ham, tuna, or salmon) to the sauce. She stirs it slowly, heats it through, and serves it, perhaps on a bed of basmati rice or on a platter of spaghetti. The 5- or 6-ounce cans of meat are just right for two people for one meal and can be easily doubled if there are four on board. The small cans cost a little more than the 10-ounce (233 g) cans but are convenient and easy to store. If there is any choice, we suggest buying the meat, fowl, or fish packed in *spring water* rather than in strongly seasoned oils of various kinds.

The white sauce can be made into a cheese sauce by adding ½ cup grated cheese and stirring above heat for a few minutes. This is good over steamed cauliflower or broccoli and makes a hearty vegetable dish. Cut gashes in the cauliflower stalks and steam 5 to 10 minutes in a covered pan over a little boiling water until tender when speared with a fork.

Tinned Roast Beef

One of our staples is 12-ounce (340 g) tins of roast beef from Brazil or Argentina. These large cans (about $1.50) are chock-full of beef and are excellent heated and served over rice, butterfly noodles, or new potatoes. We keep a supply of these cans on hand for when the weather is poor and we feel in need of a lot of quick energy without doing complicated cooking. The tins of roast beef are a little hard to find and tend to be sold in chain economy stores, but they're definitely available. When you find them, it's worth reading the labels carefully because some brands have MSG and twice as much salt (19 versus 34 percent) as others. In the beginning, buy one can for a trial.

If you make stew from scratch, it will taste very much better. Use chunks of meat from a tin of roast beef. Put them together with all fresh vegetables—potatoes, onions, and carrots. We add beef broth from a tin and seasonings that include a crushed clove of garlic and a dash of Angostura bitters. Warmed canned stew tastes exactly like warmed canned stew (mostly mushy potatoes, lots of salt, and little meat). By all means make your own.

A Plumrose canned ham or two and a couple of large salamis (if you like spicy foods) will help the meat department. Before I left Cape Town for Australia on one long trip, a kind South African gave me a smoked leg of lamb. It was great because I could whack off a piece from time to time, with no preparation and no cleanup.

Fish dishes can be served on steamed rice, mashed potatoes, or toast. Margaret often adds unusual ingredients to pep up ordinary fare. She may put a small can of crunchy water chestnuts in the beef stew. Or she may add canned bamboo shoots to an omelet. Spicy pimentos do wonderful things to fish prepared in a cream sauce.

Milk

In the 21st century, milk is no longer a problem. I have always found the taste of canned evaporated milk to be ghastly, but Parmalat (Vitamin D, Grade A, UHT long-life milk) is widely available in $^1/_2$-pint or quart boxes. It's excellent real milk with good taste.

The milk is slightly more expensive in $^1/_2$ pints, but since Margaret and I don't use much, we find the small size convenient. We open a little box every two days or so and put it on hot or cold cereal and use it in pasta dishes, white sauces, and an occasional instant Jell-O pudding (I like pistachio). Each small box comes with its own straw and a place to insert it. Children think the little milk boxes are a great treat, and it's possible to buy it in chocolate flavor as well.

The UHT (ultrahigh temperature) milk is sterilized at 284°F and will keep without refrigeration for six months if there are no extremes in temperature. The little boxes are easy to store; each comes with a prominent date stamp. Once a box is opened, we treat it like fresh milk. Four dozen boxes last a long time. We also carry a few boxes of powdered milk, but since we found UHT milk, we've stopped using powdered milk because it's less convenient.

During the past few years we've been eating lots of packaged pasta dishes, which are simple to fix and tasty. Most are packaged for two portions, need only the addition of water, milk, and butter or margarine, and cook for 7 to 12 minutes. The sealed packets are small, dry, and require no refrigeration. I have at hand three sold by Lipton: egg and spinach noodles in parmesan; egg noodles in a butter sauce with savory herbs; and ruffle pasta in a mild cheddar sauce. There are many varieties.

Curried Lentils

A lentil looks something like a flattened pea. It is close to a small bean in size but easier to cook. My favorite recipe is curried lentils, which is based on traditional directions that Margaret, who was born in India, brought from Bombay. We have it often.

1. Wash and soak 1 cup lentils for 2 hours in fresh water.

2. Put the lentils in 2 cups lightly salted water and simmer for 20 minutes. Save the lentil water.

3. Chop up a large onion and a clove of garlic and sauté them in 2 tablespoons butter or margarine in a frying pan until translucent. Then add 1 tablespoon flour and 1 tablespoon curry powder. Season with salt and pepper.

4. While stirring, gradually add 1 cup of the reserved lentil water from step 1. Simmer for 15 minutes or until the curry is thick.

5. Add the lentils and $^{1}/_{2}$ cup raisins to the sauce, simmer for 10 minutes, and serve with rice and a few spoonfuls from a bottle of chutney.

Eggplant

The easiest way I know to prepare eggplant is simply to cut athwartship slices about $^{1}/_{2}$ inch thick. Put a few drops of lemon juice on each side to prevent discoloration. Squeeze out any excess moisture between two dinner plates. Dip the slices in a beaten egg or two, and then roll in breadcrumbs seasoned with salt, pepper, oregano, and thyme. Fry lightly in a thin layer of hot vegetable oil.

The French call eggplant *aubergine* and have a dozen intricate ways to prepare this queen of all vegetables (with her glossy purple imperial gown). It can be sliced, stuffed, layered into moussaka or ratatouille, or hollowed out, cooked, and stuffed with olives, cheese, peppers, squash, tomatoes, and whatever else you can find in the vegetable locker.

Burrida

On a sail around Newfoundland, we picked up this splendid fish recipe from our boating friend Doug Hill in St. John's. It's called *burrida* and is a nice change from the usual fried fish. The recipe works best with cod or a white-fleshed fish that has just been caught. We tried it a few days ago with mahimahi and it was excellent.

For three people:

1. In a large covered frying pan, put in 3 tablespoons olive oil, 1 small onion, and 1 small clove garlic. Sauté until soft.

2. Add $^{1}/_{2}$ cup diced canned tomatoes (or fresh if available), 2 teaspoons dried parsley (or $^{1}/_{4}$ c. fresh parsley), $^{1}/_{4}$ teaspoon anchovy paste (from one of those big toothpaste tubes), and $^{1}/_{4}$ cup white wine. Cook 5–10 minutes.

3. Add $^{1}/_{4}$ teaspoon each cayenne pepper, salt, and pepper, $^{1}/_{2}$ bay leaf, and $^{3}/_{4}$ to 1 pound fish cut into chunks. Simmer 15 minutes (over a flame tamer) or until the fish is cooked. Serve with rice or pasta. This recipe can easily be doubled or tripled for a crowd.

One rule we have is for the cook to always wear an apron. It should be long (down to the ankles) and of heavy vinyl or some material that will deflect, not absorb, boiling liquids. Burns at sea are catastrophic.

Fruit and vegetables should be stored out in the open so air can circulate around them. When we're in port and come in from shopping, we take everything out of paper or plastic bags on the dock or in the dinghy. We discard all bags and cardboard boxes (because of possible cockroaches) and never bring them aboard. Once on the yacht we wash the produce with fresh water, and put the fruit and vegetables in string bags or in open plastic milk boxes in the forepeak. *Do not leave anything stored in plastic bags of any kind, because condensation will ruin the contents.* When you're buying eggs, try to avoid supermarket and cold-storage products. What you want are fresh eggs from a farmer, day-old or week-old eggs, not something that's been in a government refrigerator for a year or more. Generally, if you ask around you can find fresh, unrefrigerated eggs. As I mentioned at the beginning of this chapter, Margaret coats them with petroleum jelly, and the eggs keep for a long time.

We use both butter and margarine. Margarine is less expensive, stays fresh longer in the tropics, and is said to be better for you healthwise. Nevertheless, the taste of Dutch or Irish butter from a newly opened tin on fresh bread is hard to beat. Canned butter is available in many countries, although it's sometimes difficult to buy because of restrictive dairy laws. In California—which exports lots of canned butter but does not sell it internally—I once had to promise a reluctant supplier that I would not open the cans until I was at sea! Canned butter is easy to purchase in Europe, and I've also bought it in Northern Australia. A 1-pound can lasts us about two weeks. In the tropics Margaret and I tend to eat less bread and consequently not as much butter or margarine.

We fry food in Teflon-coated pans, which need little or no grease or butter. For frying onions or foods that we want to brown, we use oil or a white vegetable shortening (Crisco). A can lasts a long time.

Leftovers are a problem, particularly in the tropics, because it's distressing to throw away food. Our solution is to keep the remains of last night's supper and to use the leftovers for stuffing in omelets or mixing with scrambled eggs. For example, a cup of cooked rice and a few bits of spicy fish make a breakfast omelet tasty and filling. The ship's cat eats the rest. The fish get what the cat doesn't eat, because we never keep doubtful food. Trust your nose. If something smells bad, don't even *think* of eating it. Heave it over the side.

Among *Whisper*'s stores we carry small cans of Nestlé or Carnation cream (6 oz.). Canned sweet thick cream is almost impossible to find in the United States, but it's widely available everywhere else in the world; buy a few cans when you see it. Spoon a little on top of vegetables (spinach or green beans), meat dishes, and fruit. This cream is especially good with meat. One idea is to sauté a few chopped onions and cook some roast beef with button mushrooms. Then put a little cream on top of the meat and heat the whole works. Delicious! We do the whole meal in a single 9-inch skillet to avoid using extra pans.

To keep track of our edibles, we use a small spiral-bound notebook (labeled *The*

Food Book) that has two sections: the front half has a list of all the nonfresh food we have on board *by subject* (canned peaches, small tins of chicken, Cream of Wheat, breadcrumbs, etc.). Each can, bottle, or package is represented by a vertical mark after the name.

The back section lists everything *by location* (lockers 1, 2, 3, etc.). When we take out a jar of strawberry jam, for example, we cross off the marks on both the front and back lists. The notebook keeps us current with a running list of all the nonfresh food on board and the location of each item. The little book is handy for finding things and for making out a shopping list at the next port. The fresh food is more out in the open and easy to keep track of visually.

Fresh fish at sea are always good. The fish, however, tend to be of the tuna, wahoo, or dorado variety and are often two to four feet long. The trouble with catching a large fish is that you can eat only so much at the next meal or two. Usually by then you've had enough for a few days anyway.

I generally make cuts *across the fish* with a hacksaw to get steaks quickly and without fuss. In the tropics we feed leftovers to the sharks; in cooler Alaska we have kept pieces of halibut or salmon for two or three days. Some sailors talk about drying fish, but I've not met anyone who was successful at it.

Fishing gear needs to be heavy. We never had much luck catching anything until we tied up near *Fast Lady*, a Japanese yacht that we met in Western Samoa. The Japanese crew lived largely on fish that they caught, and the men couldn't understand how we could be so unsuccessful until they saw our small lures, puny hooks, and thin line.

"The fishing machinery of *Whisper* is for humor only," said the Japanese captain. "Fish of the open ocean are fierce fighters and all catching equipment must be overstrong. We wish no disrespect, but your devices are for small river fish only."

The captain of *Fast Lady* showed us his tackle, which was made up of colorful 6- and 8-inch lures that sparkled with bits of glass and plastic and bristled with feathers. Each hook was 2 inches long and fiendishly curved with a large barb. Four of these hooks were lashed together to make a fearsome trap for a fish. The line was 3-millimeter (⅛") polypropylene with a breaking strength of 200 kilograms. The machined swivels were the diameter of a pencil.

The crew of *Fast Lady* presented us with a selection of lures and line. Our fishing results improved at once. Generally, we have had our best catches near land, although we occasionally hook a tuna or a wahoo far out at sea. We gave away our fancy rod and reel and now madly haul the polypropylene line in hand over hand (after putting on a pair of cheap cotton gloves) when we hook a fish.

One reason the line and lure need to be strong is because of the forward speed of the yacht. At 5 or 6 knots, there's a lot of resistance from a large fish, and the fish may want to go in a different direction. To keep the lure from tearing out of the fish's mouth when he strikes, we put a 3- or 4-foot piece of shock cord on the cockpit end of the line. Sometimes when we hook a big fish, we slow the yacht by letting out the mainsheet.

We carry 78 gallons of fresh water in two tanks plus another 10 gallons in four plastic jugs. Our water consumption at sea is *half a gallon per person per day*. We wash dishes in cold soapy salt water and give them a sparse final rinse with boiling fresh water. We generally take water as it comes from a tap onshore; if the water looks suspect or we have been warned about contamination, we add a little domestic chlorine bleach (Clorox). The formal recommendation of the Clorox people is 1 teaspoon (or 5 mL) per 5 gallons of suspect water, but this amount must be for severely contaminated water.

We strain the water through a fine white cloth as it goes into the tanks; it's surprising how many particles of mud are in supposedly clean water. When locals see us using a cloth, they almost always shake their heads and say that it's not necessary. Yet when they see the mud afterward, their reply is: "I wouldn't have guessed it!"

"Good food and regular meals, as well served as possible, are, I think, the most important thing of all on a long voyage," wrote a famous sailor a long time ago. "It is not often that several people can live at very close quarters and at times in considerable discomfort, without feeling the strain of it after a while. I am sure that the best, and indeed the only way of having a happy ship, is to spare no pains in making the meals as wholesome, as varied, and as attractive as possible."[82]

When the weather is rough, Margaret and I (well wedged in somewhere) eat from bowls, perhaps having pilot biscuits, macaroni and cheese, and oranges. Usually, however, we eat from china plates with pretty decorative patterns. We like the feel and appearance of proper plates and silverware. We appreciate pottery mugs and elegant cloth napkins. We find their use makes our mealtimes a little nicer. After all, the yacht is our home. Why not eat with a bit of style and elegance?

Cooking fresh halibut with chopped onions, dill, and salt and pepper.

21
WHAT DOES WORLD CRUISING COST?

Iwonder if anyone today can realize how far we sailed on so little money. Sailing was more a matter of spirit than common sense. But we were young and wanted to see the world.

I know this chapter will be the first that many people will turn to and read because everyone wants to find out what world voyaging costs. I'll give you my best estimates, but the numbers are slippery because small-boat owners represent three or four economic levels. Some sailors are content to operate on an austerity basis; others demand and are quite willing to pay for what I would call luxury sailing.

To begin with, let me say that if you own a seaworthy vessel in reasonable condition with a few spares and necessary charts and Pilot books, you can go a hell of a long way if you have $10,000 in your pocket. And if you're willing to work, you can always find something. It may be humbling, but . . . well, read on.

Of course, you don't want to run out of money in some far-off country where there's no chance of employment or where you may be in hopeless competition with the locals. You always need to keep a little something on hand and to have an emergency fund in a reliable bank in case of accident or sickness or a mishap with the yacht. Yet if you live simply, spend cautiously, and keep a low profile, you can have a wonderful life and get by for very little, year after year.

We should remember that when we're on a boat for either a short trip or a long trip, the vessel becomes the place where we eat, sleep, and spend substantial amounts of time. The boat becomes our house; the miles logged by the yacht take the place of airline flights and automobile trips. Our principal entertainment is sailing from port to port and living on the boat in the harbors or anchorages at each end.

So at a stroke, we've eliminated two significant expense areas—home and transportation—and severely cut down on entertainment costs. This holds true whether we're going 100 miles along the coast of Brazil, sailing across the 9,615 miles of the Pacific between Ecuador and the Philippines, or sitting in a local marina in Boston.

Our other expenses are for food, routine maintenance, and an occasional piece of boating gear or a new sail. We also have medical costs and a few personal and miscellaneous items. Margaret and I generally don't carry insurance on the yacht unless it's required in a special case (Italy), for liability (United States), or for an unusual risk (the coast of Labrador). Then we buy a policy with a sizeable deductible. If you're tied up at a dock for the winter, why pay for expensive sailing insurance? At least you can opt for insurance for a laid-up, nonsailing vessel.

My income as a freelance writer and editorial photographer has always been up and down. Years ago we learned to operate on a cash basis and do not use installment accounts of any kind. We pay cash at the dentist and receive a discount. We use credit cards for convenience, but either pay the charge within 30 days or keep an interest-bearing cash balance with the credit card company (this is often called a debit card).

In eastern Maryland in April 2002, we spent about $95 a week (call it $13.50 a day) for food. This covered everything for two people, including meat, fish, and an occasional bottle of wine. Like most people we shop carefully and buy food specials at the market, but we don't stint ourselves in any way and have plenty of fresh fruit, vegetables, milk products, chocolate—whatever we want.

Margaret and I eat almost all our meals aboard *Whisper* because we like eating together, and we know that our food is better and more convenient than restaurant fare. We seldom go out because the food is generally middling to poor, and the present-day costs are high ($20 to $35 or more for two). On a recent Mediterranean trip, I recall that a couple on a yacht next to us in the village of Carloforte on San Pietro Island off Sardinia spent $42 "for a nice meal of fish at a waterfront restaurant." Spending $42—a typical charge—once in a while is not going to bankrupt most boatowners, but on a steady basis it can triple the food bill. If your funds are limited and you want to extend your cruising miles, stay out of restaurants or limit yourself to one meal out a month, or fewer in expensive countries.

Perfecting the galley and its equipment is a good investment. Margaret keeps a folder with all our favorite recipes.

I remember discussing the food situation on long trips with a Belgian sailor, Guy Cappeliez, when our yachts were anchored near one another in Hanamenu Bay on the island of Hiva Oa in the Marquesas Islands.

"We like to eat well, but our cruising fund is not too big," said Guy, who was sailing around the world on his blue double-ender *Procax*. "Viviane and I always buy first-class foodstuffs, which we prepare on board the ship. We feel that our meals are infinitely better than restaurant fare, and of course our costs are much less."

I wrote the last two paragraphs long ago, but I believe they're valid today and are a universal truth of voyaging in a small sailboat: *Buy first-class food, but eat on board.*

We often invite local people or other sailors on *Whisper* for meals. Margaret and I enjoy this and find that it's a good way to become acquainted with nearby residents, who may see yachts in their bay year after year but are seldom invited aboard. Having visitors on *Whisper* leads to all sorts of social life, sometimes more than we can handle.

We always ask visitors to sign our guest book and put down the date and their address. Over the years, we've filled two books with hundreds of names and little messages and sometimes a photograph, a lock of hair, or a crude sketch. These two books have become precious, and we often look at them to retrieve an address or a memory.

In Alanya, Turkey, behind the breakwater and in the shadow of the medieval Red Tower that protected the galley fleets of bygone times, we tied up next to the modern fishing fleet. There were 42 open wooden boats 6 to 8 meters long. Each was driven by a 1-cylinder diesel and crewed by noisy, proud, determined fishermen who worked on their nets day and night. The man next to us wore an orange cap, a natty sweater, and black boots into which he tucked his drawstring trousers. He was immensely strong, and when he rowed around the harbor he treated his oars like matchsticks.

*   *   *

In the remote tropical islands of the South Pacific, we found that by entertaining or doing a few favors for the locals—taking them for a sail, dealing with coral cuts, or sharing a glass of wine—we received all the fish we could eat. In Alaska we were often given a salmon or a slab of halibut (which are enormous). In Canada, it was a salmon, or Dungeness or snow crabs. In Chile, we swapped a few pesos for a tasty, meter-long *congrio colorado* or half a bushel of clams. In northern Australia it was the barramundi, one of the tastiest fish anywhere.

Certainly fresh fish (and occasionally shellfish) is wonderful and a fortunate addition to our larder, but we have learned that we can never count on it. And when we're lucky enough to have fish, there's always too much at one time. I've sailed across the Atlantic many times, but only on the last two crossings have I caught anything worthwhile (one tuna and eight dorados).

In the Cyclades and Dodecanese islands in the Aegean Sea, we spent a few drachmas for food, but not many because there simply wasn't much to eat on some of the small islands. We passed two winters in the British Virgin Islands in the Caribbean where the little shops had pathetic stocks of marginal food. Again, there wasn't much to buy. (At the public markets, the fruit and vegetables always had two prices: the lower for black people, the higher for whites.)

One cruising truth emerges: When you are on a sailing passage or visiting obscure islands and little-known coastlines, your financial requirements are low. Many of your meals will be from stores on board, and in effect you will be eating from a food bank, with a few supplements now and then. I can easily recall many two-month periods of not spending a single dollar. On a trip around Vancouver Island, our main expense was for an armload of oiled wool for two sweaters that Margaret was knitting.

To summarize food costs, I would say that at sea, and when sailing in remote areas, you tend to eat simpler, less deluxe food. You have what you need, but it's not as fancy. There is often plenty of food somewhere in third world countries if you could only get it. The reality is that the marvelous food distribution systems and supermarkets of North America, Europe, and Japan don't exist in most of the world. For average onboard, in-transit food costs in 2002, therefore, I would slice off $2 from the $13.50 figure. Let's say $11.50 for two people.

For medical care, we have simply paid cash for private doctors and dentists, which over the years (for us at least) has been quite satisfactory. Before a long trip, Margaret and I go to a dentist for X-rays and to have any doubtful teeth repaired. In past years, our experiences with private medical insurance, both domestic and foreign, have been dismal. The fine print (exceptions, limitations, cancellations, revisions) is endless, and the governing policies of the companies seem to be to argue, stall, and delay, rather than to pay.

In truth, our medical problems have been infrequent. A long time ago in Brazil, Margaret was troubled by an ear infection. She went to an excellent eye, ear, nose, and throat specialist in Recife. Once a doctor in American Samoa treated infected coral cuts on my ankles. Two years ago in Newfoundland, a dog bit me. Other times I have seen doctors in the Canary Islands and Martinique. All were first-class except for two dreadful Greek medical imposters in Cyprus. (My mistake was not going to the British hospital in the main city.) I have no doubt forgotten about other visits to doctors. We've always had an emergency fund but never used it. We've been lucky.

In most countries, medical costs and drugs are far less expensive than in the United States. In Peru, for instance, you can buy any kind of medicine over the counter. The Peruvian reasoning seems to be that if you are stupid enough to use hard drugs, you will soon kill yourself.

Medical care falls into two categories: minor problems (a burned hand, an infected cut, a dislocated shoulder) and major problems (appendicitis, kidney stones, a heart attack). For minor things, a trip to the local doctor and pharmacy may be adequate.

The major category is more difficult. Do you return to your own country from a distant island? Or head for a closer major medical center? Who pays for the medical evacuation, the specialist, and the hospital stay? Is the foreign hospital any good? Where does the patient recuperate? Will your nearest embassy or consul give advice? Once I was operated on in a hospital in Puerto Rico. The operating theatre, doctors, and nurses were first-class, but the hospital room was dreadful, and after a very hungry day, I learned that the patient's family was responsible for feeding the patient.

In 1981, a deranged local man in Bequia in the Caribbean stabbed visiting sailor Jim Holman. Poor Jim almost died from the resulting chest infection in the crude local hospital, where the care was on a witch doctor level. Jim's wife, Betsy Hitz-Holman, a former managing editor of *Cruising World* magazine, saved her husband's life by taking him to a private clinic where there was a proper doctor and competent nurses.[83] In this sort of situation, of course, you spend what's necessary.

The charges for minor medical care may be on the order of fifty to a hundred dollars. For major medical emergencies, the costs can be in the thousands. Whether to cover major problems by long-term insurance is up to each person. Medical evacuation insurance is another tough choice. When we were in Turkey in 1996, a British acquaintance on a nearby yacht had a severe internal problem. The conscientious Turkish doctors dutifully tried everything but finally recommended specialists in London. The sailor was evacuated to England by air, but the charge was the equivalent of nine first-class fares. It's easy to dismiss this until a loved one is stricken with something serious; then your attitude changes abruptly.

When you're over 65, you need more medical attention. Margaret and I qualify for Medicare in the United States, which costs the two of us $1,260 a year. We supplement it with a Blue Cross policy for $2,880 a year. The total is $4,140 a year, or $345 a month. The Blue Cross coverage offers limited medical attention outside the United States. Most countries have similar insurance.

If you're a sailor and reading this, there's a chance that you may be on a budget, which means that overseas telephone calls, rental cars, guided tours to the interior, airplane flights, and taxis should be used with caution. When you travel to distant places, you probably want to do a little sightseeing. Often you can arrange side trips without a lot of spending because you're already at your destination and—like a turtle—you have your home with you.

When I talk about costs, it may sound as if Margaret and I deprive ourselves of things. Not at all. It's simply that long ago we decided to live modestly and travel and sail at our own pace.

Over time, we have learned that once we arrive at the next port—perhaps in a big city—it's easy to produce a two-page shopping list. You are tempted to hit the fancy cafés, rush to a sailmaker, hire a car, engage a local helper, and all the rest. If your budget is X, you can spend 2X or 4X or more. In some places, you can get involved in a complex social game with high entertainment costs. How to get around this? Sailors on an economy budget should avoid big cities and yachting centers and examine each expense to see if it's really necessary.

For instance, instead of tying up in crowded marinas, we prefer to anchor out or lie alongside a private dock. The world is filled with thousands of delightful, sheltered places to anchor. Most are nicer than noisy marinas. Of course, a marina may be easier to live in than a spot where you're anchored out, but it's your choice. If it's necessary to go to a marina, we run errands for a day or two and then move on.

To find a private dock in a waterfront community or up a river usually takes a little looking around. In the United States, we ask people, pin up notices at the yacht club and grocery store (the responses go to a friend's phone or cell phone), and maybe run a small classified advertisement in a local newspaper. If we pursue all three at the same time, there's a good chance we will have several offers.

We've discovered that many owners or managers of unoccupied docks secretly wish for a handsome sailboat to brighten up their property. When you get to know the owners, you sometimes wind up keeping an eye on the dock or property in return for free dockage. However, I think it's wise to make a small payment or perform a definite service for the property owner. We all know about free lunches.

Margaret and I spent three wonderful winters in Maine tied up to unused boatyard docks (once in Camden; twice in Southwest Harbor) in return for small fees. Another time we did this in Sidney, British Columbia. In 1984, we could have passed the winter at the yacht club in Seville on the Guadalquivir River, but we decided to move on. During the winter of 1988–89, we were at the downtown dock of the fancy Hilton Hotel in Annapolis for the winter. We paid a trifling fee ($2.33 a day) and used the hotel exercise room, showers, and telephones and received our mail at the front desk. We spent another winter in Buenos Aires at the lovely grounds of the Yacht Club Argentino in San Fernando, where we were guests.

Occasionally you sail to a country where the exchange rate is grossly out of step with your own currency. Then everything is unbelievably cheap; life becomes unreal. In the past this has happened to us in Bali, Vanuatu, Chile, and Turkey. Of course, sometimes the exchange rate goes the other way. At the moment, foreign sailors shopping in Norwegian grocery stores need to take their heart medicine with them. Again, life becomes unreal.

Routine yacht maintenance is costly but part of the sailing life. It's expensive to take a boat out of the water and to clean, sand, smooth, and cover the bottom with special paint. Generally, the best time to deal with problems is when the yacht is in a boatyard because various experts and specialized tools are at hand. The propeller shaft bearing may be worn, or a bow fitting may need to be welded. You may want an expert boat carpenter for a few hours or an electrician to help solve a wiring puzzle. By temperament and preference, I prefer to do as much of my boatyard work as possible, and we can generally find a yard where this is permitted or even welcomed.

Besides general upkeep, there's an area of work that I call capital improvements. When you log a lot of sea miles, you find that over time, various major installations do not work out or need modifications. Often the cost of the change—the labor—equals the cost of the item itself. For example, when I bought our present *Whisper*, I installed a lightweight hand windlass on the foredeck. It worked OK for five years, but then broke down. It was difficult to obtain replacement parts, and when I studied the damaged pieces, I realized that I had been grossly overloading the device. I finally junked it and bought a larger windlass with more robust gearing. To mount it, I had to reinforce the foredeck and install a special stainless steel brace.

This sort of expense is usual with sailboats and needs an allowance in the budget. The money can be for improvements to the anchor roller at the bow, a bigger winch on the mast, repairs to a water tank that's developed pinhole leaks, a new sun awning, a galley pump, or whatever. The standard of maintenance on world-cruising yachts is surprisingly high because it's important for everything to work and to be in first-class order. When you're alone in distant places, there are few pull-in garages. During the weeks and months when you're under way, you should spend your expertise sailing and navigating and enjoying the passage, not fiddling with boat maintenance on jobs that should have been dealt with during the last haulout.

Elsewhere I have noted that maintenance costs escalate rapidly with increasing overall length. A mitigating expense consideration, however, is that if three or four people (or a couple with children) sail on a yacht, the vessel's expenses remain about the same as for one or two people. The food, personal, and medical costs increase somewhat, but the yacht's running expenses are no higher.

Poets claim that the wind is free. It is not, and I can tell you that to employ the wind to drive your vessel is a substantial and continuing expense. A new mainsail and jib for *Whisper* cost about $5,000 dollars. The problem is the sun, which after two or three years rots out the Dacron material. This happens particularly in the tropics— even if you carefully cover the sails when they're furled (doubling the thickness of the sail cover helps). Our two most used sails last for about twenty thousand miles; the cost works out to be roughly twenty-five cents a mile.

There's unending pressure for boatowners to buy things. Take just one: Advertisers trying to sell space-age telephones stress the importance of keeping in touch with parents, children, and friends. Some of these devices are very expensive, both for the initial equipment and the unit cost per message. Before you buy, ask for something in writing about trial periods, bottom line costs, whether the message deliveries are guaranteed, and if the device can be repaired when you're in Sri Lanka or Uruguay. And, oh yes—how long has the company been in business?

Personally, I like to write and receive ordinary letters, which are written at a slower pace and perhaps reflect a little more thinking and less chatter and small talk. But each of us is different.

Sightseeing in foreign places is part of the fun of cruising. Often you can take local buses or rent bicycles or motor scooters. Or you can walk. We have entertained people on board who were so proud of their local area that we got a grand tour the next day. In Ketchikan, Alaska, I recall that Virginia Head, the wife of a logging camp operator, not only urged us to climb the local mountain—"You must see the view from Deer Mountain"—but accompanied us to the top. Many times the local sightseeing is easy and close because you can sail in your boat to the very heart of the best places.

Yet the increasing number of cruising yachts means that they are no longer such an attraction. Twenty-five years ago, the arrival of a small boat after an ocean crossing meant a newspaper story. Today, city editors are bored with yachts unless they run into trouble or have a crew of four pretty young women and one man.

Cruising boats tend to follow well-worn trails. Numerous yacht clubs, marinas, and cities in the path of these yachts now deal with their nautical visitors on a strict business basis, rather than as distinguished guests. Today, when you pull into many marinas or yacht clubs, the manager may be standing on the dock and smiling. However, he may also have his pen out and a so-much-per-day contract in his hand for you to sign.

With reasonable preparations you can make long sailing trips without much expense. Many people have gone from the south coast of England to the Caribbean, spent a year or two, and returned without hauling the yacht or buying new sails. Afterward, however, there are usually heavy charges for a major refit and the renewal of worn or broken items. Over time, you must replace leaky oilskins and change worn halyards and sheets. You may lose an anchor, or the cooking stove may rust out. Oars may float away; someone may have swiped the dinghy. You may have to buy new zincs and have the engine fuel injectors rebuilt. The anchor chain may need to be galvanized or replaced.

The sums in our maintenance budget allow for these renewals and repairs. Not everything at once, of course, but little by little on a regular basis.

If you examine the expenses of a dozen long-time cruising couples, you will find without exception that the biggest item is the upkeep of the yacht. Painting, general repairs, the purchase of an occasional sail, and gear replacement are absolutely necessary if the boat is to make continuing and successful offshore voyages. The surprising thing is that food and miscellaneous personal costs are not high. It's a mixed bag with regard to insurance costs for health and the yacht. Some couples have both; others have none.

Here are numbers for *Whisper* over a 25-year period.

Item	1976	2001
all food costs	$100 a month or $1,200 a year	$375 a month or $4,500 a year
health plan, doctor, dentist	$70 a month or $840 a year	$345 a month or $4,140 a year*
clothes, toiletries, laundry, mail, local transport, and miscellaneous	$100 a month or $1,200 a year	$300 a month or $3,600 a year
yacht upkeep and new equipment, fuel, charts, and moorings	$250 a month or $3,000 a year	$750 a month or $9,000 a year
Totals	$520 a month or $6,240 a year	$1,770 a month; $21,240 a year*

* Note that this includes significantly higher medical costs because of the ages of the principals.

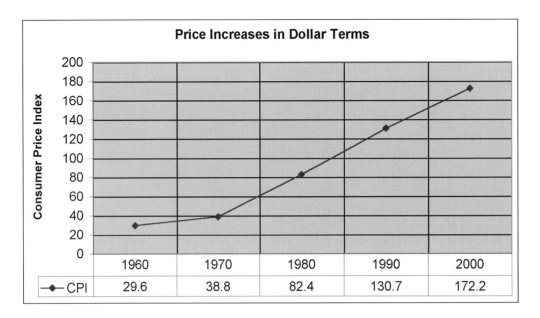

The figure of $21,240 for a yearly sailing budget seems stratospheric, but the truth is that the supposedly stable U.S. dollar buys less and less each year. Inflation and price rises grind on. The U.S. Department of Labor publishes the Consumer Price Index (CPI), a figure based on a basket of goods and services in the United States. This number is not ideal, but it's published every month, has some validity for comparative costs abroad, and gives a good idea why our savings account is worth less each year. Consider the CPI figures in the accompanying graph. These numbers mean that $100 in 1980 was worth $47 in 2001. Or $100 in 1990 would buy $74 worth of goods in 2001.

Our cruising friends Willem and Cori Stein from Holland, who live similarly to us and sail in a red 39-foot Joshua steel ketch named *Terra Nova*, reported their costs in year 2000 at $15,000. This includes $2,000 for health insurance and $600 for boat insurance ($100,000 with a 35 percent deductible).

Ex-attorney Andy Kerr, owner of *Andiamo III*, reported in 1992 that he and his wife, Susan, spent $1,500 a month on minimalist cruising on their extensive world trips. Updated to 2001, the sum would be $22,721 a year.

In 2001, we met the husband-and-wife team of Simon Brown and Beverly Pilgrim, who sailed their engineless 36-foot gaff-rigged wooden cutter *Beroë* from England to the Caribbean. Simon and Beverly then headed to the United States, Bermuda, Spain, and beyond. *Beroë* was run frugally but sensibly. That year, her owners spent $14,678.

*   *   *

I want to make it clear that this chapter is about traveling and upkeep costs of voyaging yachts that pay their way as legitimate enterprises. I suppose it's possible to bum your way around the world, scrounging meals and hospitality and taking advantage of people. However, this is not the way my sailing friends and I travel. I am not a seagoing hobo because I don't believe it is ethical. I pay for what I need or trade a skill that I have for something from others.

Many of the major voyages in small sailing vessels have been made by ordinary people with more adventure in their hearts than dollars in their pockets. As long as your vessel is sound and well stocked, you have something set aside for emergencies, and there is a little to live on, you can get by. Of course, if you're retired and receiving monthly checks, the economic pressure is off; yet there's a certain stimulus and satisfaction that comes from earning your keep as you go.

Who are the people who actually go long distances in small boats? Two of them are the English sailors Simon Brown and Beverly Pilgrim from Norfolk, who sail in a rebuilt wooden racing cutter that was designed by G. L. Watson and built in Scotland in 1887. Is an old boat slow? Not at all. Simon and Beverly averaged 137 miles per day on their Atlantic crossing, a daily total that boats a century newer would be hard-pressed to equal. Seldom have we met a couple that had such fun every day. To pay their cruising expenses, Simon and Beverly sold their landscape gardening business, car, apartment, furniture, etc. and invested the proceeds in modest rental properties that provide a small income.

If a person is diligent and willing to work, he or she can always find something. It may be teaching English or French, painting houses, or typing bills of lading. It's not the work that's important, but the cash to continue while the faraway light is still bright in your eyes. The old standbys for men (women can do these jobs as well) are diesel mechanic, boat carpenter, and refrigeration expert. For women, it's teaching school (perhaps as a substitute) or providing language instruction. There are also boat deliveries, boat supervision (while the owners are away), sail repair, fixing outboard motors and motor scooters, canvas work, and varnishing and painting. One of the best places to find work is among the large boats of the cruising fleet, where language difficulties and work permits are generally not problems. Sailors who work for others should arrange to be paid in cash on a weekly basis.

Remember that my whole case is based on sailing and going somewhere, not sitting in a marina and talking about voyaging.

Careening a schooner for bottom cleaning in a sheltered bay on the island of Bequia in the Caribbean.

22

THE CRUISING ENGINE: NECESSITY OR MONSTER?

Ever since auxiliary engines were first installed in pleasure sailing vessels, the owners have compiled long lists of reasons for both having and not having engines. At one extreme is the purist, who disclaims any alliance with mechanical propulsion. "The natural wind is good enough for me," he says loftily—until the wind dies and he wants to go somewhere. At the other extreme is the proponent of the motor sailer, whose life and often existence seem to revolve around large engines and masses of complex machinery.

Since I've sailed a 50-footer around the world twice without an engine, and I've campaigned 35-footers in many places with the occasional use of a small auxiliary engine, I will try to speak for both sides.

I believe that if you take a vessel with reasonable sail area from an anchor or a mooring in a region where the winds are generally predictable, you can manage without an engine. Long ocean passages usually don't require an engine; it's the

An engine is dirty, smelly, noisy, heavy, expensive, and hard to work on because it's jammed into a small space. Yet once installed and running nicely, a small inboard engine is wonderfully handy for docking maneuvers, anchoring help, and calm patches.

ports and headlands at each end that may demand some expert sailing. More rarely, an ocean journey may include a portion of the doldrums, where a few hundred miles of powering can take the place of a great deal of frustration and sail drill.

A small engine can be very helpful in areas where winds are fickle, in regions where tidal streams run like flooded rivers, and for ports with difficult entrances and complex docks and jetties. You may lose the wind outside a port with bad weather coming up; you may wish to transit a canal or a narrow strait. You may need to shift your berth at night with an ill wind blowing. It seems to me that all these situations are legitimate uses for a small auxiliary.

Yet the captain of a cruising yacht should be able to deal with these problems under sail alone, or at least to make a courageous attempt. With patience, clever use of the sails, a bit of anchoring now and then, perhaps a few strokes of a sweep, and the use of lines to warp the vessel around, you can do astonishing things. Instead of a panic call to the coast guard or a towing service when the wind dies and the engine won't start, you might drop a light anchor and—like our forefathers—wait for the wind.

It won't hurt you to anchor for a few hours, and it will give you time for your life to calm down.

I believe it's just as important to know how to handle a sailboat in narrow or crowded waters as it is to understand navigation or anchoring. Personally, I find that the tactics of maneuvering in difficult circumstances are a challenge, a lot of fun, and eminently satisfying. One of my greatest pleasures is to enter and leave ports under sail. Sooner or later the engine will be out of order anyway, and you will have to sail under marginal conditions. Then the practice will pay off. Competent maneuvering under sail may save your vessel and maybe even your life.

I urge you to practice at times when the winds are light, you're not in a hurry, and you're in safe, uncrowded waters. Then if you make a mistake or two, you can try again. Privately.

- Just for fun, see if you can tack around that distant buoy when the wind is 6-8 knots. You may find that a tidal stream is setting your boat one way or the other. Your course may not be as direct as you thought.
- See if you can sail the anchor out.
- When your boat is sailing fast downwind, tie a loop in the line of your worst white fender and toss it over the side. Try going back under sail and picking up the fender with a boat hook. You may find that there's more to this maneuver than you think. This exercise may give you a whole new appreciation of man-overboard drills.

You can make a distinction between (1) a pure sailing ship, (2) a sailing vessel with a small auxiliary engine, and (3) a motor vessel with auxiliary sails that are used when the wind is favorable (a sail-assisted vessel). Most accidents happen to category 3, because many owners of so-called full-power auxiliaries are more motormen than sailors and don't know how to maneuver and control their ships under sail. These yacht owners often have no concept of storm management, how to approach a harbor under sail, how to heave to, and so on.

Instead of knowledge and practice, they rely on engines that may work or may not. These expensive vessels are often built like icebreakers, with emphasis on deluxe accommodations and machinery, and typically have a cut-down ketch rig for easy handling in heavy weather. They may have battenless roller-furling sails for both the jib and the main. Unfortunately, such a rig—in combination with the drag of a large three-bladed propeller—gives no light-weather performance at all. I think this design trend is deplorable for long-distance voyaging. People who have sailed long distances know that light-weather performance is most important and that cut-down rigs are ill-advised. As I've said elsewhere, I've found that 50 percent of all winds at sea are 15 knots or less.

An engine does not substitute for seamanship under sail. The confidence that an engine gives to a new boatowner is based on the spurious logic that suggests "I'll be twice as safe with a 60-horsepower engine as with a 30-horsepower." If you own a sailboat and don't know how to operate it, you should hire an experienced man or woman to teach you or go to sailing classes and learn to sail a dinghy. In this game it's necessary to serve a bit of an apprenticeship. If you don't want to do this, I suggest that you sell your boat.

The only practical engine for a cruising yacht is a diesel. Gasoline is out of the question for three reasons:

- acute fire danger from the fuel
- high fuel consumption
- the difficulty of keeping an ignition system operating in a damp, saltwater environment

While diesel oil will burn, it's much less flammable than gasoline, whose vapors are full of liquid lightning. Years ago when I was in the U.S. Air Force, I attended a firefighting demonstration. The instructor put a flat metal drip pan that measured 4 by 4 feet on the ground near a hangar and poured half an inch of 100-octane gasoline into the pan. He then tossed a match into it. Wow! A roaring torrent of flames about forty feet high thundered into the sky. The gutsy instructor moved right in on the fire with an extinguisher and showed us how to put it out.

I've never forgotten the raging ferocity of that fire.

I was long aware of the drag of an aperture and a conventional propeller. John Brandlmayr, Whisper's *designer, suggested "an increase in rudder area and a more modern shape." Since I was in the midst of installing a new engine, I decided to close up the aperture and build a new rudder at the same time.*

Yachts with gasoline engines burn up every year. Once Margaret and I watched in horror when a gasoline-powered ex–coast guard vessel blew up with a tremendous explosion across from our berth in Sausalito. The owner was killed instantly. Timbers flew through the air, and one banged down near us while smoke and flames roared into the sky. The experience was terrible. This is why I don't carry gasoline on board or use an outboard engine.

Diesel fuel consumption is about two-thirds that of gasoline; diesel fuel is usually cheaper, so the hourly cost is about half that of a gasoline engine. At modest cruising revolutions a marine diesel of 12 to 35 horsepower will use from 1 to 4 quarts of fuel an hour, and of course a diesel requires no spark ignition system at all. The investment is more than for a gasoline engine, but the safety, greater range, and reliability compensate for the higher price.

A marine diesel will last for years. These engines are strongly made, with a massive crankshaft, heavy cylinders, and sturdy bearings. Reduction gears are usually fitted to enable an efficient, large-diameter propeller to be driven smoothly and easily hour after hour. A big fixed propeller, however, produces substantial drag when the engine is shut off and the yacht is sailing.

To get around this, many owners fit either feathering or folding propellers to angle or collapse the blades out of the way for less resistance. The best-known feathering propeller is the Italian-made Max Prop, which is made in two- and three-bladed models. They are nicely machined and work well, although they are expensive and need regular servicing because of the complicated gearing in the hub.

I like folding propellers because of reduced drag and the lesser likelihood of picking up lobster pot lines. I have used two-bladed Mar-Tec folding propellers with good results for many years.

A diesel engine weighs about 25 percent more than a gasoline engine of equivalent horsepower and requires sturdy mounts to withstand greater vibration. A small diesel can easily drive a 50-amp alternator to generate electricity for lighting and accessories as well as a belt-driven bilge pump or a refrigeration compressor.

The engines we use are four-cycle models in which the first downstroke of the piston draws in air, which is compressed on the upstroke to about 600 pounds per square inch. At the top of the stroke, a small charge of oil is sprayed into the cylinder through an injector. The heat of the compression ignites the oil, and the rapid expansion of the gases created by the explosion drives the piston downward. The next upstroke forces the waste gases out the exhaust port, and the cycle is complete.

The sole demands of a diesel engine are clean fuel and plenty of air. (With an elevated air intake, a diesel will run submerged.) To ensure clean fuel, you pass it through a series of screens and filters to

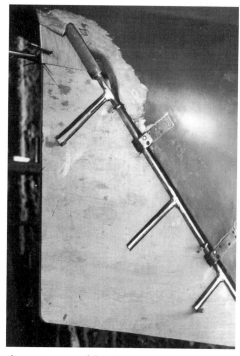

An expert welder brazed fingers to the rudder stock. I then formed the new rudder of ³⁄₈" plywood and glassed it to the metal pieces by wrapping fiberglass around the rudder stock and across the bronze fingers.

remove water and foreign matter. The slightest bit of blockage will clog an injector and, depending on the number of cylinders, stop the engine or—with a dead cylinder—make the engine shake and vibrate severely. One fuel filter is not enough; generally boats employ three. Sometimes a partially blocked injector will pump raw fuel into a cylinder. The engine will run roughly while raw fuel washes the lubricating oil from the piston and cylinder walls. Suddenly a horrible squealing followed by silence means that the piston has frozen in the cylinder. (My tuition for this little lesson was $550.) Servicing injectors and installing new tips is another expensive game.

You can guarantee clean fuel if you pay attention to the fuel that goes into the tank and change fuel filters regularly. If you install an hour meter on the engine, it will alert you to put in new filters every hundred hours or at whatever interval you decide. If you don't log a lot of engine hours, it may be prudent to change the filters every so many months. The cost of the filters is trifling compared with their importance.

I try to strain all the fuel coming aboard by slipping a piece of woman's nylon stocking over the pump nozzle. Or I filter the fuel through a felt or chamois element in a large funnel if I am pouring from a plastic jug. At a crowded fuel dock, however, it may be impossible to filter the fuel, and you may have to accept the diesel as it comes. For this reason I prefer to take fuel in jugs. Of course, in remote places, jugs are often the only way, and you may be lucky to get any fuel at all.

When I'm taking fuel I add a few drops of a microbiocide chemical (Biobor or equivalent) that keeps down slime-producing fungi that clog filters and fuel lines.

I built up the rudder with layers of fiberglass laid in epoxy. I used carefully scribed lines, a long straightedge, a red grease pencil, and a grinder to shape the rudder. I found that a mixture of epoxy and microballoons and hand sanding with a large flat block worked well for the last part of the fairing. To stabilize the final product, I put one layer of glass cloth set in epoxy over the final product.

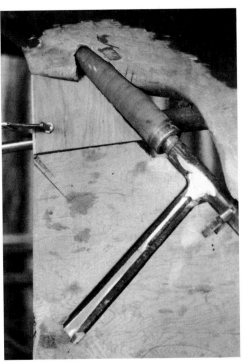

I had a machine shop knurl the rudder tube so it would bond well with the hull. Here I'm adding a piece of plywood as a base for glassing to fill in an area at the top of the old rudder cutout. I have partially filled the old aperture.

You need only a tiny amount—135 to 270 parts per million. Dilution directions come with the chemicals, which are sold in clever application bottles.

When the tank is full and has sat for a few days, I drain a pint or so of diesel oil from the bottom via a petcock, whose handle I keep tied in place with safety wire. This step draws off any water and impurities that have settled to the bottom.

If the base of the fuel tank is not accessible, it may be possible to pump a little fuel from the bottom of the tank by going in the top with a long piece of ⅜-inch-diameter copper tubing or a stiff rubber hose connected to a small hand pump. If

Here I am building up and fairing the hull by gluing small pieces of plywood in place with epoxy, carefully grinding them to shape, and then adding layers of fiberglass. I have closed the old propeller aperture. I had a machine shop make a longer stem tube so the propeller will operate aft of the rudder. In order for the propeller shaft to miss the rudder tube, I angled the engine five degrees to port. This offset about equaled the torque of the propeller to starboard.

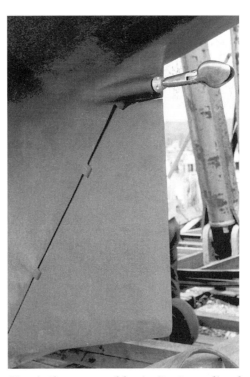

Here's the new rudder in its streamlined and enlarged form. All these changes worked out nicely. At normal cruising engine revolutions the boat traveled in a straight line. At low speeds with the propeller blades folded, she definitely sailed faster. We traveled around the world with this arrangement. Crab pot lines merely slid past the propeller.

you move this pipe or hose around a little as you work the pump, it will vacuum the bottom of the tank and suck up water and particles of sludge. This is crude, but it's surprising how much junk you pick up.

From the tank the fuel goes through three filters. The first is a high-quality primary cylindrical filter (4" in diameter and 9" high) with a drain at the bottom. I use the excellent Racor 500 FG device, which employs a paper element and a complex filtering scheme to take out water and suspended particulate matter. It's best to mount the filter near the forward end of the engine or in a place where the filter can be seen and serviced. This makes it easy to change elements and to inspect the clear plastic bowl (with a flashlight) to see how much crud has fallen to the bottom and whether the filter needs draining.

I change this filter every six months. I have found that it's best to use a Racor element with a Racor filter (or an X element with an X brand filter) simply because there's a better chance that they will fit together. A dozen companies make replacement filters at discount prices, but they all use such complicated numbering schemes that there's a good chance that the replacement filter will be too long or too short. I try to keep a couple of genuine elements on board.

The second filter is a microscreen on the engine fuel pump. The third is the final fuel filter, another cylindrical device with a replaceable paper element. By this time, the diesel oil should be perfectly clean.

For some fuel arrangements, it's helpful to keep a slight positive fuel pressure in the line between the tank and the injector pump. In the past, I have installed a black neoprene squeeze-bulb hand pump from an outboard engine in the diesel fuel line. A few squeezes on the bulb gives enough pressure to draw fuel from the tank, fill the filters, and reveal any leaks in the various lines and connections after the system is bled of air.

Fuel delivery to the engine can be interrupted by air in the filters or in any of the lines between the diesel tank and the injectors. To get rid of the air you generally go through a simple but messy procedure in which you pump a little fuel while you loosen the injector lines or a special bolt on the final fuel filter. This allows bubbles of air and diesel oil to escape until the fuel system is free of air. Some engines deal with this automatically. The engine instructions will tell you how to bleed the fuel system, or you can hire a mechanic to show you. Don't leave the dock without this knowledge.

I don't mean to scare anyone with all this talk about filters and bleeding, because if you keep the fuel system of a diesel in order, the engine will run with remarkable reliability, year after year.

Inboard engines are almost always water-cooled. (Air-cooled engines are unbelievably noisy.) A saltwater pump delivers cooling water into a mixing area or elbow at the outlet of the exhaust manifold. The pressure of the exhaust gases coming from the engine then pushes the hot water and exhaust gas mixture overboard. On its way over the side via a large-diameter (say, 3") thick-walled hose, the exhaust gases and water usually go via a waterlift muffler, which reduces heat and noise. Since hot exhaust gases and salt water make a particularly corrosive combination, waterlift mufflers are generally made of fiberglass or heavy ($^5/32$" or 4 mm) stainless steel.

There are two problems with wet exhaust systems.

First, since the engine and exhaust are usually at the waterline or below, seawater is liable to run back down the exhaust system from the outside when the engine is not running.

The usual remedy is to put a high loop in the exhaust hose on its way through the transom area so that any incoming water from the outside will have to climb a steep hill. Since this is not 100 percent effective, it's often augmented with a large flapper valve (either on the transom or along the hose), so that water and gases can run out but not in. A few sailors use a gate valve or lean over the transom and shove a tapered plug into the exhaust outlet, but these both have

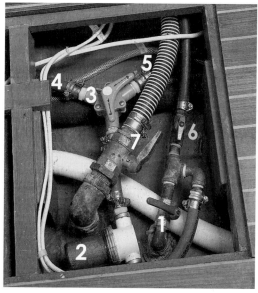

There are many ways to arrange bilge plumbing. Here is what I have done in one area of Whisper's *cabin just forward of the companionway steps. Number 1 is the saltwater intake and shutoff valve for cooling water for the engine. The cooling water goes through a simple filter (2) and then through a Y-valve (3) to the engine via line 5. If I should elect to pump the bilge with the engine (a low-capacity arrangement), I turn the Y-valve to its alternate position. This draws water from the bilge via hose 4. Valve 6 is the shutoff for the galley saltwater foot pump. Number 7 is the shutoff for the galley sink drain. The two large hoses underneath are to and from bilge pumps. In all, four valves and a filter are handy and accessible.*

the disadvantage that you have to remember to do something. The high loop and the flapper valve actions are automatic.

Second, when the engine is shut down, the normal cooling water can continue to flow to the exhaust manifold by siphon. This is the seawater that normally is forced overboard by the exhaust gases. When there's a siphon problem, however, the water comes in via the saltwater inlet in the bilge, through the saltwater pump, to the exhaust manifold, and into the heart of the engine through an open exhaust valve.

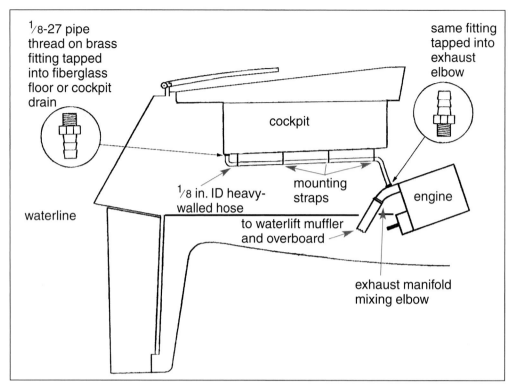

To prevent cooling water from siphoning into the engine when it is shut off, I bleed off a small percentage of the cooling water via a small hose that goes to a back corner of the cockpit. When the engine is running, it is easy to glance down and see whether the cooling water is flowing. When the engine is off, air runs back down the hose and prevents siphoning. This arrangement is automatic and requires no attention. Thick-walled hose, sturdy fittings at each end set in permanent bedding compound (3M 5200), and the usual stainless steel hose clamps ensure reliability and long life.

If you close the engine saltwater intake when you shut off the engine, the problem is solved. However, it's easy to forget to do this (just as it's easy to forget to turn on the water when you start the engine) because you are generally setting and adjusting the sails and are busy with navigation and traffic after you shut off the engine. You need an automatic arrangement. I have found commercial siphon breakers unsatisfactory because they tend to plug up, dribble, and corrode fittings and wires around them.

I have worked out a much better system. To break the siphon when the engine is shut down, I drill and tap a small hole in the top of the exhaust manifold mixing elbow (see illustration). I then install a threaded brass fitting and run a ⅛-inch-inside-diameter (3 mm) thick-walled rubber hose up through the cockpit floor to a convenient back corner (via another brass fitting). Just inside one of the cockpit drains is a good place. When the engine is running, the hose bleeds off a small portion of the exhaust water in a steady stream (which the helmsman can glance at to check that the cooling system is functioning normally). When the engine is shut off, air finds its way back down the small hose to the exhaust elbow and breaks the siphon. I have used this scheme for many years; its advantage is that once it's set up, it requires no thinking or action by the crew.

There is one other slight hazard with the usual exhaust system. If you do any prolonged cranking (if you're having problems with the fuel system, for instance) and the engine doesn't start right away, incoming salt water (via the engine saltwater pump) can build up in the waterlift muffler and back up into the engine. Normally this water is blown overboard by the hot exhaust gases, but if the engine is not running, there's no way for the water to get out. Solution? Shut off the saltwater intake valve to the engine until it starts. Then turn on the water.

What size engines do 25- to 55-foot cruising yachts require? Gasoline horsepower is based on intermittent duty calculations while diesel ratings are figured on continuous duty. This means that the power of a 15-horsepower Lister diesel, for example, roughly equals an Atomic Four gasoline engine rated at 25 horsepower.

I believe 2 horsepower per ton of displacement is adequate power for an auxiliary engine. When naval architect Tom Colvin designed and built his 42-foot *Gazelle* (11 tn. displacement), he installed a 10-horsepower Sabb that gave the boat a steady 4 to 5 knots in calm water. I have seen the same design with a 50-horsepower Perkins 4-108. Of course, the larger engine drives the yacht faster and can stop the boat more quickly at a dock. However, the 4-cylinder Perkins uses at least three times as much fuel and is bigger, heavier, and more costly in every department. Is it really necessary to go 7 knots instead of 5? I've heard owners complain that they needed a larger engine because they "had to motor into a chop." If there's a chop, it suggests wind. Why not put up some sails?

Twelve- and 15-horsepower engines were ample for our first *Whisper*'s 6 tons. On her circumnavigation, we had a 1-cylinder 12-horsepower Farymann that was perfect. The little engine had reasonable power for maneuvering and was easy on fuel. It had an electric starter, but the engine was a cinch to hand crank if the battery was down.

There is an excellent range of small diesel engines available: Bukh, Farymann, Kubota, Perkins, Sabb, Sole, Volvo, Watermota, Westerbeke, Yanmar, and more. These range in size from 12 to 40 horsepower, are reliable, and are well suited for auxiliary power for vessels of moderate displacement up to 55 feet. The engine in my Santa

Cruz 50 when I sold her was a 24-horsepower, 3-cylinder Yanmar that drove her along at 5 to 5½ knots.

Engineers tell us that the higher operating temperatures of freshwater cooling systems make the engines more efficient. Yet raw seawater cooling seems quite adequate for these small engines and is cheaper and simpler. Freshwater cooling requires an extra pump, a heat-exchanger device, an expansion tank, more plumbing, and sometimes an oil cooler. Saltwater cooling systems have served me well for a long time, and I find the argument about preventing corrosion in the cylinder head unconvincing because the cylinder heads are usually made of thick-walled cast iron.

Water-cooled models of the small Farymann diesels attempt to get the best of both worlds by surrounding the engine cylinders with water-filled plastic jackets (through which seawater is pumped) that are in contact with the cylinders for cooling but whose plumbing is separate from the engine. If a leak develops in a cooling jacket, the water simply runs into the bilge instead of inside the engine.

Another criterion for engine choice is the availability of parts. In spite of the claims of manufacturers, it's often impossible to get engine parts in remote places. The big companies claim to have "worldwide networks of dealers"—but they are mostly dealers who don't stock the part you want, are not excited about your small order, and often need to be pressured into ordering your valves or big end bearings or whatever. The regional dealers will order the parts. But to ease the shipping and customs charges, the dealers may wait until they put together a sizable order. In Newport Beach, California, I once marked time for seven weeks to get a tiny thermostat that could have been airmailed from Sweden in three days. The irony is that in the days before the dealer network, I could have purchased directly from the factory and had both immediate airmail service and lower factory prices. Today the factory won't sell to me "to protect its dealers."

The best plan is to order a comprehensive set of spares months in advance, perhaps through a friendly boatyard. Buy a complete set of gaskets, fuel pump parts, saltwater pump impellers, valve springs and keepers, a starter solenoid, and so on. Don't be hesitant about acquiring a few complete assemblies—a water pump, fuel injectors and their metal plumbing lines, an alternator, and maybe *two* voltage regulators. *Be sure to purchase all the service manuals.* Perhaps the most important spare part is a rabbit's foot for frequent stroking.

If the engine parts catalog shows any special tools, I would buy all the small tools and carefully look over the larger items. I feel it's better to spend a hundred dollars now than to be stuck without a special tool in some remote place and have to *make* the needed puller or wrench or whatever. I once had to remove the flywheel of a Volvo Penta to replace a front oil seal, and without the special flywheel puller, I wasted days and in the end spent about three times the cost of the factory-made puller. Some of this stuff you'll probably never use, but all insurance is a balancing act.

If it weren't for the noise problem, you could make a case for an air-cooled engine in a yacht. Out on the Egyptian desert in the Middle East, I've seen the excellent air-cooled English Lister diesels at full throttle running pumps and generators round the clock for months. But the noise is mind-deadening.

A fundamental fault of a water-cooled engine is that you introduce a hostile, alien substance into the vitals of the engine, certainly the last place you want a fluid that can easily destroy the bearings and delicate machined parts. It seems logical to keep water as far from a marine engine as possible. Few marine engines wear out; they are destroyed by corrosion from water that gets inside—from a faulty head gasket, bad seals on a saltwater pump shaft, or water backing up into the exhaust system. (Incidentally, lubricating oil in a diesel is usually a rich, thick, lustrous black; if it appears grayish and thin, look for an internal water leak.)

Smaller sailboats can use outboard engines in either two- or four-cycle models. Often these need to be long-shaft models so the propeller will reach sufficiently deep into the water. Using an outboard means keeping gasoline on board. If you must have it, gasoline is best stored on the afterdeck or the top of the transom in a sealed plastic container kept in a deck box that drains over the side (not belowdecks). In the BOC and Around Alone offshore races, a number of 60-foot yachts have used outboard engines to move around in port and during trial sails. Steve Pettengill delivered one of these big yachts from Newport, Rhode Island, to California and took the vessel through the Panama Canal with an outboard. A variant of this is an outboard diesel. Yanmar makes a 27-horsepower model, but the weight is a staggering 207 pounds, twice the weight of a gasoline outboard of the same horsepower.

When you're buying a boat or thinking about a new engine, consider the size of the power plant in relation to its space. The best mechanic in the world cannot service the best engine in the world if it's shoehorned underneath a galley sink or jammed beneath a cockpit with tight-fitting berths and lockers on each side. Some of the engine installations I've seen are impossible to service; the vitals seem reachable only by midgets under hypnosis.

I wish that some of the architects had to service the engine installations they design. I am forever being asked: "How many people does your yacht sleep?" I am never asked the following questions.

- Can you change the engine oil and filter easily?
- If you need to adjust the engine alignment, can you reach the motor mount bolts with a wrench or a socket and have space enough to use the tool?

- How tough is it to remove the starter solenoid or the starter itself?
- Can you reach the stuffing box to add new packing?
- How do you change the oil in the transmission?
- Can you get at the back of the alternator to check the wiring?

And so on.

Certainly the prospective purchaser of a yacht should take a hard look at the engine installation. How much trouble would it be to improve access to the engine? Consider each side, the top, and the area around the connection between the engine and the propeller shaft. Can various panels be made removable or hinged or changed to facilitate entry? Can you remove and replace the impeller of the saltwater pump? Are the fuel filters accessible? How do you change the oil? If you drop tools, where will they fall? Look at each major part (heat exchanger, injectors, expansion tank, alternator, etc.) and consider whether it can be dealt with in the present installation.

I wrote some of this chapter at Isla Fernandina in the Galápagos Islands while Margaret and I were anchored next to a jaunty, 43-foot motor sailer named *Vagabond*. She was built in Holland and owned by a Swedish couple named Lennart and Inga Jorneus-Martinson, who were sailing around the world. Lennart and Inga lived in Switzerland, where Lennart ran several businesses.

Inga was always scrubbing and polishing the boat, which gleamed from her efforts. Lennart mostly supervised from a deck chair while he drank iced tea. Lennart was a vegetarian, and Inga loved meat, so when they came to dinner on *Whisper*, Lennart gnawed on vegetables while the rest of us knocked off a roasted chicken.

Their sturdy blue-and-white steel vessel was filled with all kinds of machinery and systems—generating plants, ham radios, an electric stove, pressure water pipes, a complex heating system, and so forth. Lennart's elaborate electrical panels looked like they belonged in a nuclear factory.

"Everything works," my neighbor told me, "but the price of all this"—Lennart waved his arm disparagingly at the boat—"is that I am forever fixing something. It's too much and is seriously interfering with the enjoyment of my world cruise. If I were to do it again, most of these things would remain on the dealers' shelves.

"It's only gradually that I have begun to realize that one's enjoyment is inversely proportional to the time you waste on mechanical annoyances. When maintenance and frustration turn a pleasure trip into drudgery, it is time to reevaluate one's equipment and vessel."

Lennart called to Inga from his comfortable chair, "Bring me another iced tea."

Whether it's in Greece, the Seychelles, Chile, or the Azores, children always come down to the yacht to see us, to play around the boat, or maybe to go below for a look. We met this sweet-faced charmer in Atka, Alaska. She and her brother had been turning over smoked salmon filets that were drying in the sun. When they finished with the fish, they went running up and down the hills. She was full of smiles, enthusiasm, and all the delights and wiles of a little girl.

23

SCHOOLING AT SEA

Some of the queries we've heard most in our travels concern children on board. What about their schooling and safety? Are there any special problems? How old should they be?

Whisper's great friend is Mary Adams, who was 11 when we met her. She'd been living on the 40-foot Canadian ketch *Eileen* for almost two years. Her father, Doug Adams, is a doctor, and her mother, June, is an attractive shipboard wife who keeps *Eileen*'s brass lamps polished brighter than any others we've ever seen. We met the Adams family in Canada when they were moving aboard and getting ready for a long cruise. At that time, Mary was a bit shy and introverted. We used to see her coming down the dock at Van Isle Marina on Vancouver Island, but she seldom had much to say.

Eighteen months later when we met *Eileen* near the U.S.-Mexican border, the change in young Mary was surprising. No longer was she the bashful and diffident girl we had known in Canada. The Mary we now met was friendly and outgoing. Of course, the change in her behavior and attitude may have been simply one of growing up a little. But I like to think that living on board, traveling to new places, shar-

Mary Adams busy with schoolwork aboard Eileen.

345

ing a little of the responsibilities on *Eileen*, and meeting a variety of children in similar circumstances had something to do with it.

Mary, a fifth grader, spent each morning from 0900 to 1100 or 1130 studying her elementary correspondence school lessons from the Department of Education in Victoria, British Columbia. Since the Adamses were taxpayers and residents in the province, the school department supplied all the teaching expertise and materials at no cost, except for a few small fees. When Mary's parents signed up for the program, they received several big packages of books, lessons, examinations, teaching instructions, and even specimens (such as a preserved shrimp) for science.

Included among the books was a short stack of paperbacks. Mary also received a hefty atlas, a large dictionary, a book of poetry, and various hardbound textbooks. The Adamses learned that they could often borrow supplementary books from a local library—if one was near.

In short, the yacht had become a traveling schoolroom. All the parents needed was a dose of patience to keep an alert eye on the whole business.

"When we first left Canada, Mary missed her friends at school," said June. "She was unhappy for a few days but soon got over it. We discovered that children waste an inordinate amount of time at school. The lesson plans of the correspondence courses are excellent; Mary could accomplish more in two hours in the quiet saloon of *Eileen* than she did in five hours at school. To make up for the lack of social life, we found that she soon made friends in each port that we visited.

"Make no mistake about the parent's role," June continued. "Even with the teaching instructions written out by experts, there is quite a bit of reading to do. It's amazing how much *I've* learned. We find that a child should have reasonable reading skills, because most of the instructions are detailed and need to be followed closely. There are many composition-type exercises that cover topics of different choices—stories of the trip, new friends, personal experiences, that sort of thing. Laboratory science situations are sometimes difficult, but there are various alternative lessons. We were told that correspondence lessons don't work for some children, so we tried the system out a little before we left.

"Both the parents and the child need a bit of organizing," June said. "It's surprising how many things must be completed before a set of lessons is ready to be mailed. Mary always breathes a big sigh of joy when she finally puts a lesson envelope in the mail."

Some of the Canadian correspondence pupils are in the Arctic, some live in Africa, while other children travel with parents who are engineers, doctors, diplomats, military advisors, or U.N. consultants.

Dawn Lupton, one of the teachers in Victoria, works with a small group of other instructors to look after the educational needs of 45 young people who come from her district of British Columbia. "I thought that by 2002, all the lighthouses would have been automated," said Lupton when I spoke with her recently, "but we still have one family along the coast. We also have a family that runs a bed and breakfast in Bali, Indonesia."

In recent years there has been a phenomenal growth in home-schooling—that is, parents who teach their children directly without access to a formal school. In 1994, the U.S. figure was 345,000 students. In 1999, the most recent year studied by the U.S. government, the figure had grown to 850,000. That's only about 4 percent of the total school population of kindergarten through 12th grade, but the five-year growth rate of 2.46 times is impressive. Home-schooling has been legal in all 50 states since 1993.[84]

Coincident with this has been the phenomenal acceptance and the rising use of the Internet and e-mail. When I naively suggested that e-mail might be a good learning exchange medium for older pupils, I was brought up short. "Dead wrong," said Dawn Lupton. "Even with their limited reading and writing skills, the kindergartners and first graders understand e-mail and the Internet perfectly."

If possible, the teachers like to meet their foreign charges before they set off on their distant journeys. If not, the teacher and pupil at least exchange a snapshot or two. A student has the same instructors all year, and the teachers and their charges send little notes back and forth. In other words, the school staff tries hard to make the student and teacher—who may be separated by half a continent or more—a little closer in spirit. A brown envelope can be pretty impersonal.

"Sometimes it's hard to keep to a regular schedule," said Mary's father, Doug. "Things are a little more hectic and irregular on a boat. Guests and workmen and officials arrive without notice, or we may have the yacht hauled out of the water while we paint her bottom. But by and large, Mary puts in the required hours. I see to that."

The school prefers to have tests administered by a responsible disinterested person (lawyer, local school official, port captain). However, the arrangement is flexible as required.

The Canadian school is only one of many correspondence programs that are used by children and adults of every age. Practically all countries have correspondence schools of some kind—programs for elementary, junior high, high school, and beyond. State universities often have extensive programs and will send a thick catalog in exchange for a postcard.

Many American and foreign children on cruising yachts and in foreign places have been educated by the Calvert Education Services, 10713 Gilroy Road, Suite B, Hunt Valley, Maryland 21031 (www.calvertschool.org). The Calvert school was founded in 1897 and offers instruction from kindergarten through eighth grade by a teaching staff of 54. Over the years, Calvert has taught more than 400,000 students.

In one memorable letter to Calvert, the young daughter of an American missionary in Africa wrote to apologize that she was behind in her home-school studies, because "the lions roaring all night keep us awake."

Educational experts on Calvert's staff constantly update the courses and offer the latest in the teaching of mathematics, basic reading practice and drill, and dozens of other subjects. For example, the third-grade course includes reading, phonics, spelling and vocabulary, composition, mathematics, science, poetry, history and mythology, geography, and art. This is a stand-alone program and comes with both general instructions and daily lesson plans.

As a supplement, Calvert has an optional advisory teaching service to give additional help to the home teacher, who often has no experience. This extra teaching aid offers the support of a regular cycle of testing and correspondence to help keep learning on schedule. A supervising teacher returns each test with a personal letter to the student with specific comments on what the child has done and recommendations for further study.

In addition, Calvert has specially trained education counselors available by telephone or e-mail to offer assistance to pupils or parents stuck with a problem or procedure. The use of e-mail makes it easy and quick to talk back and forth to odd corners of the world. At the moment, e-mail communication to yachts at sea is rudimentary and slow, but each year it is improving.

The Calvert School is a nonprofit organization approved by the State of Maryland. Most authorities accept the school's certificates of completion.

What does it cost? The tuition for the third grade for a school year with Calvert was $541 in 2002. This includes the educational materials and supplies for all subjects. (The shipping weight of a typical Calvert course is 22 pounds.) The advisory teaching service was an extra $281.

"The Calvert people are not kidding when they claim to furnish everything," said Adam Stapley, the owner of *Silver Flute*, a sleek, light-blue 46-foot steel yawl built in Canada and based in Miami. "When we enrolled our girls, Sheila and Susan, in the fifth and seventh grades, we were flabbergasted at the mountain of things that arrived. The girls received hard- and soft-cover books, paper, pencils, crayons, rulers, drawing paper, compasses—everything except thinking caps.

"We soon found out that the supervision aspect requires considerable adult time," Adam said. "The instructions are planned for a nine-month school year with each of our two girls working five days a week for two to five hours a day. A typical instruction plan starts out with the phrase 'Today your student will study. . . .' We think the girls are getting excellent schooling in both hard-core and cultural subjects, although we realize that correspondence work doesn't replace a normal school.

"Preparatory to enrolling at the Calvert school, a student takes a test to evaluate his knowledge," Adam explained. "Sheila was OK for arithmetic but a poor speller, like her father. Susan needed help with composition and handwriting."

Schooling in distant places can be leisurely or more rushed, depending on the student. When I talked to Liev Kennedy in Vancouver, she recalled her son's schooling in Australia aboard *Kelea*. "One morning, less than a week after our arrival in Gladstone, a shout sounded from the after cabin. 'Hooray! I've finished grade five.' We all cheered. Curtis had done well. Working only while in port, he had waded through thirty-six lessons of arithmetic, English, social studies, science, and spelling. His working day would generally start around seven and continue into the afternoon. He would always join us, however, on any excursion we might take to a new area. He was his own boss and set up his own work schedule; it was up to him how much he got done."

When I began to collect material for this chapter, I had no idea there were so many children on yachts and elsewhere being educated by correspondence or the Internet. Home-schooling is big business. I found out that there are dozens of schools (for more names and addresses, check any library or type *home schooling* into an Internet search engine). The two that I've detailed are typical, however, and have been well tried by the children of the sailors to whom I've talked. Many home-study schools are concerned with high school completion for adults.

An Australian sailing couple, Laurie and Carole Pane, set off with their son, Ryan, aged eight. The Panes were determined to see and enjoy the world in their 53-foot sloop *Dolphin Spirit* and to educate Ryan at the same time. The first year Ryan was in the third grade, and the Panes used the Calvert system. Carole Pane, formerly a veteran primary schoolteacher, liked the Calvert approach, but she found it too rigid. She decided to write her own curriculum for Ryan based on the history, geography, culture, and language of each country that *Dolphin Spirit* visited.

The Panes feel that their involvement with their son's learning is important, and the whole process is a family affair. Every day, Ryan's mother makes a lesson plan that Ryan follows until he has mastered it. If there's a lack of understanding, the teacher is there to guide her pupil. With the ratio of teacher-to-pupil on a one-to-one basis, the learning situation is ideal and is more like a seminar arrangement with a tutor than a schoolroom.

When the Panes are sailing, Ryan studies every day—including weekends. This keeps him up-to-date in his studies or a little ahead. This means that when the weather is rough, the family takes a trip on land, or Ryan wants to play with other children in port, he can take a few days off without falling behind in his reading, math problems, or social studies projects.

Ryan uses a computer, tapes, and videos to advantage and has learned typing, piano, guitar, and languages from them.

In four years, the Panes have sailed 25,000 miles and visited 30 countries. Ryan—who is now 12—has studied the history, geography, culture, and language of each country. The secret to success, say the Panes, is the involvement of the parents and a structure and consistency to the teaching effort. "Teaching is time-consuming," writes Laurie, "but the rewards, for both parents and children, more than compensate for all the effort."

Laurie continues: "having children around is by far the best way of getting to know new people, both cruisers and locals. Within seconds of the anchor going down or the dock lines being secured, Ryan is off, introducing himself to cruisers and locals. I have become accustomed to being known as 'Ryan's Dad.' We have had many wonderful experiences that would have been missed if Ryan hadn't been there to break the ice. Having him learn about each country has given us more insights than we perhaps would have gained without that incentive. Overall, for us, the whole experience with Ryan has been quite wonderful, bringing us firmly together as a family, more than we ever anticipated, or hoped. Long-term cruising is not for everyone, but having children should be an incentive, not a deterrent."[85]

Carol Hogan wrote about her children's schooling in *Sail* magazine: "The Kids Made the Cruise." The Hogan family had a 9-year-old girl and an 11-year-old boy to educate during the cruise but no money for formal correspondence courses. While the cruise was still in the planning stages, Carol Hogan asked the principal at the school her children attended for advice. The principal thought the proposed cruise was the best possible education and helped Carol prepare an extensive study outline. The principal gave her 75 books, including teacher's editions.

For the first six months, the Hogans tried to maintain regular study periods. ("OK, everybody down below for some arithmetic.") In Panama, however, after the children had passed achievement tests with ease, the approach was changed to put more emphasis on current experiences and less on schoolbooks. Instead of writing on abstract topics, the children were encouraged to prepare compositions about their trip and the things they were experiencing. The Hogan youngsters read from children's literature, including fiction and the classics in paperback. Geography and language books helped develop other skills, while foreign-language practice was easy with local children when the yacht was in distant ports. Carol supplemented the ship's library with additional books and pamphlets from the U.S. Government Printing Office and the Pan American Union, both in Washington, D.C.

> After the first few months of cruising, [wrote Carol] the year ended and we didn't have a calendar so we improvised with a home-made one. These were always colorful and had pictures and notations added by the whole crew. We kept careful track of days spent at sea and noted special events, which could be anything. Our daughter

became publisher/editor/reporter, and typed a weekly newspaper entitled *Discovery Press*. It contained poems, straight news, special events, and lottery results. Small prizes were awarded for accurately guessing ETAs, and winners were announced in the paper. Other diversions at sea included cards, puzzles, and games. Scrabble was an educational favorite.

Birthdays and holidays were exciting events. We always managed to bake, and we had a supply of candles and cake decorations. Boat-baked cakes became works of art. To accompany the cakes, the children filled many hours designing and creating holiday decorations and cards from our supply of crayons, colored pencils, glue, and glitter. Additional craft items aboard included a watercolor set, construction paper, wrapping paper and ribbon, writing paper, masking tape, Scotch tape, oil paints, small canvases, and even a supply of mosaic tile and cutters. We kept a list of birthdays of family and friends, and we mailed cards and gifts made at sea from the next port.

Even on the high seas we celebrated Christmas with a small, stowable, artificial tree hung with brightly-colored, home-made decorations. The cabin lamp was usually hung with paper trees and bells.

We had a small portable sewing machine on board, and using a gasoline generator on deck for power, we could sew on calm days at sea. The sewing kit included embroidery hoops, thread, every kind of sewing notion, and extra blue, green, and red yardage, which we used to make our own courtesy flags before entering ports. For reference we used a United Nations flag chart.

Once in port the local stores supplied small playthings of interest to the kids. Almost every town had souvenir items that made good toys. In Mexico, Sharri bought small pottery dishes for a few pesos. On board, she played with her small dolls and pots for hours, and every item imaginable went into making doll clothes and doll houses.

The children had a few small pets on board, and in foreign ports they became fishermen and local explorers in the sailing dinghy. There was hiking, surfing, and swimming with fins and masks. The children also collected shells, which they cleaned, categorized, labeled with correct Latin names, and stored. At sea the youngsters towed a plankton net and inspected their daily harvest with a simple microscope. As the yacht's latitude changed, there were new constellations of stars to identify. When the Hogan family crossed the equator, a fatherly King Neptune made his appearance—bearded, crowned, wearing a white sheet, carrying a trident—and solemnly presented hand-lettered shellback certificates. Obviously, the conscientious parents had as much fun as the children.

> The major teaching problem turned out to be the everyday distractions involved with cruising, [wrote Carol,] e.g., a reading lesson interrupted by my husband catching a fish, with the result that reading turned into biology. Because of this we realized the need to be flexible, and whenever possible we made everything into a learning situation, not getting frustrated by interruptions. We found we needed books to cover every topic from astronomy to zoology. I recommend an encyclopedia set published by the World Publishing Company called *The Ocean World of Jacques Cousteau*.

Carol Hogan learned that with the whole world as a classroom, you don't need formal teaching credentials to wind up with some fairly well educated children at the end of a voyage. It's not necessary to be a nuclear physicist to teach a nine-year-old a little arithmetic.[86]

Margaret and I have seen young people of all ages on yachts. Three times we have met children who were born afloat. However, very young children require a good deal of care and attention. Special food and medical attention may be problems. At walking age, the children are liable to crawl up the companionway steps and toddle right over the side unless an adult keeps an eye on them. Certainly youngsters should be obliged to wear life jackets whenever they go on deck.

From four or five years of age and onward, I think a child can fit in nicely with life afloat. He or she can learn simple jobs at first and gradually master more complex procedures with age and experience. The children can soon learn to steer and to take daylight watches. In fact, to keep up crew morale and interest, it's good for everyone—spouses, children, friends, in-laws—to participate in some phase of running the ship. Certainly all hands should have safety harnesses and should practice man-overboard drills and recovery.

If young people are given their head, it's surprising how much they can learn about navigation and pilotage and sail handling. I immediately think of Curtis Kennedy, Reid Griffith,* and Ronald Mitchell, respectively a Canadian, an American, and an Australian, who started sailing with their world-cruising parents when they were small boys. Later with tens of thousands of sailing miles behind them, these youths were no longer boys, but experienced and resourceful men. Each had a well-developed sense of judgment and achievement and an enviable background of visits to the far corners of the world—the unique reward of life under sail.

---

*Tragically killed in a climbing accident in the Marquesas.

I think also of the daughter of a friend who has taken his family on one long sailing passage after another. The daughter was 17 and her beauty and figure were breathtaking. Her smile would have opened the door to heaven itself. At each island where the yacht stopped, a swarm of suitors soon collected. The daughter fell madly in love with one young man and announced that she was staying. Her father countered that the yacht was leaving on Tuesday and that she had better be ready to leave with it.

"But, Father," she wailed. "You can't. I'm in love!"

"It's Tuesday, child, and that's final," said her father in a stern voice. "We're leaving right on schedule."

On Tuesday the yacht left with a weeping and miserable daughter who was prostrate with grief. ("Oh, Daddy, what'll I do?")

On Wednesday she was standing watches as usual.

On Thursday she had forgotten her suitor's name.

On Friday she was eagerly scanning the horizon for a new landfall.

Sometimes the things we've seen on our travels are starkly beautiful, like this tiny church set behind four palm trees and a wall of lava stones along the edge of the sea. Kamaluu, Maui, Hawaii.

When the 55-foot Nicholson fiberglass yawl *Lord Trenchard blew up in Poole, England, at dawn on a clear summer day in 1999, people four miles away heard the explosion. Not only did the mishap trash a handsome yacht, but the captain, Colin Rouse, had his left leg torn off. The mate, Gavin McLaren, asleep in a quarter berth, was suddenly blown out of his berth. McLaren was cut, gashed, and covered with blood and wreckage from the interior, which a moment before had been a deluxe yacht ready for a channel crossing to France. Minutes later, the vessel was half full of water and diesel oil. The interior was unrecognizable. Joinery, bulkheads, portlights, and the cabin sole were blown out. The front hatch was torn off. The whole afterdeck and cockpit were gone. The entire deck had been lifted, and the steering wheel and binnacle had been blown high in the air. The cause was threefold: There were two 9-pound propane gas bottles. The evening before the accident, bottle 1 ran out. Bottle 2 was turned on, but the connection was loose, which allowed gas to leak into the propane locker. This should have drained overboard, but somehow the locker was not gastight. Instead of draining properly, the propane went into the bilge area below the cockpit. A gas alarm should have detected the propane in the bilge, but the alarm failed to work. When the captain started the generator, a spark from the starter ignited the propane which blew up the boat.*

24
HEAT AND COOKING

LIQUEFIED PETROLEUM GAS

Ninety percent of the people who sail long and short distances do their cooking with liquefied bottled petroleum gas (LPG) because modern propane stoves are efficient and convenient. As long as propane (or butane) is kept under control and handled properly, it's a miraculous fuel.

Unfortunately, LPG is heavier than air. If it accidentally leaks into the interior of a boat from one of the small metal tanks where it's kept under pressure or from any of the plumbing, the gas will settle into the lower areas and bilges. Then if ignited, perhaps by a spark from a motor, it can blow a vessel apart with force comparable with exploding dynamite or TNT. This has happened many times.

To utilize the advantages of gas, but to minimize its dangers, sailors and engineers have worked out a series of safe practices. You can be sure that each detail is important and has been added to the list only after tragic experiences.

1. Store the gas bottle or bottles in a gas-tight locker or box with an over-the-side drain leading from the bottom of the container. This is necessary so that if there are any leaks in the bottles, regulators, shutoff valves, or plumbing, the heavier-than-air gas will drain overboard and dissipate. In practice, the locker is usually a small fiberglass compartment with a tight-fitting lid.

2. It's important to seal the opening in the locker where the gas pipe or tubing exits, so there is no possibility of gas leaking into the interior of the yacht. This can

be done with bedding compound, or better yet with a special threaded vapor-tight nylon and rubber seal built for this purpose.

The overboard drain for the locker is usually made of ¼- or ⅜-inch-inside-diameter heavy-walled rubber or reinforced plastic tubing. This drain should be plumbed

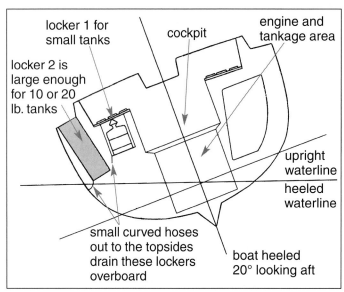

Looking aft through a cross-section view of the cockpit area and stern section of a modern, 40-foot sloop that's heeled 20 degrees. The problem is where to store the propane tanks and whether the lockers will drain when the vessel is sailing at an angle. Locker 1 shows a minimal arrangement with two 4- or 5-pound tanks for limited cooking. A locker (2) required to hold two 10- or 20-pound cylinders measures 20.5 inches high, 30.5 inches long, and 16 inches deep. Two 10-pound tanks fit in a smaller locker (12" deep), but the problem is where to locate the box so that it will drain properly when the boat is heeled. Obviously, the best location is in a stern locker on the centerline of the vessel just forward of the transom, but this may be difficult if the design demands maximum accommodations, which tend to push the cockpit close to the stern. Whatever the propane locker arrangements, the drain hose should be arranged so that seawater cannot stand in a curve of the hose and block propane drainage in case of a leak. If the locker is located away from the centerline and the boat heels, seawater may find its way into the compartment. It's not feasible to put a one-way flapper valve on the drain line because it will interfere with propane drainage. All these difficulties argue strongly for locating propane tanks in an open box on the coachroof.

so that it gently curves as it leads to a small through-hull opening, which should be well above the waterline (see illustration). If the drain line is too long, it may curve below the hull opening on the inside of the hull. The resulting half loop can form a water trap and stop any leaking gas from draining overboard.

In many yachts there may be a problem finding sufficient vertical room for a locker to take the bottles and still be high enough above the waterline for the locker to drain when the vessel is heeled.

Let's not forget that in the real world, people eat and use cooking stoves when yachts are heeled. If the locker drain exit is underwater, the whole point of the locker may be invalidated. Or said another way: in their quest for smooth lines to the eye and a wish to keep such mundane things as gas bottles out of the way, designers often locate the gas bottle locker too low for it to drain properly at all conditions of heel. I believe this is a good argument for keeping gas bottles on the coachroof or deck, or in a coachroof or deck locker with drain openings at the bottom.

These points may seem niggling, but each is extremely important.

3. The copper (recently annealed) or rubber line (a better choice) that runs from the gas bottle locker to the stove should be of the highest quality. The usual LPG hose is designed for use at 350-pounds-per-square-inch pressure while the actual gas pressure (after going through the regulator) is only 0.5 psi. This means the hose is actually using only $\frac{1}{700}$ of its normal pressure capability. This line should be one continuous piece, carefully sited, and fastened so that it doesn't chafe on anything. This usually means there needs to be a little slack here and there. When the line is connected to the stove (with either a special threaded fitting or two hose clamps), the joint should be tested under pressure with a soap solution. When you're fitting this line, allow enough slack so that a gimballed stove can swing easily between its extreme limits of movement.

The electric wires for the on-off solenoid in the propane locker need to be properly bedded or run through a special seal where they pierce the locker wall.

4. All the pipe fittings inside the gas locker (regulator, pressure gauge, solenoid control valve, pigtails, adapter fittings) should be connected to one another with Teflon tape or special thread compound and carefully tested—under pressure—with soap solution. The sole function of the pressure gauge is to spot leaks in the system. (The pressure gauge has nothing to do with the amount of gas in a cylinder. This is determined by weighing the gas bottle when empty or full.)

5. It's well established that a remote on-off valve controlled by electricity and placed near the tank is an additional safe measure. This device is usually an electric solenoid mounted inside the gas-tight locker and starts or ends the gas flow. The on-off switch for this valve—which includes a prominent red light placed at eye level—is located in the galley. When you're ready to use the stove, you start the gas flow by flipping the switch to "on," which also turns on the red warning bulb. You light the stove and proceed with cooking.

When finished with the stove, but while a burner is still alight, you turn off the switch, which closes the solenoid in the gas-tight locker. The flame in the burner continues until it uses all the gas in the line. When the flame goes out, you turn off the burner valve, and you're done. The stove is out and the gas has been shut off. Everything is safe.

Note that the gas has been shut off at the bottle *inside the gas-tight locker*. Additionally, the solenoid is constructed so that in case of a general electrical failure, the valve will close. Many people take the additional step of going to the propane locker and physically turning off the gas at the bottle.

6. If there are two gas bottles in the gastight locker and one becomes empty, the gas flow stops. You have to go to the locker and either turn a valve to connect the other bottle, presumably full, or physically disconnect the empty bottle and connect the other. Note that the tank and mating pigtail gas line have *left-hand threads*, which means that you turn the wrench in the opposite direction. (Keep the special wrench for this job in the locker.) Now is the moment to pay attention to the pressure gauge that is generally part of the regulator. When you change from an empty cylinder to a full cylinder, check that you have the solenoid closed (red light off). Then do the following:

> A. Open the main valve on the new gas cylinder to charge the lines, regulator, and pressure valve inside the gas-tight locker with gas under pressure.
> B. Close the main valve on the gas cylinder.
> C. Note the pressure gauge reading, which should not change during a three-minute period. If it changes, something is leaking.

7. Consider installing a gas detector in the bilge of the boat. Then in the unlikely event of gas leaking into the interior of the vessel, an alarm will sound and a red light will flash.[87]

8. You can make a strong and compelling argument for mounting a gas bottle out in the open *on the deck or coachroof*. Then if the LPG bottle or plumbing leaks, the explosive gas will flow harmlessly overboard. A high-quality manual shutoff valve can be fitted near the tank. Depending on where the tank is mounted, it may be possible to reach a hand out through an opening hatch or portlight to turn the gas on or off. Or you may have to climb on deck. This is a safer arrangement than using a locker whose drain line can be blocked, either by poor design, improper fabrication, or a quarter wave when the yacht is heeled and sailing fast.

Additionally, a manual shutoff valve is simpler and more positive than an electric solenoid.

Of course, a gas bottle mounted above the galley on the coachroof next to the boom gallows or aft of the cockpit is much less attractive than if it's tucked away inside a hidden locker. The bottle can be disguised by covering it with a plastic storage box (a milk box with open-mesh construction) held down with a couple of pieces of shock cord. Often exterior bottles are mounted on deck behind the cockpit, with the in-use bottle on one side and the spare on the other. Such bottles need stout metal mounts and perhaps a line guard.

About twenty-five years ago, compressed natural gas (CNG) was introduced to the boating market in the United States. CNG was lighter than air, which meant that it would dissipate upward and not flow into the bilges of boats if there was a gas leak. Everyone thought that CNG (with a specific gravity of 0.67, a bit more than half the weight of air) had a great future because it was so much safer. Certainly it would eclipse the bottled gas market. Regrettably, CNG, in spite of its inherent advantage, failed to catch on, and like the Edsel car and the smokeless cigarette, has faded from the scene.

How much propane should a person take along? The rule of thumb is that one person will use 1 pound of gas to cook meals for 1 week. According to this, a 10-pound gas cylinder will supply cooking for two people for 5 weeks, three for 3.3 weeks, and so on. However, additional people have proportionally less effect on the amount of time the gas will last since one cooking of spaghetti (or whatever), even with more in the pot, will do for the whole crew. Many cruising yachts carry two 20-pound bottles.

Another example of the dangers of bottled gas in restricted spaces. This is the power yacht Intrepido *on pier 3 at the Sausalito Yacht Harbor in California. A friend and I were walking down the dock at night and were about seventy-five feet away when* Intrepido's *propane heating system blew up. I took this photograph the next morning. The force of the exploding gas lifted the deck, pushed out the hull, and split open the stem. The front hatch is entirely gone, and the cabin has been destroyed. A woman was asleep on board when the explosion took place. Fortunately, she was uninjured, but she cut her feet on glass from the broken windows when she climbed to the finger pier in her nightgown. The choice of cooking and heating fuels is a personal choice, but is it necessary to carry products that can explode with such force?*

I have inquired among my friends about propane consumption, but the answers have been so varied and vague that I hesitate to give any hard numbers. I suggest that you keep a record in the ship's book (see page 381) each time you change and fill the gas bottles. Make a notation of how long they last with your system and your cooking habits.

When a yacht goes to the high latitudes, her crew invariably uses more cooking fuel because the people on board want bigger meals. Everyone eats more in Antarctica or Spitsbergen, where the weather is cold. Friends who have sailed to the Palmer Peninsula have reported running out of cooking gas and having only one hot meal a day, a dreary prospect.

In addition to liquefied petroleum gas, there are six other cooking fuels: alcohol, electricity, wood, coal, kerosene, and oil. Margaret and I have been on yachts where each of these has been the mainstay.

ALCOHOL

I totally reject alcohol because in most places—particularly in remote areas—it's extremely expensive and usually not available. In addition, the heat output is so poor—only half that of LPG—that it takes forever to boil a kettle of water or to cook something. For an occasional meal on a Sunday afternoon sail, alcohol may be OK, but for food every day year after year, it's unsuitable.

ELECTRICITY

On the plus side, electricity is clean, safe, and quick. On the negative side, it generally means starting a generator or living with the drag of a propeller to generate current while under way. I recall spending time on San Francisco Bay aboard a wonderful old Winthrop Warner yacht named *Blue Sea*. She was traditional in every way except that if you wanted a cup of coffee and turned on the stove, a generator sprang into life and was so noisy that it even scared the seagulls.

During a trip to the Galápagos Islands, Margaret and I had a meal aboard *Benedic*, a deluxe Ocean 71 yacht from England owned by a land developer named Dick Dusseldorp, a charming fellow from New York. The big ketch had electric cooking powered by two professionally soundproofed Volvo generators that were isolated in special cockpit lockers. *You could not hear them running.* I suspect the installation and soundproofing cost thousands of dollars.

WOOD

Both Joshua Slocum and Harry Pidgeon cooked and heated their vessels with woodstoves. These are excellent in the high latitudes but sometimes a little warm for the tropics. The problem of replenishing the fuel is easy if you're anchored off a beach full of driftwood and you're handy with an ax and a saw and have some time. It's not so simple when you're tied up in a city. Friends have used Presto logs (made from compressed sawdust) bought in a grocery store once a week. Some people (Margaret) are allergic to wood smoke and begin sneezing as soon as they get near a woodstove. Wood is the least expensive of all fuels, but to keep the wood box filled, you've got to find it, cut it, maybe dry it, and row it out to the yacht.

COAL

In years past, Warwick Tompkin's famous 83-foot pilot schooner *Wanderbird* had a big Swedish AGA Cooker that burned anthracite. And just last winter we had a few meals aboard the English cutter *Beroë*, a 36-footer that had a small anthracite heating stove that kept the yacht warm and dry and pleasant when she was iced in at the Chesapeake Bay Maritime Museum in St. Michaels, Maryland. My objection to coal is that it imparts a slight smell to everything aboard that you notice as soon as you enter the cabin. I remember this odor from my boyhood in Cleveland when my family's house was heated with soft coal.

KEROSENE

Kerosene is a favorite of veteran long-distance sailors because Primus pressure stoves are simple to use and the fuel is widely available. Whatever far corner of the world you visit, you will find a few diehard sailors and locals who cook with Primus stoves because no matter what happens, they can always heat up something and make a cup of coffee.

A Swede named Frans Lindqvist invented the Primus stove in 1882. It was an immediate success, and over time millions were sold in more than ninety countries. Amundsen carried one to the South Pole. Hillary and Tenzing took a Primus to Mt. Everest. Thousands of sailors have cooked with the stove. LPG stoves are easier to use, but they're not as portable, and fuel is difficult to find in remote places.

A proper Primus flame is blue and hot, and its familiar hiss will turn a liter of cold water into a boiling fury in six and a half minutes. Since half the world still cooks, heats, and lights with kerosene, you can buy the fuel—sometimes of varying quality—almost everywhere. Once you find some that's satisfactory, it's easy to put 10 gallons on board, enough for at least three months of cooking for two people. We pour our kerosene through a piece of thick felt in a funnel to filter out water and impurities. My friend Noel Barrott from New Zealand, a sailor of great experience, adds 30 percent paint thinner to his kerosene and reports improved burning.

In spite of all this rosy talk, pressure kerosene stoves are high-maintenance items. Certainly if you're going to live with kerosene, you need to keep several spare burners on board along with a few nipples, prickers, cleaning needle spindles, fiber washers, and so on. A two-burner stove may run perfectly for months. Then one burner may suddenly quit. Usually it's because the combustion of kerosene has built up tiny deposits of carbon in the main metering jet.

Most Primus units have self-pricking burners. With these you turn the control knob backward to force a tiny built-in cleaning wire through the jet to clean it. This takes only a few seconds and can be done while the burner is alight. In a so-called roarer burner, which is simpler, you use a small pricking tool to manually force a thin piece of wire through the jet to clear it.

Primus stoves work on the principle of burning the vapor of superheated kerosene. To light a burner, you heat it enough to vaporize the kerosene inside it. The procedure is to pour a little alcohol into a priming cup underneath the burner and light the alcohol. Or you can saturate a Tilley wick (see photograph) with alcohol and clip it around the burner. We use the Tilley wick system, which uses a measured amount of alcohol and a burning scheme that cannot backfire into a container of alcohol.

If a Tilley wick is not available, it's possible to do the same trick with a 1-ounce (30 mL) bottle (the size that sample shampoo comes in). Simply fill several of these tiny bottles with alcohol. Then if you dump the contents of one bottle in a priming cup, you have enough alcohol to preheat the burner. With this system there's no way the fire can get out of control because the fuel is limited. You can also preheat a Primus burner with a butane soldering torch, which is useful if someone on board does not like the smell of burning alcohol.

When the burner is hot enough to vaporize the kerosene, you open the control knob and light the burner. Once it's going, the hot burner continues to vaporize the fuel, a self-perpetuating arrangement. It's possible to adjust the flame somewhat with the control knob, but a Primus fire tends to be all or

We prime our kerosene stoves and lanterns with a Tilley wick. This is a finger-sized clip-on cup device that holds a small amount of alcohol in a wadded-up pad of fiberglass cloth. We store the wick in a 4-ounce jar of priming alcohol, which keeps it saturated with alcohol and ready to use. Note: When we remove the wick from the jar, we screw the lid back on the jar before we light the wick. The advantage of this little device is that when you light the wick, you have only a measured amount of combustible fluid available. The fire cannot spread because there is no more fuel. Beware of preheating arrangements with a rubber tube leading from the top of a plastic detergent bottle full of alcohol. If you need to reprime, it's easy for an unseen flame to shoot up the rubber tube and cause the plastic bottle to explode.

nothing. To reduce the heat, it's helpful to insert a metal flame tamer between the cooking pot and the fire.

The main cause of trouble with Primus stoves is inadequate priming. If kerosene under pressure floods into a cold burner, the unvaporized kerosene will flare up with a large smoking yellow flame and a great hissing sound. This happens because the burner is not hot enough to vaporize the fuel. You need to reprime or to prime more in the first place. *There is no other solution.* Shut off the burner and start again. If you prime properly, you won't have flare-ups.

Margaret has cooked thousands of meals on kerosene stoves and seldom has trouble. "But I'd be less than honest if I didn't admit that the stove acts up once in a while. Generally, one burner conks out and I'm down to cooking with one burner until Hal fixes it," she says.

Since kerosene cooking is not popular today, it's difficult to buy stoves. We have used a two-burner Taylors 028, which has a small warming oven and an external tank. This is available from Blakes (Sales@Blakes-Lavac-Taylors.co.uk). I do not recommend the 029 model.

I prefer the Optimus 155W. The website is www.optimus.se/products/nova/. This is an excellent two-burner stove of stainless steel with a built-in $1\frac{1}{2}$-liter brass tank and pump. It's all one unit, nicely fabricated, easy to keep clean, and can be ordered with gimbals. The Primus Company of Sweden has not manufactured kerosene burners since the early 1960s. Optimus makes kerosene burners of a new design with a cast body. The only traditional Primus-type burners that I know of are made in Portugal. These are available in Canada from Force 10 Marine Ltd. in Richmond, British Columbia, at sales@force10.com; an English source is spares@base camp.co.uk. I have had good service from these burners for many years.

All vessels that go to sea—no matter what their fuel—need clamps, fiddles, or guards on the top of the stove to keep pots in place. If the guard is in the form of a two-inch fence around the edge of the stove, the front fiddle should have cutouts or corner spaces to accommodate the low handles of frying pans.

Kerosene, alcohol, and gas stoves are usually gimballed with the pivots placed in a fore-and-aft direction to keep the top of the stove level, no matter what the angle of heel. This gives a flat, always horizontal stovetop on which to set hot cups of coffee or soup or whatever.

The axle of the pivots or gimbals should be roughly even with the top of the stove so that the stove will pivot as a seesaw. If the pivots are too high, as they often are, the motion becomes that of a pendulum. Then the back-and-forth stove motion becomes violent, and the pots or their contents may be thrown off the stove. Eric Hiscock pointed this out more than fifty years ago, but nonsailing stove makers persist in making the gimbal pivots too high. Often a hefty chunk of lead bolted to the

The Taylors kerosene heating stove uses a Primus-type burner to heat a series of ceramic elements inside a 7-inch-diameter cylinder. The flue leads vertically upward to a vent in the coachroof. Since it's easy to grab the hot flue pipe when the boat rolls, it's good to surround the flue with a stainless steel guard spaced around but separated a little from the hot pipe.

bottom of a nervous stove will do wonders to stabilize its motion.

As good as our little cooking stoves were, they didn't heat the cabin. We considered various heating schemes and rejected coal, wood, and charcoal. The problems of stowing enough fuel for long voyages seemed insoluble unless we towed a barge laden with anthracite, fagots of pitch pine, logs of pressed sawdust, or sacks of charcoal. We knew these fuel sources were dirty, often unobtainable, and not really suitable for long-term daily use. We had sometimes enjoyed a charcoal fire on a friend's yacht, but such a fire was an occasional proposition, not a day-after-day necessity. One-third of a bag of charcoal for a single stove loading was ridiculous. Besides, the heat was hard to control, and there was a mess to clean up.

We elected to continue to use kerosene, so we purchased another Taylors stove.* This model had six ceramic elements that fitted inside a cylindrical brass can 11 inches high and 7 inches in diameter. A single Primus burner mounted underneath heated the ceramic elements, which soon glowed red and radiated heat in all directions. A 1-inch copper pipe topped with a miniature stove stack conducted the fumes outside. The stove was neat, compact, reasonably clean, and, for nights that didn't fall below 25°F or 30°F, the unit put out ample heat for *Whisper*'s living area, which very roughly measured 8 by 23 feet. We mounted the stove near the cabin sole to ensure warmth at foot level.

The heat was adequate for winters at 40° N and during chilly or damp periods in the tropics. At sea the stove burned at any angle of heel. Pitching didn't bother it. Occasionally we had trouble with a wave falling on the stove flue. We solved this by surrounding the outside part of the stack with a scrap of plastic plumbing pipe that we glued to the coachroof (see photograph opposite). When we didn't use the

*Force 10 makes a similar heating stove for use with kerosene, diesel oil, or propane. If the propane heater is used for long periods, however, the consumption of LPG is excessive.

stove for long periods during the summer, I covered the plastic pipe with duct tape.

I emphasize that nothing must interfere with the exit of the cabin heater fumes, whether it's a sailbag accidentally piled on top of the stack, a misaligned gasket, or anything else. The stack must work; otherwise, someone could be overcome by carbon monoxide. A gas alarm in the cabin will give added protection.

I can hardly tell you the feeling of warmth and comfort we enjoyed from the permanent installation of a stove that was easy to use. For years we lighted the Taylors heating stove every night and morning during the cold months. We came to know and welcome the familiar hiss of its Primus burner.

Often visitors came to *Whisper* for dinner during cold weather. Our guests would arrive wearing layers of woolens, ready for an evening of discomfort. But once they were aboard, we invariably heard the same words: "Gosh, it's pleasant down here. You're quite warm and snug. I had no idea. . . ." And off would come the sweaters and the expressions of uncertainty and doubt.

It's important not to block the flue in any way. Nevertheless, to keep water from running down the pipe, I glued a piece of plastic pipe on the outside to serve as a barrier.

At sea a source of dry heat can make the difference between a wet and dismal passage and a dry and pleasant trip. We installed a few brass hooks on the overhead above the stove, and many times we had a line of gloves or woolen socks or a sweater drying there (after a quick rinse in fresh water). Margaret and I can't think of anything more horrid than a long trip in cold weather without dependable heat.

I believe that comfort on a small vessel in cold weather requires dry heat, insulation, and good ventilation. All are important and help defeat condensation. On our yachts with single-layer fiberglass hulls, we have carefully insulated the entire interior with two layers of ¼-inch indoor-outdoor synthetic fiber carpet (Ozite) tacked on with contact cement (buy it by the gallon). The job is tedious because each piece has to be cut and fitted. In addition, we drill dozens of ¾-inch ventilation holes through various lockers and bulkheads and install high-quality hatches and as many opening portlights as possible.

During my sailing career I have had no luck with ventilators, whether they were Dorades, fancy French jobs, the best from England, or patented Canadian designs. When going to weather—at least in my experience—if the boat takes a solid wave, *all ventilators leak*. I cannot tolerate wet stores and ruined books. My friend Peter Tangvald came to the same conclusion years ago. "You must seal up your boat like a bottle when you go against the sea," he said. I agree.

Dead, damp air is conducive to condensation and mildew. Dry, warm, moving air is what you need for comfort. I am all in favor of lots of air and ventilation, but I get it by cracking portlights and hatches as soon as the boat gets off the wind.

We were quite content with our kerosene cooking and heating stoves until we spent an exceptionally cold winter in British Columbia. The Taylors heating stove performed valiantly and put out its 10,000 BTUs, but it couldn't combat the rigors of snow and ice on deck and the frigid drafts that sometimes raced down the main hatch. When we decided on a trip to Cape Horn, I began to look for a source of greater heat, and something we could run for long periods.

Oil

Oil stoves have a chamber in which a small amount of incoming oil and a large volume of air are mixed and burned. The rising heat is vented to a chimney that provides an upward draft that accelerates the combustion and allows gases and smoke to escape. The efficiency of a stove depends on its design and the completeness of combustion. Sometimes a small electric fan is used to help the performance. The advantage of an oil stove is that it can be used for both cooking and to heat the yacht. There's an oven for baking, and if you put a kettle on the back of the stove, you always have hot water.

In 1971, I bought a Dickinson Pacific oil stove in Canada and installed it in our first *Whisper*. The stove weighed 120 pounds, and the installation was a big job. Not only did the unit require a substantial bolt-down mount, but I had to fight the battle of the tank, the flue, and the plumbing. The stove had a 5-inch-diameter chimney that was $5\frac{1}{2}$ feet long. The combustion chamber, or pot, was about 10 inches in diameter and finished in fire clay that was almost white. We ran the stove on kerosene or light diesel oil from a gravity tank. (Fuel can also be pumped from a bilge tank with a small electric auto-pulse pump—the type used in Jaguar automobiles.) A small adjustable needle valve furnished a steady drip, drip, drip of oil. The stove performed flawlessly for 15 years, and we used it for both cooking and heating. We sold the yacht in 1986, and as far as I know, the stove is still working for the present owner.

On a trip around South America, we ran the stove for seven months without shutting it off. We spent three winters aboard the yacht in Maine and were always warm. The pot chamber burned perfectly clean (we could see the almost white fire clay) with a large blue flame that sometimes had a tiny touch of yellow at the top. We generally ran the Dickinson at its lowest setting but sometimes turned it up a little when baking or when the weather was extra cold. There was no soot. No filth. No problems.

In 1986 when I was fitting out my Santa Cruz 50 for her first trip around the world, I bought what I thought was an identical copy of the earlier stove. Unfortunately, the makers had "improved" the combustion chamber. Now it was made of stainless steel with a separate metal superburner. I was assured it was better. I installed the stove as before, but I found that it worked poorly and produced masses of soot. Various experts worked on it, but the performance only worsened. Regrettably, I chucked it out and sailed without heat.

When we bought our current *Whisper* in 1992, we spent a particularly severe winter on Chesapeake Bay. We had violent ice storms, a foot of snow on deck, and children were playing ice hockey next to us. In order to survive, I installed a German truck heater called an Espar. It runs (we still have it) on diesel oil from the engine tank and has a multispeed electric blower. The stove works well, although it draws 25 amps for about five minutes when first turned on.

There is absolutely no soot, and in spite of my initial horrors about the current draw, we have managed to live within its demands. I mounted the heater beneath a quarter berth in the aft part of the yacht. The German furnace produces hot air that is piped forward via a 4-inch-diameter flexible aluminum hose that snakes its way through various lockers on the port side. We have hot air outlets near the chart table, in the main cabin, and in the forepeak.

In 2000, Margaret and I decided to sail around the big island of Newfoundland and to Labrador. We would be in the cold Labrador Current near icebergs and pack ice and would need reliable heat. We had been using the Espar, but I worried about the electricity demands. If only we could emulate the performance of the first Dickinson stove in our old 35-footer!

I called the Dickinson company and was told that all problems had been solved. I ordered another stove, but when the shipment arrived and I looked inside, my heart froze. The new stove had the separate stainless steel afterburner and looked exactly the same as the 1986 Dickinson. I carefully installed it, but the stove never worked properly, at least with a $5\frac{1}{2}$-foot chimney, which was recommended. We had terrible soot problems during the trip, and in order to cook meals, we mostly used a spare Primus stove. For heat we turned on the Espar. With regrets, I junked the Dickinson.

My friend John Armitage, a retired IBM scientist, spent a dozen years mostly single-handing a 38-foot Amel sloop named *Kyrah*. John's adventures included ten years of sailing along the coast of Norway—from the southern tip to the remote Arctic island of Spitsbergen. A few times he sailed with his young son Ben, but mostly he traveled by himself. John has written a sailing guide to the Norwegian coast.

He wrote me about his heating arrangements.

"My diesel heater is a Sigmar 120 (www.sigmarine.com) with a so-called 'balanced draft' feature. The heater ($19 \times 8 \times 9\frac{1}{4}$ inches) has a normal three-inch-diameter vertical flue at the top, but in addition has a second vertical flue pipe that runs outside the stove and curves around underneath the stove to allow air from above deck to be fed into the combustion chamber from below. (See illustration.) This reduces the effect of gusts.

"The stove has a little float and needle valve. I have an electric pulse automotive fuel pump to supply diesel oil or kerosene (or a gravity tank can be used). This arrangement has given me no trouble in twelve years of heavy use. The feed is a controlled leak from the float chamber, a very simple system, again without trouble. The stove will run in all conditions, even when heeled under sail in a gale.

"The secret to this is a $3 \times 3 \times 1$ inch, 12-volt 'muffin' fan in the inlet air tube, which pre-

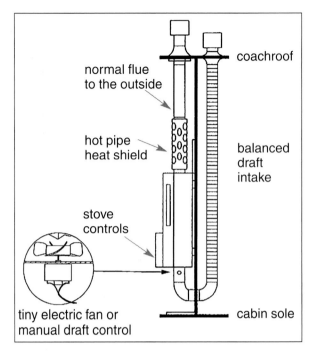

Diagram of Sigmar heating stove with balanced draft arrangement to deal with gusty winds and back drafts. The use of a tiny fan is helpful.

vents back drafts. The little fan is square with rounded corners, is made of black plastic and costs $15 at Radio Shack, part number 273-243. I usually run it at less than half speed, with a four-position switch and three voltage-dropping resistors so I can choose full speed or just a whisper. Probably a 2-inch fan would be enough. I simply cut a 2-inch long section out of my 3-inch diameter air inlet tube, placed the fan in this gap blowing in the direction of the furnace, and used lots of silver duct tape to position the fan in line with the tube and keep everything airtight. Crude, but easy and effective. If the fan dies, it is easy to remove the tape and put in a new fan. The current draw of 0.150 amps is negligible.

"Today," continued John, "I gave my Sigmar 120 its cleanout which is needed every year or two, depending on usage. The heater was slow coming up in the morning and slow to respond to a change in fuel flow setting, which made me suspicious. You lift out the top ring and the superheater and knock loose the residue on the bottom of the chamber. I sucked out all the junk with a little vacuum; although, really, the foreign matter does not seem to hurt much until it closes over the inlet hole.

"Untypically, I also had to clean out the fuel entry tube using a wire and syringe because some crud had fallen into it. You can tell when this has happened because the flame height responds sluggishly to a change in the fuel flow setting and it is hard to get a big flame. This is only the second time in twelve years of intensive use that this has happened. You remove the little hose under the heater and poke and prod until you can syringe a few ounces of clean diesel down from above and have it drop out the bottom cleanly.

"If I use latex gloves and a big plastic bag and lots of little clean rags, I can manage all this easily with no mess. I need to replace the superheater for the second time—it is a sheet metal rocket-ship-shaped affair that often gets red hot. After a few years, it starts falling apart, but it still works even when partially ruined. I'll order two replacements next winter, one for a spare. The other spares I like to carry are ones I cannot replace locally: the isinglass window, the asbestos-like gasket strip, and the rubber-lined seat for the float needle. The stove is very simple inside, hence easy to fix by crude methods if necessary."

A lovely anchorage in Daniel's Bay on Nuku Hiva in the Marquesa Islands in French Polynesia. The slopes of the mountains are an incredible dark green, and the trees are like enormous ferns.

NINE IDEAS

1. DEALING WITH TOOLS

With luck, you can complete a long cruise with a pair of slip-joint pliers and a slot screwdriver, but don't count on it. The more tools you keep on board, the better because in distant places or at sea, you will probably be making all the repairs yourself. Without the proper tools and a supply of fastenings, a bag of hose scraps, a few odd pieces of metal, a string of hose clamps, and some bits of wood, you may not be able to keep up with the mending and fixing of your home afloat.

Some of the repairs thought up by voyaging sailors—to the sails, rig, hull, and engine—are remarkable, and every year we hear about new heights of improvisation; certainly the keys to these successes are plentiful tools and the little odds and ends that veteran sailors tuck away.

But what do you tuck away? Where's the dividing line between necessary tools, overkill, and just plain junk? What about weight and cost? Where do you store all the stuff? And how can you quickly find those tools and nuts and bolts that you're sure you have on board somewhere when there's a real problem?

A few years back, the English sailor Bill King left Fremantle, Australia, for Cape Horn and was near Cape Leeuwin when his boat collided with a whale. The hull

Ordinary tools should be handy and easy to find day or night.

was stove in on the port side forward. A frame had buckled inward, and water poured in through a dozen cracks in the four layers of cold-molded mahogany. King threw his boat onto the opposite tack, which brought the damaged area just above the water. In between pumping, he managed to rig three wooden shores to support the area from the inside. King then rigged a collision patch on the outside, held by lines that he pulled right around the hull. Dealing with the patch took three days before the captain turned toward land. How important it was for King to have found his tools quickly during the emergency![88]

At one time I kept my tools in metal fishing tackle boxes that I stowed in cock-pit lockers or below in the cabin. All sorts of gear got piled on top of the boxes, and not only was it hard to pull them out, but I often had to unload half a box before I found the right tools. Usually I left the box out so I could put the tools away. Then it was easy to trip over the box or to upset it when I was in a hurry and forgot to clasp the top. Sometimes I bashed a heavy toolbox into the woodwork. I finally real-ized that it was stupid to drag out a heavy box when all I wanted was a little ham-mer or a pair of pliers.

I never seemed to have enough room for all the tools, and after I half filled the boxes with salt water a couple of times, I chucked out the rusty toolboxes. I con-sidered plastic toolboxes, but again this didn't touch the real problem. Why handle dozens of things to find a couple of small tools?

I changed to a scheme that uses *a handy compartmented drawer* to hold the tools that I employ most frequently. I found it best to have the tools at chest level with a light above that shines down into the drawer so I can find what I'm after, especially at night. It may be possible to have a quick-access tool compartment under several of the companionway steps, but this is generally a high-traffic area and sometimes there's water flying around. I've found it best to have the quick-access drawer in the aft part of the main cabin, where it's dry and away from salt spray.

Section 1 of my three-compartment drawer houses a selection of screwdrivers: four sizes of Phillips or cross-points, half a dozen standard slot (flat-blade) screwdrivers plus a couple of stubby slots, a stubby Phillips, three offset screwdrivers (one a Phillips),

It helps to have a light that shines down on the tools.

and a set of six miniatures for tiny screws. If you have a Canadian boat with Roberts fastenings dotted about, you'll need four Roberts screwdrivers plus spares. I cringe at the number, but this list already totals about *thirty* screwdrivers (plus three more large ones stored with what I call "the big tools" that I will talk about in a moment).

Section 2 of the drawer is for pliers: a couple of pairs of ordinary slip-joint pliers, two sizes of needle-nose, two pairs of side cutters (often called dikes), a pair of slip-joint water pump pliers, a pair of Vise-Grips, and electrician's pliers for stripping wires and crimping terminal fittings.

Section 3 contains general small tools and a set of 13 Hansen drills ($1/16$ to $1/4$") that come in a little yellow plastic case. In this area I keep a small ball peen hammer; a center punch; a large, fine-grade flat file; adjustable crescent wrenches (tiny, small, and medium); $1/4$-, $1/2$- and $3/4$-inch wood chisels (with guards); a razor blade scraper; giant tweezers; 2 inspection mirrors at the end of telescoping handles; a couple of tape measures; 2 small brushes with metal bristles; an old toothbrush; and several spare pocketknives. The yacht has a few fittings that need frequent adjustments, so I keep 10-millimeter and $7/16$-inch box-end wrenches in this section as well.

With the exception of an electric drill, the tools in this three-sectioned drawer take care of perhaps 70 percent of ordinary jobs. For the other 30 percent, I need "the big tools," which are stored in a less handy place because of their size and bulk. In *Whisper*, I keep them under the head of the berth in the aft cabin.

The big tools include hammers, a rubber mallet, a small vise, two jumbo slot screwdrivers (for mast fittings), a large crosspoint screwdriver for the engine, two eggbeater hand drills, pry bars, a combination square (with level), a large carpenter's square, and two 24-inch mechanical fingers for picking up objects in the bilge (mine cost $1 each twenty years ago and are great tools). I have 15- and 18-inch adjustable crescent wrenches and a Ford wrench that open wide for the big nuts on the stuffing box on the propeller shaft, large turnbuckle nuts, and the engine mounts. There's a hacksaw with high-speed steel blades of 18, 24, and 32 teeth per inch (plus spare blades). I also carry a 30-inch crosscut wood saw with sharp teeth, a Japanese pull saw, an 18-inch wood saw with fine teeth, and several keyhole saws. The assortment includes a pair of 22-inch water pump pliers, a selection of Samson splicing fids and pushers, and a special handle that holds one end of a hacksaw blade for sawing in tight quarters. In the mix are big scissors for cutting fiberglass materials, an S&F Nicopress swaging tool, and a Stilson pipe wrench. I keep punches, cold chisels, a small socket set, and lots of extra drill bits in small plastic boxes.

Other big tools include round and flat wood rasps and metal files, large metal drills, threaded rod, a small wood plane, and a 100-foot tape measure. A particularly handy tool is an adjustable bevel, which is good for checking the angles between the mast spreaders and the upper shrouds.

An important big tool is a Makita right-angle battery drill that takes drill shanks up to $\frac{3}{8}$ inch. This gutsy, powerful little drill is a great seagoing tool and one of the handiest devices ever invented because you can drill holes in confined places that are impossible for hand drills to reach. For years I used a hand eggbeater drill until on a voyage to Cape Town, Otto Kindlimann put me on to the Makita cordless angle drill (model DA 391D). The 9.6-volt nickel-cadmium battery lasts for years and is easy to charge on a 12-volt system.

There are a few tools that I think are necessary to have on board but are rarely used. These include a large accordion-style rivet gun for setting $\frac{3}{16}$- and $\frac{1}{4}$-inch pop rivets, boxes of stainless steel rivets, an impact wrench, a brace and bits, 22-inch-long Felco wire cutters (which will slice through $\frac{3}{8}$-inch-diameter rigging wire), a punch for making holes in leather or thin plastic, the hand crank for the engine, and so on. We oil all these tools, put them in several plastic bags, and tuck them away in a forepeak locker.

West Epoxy, cans of Marine-Tex (a kind of superepoxy with a filler that is excellent for underwater cracks, general repairs, and fairing), various paints and varnish, bottom paint, acetone, paint thinner, brushes, sandpaper, and so on all fit in the bosun's locker under one of the cabin seats.

The metric system has gradually taken over the world (including Mexico and Canada) and is obliging a kicking and screaming United States to follow. Since most small marine diesels are made in Europe, China, or Japan, you need wrenches from 5 to 25 millimeters. The engine accessories and some plumbing fittings require wrenches from $\frac{1}{4}$ inch to $1\frac{1}{2}$ inches. I find that all these wrenches in a single box are too heavy and get mixed up, so I keep metric and English unit wrenches in separate plastic boxes. When buying wrenches, by all means purchase them in sets. You can often buy a complete set for the price of several separate wrenches. Many tool stores (e.g., Sears) sell small flat *plastic* boxes that are ideal for wrenches and socket sets. Metal boxes soon rust. If possible, try to keep each category of tools (a big socket set, electrical wire, tubes of glue and bedding, the sail-mending kit, plumbing parts, metal pieces, etc.) in separate, labeled containers. If the contents are heavy and the catch for the top is doubtful (most are), tie a piece of $\frac{1}{8}$-inch line around the box so you won't dump the container when you pick it up.

Fastenings constitute the other half of the tool story. Just about everything on a boat is screwed, nailed, or riveted to something else. And it seems that each fastening is different from all others! To keep track of nuts, bolts, screws, and so on, I separate them into the classes listed in the accompanying sidebar and put them into small plastic containers. For the bulky categories I try to find square, wide-mouthed containers with screw tops, not snap-on lids. I store them with the most-used containers on top. These are only suggestions, but the scheme helps me classify what's on board and makes it easy for me to find what I want quickly.

I also have a box into which I put small containers with seldom-used hardware. Often I don't go into it for months, but when I need a lock washer or a finish washer or a copper brad, I can find it in a couple of minutes. (See second list.)

Of course, all these containers need labels to keep them sorted out. I have a little labeling gun (Rotex 780). Unfortunately, the labels stick poorly to plastic lids even if I rough them up with sandpaper. I have tried putting a piece of duct tape on the lids and then sticking the label on the duct tape. This works somewhat, but I am looking for a better scheme.

I've built up my tool collection over a long time, gradually discarding useless items (large plane, big hand saws) and buying a few new things each year (adjustable block plane; metric/U.S. tape measures). I am an inveterate fastening picker-upper, especially in boatyards, where few people bother to bend over to collect stainless steel screws and bolts that someone has dropped. When I buy fastenings, I always order a few extra. And when I remove an installation (wooden shelf, plumbing fitting), I save the old fastenings that are in good condition and sort them

---

Fastenings Lists

Frequently Used Fastenings	*Occasionally Used Fastenings*
round-head screws 1" and under	copper tacks
round-head screws over 1"	brads
flat-head screws 1" and under	grub screws
flat-head screws over 1"	O-rings
nuts and bolts under $\frac{1}{4}$" dia.	galvanized nails
$\frac{1}{4}$" dia. nuts and bolts	lock washers
$\frac{5}{16}$" dia. nuts and bolts	finish washers
nuts and bolts over $\frac{5}{16}$" dia.	circle clips
washers	screw eyes
unusual washers (plastic, fiber, etc.)	copper washers
cotter pins under $\frac{1}{8}$"	Nicopress fittings
cotter pins $\frac{1}{8}$"	springs
cotter pins $\frac{5}{32}$"	Sta-Lok fittings
taps	hinges, latches, and lifts
dies	teak plugs for joinery
Allen wrenches (metric and U.S.)	grommet kit
hole saws	

into their proper box or jar. Result? A handy supply of all manner of nuts and bolts that will, one day, be useful on board or helpful to others.

Reading this over gives me the scary feeling that I'm running an onboard hardware store. This is not my idea at all. All I've done is classify my tools according to frequency of use, store them so that I can find them in a hurry, and sort the fastenings (in whatever quantity) so that I can pull out four 1¼-inch number 8 flat-head stainless steel screws without wasting half an hour. Am I a fusspot? Perhaps.

2. FILLING WATER TANKS

In the trade-wind zones, the easiest way to fill the freshwater tanks is to set up a water-catching awning or to use the mainsail. There is usually plenty of water around high islands and atolls in the tropics, but the problem is collecting it. Sometimes you may be anchored a long way out from shore in a shallow lagoon. This means you must row the jugs ashore and carry them to a suitable place along a stream (above where the women are washing) or go to a cistern where you can draw water. This is generally beneath the roof of the church, the building with the largest catchment roof on the island. To get eighty or a hundred gallons of water may take an entire morning. You row half a mile to shore and walk a long way to the church. Then you fill the jugs and lug them back to the yacht.

It's easier to use a water-catching awning. Not only is it simple, but once set up, it takes care of itself. The water is purer because you don't draw it from a cistern of doubtful purity or take it from a stream whose upcountry customers you may or may not like.

An easy scheme to fill the water tanks is to use a couple of buckets during a rain shower, a system that has been in use since Year 1. Crude but efficient. It's a far cry from a modern osmotic watermaker, but the bucket system is simple and dependable as long as it rains occasionally. Watermakers are excellent when they are working, but they demand care and regular maintenance.

Practically all yachts have a sun awning of some kind that can be adapted to catch water. On *Whisper* our awning measures 10 by 17 feet and rests on top of the main boom. We use four athwartship battens to support the awning. At the forward end, the awning is secured to the lower shrouds and the mast; I tie the middle part of the aftermost batten to the backstay; we tie light lines between the lifelines and the ends of each batten to keep the awning from flapping. We have a small triangular pocket at the forward starboard corner that takes a hose that leads to a water tank. During a rainstorm we tilt the awning a little so the pocket area is low, which allows the water to collect and run down the hose. If we put a clamp on the hose, we can take a shower by kneeling underneath and releasing the clamp after some water has collected. If the water stands for a while, the sun will heat it.

A problem with the big awning is that a good deal of wind often comes with strong rain squalls. This makes it necessary to roll up the awning. To get around this difficulty and to be able to catch water in places where we don't use the big awning (away from the tropics), we have a smaller awning especially to catch rain.

This funnel under the main boom gooseneck leads to the water tanks. A square funnel is a little easier to mount. Plastic is the best material.

This awning goes along one side deck and is 9 feet long and 2½ feet wide. It is arranged to be lower at the forward end, which is over the deck opening for the tank. Short ties hold it between the lifelines and the coachroof handrail. A sewed-in plastic funnel and short hose lead directly into the filler pipe. To keep the awning from flapping in the wind, we weigh it down with the boat hook.

Another plan is to use the mainsail for water catching. You can do this when either sailing or at anchor. (You may need bow and stern anchors.) Ease the halyard and take up on the topping lift a little to make a big bag of the mainsail. This will direct all the water to the front of the sail and the gooseneck area. The water then pours into a large funnel that we hold against the back of the mast underneath the gooseneck with a piece of shock cord. A square plastic funnel is best and can be bought for a few dollars at an auto parts store. Mark this funnel plainly or buy a special color and reserve it for water catching; don't use it to transfer kerosene or diesel oil.

Does it rain in the tropics? I remember a rainstorm about halfway between Mexico and French Polynesia while we were sailing hard in the northeast trades. Did it rain? Oh yes! In the darkness of night, Margaret and I eased the main halyard a little and lifted the main boom slightly with the topping lift. The wind was fair and the rain thundered into the sail and cascaded on deck near the mast. After the first few minutes the sail was washed clean, so we directed water into the freshwater tanks, which were soon full. We filled the teakettle, the sink, the water jugs, and the buckets and took long drinks of the delightfully cool water. We washed our hair, wiped down the cabin sole, and, after plugging the cockpit drains, started doing the laundry. Even the cat got a bath. Did it rain? Two hours later it was still pouring. Talk about an unnautical scene! Naked bodies, laughter, laundry flapping, and a meowing cat that looked like a rat—all while we footed along at five knots with a silvery wake bubbling behind us. All we needed was a man playing the flute!

Still another way to catch water is to use the coachroof or a section of deck and to surround a flat, level area with low battens. Then, with a through-deck drain, a petcock underneath, and calm sailing, you can pipe the water to the tanks. Blondie Hasler used this idea on his famous *Jester*, and I have seen a similar scheme on a ferro-cement yacht in Samoa. I suppose you might catch drinking water in an upright-stowed dinghy if it were cleaned out thoroughly. During his many high-latitude adventures, Bill Tilman often ferried water from freshwater streams to his big wooden pilot cutter *Mischief* by means of a rubber dinghy that was washed out, filled to overflowing, and carefully towed out to the ship behind another dinghy.

3. FLASHLIGHTS

The trouble with conventional two-battery D-cell flashlights is the *switch*, which so often fails in a saltwater environment. I've bought flashlights made in the United States, England, Spain, Japan, Mexico, and Hong Kong for years and years. None has been any good over time. The flashlights work nicely the first day or maybe for a week or two. Then dampness invades the switches, and to make the lights go on, you resort to tapping and banging to try to get the damned things to work. At one time I thought the answer was a French underwater flashlight whose switch mechanism was a screw-down affair beneath an O-ring. I decided this was a foolproof design and bought several flashlights at vast prices. They too failed. The black flashlights carried by police officers were another disaster. I got tired of sandpapering the ends of batteries, the coiled spring at the bottom of the case, and the various brass contacts as well as trying to fix damp switches.

In 1986, Duracell passed out a few samples of a plastic penlight that used two AA batteries. Instead of the customary large flashlights, we tried carrying these little 4-inch-long flashlights that have a particularly good stainless steel compression switch that is simple, easy to get at, and seems idiot-proof. Push for contact; relax for off. The battery contacts are made of stainless steel, which is superior to brass that corrodes. Even when these hand-sized lights get a blast of salt water, it's easy to rinse them off and dry them out. It was about in 1986 that alkaline dry batteries began to be widely used, and these made quite a powerful light. Then a few years later, krypton bulbs became available. With both improved batteries and bulbs, the light from these penlights is exceptional.

The bottom line? We have three regular two-battery D-cell flashlights on board, but we haven't used them in years. We have a dozen or so extra D-cell batteries on hand, but they're moldering in a drawer.

Instead, at night or in dark corners, we use the little penlights, which are easy to carry and switch on. If I need two hands for a job, I hold the light in my mouth. We can slip them in a handy pocket, where they're available in a few seconds. I think we have eight or ten of these small flashlights on board and at any moment a couple of them are stuck in various jacket pockets. No, I'm not on Duracell's payroll. I buy the penlights in a grocery store for six bucks each and put in alkaline batteries and a krypton bulb. Try one. You'll be surprised.

4. MAST STEPS

Margaret and I go up and down the mast on metal steps that are fastened every 20 inches on alternate sides of the spar. Our 24 steps extend to just below the masthead, where we have a fitting on each side—opposite one another—for convenience in working at the top or for looking ahead. In practice we find that we keep the rigging in better condition because inspections and work aloft are easier. For big jobs when you need many tools and a comfortable seat, it's still necessary to use a bosun's chair, which I hoist to the appropriate height and then climb to on the steps. Or you can get into the bosun's chair on deck and someone can hoist it while you climb the steps.

I think steps are superior to ratlines on the lower shrouds, which move around and are dangerous to climb if the vessel is rolling. Ratlines of thin line are impossible to climb barefoot.

An important advantage of the steps is the ability to go aloft at sea when there's a rigging problem or a spinnaker wrap. Mast steps are quicker and simpler to use than a bosun's chair or a rope ladder, although no scheme is 100 percent safe on the moving ocean. Going aloft requires your full attention and should be avoided if possible when the boat is rolling or pitching severely because of the danger of getting slammed against the mast or even getting whipped off. If the yacht is rolling heavily, you won't be able to do any significant work in any case because you'll be using all your strength to hang on. In light airs on a smooth sea, however, it's easy to climb to the masthead.

If you are planning to install mast steps, I suggest that you try climbing the steps on another mast beforehand if possible. People vary quite a bit in their leg and thigh strength, and some otherwise athletic people are simply unable to climb mast steps. In addition, the spacing may be too little or too much for your leg and thigh length. When we put steps on the first *Whisper*'s mast in California, there was a lot of curiosity about them. Many people tried climbing up, with surprising results.

There is a slight problem of getting halyards around mast steps, but we have

We like mast steps because getting aloft is quick and simple.

learned to keep the slack out of the halyards and to look aloft frequently when hoisting the mainsail. It's possible to eliminate this problem by drilling small vertical holes in the outer part of the steps and running a light line or wire from the bottom to the top step. However, I don't find this is necessary.

There are so many things on a mast that I hate to clutter up the spar with metal steps, but I feel the quick accessibility to the top is worth it, particularly on shorthanded vessels. The head-on windage is small; you can hardly see the steps from forward or aft from a distance. The steps make it easy for a lookout to climb to the spreaders to look for a way through coral reefs or to take a photograph from a high point.

I had my steps fabricated of 0.085-inch marine-grade stainless steel 1 inch wide except for the footstep, which is 1½ inches wide and slightly rounded. (You can climb the steps barefoot, but it's best to wear shoes.) Each step is 5 inches wide at the tread and measures 10 inches from top to bottom. The individual steps weigh 7 ounces and are held to the mast with six hefty stainless steel screws (for wooden masts) or ³/₁₆-inch-diameter stainless steel pop rivets (for aluminum spars). There are more streamlined Canadian folding steps, but these require you to reach up and either unfold or fold the steps and introduce one thing more to do. I prefer to concentrate on the climbing. In addition, I like to have my feet inside the confines of a steel strap. But to each his own.

If you decide to install mast steps, it's probably easiest if you work up and down from the lower spreaders and mark the position of each step and its holes before you drill anything. I suggest that you do this from a bosun's chair while the mast is up with all the standing rigging in place. Usually it's necessary to move a couple of the steps a little sideways around the mast where a shroud fitting is fastened to the spar. Otherwise, you may not be able to insert your foot into the step. *Plan and mark everything before you drill any holes.*

5. Nonskid Surfaces on Decks

For secure footing on the decks, cockpit floor, cockpit seats, bridge deck, and coachroof, we add coarse sand to the deck paint. Some of our visitors think our decks are too rough, but no one has slipped yet, a statement that can hardly be said for many fiberglass decks with supposedly skidproof patterns molded into them. Most boatbuilders never go sailing and have no idea what's necessary. A nonslip surface is essential, and it's an important safety feature. It's better to err on the side of an overrough deck than to risk slipping and injury.

We paint the decks with ordinary one-part polyurethane paint and sprinkle the sand from a 3-inch-diameter saltshaker. Our routine is to paint a patch about three feet long, and sprinkle sand on it. We let the paint dry a few minutes and then stipple on a second coat before moving on. The next day we overcoat the earlier painting with a third coat. We try to stay off the decks for a few days to let the paint harden.

This technique is quick and easy and combines with the sand to make a filelike surface that either bare feet or boating shoes can grip. We have found that a coarsely roughened surface is easier to keep clean than a lightly roughened surface.

6. Ship's Book

I use a small spiral-bound booklet to keep track of all boat data. It's helpful to know that when I'm replacing a jib sheet and hunting for a suitable line, the correct length should be 55 feet. The jib furling line should be 65 feet long, and the second reefing pendant is 41 feet. Over time I have noted the correct lengths for most of the running and standing rigging. I see that the engine reduction gearbox is 2.4:1, and the area of the small storm jib is 79 square feet. The ship's book has the part numbers for the engine fuel injector tips, and I can find out the serial numbers for both head parts and the paper filters for the diesel fuel filter.

I once measured the luffs of the spinnaker (46 feet) and think I know the area from a formula that I copied into the book. (The parachute spinnaker area is 76 percent of a rectangle whose length is the luff length [46'] times the J measurement [14.75'] times 1.8. This becomes $14.75 \times 1.8 \times 46 = 1,221$. Seventy-six percent of this number is 928 sq. ft. I hope this formula is right.)

The ship's book has both the yacht's U.S. Coast Guard documentation number and the bottom paint type and number, plus radio call signs and radio license numbers. I have the name, address, and telephone number of a sailmaker at Horta in the Azores and the name of the harbormaster in Northeast Harbor, Maine. I have the address of *Whisper*'s boatbuilder in France in case I need parts for the yacht. I have the length (52') of a spare piece of $5/16$-inch-diameter 1×19 standing rigging wire that I carry in case of an emergency. The little book has the name and contact information for the mast maker in Sweden, his English agent (where the mast came from), and the U.S. counterpart.

In other words, all data, people contacts, special gear, equipment styles, the date of entry, and unclassified information go into the ship's book, which I keep next to the chart table.

7. COCKROACHES

These fast-moving little devils are the plague of all human habitations in the tropics and nearby zones. Ships of all kinds are especially prone to infestations because of warmth, dampness, darkness, food, lots of places for the pests to live free from harm, and the difficulty of fumigation. Seasoned voyagers to the tropics go to great lengths to avoid bringing cockroaches on board. Old hands prefer to anchor out, never bring cardboard boxes aboard, and scrupulously inspect all foodstuffs coming by dinghy, including dipping potatoes and bananas in seawater and scrubbing and rinsing all suspicious food.

What do you do if cockroaches are on board? Besides clobbering them with a tennis shoe whenever one appears, the best remedy that I know is to spread boric acid around the edges of the galley and the perimeter of the cabin sole.

Insect powders come and go; boric acid, however, is effective and cheap. More than thirty years ago, scientists at the University of California made exhaustive tests of various poisons, powders, and repellents. The experts confirmed that boric acid was "strikingly superior to other insecticides in long-term residual effectiveness." The tests included lethal chemical insecticides, which the cockroaches often learned to avoid. Entomologist Walter Ebeling said that it did no good to add chemical insecticides, sugar, or flour to boric acid. All the additives tended to repel the cockroaches and clearly weakened the effectiveness of the boric acid by itself. I have found no recent information to dispel these findings.[89]

My old Caribbean sailing buddy, the late Fritz Seyfarth, counseled that the best way to deal with cockroaches was to put a pinch of boric acid in little wooden matchboxes, then place a number of the slightly opened boxes around the cabin sole and galley. "The cockroaches are naturally curious and like to go into strange corners," Fritz said. "The boxes hold the poison and keep the boat neat. Once the critters go in, they never come out."

8. AN EASIER-TO-USE TOPPING LIFT

With a heavy main boom and a large mainsail, I run the topping lift from the main boom up to a block at the back of the masthead and then down along the standing backstay to the transom area behind the cockpit. This routes the line away from the mast (one less line), and it is handy to be able to adjust the topping lift from the cockpit. Because the lift is sometimes hard to haul on when a 500 or 600 sq. ft. sail is full of wind when reefing, I add a single purchase to the fall of the topping lift. This purchase is merely a single block that rides up and down the backstay on a 2-inch nylon ring about 10 or 12 feet above the deck. I splice the fall of the topping lift to the eye of the block. The standing part of the purchase is tied to the stern pulpit. The hauling part leads down from the block and goes through a second small block on deck (to turn the line 90°) and thence to a cleat on the outside of the cockpit coaming at a convenient place. To deal with the topping lift, I merely lean over the cockpit coaming and either haul on the line or ease it. Once arranged, this setup works well and seldom needs attention.

As Eric Hiscock suggested long ago, we use ⅜-inch-diameter three-strand nylon line for the entire topping lift. This line is strong, has ample stretch, and has little chafing tendency on the leech of the mainsail. The line lasts for a long time. The block at the masthead needs to be of a type that cannot revolve; otherwise, the two parts of the topping lift may twist together. In an emergency the topping lift can be used as a main halyard or for other purposes, so the masthead block should be strong and securely mounted. I always

To gain power when using the topping lift, I use a single purchase on the hauling part. This goes to a small deck-level block and then to a handy cleat on the outside of the cockpit. The nylon ring on the backstay keeps the fall of the topping lift out of the way of the sail and allows the block to run up and down. The ⅜-inch-diameter nylon line in the photograph is slightly worn but has been in use for ten years and is still perfectly good.

take up on the topping lift a little when the mainsail is being raised or lowered to prevent possible strains on the leech of the sail.

9. Stuffing Box Leaks

If you're sailing and have a severe leak in the stuffing box for the engine shaft, you might consider the ACE bandage treatment. Take the yacht alongside a dock or put her on a grid where there's a sufficient tidal range to let her dry out—at least down to the propeller. Then working outside the hull, wind an elastic Ace bandage (for sprained ankles) around and around the shaft and stern tube (presuming that it sticks out a little) to stanch the incoming flow. On the next flood tide she will be afloat, and no water will leak into the interior. This means you can repack the stuffing box or work on whatever shaft system your boat has in place. Repairs done, on the next ebb you ground the yacht out again and remove the Ace bandage. I suppose you could do this with scuba gear.

I have also heard of sailors winding an Ace bandage around and around the shaft and stern tube *on the inside of the boat* to stop a severe leak while under way and far out at sea. This of course stops engine propulsion but may save the vessel. I have heard this suggestion repeated by sailors in widely separate parts of the world, so it must be true that desperate minds think alike.

Every 18 to 24 months we take our yacht out of the water at a boatyard and spend a couple of days sanding the bottom to clean off marine growth and old paint. We do this job carefully, which forces us to inspect every bit of the bottom. We check all the through-hull fittings and shutoff valves and deal with the speed indicator, depth sounder transducer, and propeller. We find the best tool for this is a large sanding block and grade 125-grit wet and dry abrasive paper. The job is easier and cleaner if you have access to a freshwater hose, but it's possible to do the work with a bucket and salt water. An air-driven orbital sander will speed the job. Don't try it with an electric sander because with all the water flying around, you're a perfect ground, which means there's an excellent chance of electrocuting yourself. Margaret took this photograph in Malta, but we've done this job in a dozen countries. A perfectly smooth bottom, flush through-hulls, carefully faired rudder fittings, and a folding or feathering propeller do wonders for light-air sailing.

26
THE DINGHY PROBLEM

A dinghy or yacht tender has four main uses and a less frequently used fifth:

- To take the crew and supplies to and from the shore.
- To lay out a second anchor if bad weather comes up, or to run a line ashore.
- If the yacht goes ashore for any reason, you need a dinghy to carry out an anchor so you can pull the vessel off. Sooner or later all yachts run aground; prompt anchor work can generally get the vessel off. Even if you sail from a marina dock, you can make a strong case for carrying a dinghy in case you go aground.
- Sometimes it's nice to do a little sightseeing from your small boat.
- If there's no wind and the yacht has no engine or one that's out of order, it's possible to lash the dinghy alongside, fire up the engine, and proceed at a few knots. This technique may seem ridiculous

Twenty yacht tenders tied up at a crowded dock. Four are hard dinghies (one collapsible). Outboard engines are in at least half the boats. Oars (in one case, a single paddle) propel the rest. In several I see an outboard but no backup oars, perhaps suggesting hope over common sense.

to some, but in a pinch it works extremely well and is worth tucking away in your bag of sailing tricks. The Maine charter schooner fleet has been doing this for more than fifty years.

A general-purpose *hard* dinghy is $7\frac{1}{2}$ to 10 feet long and weighs 45 to 135 pounds. It's usually made of fiberglass—or less frequently of flat panels of plywood or cold-molded—and is powered by oars or a small outboard. A few experts scull dinghies with a single oar in a transom notch or rowlock.

In reality a $7\frac{1}{2}$-or 8-foot boat is only a tolerable dinghy at best; a 9- or 10-foot tender is much more satisfactory because it is safer, easier to row or motor, faster, and has a larger carrying capacity. If you have the room, by all means take the largest small boat you can.

With regard to design, the late Hamish Davidson of Vancouver, British Columbia, who built 8,000 dinghies during a long career, liked plenty of beam and freeboard to help the load-carrying ability of his boats.

"In addition, I favor a modestly pointed bow to help the craft slice through small seas," Davidson once told me in his West Georgia Street shop. "I feel that a dinghy needs a flattish floor, a transom stern, and a modest keel carried back to the transom in the form of a straight skeg to keep the dinghy on course. I like ample sideways and fore-and-aft curvature of the hull lines at the stern to allow the water to flow away easily."

A second design type is a pram, which has a flat transom at each end and hard-chine construction, with a slightly V-shaped and cambered bottom. Generally $7\frac{1}{2}$ to 9 feet long, they are easy to make from kits or sheets of plywood, row reasonably well, and can be sailed. They are lighter in weight than fiberglass dinghies but more fragile.

In 2002, I looked at the offerings of eight companies whose hard dinghies cost from $730 to $2,100. All had built-in flotation, bumper strips around the gunwales, and room for two or three people. Six of the eight were made of hand-laid-up solid fiberglass and should be good for twenty years or more of banging into docks and knocking around stony beaches. Two of these builders made fiberglass hulls with lapstrake-type construction, which is particularly stiff and strong. The seventh dinghy—the lightest of the lot at 45 pounds—was a pram that was nicely constructed of thin plywood with epoxied fiberglass tapes on all the seams. All seven would be easy to repair.

The eighth company offered a tender constructed of inner and outer shells of thin fiberglass separated by an air space. Certainly this construction will not stand up to hard usage, besides being tedious to repair. Another firm advertised dinghies that sold for about half of the above prices and were made of injection-molded polypropylene or heat-formed polyethylene and were more children's toys than tenders for long-distance cruising. These boats also had marginal flotation.

Fiberglass dinghies are often constructed of thin moldings—say, $\frac{5}{32}$ of an inch or 4 millimeters—that have little strength in unsupported panels. However, with the addition of a few stringers, molded-in buoyancy tanks, seat supports, knees, transom braces, mast steps, wooden gunwales, and so on, the strength increases rapidly (as does the weight and cost). Many sailors like wooden cold-molded construction with perhaps three layers of 4-inch-wide strips of $^3/_{32}$-inch wood glued over a male mold to make form-following plywood that is surprisingly rigid. My friend Raith Sykes borrowed a fiberglass dinghy, used it for a male mold, and built a splendid 9-foot cold-molded tender that, when varnished, was both handsome and lightweight.

A hard dinghy needs a brass or stainless steel (not iron) rubbing strip on the bottom of its keel to help protect it from rocks, coral, and gravel when the boat is pulled across beaches. On one 8-foot tender, I used a 9-foot length of $^3/_4$-inch stainless steel half round that began at the bow towing ring (which held it at the forward end), curved down to the keel, and ran back to the transom. I fastened the strip along its length with 10-24 bolts and stainless steel self-tapping screws set in Marine-Tex epoxy to make a tough bottom skid.

A tender should have an encircling bumper strip of old fire hose, 2-inch diameter manila line, or split vinyl hose fitted entirely around the gunwale and transom to ease knocks, chafe, and noise. It's worthwhile to fasten bumper strips carefully at close intervals. I've had excellent results with $^3/_4$-round polyester-covered rubber gunwale guard, a commercial product. All dinghies need built-in buoyancy to prevent them and their occupants from sinking. The buoyancy can be provided with flotation bags, large pieces of closed-cell foam, plastic or metal tanks, or closed areas built into the hull.

There's no sense denying that the basic difficulty with a hard dinghy is that it's big, awkward, and terribly in the way when stowed on the deck of a sailboat. The problem is like parking an automobile in the downtown section of a crowded city; it would be ideal if you could rub a magic lamp and have a genie whisk the dinghy away, only to have it magically reappear when you clap your hands.

Usually a hard dinghy is placed upside down ("capsized") over the coachroof of the yacht with the tender's long dimension parallel to and underneath the main boom, with the bow forward and perhaps touching the mast. Placed like this, the capsized dinghy fits over the coachroof skylight, which often can be left open for ventilation.

You can store a hard dinghy right side up, but this requires special chocks and more vertical space. This reduces forward visibility, and even with a cover, the tender becomes a general repository for scrap lumber, empty bottles, half-full paint cans, and odds and ends of junk better stowed elsewhere or tossed out.

Depending on the size of the craft and the rigging arrangements, the tender may fit ahead of the mast and over the front hatch. The larger the yacht, the easier the stowage.

A few sailors store their dinghies on stern davits, which allow the small boat to be launched and recovered quickly and simply, and kept secure. However, most people object to davits for aesthetic reasons because a bulky dinghy above the transom spoils the appearance of a yacht. Additionally, it may be hard to mount davits if there's a wind-vane steering device or a mizzen boom. Finally, the windage aft may interfere with steering in strong winds, and if the sea is rough, the dinghy in davits may be difficult to keep from swinging around and being threatened by overtaking seas. Depending on the rig, a larger yacht may be able to fit davits on a side deck.

Consider the *placement* of a stored dinghy. An 80-pound tender on the foredeck of a small yacht in a seaway will definitely slow progress to windward. The same penalty applies to stern davits, although the windward penalty isn't so drastic. Ideally, heavy weights should be placed amidships. An adult crew member on the foredeck of a 25-foot Folkboat noticeably upsets the balance of the boat. It's less on a 40-footer, but still a factor.

An inflatable dinghy would seem to solve all the above problems. You let out the air, roll up the bundle, and toss it into a locker. It's gone and out of the way. When you want to use the dinghy, you unroll it and pump it up. The inflatable is unsinkable, won't capsize, has smooth sides, and can carry large loads. What could be better?

Inflatables are perfect for visitors not used to tippy hard dinghies and for landing on surf-washed beaches or rock-strewn shorelines. Their fabric materials are surprisingly tough and durable. The smaller models are quite easy to haul up on land or a dock and to store with a friendly shopkeeper or harbormaster.

Unfortunately, the story grows more complicated. Inflatable dinghies are essentially giant inner tubes that float on top of the water like doughnuts. Unlike conventional boats, these air-and-fabric creations have no keel and therefore no grip on the water. This is why inflatables row so badly—particularly in a wind—and why it's usually necessary to use outboard motors with them.

An inflatable is difficult to construct because it's made of curved cylindrical tubes of sun-resistant rubberlike fabric with hand-glued or welded seams. Due to the labor and special material required, the cost of inflatables is high, to which must be added the cost of an outboard motor and a mounting arrangement.

When you stand on the fabric floor of a basic inflatable dinghy, it's like walking on Jell-O. To overcome this, the makers have designed plywood panels or roll-up athwartship aluminum or plastic slats that fit along the bottom and serve as a floor. This roll-up dinghy deflates to a modest package, but because of the bulk of the floor slats and the rigid plywood transom, the bundle is larger than an all-fabric inflatable. There are also models with high-pressure inflatable floors and small inflatable keels that project a slight V-bottom for better performance.

To help inflatables track well and perform like regular small boats, naval architects have designed deeper V-bottom fiberglass or aluminum hulls with 16-inch-diameter (or thereabouts) inflatable cylinders along each side and at the bow. These rigid inflatable boats (RIBs) are first-class performers and can easily plane with small outboard motors. However, the fiberglass or aluminum hull—with its keel and floor—does not collapse or fold up. This means the basic advantage of the inflatable—the wonderful stowage—has largely been lost.

The ability to store RIBs is limited to the length and width of the rigid hull, plus the deflated side chambers. This bulky package is a long way from the inflatable that you can stuff in a bag and put on your shoulder. It seems to me that you're far better off with a hard dinghy that costs less, lasts longer, is easier to repair, and performs well with either oars or an outboard motor. Of course, the big advantage of the RIB is that with its surrounding flotation cylinders, it's almost impossible to capsize.

The best answer to easy dinghy stowage and reasonable performance that I know of is this Tinker Foldaway rigid inflatable boat (RIB). The fiberglass bottom is hinged athwartships in two places. This allows the rigid bottom to be folded in thirds. When the dinghy is unfolded and the side tubes are inflated, the tubes hold the opened-out floor together in a firm, one-piece unit with a slight V-bottom. This clever design feature solves the stowage problem of a normal RIB, whose stowage dimensions are not much different from a fully inflated dinghy. The Tinker that I examined and tried was made of Hypalon and well constructed. I rowed it with 6-foot oars, but 7-foot oars would be better. With the rigid floor, the dinghy was easy to use and move around in, and it rowed much better than a soft-bottom inflatable.

The Tinker Foldaway RIB partially stowed. Ed Zacko is about to fold the boat in thirds, which reduces its stored dimensions to 39 × 33 × 17 inches. The weight is 56 pounds. Its overall inflated length is 9 feet, and the beam is 5 feet. The fiberglass molding has two small plastic wheels on the transom so the dinghy can be pulled around like an airport suitcase.

I have looked at 12 inflatables made by Avon and Zodiac, two leading manufacturers. The dinghies were from 9 to $10^{1}/_{2}$ feet long, weighed 63 to 150 pounds, and in 2002, cost from $900 to $2,800, with an average price of $2,029. The recommended outboard horsepower for the 12 inflatables ran from 4 to 15, with an average of 9.75. An 8-horsepower two-stroke-cycle Mercury outboard cost $1,490. The price of a 9.9-horsepower four-stroke-cycle Mercury outboard was $1,930. According to these figures, the all-up total for an inflatable with an outboard ranged from $2,390 to $4,730.

Almost everyone agrees that the rowing performance of inflatable dinghies is poor to abysmal, although it can be helped with longer oars and firm rowlocks. This means that in strong wind and sea conditions, it may be impossible to lay out an anchor with an inflatable and oars, which, as we have seen, is a vital function for the tender of a cruising yacht. The glib-tongued sellers of inflatables try to gloss over this basic fault, and the advertising photographs are always taken in smooth water with a smiling, pretty young woman using the oars, which are always too short, with small blades and flimsy rowlocks. The pictures never show a cold and wet sailor trying to manhandle a fifty-pound anchor on a windswept night.

However, with a 6- or 8-horsepower outboard motor and easily handled forward, neutral, and reverse controls, an inflatable becomes a completely different boat. A skilled and practiced operator can easily run out a long line to windward and toss over a heavy anchor if there's enough water depth for the outboard.

Such an inflatable craft is quite good for traveling long distances around harbors and islands. However, an inflatable and an outboard represent a good-sized investment and are highly attractive to thieves. Some owners make it a policy to put the dinghy aboard every night. When ashore, they may lock the engine and dinghy to a pier or dock with a steel cable. (Watch out for a rising tide.)

Inflatables are extremely popular, and most cruising yachts carry one. Many have larger outboards than recommended because the owners and their children like to buzz around anchorages and marinas at full throttle. They even do this at night and often don't carry the white all-around light that is mandated by international rules and common sense. Since no one cares to police these people, the best way to avoid these high-speed bullets and stay alive is to anchor away from crowded yachting centers. St. Thomas in the U.S. Virgin Islands in the Caribbean is one of the most dangerous harbors in the world because of reckless inflatable dinghy use; people have been killed, and there have been all kinds of ghastly accidents. Yet this stupid behavior goes on.

If you need to carry gasoline for an outboard motor, I suggest that you put it (say, five gallons) in an extraheavy-plastic jug stored at the back of the afterdeck or in a dedicated locker on the transom. Arrange the jug so that if it leaks, the gasoline will drain directly over the side. *Don't even think* of storing gasoline below or in a cockpit locker.

A good many new boatowners naively believe that there are fancy marinas with running water and electricity all over the world. No belief is more mistaken. Margaret and I are well used to ferrying water in jugs or catching rainfall in an awning. Plus hustling food shopping, taking buses, and hunting up customs and immigration officials. Except for a few boatyard jobs, we haven't had shore power aboard in years. In most ports, we have anchored out or tied up with fishing boats. I think of Cádiz, Rio de Janeiro, Western Samoa, the little ports along the coast of Labrador, Valparaíso, Carloforte, Port Sudan. . . .

When we first sailed to foreign places, we were surprised at how much we used a dinghy. In most parts of the world, vessels without important dock business anchor out (if indeed there is a dock). For yachtsmen, this is better in many ways. People trouble you less when you're at anchor. Generally, the view is better and your life is quieter. In the tropics there is more breeze at anchor and the vessel can swing head to wind so you can open the front hatch to funnel air into the cabin. You don't scratch and gouge the topsides by banging against rough docks. Insect visitations may be less frequent, and you avoid rodents completely. If there's a wind change, you won't be pinned against a wharf. Finally, it's easier to get under way from an anchor.

It's possible to tow a dinghy from place to place. However, *experienced sailors never tow dinghies*—hard or inflatable—because if the wind increases and the seas grow large and lumpy, there's a good chance the dinghy will fill and sink, or almost sink, and have to be cut away. Beginners sometimes think that if the weather worsens when they're towing a dinghy, they will simply haul the tender on board. This almost never happens because when squalls or a storm comes, the crew is busy sailing and shortening sails. At that moment the crew has no time to fiddle with the tender, which may be half full of water, impossibly heavy, and, with the sea conditions, too risky to bail out. Or the crew may get into more serious problems (going off course, experiencing accidental gybes, going aground) from inattention because of fumbling with the dinghy in worsening weather.

You can get away with towing a dinghy nine out of ten times, but the odds are that you will get the painter around the rudder or propeller and lose the dinghy if you persist in towing it. Note: Dinghy covers are not effective in keeping out water.

It should be part of the regular sailing routine to put the dinghy on board before you get under way. This takes about ten minutes.

When I'm ready to put the dinghy on *Whisper*, I pull it alongside, jump down into it, and lift the oars, 5-pound anchor, bailer, and sponge to the deck of the yacht. Back on the yacht, I tie the bow painter to the main halyard and winch the dinghy vertically upward until it's clear of the water. Then I dip a few buckets of seawater and slosh out the mud, grit, and sand. I hoist the dinghy over the lifelines and turn it so that its bottom faces aft, which is easy with the halyard holding the weight. I then pull the stern of the dinghy aft toward the cockpit and lash the stern lightly to anything handy, which angles the dinghy at about 45 degrees. If I then lower away on the main halyard, the dinghy drops, inverted, on the coachroof. (This reads harder than the job is.) Once on board, we lash it in place with a length of ⅜-inch-diameter line crisscrossed between the handrails on the coachroof.

Margaret and I like to carry two tenders: a hard dinghy that rows well for our principal shore boat and an inflatable for a spare or second. We store the inflatable underneath the forepeak area. If we are at anchor and Margaret wants to go on land, I row her ashore. When she's ready to come back, she blows three short beeps on her whistle and I pick her up. And vice versa. But sometimes one person takes the dinghy ashore or to another boat when the other person wants to go elsewhere. Then the inflatable is handy. In addition, we have a second choice if one boat is damaged (or stolen, which has never happened). Years ago in Guam, we had to tie up at an incomplete U.S. Navy pier with enormous metal projections. We blew up the spare dinghy and hung it over the side as a giant fender to protect the hull from damage.

I find that one-piece spruce oars are quite good and last a long time. For an 8-foot dinghy we use 7-foot oars. I prefer one-piece oars, because the glues in laminated oars do not stand up to continual wetting, drying out, and prolonged sun. I have had some luck reinforcing the tips of the blades of oars with a couple of strips of 1-inch-wide fiberglass placed across the ends.

Oarlocks or rowlocks are hard to keep on board. In order not to lose them, I slide circular, not horned, oarlocks over plastic oar collars, which I tack to the oars with a few barbed brass brads. To keep the rowlocks from sliding off the other end, I put a stainless steel hose clamp, a single large round-head screw, or tie a Turk's head knot at the end of the oar collar (see photograph). This way the oarlock cannot slip off the oar and fall over the side or be misplaced. The hose clamps also help hold the oar collars in place.

An oar dropped over the side will always float and can be recovered, but if you drop a loose rowlock over the side, it's gone. Our spare pair of oars also has oarlocks in place, arranged so they can't slip off the oars. At one time I varnished oars, but I found that if I dropped an oar in the water at night, it was invisible. You can see oars and the boat hook much better if they're painted white. I have tried coating oars with epoxy, but it's unsatisfactory and peels off.

Most oarlock sockets are made of soft brass, and the bearing holes eventually become oval-shaped with wear. If the sockets are galvanized iron, the wear works through the zinc coating, and the bearing surfaces become rusty. However, the wear is slow and the oarlocks still work reasonably well in worn sockets. A touch of Vaseline helps.

The greatest fault with rowlock sockets is that they are almost always secured with short, easy-to-pull-out wood screws. If a rowlock socket comes adrift when you are rowing out to the yacht during a spring ebb or a fresh offshore wind, you could be swept out to sea. To get around this difficulty, I had special rowlock sockets made up of small stainless steel plates $\frac{1}{8}$ by 2 by $3\frac{1}{2}$ inches with 2-inch stainless sleeves welded to the plates to take the rowlocks. I secure the plates to the hull with four 10-24 bolts and washers. This way I have large bearing surfaces on the dinghy hull to resist the pressures of rowing, and rowlock sockets that are extremely secure and long-wearing.

I've been using these oarlocks for 25 years and they're still as good as when they were made. The mounting plate on the socket part is large enough so that the load on the thin hull is spread out. Instead of wood screws or self-tappers, I use through-bolts. Note that I cannot lose the male part of the oarlock over the side since it can't get off the oar because of the plastic oar collar, which is held in place with a few barbed brass brads and a hose clamp. The plastic oar guard keeps everything quiet. This arrangement ensures that the oarlock is always safe, in position, and ready for use. The oarlock needs a little slack on the oar collar and a touch of grease or Vaseline occasionally. If you can't find oar collars, put a hose clamp on each side of the oarlocks, because they're fittings you don't want to lose.

If you choose commercially made rowlock sockets (the best are Wilcox Crittenden), I suggest that you bolt them in place. If bolts are not possible, use long stainless steel self-tapping screws and install them in wet Marine-Tex epoxy.

In a pinch, a useful idea to remember is that you can make a vertical tholepin out of a small stick (even a ballpoint pen). If you cut two small holes through the hull just below the gunwale with a knife, you can lash the tholepin to the boat with a shoelace or a strand cut from the painter. If, in turn, the oar is lightly lashed to a single tholepin (or between two tholepins), you will find that it will do very well for an emergency rowlock and rowlock socket.

Of course, it is handy to be able to scull, a technique I am trying to teach myself. A transom sculling notch is also useful to lead a warp through when running out a line or recovering an anchor.

To keep the dinghy quiet while *Whisper* is at anchor, I usually drop a fender between the yacht and the tender and tie it up alongside with the bow and stern painters. If there is any wind or tidal stream, we let the boat go aft. If the dinghy persists in being unruly, we put out a spinnaker pole and haul the boat away from the yacht a foot or two with an endless line rove through a block at the end of the pole and tied to one end of the dinghy. It's possible to hang a block on a stern anchor line and do the same drill.

Dinghies have been a problem for sailboats for a long time. I once read an account in an old sailing book (1880) that mentioned essentially the same laments that we have today. The author wanted something big (hard to stow) and strong (heavy) with high performance (needing expert sailing and rowing); he also wanted a tender that was small, light, and easy to handle—almost totally opposite requirements.

A lot of bright minds have worked on the dinghy problem. One clever idea has been to make a hard dinghy that disassembles into two parts (across its short dimension) using bolts and wing nuts. The boat becomes two floatable halves, one of which stores inside the other. A 10-foot "cup and saucer" tender turns into a 5-foot unit that's easy to store. This idea has reappeared from time to time but has never caught on, probably because the market is too small.

Another notion was for a plywood and canvas pram that folded or collapsed sideways (by turning the seats). The Prout dinghy was made in England for many years but is no longer available. I have seen a large custom yacht whose cockpit slid out the transom to become the ship's tender. (What would happen to the main ship if somebody swiped the cockpit?) Sixty-foot yachts can slide a large inflatable into a transom compartment (known as "the garage").

The twin problems of yacht tenders are performance versus stowability and oars versus the outboard motor. The reality is that yachts under 30 feet are always going to have trouble fitting an adequate dinghy on board unless the tender deflates or collapses or can be taken apart in some way. A 50-foot vessel can easily take a 10-foot high-performance tender. The second problem is often answered by the love affair between sailors and the internal combustion engine. Most yacht types (not all) would rather use an outboard engine than row, and simply adore zipping around harbors at high speed.

It seems to me that the most logical line of development is for inflatables with a blow-up floor and keel, and perhaps with a narrower beam and more modest side chambers to reduce wetted-surface area and drag. But I don't think this is going to happen because inflatable manufacturers want to sell thousands of dinghies to a mass market that doesn't exist for a specialized dinghy.

Meanwhile, I am rowing my 8-foot hard dinghy.

*The traditional saveiro on Bahia de Todos os Santos in northern Brazil.
These boats haul bricks, sand, and lumber, and use the southeast trade wind
to cross from Salvador to Itaparica and elsewhere. The mast (a special wood)
is unstayed. Often the sailors hang blocks on branch stubs that are left at the
masthead. This saveiro is intriguing because the standing lugsail ahead of
the mainsail increases the pressure on the big sail. Additionally, these sailors
have a pole out ahead of the lugsail to pull its luff straight. Clever!*

27

QUESTIONS AND ANSWERS

Spare Sail • Night Watches • Long Keels • Rallies • Too Small
• Laundry • Security • Strength • Money and Mail
• GPS Alternate • Keeping Clean • New Skills

"What's the most important spare that you take along on your voyages?"

That's easy: an extra mainsail. It's the basic sail, and you can always keep going somehow if you have one along. If your good mainsail is blown out or destroyed, it puts you in a bad position. The spare mainsail doesn't have to be new, just so it's functional. The next time you buy a new mainsail, have the old one repaired so you can put it up in a pinch. If there's any choice, I would select a spare mainsail with short battens because they're easier to deal with when conditions are poor.

Even if it's well used and half rotten, an old sail is better than no sail at all. Another idea is to purchase a used sail from a broker (Bacon of Annapolis, Maryland, is one place). Be sure to bend on the spare sail and use it a little so that you have the foot and luff slides and reefing lines worked out. When you need the spare, you generally need it in a hurry and don't have time to deal with problems.

You may never use the spare mainsail, so you can store it in a hard-to-reach

The Rio Guadiana separates the southern extremities of Portugal and Spain and is navigable for 40 miles. During the summer the waterway is usually calm and quiet, and it's delightful to wind slowly through rural farming country to tiny, isolated villages where strangers are regarded with watchful curiosity. Except when there's an upstream cloudburst, rivers are usually free of waves and swells. The main business of sailing involves using the tidal streams, checking the depths, allowing for current, and catching up-and-down river winds.

place, but it's good insurance. Before you store the sail, hose it down with fresh water and dry and fold it carefully because it may be in storage for a long time. Our current spare main has four short battens that we manage to leave in place during the folding. We wrap the sail in three or four black plastic garbage bags to keep it dry.

In 1990, when I set off from Newport, Rhode Island, for Cape Town, South Africa, I had perfect, brand-new sails from North. Four days out, three of the five full-length battens disintegrated into long spears of razor-sharp glass. Someone at the loft had put in flimsy plastic hardware at the front of the batten pockets instead of the sturdy metal parts that I had ordered (and failed to check). My beautiful new 585-square-foot mainsail was ripped and shredded in dozens of places. Fortunately, I had a spare main with short battens that I was able to use.

"Do you really sail at night? How do you keep from falling asleep? Be honest."

Some people think that we take down the sails and go to sleep. Others believe that we carry five miles of chain and anchor every night out on the ocean. On *Whisper*—as with most vessels at sea—we carry on around the clock. If we stopped at dark, our progress would be halved, and we would never get anywhere.

We can generally make the vessel steer herself, which means that someone doesn't have to hold the tiller every minute. If the weather is settled and the yacht is going well, we don't touch a thing when the sun goes down. If nasty-looking clouds are around, however, and we have been on the verge of a sail change, we sometimes pull down a reef in the mainsail while it is still light.

At night we keep a careful lookout, especially in shipping lanes and in fishing areas, much more than during the day, when other vessels can see our sails. Staying up half the night means that we sleep a lot during the day. This generally means a couple of long naps. Our sleeping time totals about 7 hours in 24. If for some reason we haven't been able to sleep during the day and are falling asleep, I simply wake up Margaret after, say, two hours or so. I then take a brief nap until we get back on schedule. She does the same with me. Standing watch and watch has to allow for interruptions and crises. On a recent trip from Gibraltar to Turkey, we stood watch and watch for 16 days and had no problems.

Margaret and I know *Whisper* well, and we can easily roll up the jib or tie in a reef in the mainsail in the dark in case of a squall or a wind change. Except for the masthead navigation lamp, we don't turn on any lights because we can see quite well at night after our eyes have become used to the low light from the moon or the sky. If necessary, we use a small flashlight or switch on a deck light if we need to sort out something complicated.

When conditions require us to steer, Margaret and I take turns, three to four hours at a time. If the navigation demands attention and your watch is occupied with lights and buoys and shipping, the time passes quickly.

To improve night vision, we use a tiny red-coated bulb in the compass. Sometimes I turn on a dim white light over the chart table for a little general light in the cabin, but I try to banish strong lights. I write a few notes in the ship's log every hour—the compass heading, wind, weather, sightings of birds, fish, ships, land . . . whatever's going on. Nothing takes the place of a reporter's notes made at the time.

I like night watches. In the tropics, it's lovely and cool. I spend hours standing or sitting in the companionway at the front of the cockpit with my elbows on the hatch runners. I check the compass course, look around, perhaps watch the disappearing lights of a ship, and see how many stars and planets I can identify. In many ways, the quietness of night is the best part of the 24 hours.

*"Is a long-keeled yacht a better proposition for a cruising
boat than a fin keel and spade rudder?"*

People have strong opinions about the keel shapes of sailboats. I've sailed around the world on yachts of each type. In truth, the fin keel–spade rudder is a little faster because there's less below-the-water area to drag through the sea (and a smaller area to paint). The long keel is claimed to be steadier in directional stability, but I have found the course-keeping ability of both types to be equal. Remember that the rudder of the fin keel–spade rudder combination is located near the stern, where it is very effective. The long keel is easier to dry out alongside a dock for painting because there's more keel to lean on. Certainly the boat is less tippy.

Many long-keeled yachts have exterior ballast keels of lead or iron that extend a fourth or a third of the length of the vessel and provide excellent protection during groundings. You can make a reasonable argument that rudder that is fastened to the back of the long keel (usually at an angle) is stronger than a spade rudder that hangs from a single shaft or tube.

With fin keels, the keel bolt arrangements are more critical and stressed, depending on the size and design of the keel. Many modern fiberglass yachts with the ballast inside the shell have no protection at all during groundings. The hulls are constructed this way because it's quick and cheap. The fin keels of some extreme racing boats are merely long struts with ballast bulbs at the bottom. It seems to me that such designs are completely unsuitable for cruising because of (1) structural considerations and (2) the difficulty of drying out for bottom work in remote places.

Finally, a yacht with a long keel is usually impossible to back under power, particularly in a crosswind. With a spade rudder (or a rudder on a skeg), I can control backing very well and am able to maneuver the vessel around all sorts of tricky docks and wharves. With a long-keeled yacht in a tight spot, it's generally safer and more seamanlike to turn her with a couple of lines or to drop an anchor and heave a line ashore. Once turned, you can then motor ahead.

Long-keeled yachts tend to be of heavier displacement, which requires a bigger rig, larger sails, and additional maneuvering effort. Lighter displacement means a smaller rig and reduced handling forces. For this reason I would choose a fin keel and spade rudder, if the rudder was made by a reputable company.

"What's your opinion of yacht rallies?"

Something new in the sailing world is the yachting rally, a collection of private yachts, each one of which pays a substantial fee to an organizer to arrange a cruise from one place to another. The cruise can be across the Atlantic, around the world, or along the coastlines of neighboring countries.

For example, the Atlantic Rally Cruise is a collection of boats that follow a course from Las Palmas in the Canary Islands on the east side of the Atlantic across to St. Lucia in the Caribbean, a distance of 2,700 miles. The organizers set up dates, plan an easy schedule during the best weather months, and offer discounted marine berths at each end. They arrange safety lectures, local shopping for food, cocktail parties, weather information, a position-reporting radio network, help with formalities, and so on. The announced goals of the rally are for the participants to stick together for safety, to have frequent radio chats, for newcomers to learn from the experts, and for everyone to have a good time.

As you might expect, the hotels, airlines, restaurants, boatyards, and supermarkets at each end of this transatlantic affair are enthusiastic boosters of such a nautical gold mine. While the sailboats are in port there are beginning and ending banquets, crew people flying in and out, interludes in hotels, car rentals, and last-minute equipment purchases. Before the yachts set out, there is even a fireworks display, and each vessel flies a rally flag.

Five months before the Atlantic Rally Cruise began in 1993, 237 yachts had signed up. Many were big boats (34 were over 60 feet, including 5 sailboats over 90 feet in length). The average size was 48 feet; boats of this length paid an entry fee of $825 plus $81 per person. With a crew of six, the total entry fee was $1,310. If this is multiplied by the number of entries (237), the organizer's revenue was on the order of at least $310,000 plus subsidiary income and suggests that such affairs have become big business (figures from www.worldcruising.com/arc/english.htm). In addition, the entrants had to agree to carry advertising, to forgo film rights, and to absolve the organizers from liability claims of any kind. Even with all this, it's amazing how many people signed up. The Germans, who like to be organized, love these rallies and flock to them in great numbers.

I totally reject this kind of herd sailing. The premise of safety in numbers is nonsense. Once at sea, each boat is on her own; no one else has any responsibility for another yacht's well-being, and the rally organizers demand that participants agree to this in writing from the beginning. Of course, the less experienced can learn from the experts, but this happens on board a single vessel where the captain or mate teaches the novices. Learning about sailing has little to do with yachts that are over the horizon.

Personally, when I hear that a fleet of two hundred yachts is crossing an ocean, my first impulse is to sail in the other direction. Oceans are big, but thinking about two hundred nearby potential collision problems scares me to death.

The big boats in the rally dominate the smaller, which are made to feel inferior and slow. ("How many days did you take?") The boats tend to race one another, and the whole thing turns into competitions of various kinds—the tallest mast, the best varnish work, the shiniest paint, the prettiest women. The sailors on the rally boats establish a social life with one another but fail to meet the local people in a port, which seems a pity to me.

Another type of group cruising is the Eastern Mediterranean Yacht Rally (EMYR). This is much smaller, less expensive, and arranged to minimize customs, immigration, and security problems. The EMYR costs 150 euros per person and facilitates visits to 19 ports in Turkey, Northern Cyprus, Syria, Lebanon, Israel, and Egypt. In 2001, the EMYR ran from April 15 to June 1 and had 55 yachts. Two 100-foot Turkish coast guard ships accompanied the fleet. The fees included all marina costs, cocktail parties, dinners, dancing, and tours to historic sites.

At each stop, the locals made a big effort to make sure that everyone had a good time. The emphasis was not on sailing, but on scheduled touring. In many ways, the rally was more like a bus trip.

Participating in rallies is the most expensive way of cruising because in addition to the entry fee, there's constant pressure to keep up with the fleet, whether in sailing gear or entertainment ashore. A participant may have to purchase special emergency equipment and radio gear to comply with the demands of the organizer. Ashore, social decisions tend to be made by the owners of the largest yachts, who are usually the most affluent.

Besides the expense, I see three other problems with rallies:

- One of the most basic delights of voyaging under sail is to throw away the calendar. When you're obliged to follow a rigid schedule, you lose that independence and the pleasure of making your own decisions and traveling at your own pace.

- The number of people and yachts in a rally overpowers the facilities of small harbors.
- The rally participants talk to each other, not the local people. If you want to meet the natives and find out about a country, you need to travel by yourself.

"I have a custom 24-footer. Do you think . . ."

No, she's too small! I've mentioned this elsewhere, but let me repeat the answer. One or two people can make long trips in a yacht less than 30 feet long, but it will be hard if for no other reason than the difficulty of fitting on board all the things you need for cruising. The dinghy, oars, anchors, extra lines, food, books, charts, tools, clothes, bedding, personal stuff, cooking arrangements, first-aid kit—it goes on and on. You can do it, and people have and have written marvelous books about their experiences, but the comfort level is low, and the wear and tear on the human body is considerable.

You will spend a good deal of time simply moving stuff from one side of the boat to the other while you try to find what you're after. What happens when a friend shows up and wants to go along for a few days? If you're sailing with your significant other, it may be the end of the relationship, no matter how much you love your partner.

I would sell the custom 24-footer and buy a beat-up 30- or 32-footer—or larger. Maybe you will have to save up for an extra year. Perhaps your partner will kick in. The bigger boat will be faster, more comfortable, and much easier to live on.

"How do you handle laundry on board a yacht in out-of-the-way places?"

Laundry is a problem because in many areas of the world, there are no washing machines and no commercial laundry facilities. In addition, fresh water is usually limited on board.

In some places you can take a bag of laundry ashore, find a sparkling stream—often in beautiful surroundings—and then carry on in the time-honored way with a bar of soap, scrubbing on a smooth rock, rinsing well, and then spreading the clothes on bushes to dry. An old-fashioned washboard is easier on the clothes than a rock, which takes a heavy toll on buttons.

Another scheme is the two-bucket system, either on the foredeck or at the village pump. If you do the washing on deck, it helps to soak the clothes overnight in soapy water to loosen the dirt. Rub in additional detergent on the extrasoiled places and use a little bleach in the soaking water because clothes washed in cold water tend to become gray after a while. The problem with the bucket system on deck is not the washing, but the rinsing, which takes a lot of water. Salt water can be used for washing and the first and second rinses (to get out the soap), but the salt water must be followed by a thorough rinsing in fresh water; otherwise, the clothes will never dry.

Bernard Moitessier claims that if you let clothes or towels flap vigorously in a breeze, the salt crystals will fly out. I have my doubts about this and have lost too many clothes over the side to allow washing to do much violent flapping. Besides, I can't stand the noise.

For heavily soiled laundry, you can put a galvanized iron bucket of soapy water and clothes on the stove and boil the water for a few minutes. Be careful that the heavy bucket of clothes doesn't overbalance a gimballed stove and tip over.

One advantage of a sailboat is that the lifelines are a handy clothesline, and the mast and main boom have a dozen places to put up hangers. If you clip up hangers with dripping shirts or blouses, it's imperative to loop a short tie through each hanger and around a secure point so the hanger can't escape from the yacht. Without a tie, as soon as you turn your back, the wind comes up and whisks your clothes away. Don't ever throw wet oilskins over the main boom without tying them in place. It pains me to think of the clothing that I have lost.

Use plenty of clothespins when you hang things up along the lifelines. Keep a supply of clothespins on board, for they are forever falling over the side. We have found that ordinary wooden clothespins with galvanized spring clips—cheap and widely available—work better than plastic clothespins, which often break. In the high latitudes, drying clothes is more difficult; sometimes the space above our stove is festooned with socks and underwear.

During passages with a tropical downpour, we sometimes do laundry by plugging up the cockpit drains and using the cockpit as a tub. We wash only small items because drying sheets at sea is impossible unless the yacht is large. At anchor in the tropics, it's easy to dry clothes in the sun, which bleaches the cottons and makes them smell fresh and nice. In the warm zone the laundry is mostly sheets and towels—not many personal clothes—and it's easy to wash a few things every day or two to stay up-to-date. If you take a freshwater shower ashore, wash out the clothes you take off at the same time.

Often when the yacht is anchored with the dinghy alongside or behind, a heavy rain will fill it with fresh water. This is a perfect time to wash out a few clothes because bucket after bucket can be dipped out (from the deck if the bucket has a long lanyard).

In Japan, there are three kinds of detergents: for washing dishes, for vegetables, and for laundry. Once in the Inland Sea, Margaret had two buckets going on a dock with a freshwater hose when two Japanese students stopped by to look at the yacht. The young men began arguing about the label on the Japanese detergent box that

Margaret was using. Obviously there was a problem. In spite of the language difficulty, we learned that we had the wrong detergent. The students offered to accompany us to a store where we could buy the proper detergent that would ensure that we got our clothes clean. "Vegetable box weak. No good for laundry. Need more power."

Of course you always hope there will be a convenient self-serve laundry in the next port—a clean place where you can shove in coins and powerful machines will gently wash and dry your clothes. A few times after long sea passages, Margaret and I have taken big bags of soiled laundry to commercial laundries, where our experiences have been poor. (Greece and Brazil come to mind.) The results were perfect, but the charges were unbelievably expensive (four to five times more than our highest guess). It seems embarrassing to ask about the price of laundry, but if the man behind the counter begins to list each item of dirty clothing as if it were a check in a bank deposit, beware!

Margaret has a kerosene iron that she uses to touch up our shore-going clothes from time to time. Not many people have seen kerosene irons, and the few times visitors have been on *Whisper* when Margaret was ironing, they were amazed at her nifty little red Tilley iron and the neat pile of nicely ironed laundry. The technique may seem Stone Age, but the results are good.

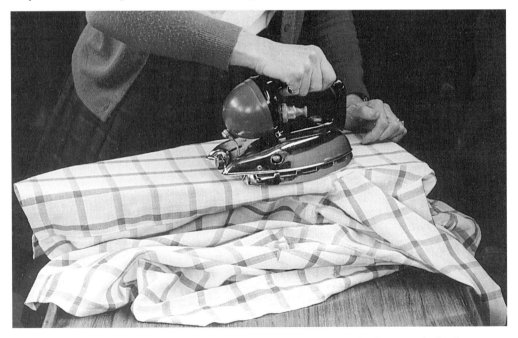

Margaret likes to keep some of our clothes pressed and smart-looking with this kerosene-powered Tilley iron.

"What about security?"

We always lock the boat when we leave her. If we happen to be in an urban area where there might be mugging problems, we dress down, try to blend in with the locals, and walk fast. In other words, we try not to look like tourists.

If possible, stay away from big cities and places with bad reputations (Buenaventura, Colombia, for example). I don't carry a billfold. I put a few small bills in my pockets, and I carry large notes and a credit card (if needed) in my shoes. If I have a camera, I stuff it into a beat-up canvas bag. (This is particularly wise in some Muslim countries where cameras and their owners are despised.) We sit in the backs of buses.

Anchoring out is fairly safe because it takes some enterprise to find a small boat, row out, and come aboard. If you're in a marginal harbor, it's a good idea to lock the yacht from the inside or put up a couple of security bars on hatches and entry points, particularly if you're sleeping. On two trips we were advised to take guns, but we found them a waste of time. Guns are much trouble in many countries because you have to declare all weapons. If you carry a gun, the best choice may be a shotgun (with slugs and buckshot).

Put the dinghy on board if you suspect any risk.

During our travels, we've been robbed only once. We were in South America and a pickpocket on a bus took two chronometers from Margaret's shopping bag while she was taking them to a jewelry shop for cleaning.

If toughs demand your money, give them everything. Don't argue.

"My husband is very strong. Unfortunately, I am not. How can a 100-pound woman sail a 43-foot ketch with heavy gear?"

If the gear is too heavy, you need mechanical assistance—winches for the sheets and halyards and a windlass to recover the anchors and chain. On *Whisper* we have nine mechanical aids:

- two powerful #46 two-speed sheet winches
- two #40 two-speed winches, principally for the running backstays
- a small winch for the mainsheet
- two small halyard winches
- one mainsail reefing winch
- a two-speed hand-operated anchor windlass that can pull 1,000 pounds

I consider these devices indispensable. I could manage without the mainsheet winch because the mainsheet is already a powerful tackle. On your ketch you might want small winches for the mizzen halyard and perhaps the mizzen sheet.

The nastiest job on a yacht is to lift the anchor (often dripping with black mud) on deck after the anchor has been raised to the stemhead by the windlass. If you do this last step by hand, you have to lift 50 or 60 pounds at a bad angle while leaning over the pulpit, and you're liable to strain your back. It's not hard to design a bow roller scheme so that you can use the power of the windlass to pull the anchor on deck *underneath* the pulpit or on top of a roller on the bowsprit of a ketch. Such a system also makes it easier to let the anchor go.

Another awkward lifting job is the dinghy. Margaret and I routinely hoist our rigid 8-foot dinghy—which weighs 75 pounds—on board by tying the bow painter to the main halyard, which we then put on the main halyard winch. We lower the tender the same way except that we secure the halyard to a mid-dinghy bridle so that we can lower the boat horizontally to the water.

I would plan on two large sheet winches and a powerful anchor windlass from the start. The size of the halyard winches is not so important, and often it's possible to work in a rope purchase to increase the power of a small winch. If you budget the cost over several years, the shock is not too great. By all means, try to buy self-tailing winches with adjustable jaws (for different-size lines). I hold no brief for small, overloaded winches that ruin sailing pleasure by making tacking an event for supermen.

If your husband won't budge, give him a pair of big winches for Christmas. He'll be so pleased with the polished stainless steel and the clicking ratchets that he may not faint when the bill comes on January 15. You can halve the cost of two sheet winches by mounting a single winch at the back of the cockpit (or elsewhere) and leading the sheets to it in turn. I suggest two-speed winches. Three-speed winches are too complicated.

You might learn to use a handy billy, a portable multiple tackle with short rope tails at either end. When you need more pulling power between two points, simply tie the tackle in place with rolling hitches on each end and haul away. The handy billy will increase your power by four (minus a little for friction). Tackles are more cumbersome and slower than winches, but the lines and blocks are usually on board. If you have enough ¼-inch-diameter line on board to rig a six-part tackle, you can easily haul yourself to the top of the mast. A tackle is a simple way to gain power, but you pay for it by using more line. A six-part tackle for a 60-foot mast needs 360 feet of line, plus a little extra to tie a knot at one end. This is a long string to keep in order.

Learn to say "no!" when a lifting task is too much for you. Instead, look for an alternate way. If your husband wants you to haul him up the mast with a small halyard winch, remind him that if you use a couple of snatchblocks on deck and run the halyard to the anchor windlass, which has some real power, it will be easy to crank him skyward.

If you can't lift a big sailbag in the forepeak out of the front hatch, don't even try. Instead lead a spare mast halyard into the forepeak and tie it to the sailbag. Then go on deck, put the halyard on a winch, and crank away. Or ask for help. It's amazing what extra hands can do.

In Peru we had trouble with our new engine. Fortunately, it was still in warranty, but the engine had to go to the Lima Volvo factory. I despaired because we were on a mooring three-quarters of a mile from shore.

"No matter, we'll send a boat," Volvo said. I envisioned a big fishing vessel with a crane.

I was surprised when a 15-foot dinghy pulled alongside, but I was astounded when five husky Peruvian workmen calmly picked up the 400-pound engine, lowered it into the boat, and left. Two days later the repaired engine was back and the men did their act in reverse. I took some of the load with the main halyard, but the men did most of the lifting and guiding. Moral: Get extra hands.

"How do you deal with money and mail when you go off on long trips?"

We carry $300–$400 in cash in small-denomination U.S. bills. We take additional funds in $20 and $50 American Express traveler's checks. The reason I select American Express is that the checks look familiar and are widely accepted. No, I am not a hireling of American Express, but I have seen checks of Thomas Cook, National City Bank, Bank of America, and others refused because the checks looked strange. My wife and I each take half of whatever funds we have so that either of us can deal with money matters if the other person is absent or ill.

Forget letters of credit. The sums are too small, the correspondent banks are often found only in distant metropolitan centers, and the routine is antiquated. I once had funds sent to the Far East, but the receiving bank did not have my home bank's authorized signature on file. The bank officers were sorry. I was stuck in a strange city without funds after a long train ride from a coastal port.

If you have money mailed to you directly, be sure to specify a formal bank check; some savings-and-loan associations issue glorified personal checks that are nonnegotiable in foreign places. Don't forget that every time you change currencies, you pay a fee. Each time a bank negotiates a foreign check, there's a charge.

The modern way to deal with money, of course, is with credit or debit cards. An added advantage for travelers is that you can charge items in foreign currencies, and the credit card company will convert the foreign charge into your home currency, sometimes at a good rate.

Be sure that you have adequate funds and that you're familiar with ATM use. (Read the directions and the fine print.) Cash machines are fantastically popular all over the world. The advantage is that you don't have to carry large sums of money because it's easy to take out small sums more often. If there is any choice, try to withdraw money during the day in busy locations, or from a machine in an inside location. Beware of isolated locations at night.

It's useful to have the telephone numbers of the credit card company so that you can call if there are problems. Often there are toll-free numbers for international calls. It's worthwhile asking credit card people and banking officials the best way to deal with money for a specific trip. They may help you negotiate the minefield of extra charges, delays, and different currencies. For example, if you are going to be in English waters, it may be convenient to set up a sterling account (with one large check from your home bank) so you can draw on an English bank (to pay twenty-five local bills).

Another useful dodge is to buy a little currency of the next country on your itinerary ahead of time, particularly if you plan to stop at outlying islands before you reach the main business areas. The storekeeper in a small village may not accept your national currency, but if you had the foresight to buy some of his local currency, you can deal with him. For example, you may have to pay a slight premium to buy $150 worth of French Pacific francs in New York, but when you arrive in the Marquesas or Tuamotus, you can buy groceries.

Of course, one blessing of remote places is that you can't spend much money. You are obliged to be frugal whether you want to or not.

Mail is a problem that I have not solved. A friend picks up our mail. He opens everything, throws out the junk, puts a collection of letters and magazines into a big envelope, and airmails a single parcel to us after we have sent our latest address. If we are waiting for mail, we can leave as soon as the single parcel arrives because we know there won't be a second.

We leave our friend a sum of cash for postage and special purchases. He deposits any incoming checks at our bank. He does not forward mail unless he has definite instructions. This arrangement seems foolproof; in practice it is not.

The mail systems of the world seem to be more cluttered and dilatory than ever in spite of high postal rates. Delays can be tolerated, but disappearances cannot. The present mail arrangements in the Galápagos Islands, for instance, are hopeless, and on a recent visit I elected to have no mail sent there at all.* In Peru, half the time the mail from New York or Europe comes in three or four days; the other half of the time it simply doesn't arrive. In Chile, the clerk at one post office

---

*We saw the president of Ecuador in Academy Bay, where he concluded a speech by saying: "Mail me your suggestions for improvements."

"But how will you get the letters?" wailed the audience.

window charges rates that are different from the rates charged at the next window. In the heart of metropolitan Rio de Janeiro, a mailbox may not be emptied for a week or longer.

I have received mail at American Express offices in Papeete, Denpasar, Athens, Valletta, and Fort-de-France. While there, credit card holders can also cash small personal checks.

Packages—all packages arouse suspicion—are another difficulty because they are promptly impounded by customs. The packages may contain urgent and important items, but the customs people of the world know no urgency. All you can do is argue and hope. Once you have found out that the package has arrived and exists, at least you have a chance. Much of the time, the package simply disappears. If it is really important, air freight, though costly, is safer. If you have the waybill number in advance, you can meet the plane and, with luck, persuade the customs man to let you take the package on board your boat as you sail away.

Most Americans bristle at the thought of paying a bribe, but in the real world, bribes (diplomatically called handling fees or processing charges) are common. At the airport in Buenos Aires I was obliged to pay a freight forwarder $150 to take delivery of a steering vane from France. I could see my box, and I screamed and argued and cajoled, but there was no other way, particularly as I was in a hurry to get the shipment. More recently in Turkey I had a small part air-shipped by FedEx from the United States. The correspondent FedEx freight handler in Turkey demanded a bribe. Fortunately, I was in no hurry and managed to wear him down by complaining to FedEx in the United States. By the time I had made a dozen phone calls and subjected myself to much aggravation, I would have been wiser to have paid the $50.

My advice about bribes (reluctantly given) is twofold. First, avoid shipments from abroad. If you must have something, try to have a crew member or friend bring it as personal luggage. If you can meet the shipment at a major airport, you may be able to avoid middlemen. Second, if you're in no hurry for the item, you may be able to win by stalling or putting on pressure by complaining to various superiors, the tourist bureau, or the shipping company in your home country. I wouldn't be too aggressive, however, because departments can close ranks and cause you trouble with your visa, tourist permit, and so on. You don't want to make any enemies, no matter how right you are. All this gets stickier when there are language problems. Remember that people who own yachts are classed as millionaires in many countries. The Indonesian soldier who is guarding the customs shed earns the equivalent of about two U.S. dollars a month. So before you get too enraged, consider the alternatives.

To succeed with money and mail in foreign lands, you need patience and an unflappable nature. I have neither.

"Do you trust GPS? What if there's a problem?"

Today nearly everyone navigates by means of the global positioning system. For offshore sailors, the development of GPS was like the invention of electricity. You buy a small set (whose cost has dropped to as low as $100), which integrates information from a network of 24 orbiting satellites put up by the U.S. military. After you switch it on, a GPS set gives you a precise location in a minute or two. This information is used by military planes, submarines, ships at sea, missiles, and tanks in the field. It is also used in the civilian world by central offices to keep track of trucks, buses, and railroad cars. Most ocean-crossing sailors carry a main GPS set and a secondary backup set on board.

I have used GPS positions with complete success. Not only is the information precise, but you can receive it at night, under overcast skies, even during storms. The only drawback that I can see is that someone might switch off the system because of a military problem, or the system itself might break down.

For this reason, I carry a sextant, a precise timepiece, and a Celesticomp V pocket computer. The little calculator has a built-in nautical almanac for many upcoming years and can handle the numbers to enable me to work out my position, just as I did years ago with HO 249 before GPS and the earlier satnav.

With a sextant you measure the angle between the horizon and the sun, moon, a planet, or a bright star at a certain moment in time. The positions of all these heavenly bodies are, in effect, listed in the nautical almanac for each second of time for an entire year.

An observation of a heavenly body results in a position line. Two observations give two position lines. Where they cross is where you are. Generally, you make a third observation to check on the accuracy of the first two. Ideally, the three lines should cross at a single point; in practice, they generally make a small triangle that's known as a seaman's cocked hat. Celestial navigation takes a little study and practice, although the mysteries of the sextant and the calculations are much exaggerated. Even if you don't understand how to use a sextant, you can make a reasonable argument for taking a sextant, a small radio for time signals, a specialized calculator, and a set of directions.

"I'm embarrassed to ask, but how do you deal with bathing on board?"

It's possible to use a bowl with a little hot water, a washcloth, and soap to have a sponge bath. However, I never feel really clean or that I can wash and rinse my hair properly.

I prefer a shower because it's both refreshing and helps me wash myself. However, showers are complicated aboard a yacht. When we bought our present boat,

We like to take lots of showers and find that this 2-gallon spray bottle and integral pump work extremely well. To have hot water, we heat a little water on the cooking stove, pour it in, shake the container, and check the temperature.

the inventory included a 5-gallon stainless steel hot-water heater that transfers heat from the engine when it's running. It takes about twenty minutes of engine time to heat water for a couple of showers. Or we can plug the heater into shore power. This system requires a water pressure pump, a pressure regulator, two shutoff valves, a special mixing valve, and a thumb-operated showerhead spray fitting at the end of a hose. Plus the appropriate plumbing to tie the engine, hot-water heater, and head area together.

A much simpler arrangement for showers is to buy a new 2-gallon plastic insecticide spray bottle (see photograph above left). Mine was made for Roundup, cost $20, and came with a nifty, built-in plastic pump and discharge spray wand. The wand was not suitable for a shower, so I substituted a black plastic spray head made for rinsing dishes (see photograph above right) that works with a simple thumb button. I had a machine shop make a threaded fitting to connect the spray head with the $5/16$-inch-inside-diameter hose that comes from the 2-gallon bottle.

I fill the big plastic bottle about one-third full of fresh water and dump in a kettle of hot water. Next I screw on the top, give the 18-inch-high bottle a shake, and pump a dozen strokes to build up a little air pressure.

My procedure is to wet myself with the spray. Then I put shampoo on my head.

If you're in the tropics, the easiest way to keep clean is to pour a couple of buckets of seawater over yourself every morning.

Next I wash the rest of me. Finally I rinse off, starting at the top and working down. An entire shower uses less than a gallon of water because the water flows only when I press the thumb button. If I want an extra rinse, I use a little more water. This system works so well that I wonder why we didn't think of it years ago. It's much faster than a sponge bath, certainly more thorough, and refreshing as well.

Part of our head compartment is a plastic molding, so we simply let the used shower water drain into the 3-inch-deep floor pan, which has a teak grate over it. When we're through with the shower, we empty the floor pan with a small bilge pump next to the head sink. The pump forces the water out through a T-fitting I put in the head sink drain. Four or five strokes of the pump empty the pan. Draining shower water into the bilge is not a good idea.

This entire shower system is extremely simple and satisfactory. Since the plastic sprayer is marked, we know exactly how much water we've used. With the more elaborate former system, we had no idea how much water we drew from the tanks. Since we keep better track of the water, we tend to take more showers.

We have a small thermometer to check on the shower temperature. I have settled on 105°F, but Margaret prefers 115°F. She particularly likes using the shower to wash her hair. We store the shower bottle in a corner of the head with a piece of shock cord stretched between two screw eyes.

> *"We're almost ready to set off on a long cruise, but I'm nervous about*
> *my lack of skill with ropework, engine repair, sail sewing, etc. Is*
> *it possible to pick this up along the way?"*

Absolutely. Nobody knows it all. It's amazing what you can do when you're faced with repairs and general fix-it situations. The main thing is to have enough tools and adequate instructions on board. For example, since most lines are of braided construction, you should learn how to make an eyesplice. This is a little tricky the first time, so take along a pamphlet from one of the rope companies and the necessary pushers and fids. If you can mend a rip in a shirt, you can repair a tear in a sail. You will be eating your own cooking, so your food preparation is bound to improve.

An exception is how to bleed the fuel supply line for the diesel engine. You should learn how to do this on the day you buy the boat. Hire a mechanic for an hour to teach you. If you're unsure of yourself, write down the instructions. (At the same time, ask the mechanic to review changing filters, belts, and the voltage regulator.)

It's a rule of the sea to help one another, and in your travels you will meet other sailors who can assist you with problems and teach you many things. Don't be too proud to ask for assistance. If I'm able, I make it a policy to help those on other boats and to give them hose clamps, shackles, a length of hose, a piece of line, Dacron patches, a few potatoes, or whatever. I never ask for payment but tell the other sailor to pass on the favor.

What do foreign ports look like? Here's the little harbor of Alanya, Turkey. Snug, noisy, intriguing, and full of people as curious about you as you are of them.

28
FOREIGN PAPERWORK

One of the mysteries of modern travel is that you can fly all over the world and whiz in and out of country after country and hardly ever spend more than a few minutes dealing with entrance and exit formalities. Yet when you switch from the air to a small pleasure boat, the same country-to-country border formalities become tedious and complex. Your welcome seems based on the procedures of a century ago when sailors hoisted colored signal flags to ask permission to enter a country. Indeed, it wasn't long ago that foreign ships were fumigated with pots of burning sulfur.

The easiest country for a yacht to enter is Canada, where you can dial a toll-free telephone number and clear customs and immigration in less than two minutes with no charges and no forms to fill out. The most difficult place is Australia, where an incoming yacht flying a yellow flag is treated like a commercial merchant ship.

In spite of much talk about simplified travel, yachts and their crews are sometimes subject to a good deal of paperwork. Australia—perhaps the world champion of bureaucracy—treats yachts like commercial ships and hands an incoming captain forty pages of forms to complete. Japan is a close second.

CUSTOMS

A vessel entering a foreign country must usually satisfy four classes of regulations: customs, immigration, health, and agriculture. Customs deals with tariffs on many items—machinery, whiskey, foodstuffs, tobacco, clocks . . . thousands of things. Of course the gear, fittings, and spares of a transient vessel are exempt, but you must be scrupulous in not selling things from the ship to locals without telling the customs people. The penalties range from a small fine to seizure of the yacht herself. If you want to help someone, it's better to give the item away, but even then, you should inform the officials. If you plan to sell or charter your yacht, you may be liable for import duties.

Not only are there possible charges and penalties for evasions, but you ought to think of the sailors and travelers who come after you. It can be very nasty to follow a yacht whose crew has misbehaved.

Most countries have restrictions on firearms. The customs officials in the Seychelles, Japan, Bermuda, and elsewhere will ask for all guns and take them from you. In exchange, they will give you a formal receipt that will be honored for the weapons when you leave. Canada allows rifles but no handguns. Other countries have varying restrictions.

It's best to declare firearms right away because customs people sometimes search foreign vessels for forbidden items. If you declare no weapons and the customs agents discover a shotgun, you're in big trouble. On one trip, customs examiners searched our yacht in Japan. Another time in Turkey, a customs man in a neat blue uniform found what he thought was a forbidden scuba tank ("Ah-ha!"). To convince the inspector that the tank was a carbon dioxide fire extinguisher, I had to light a match and put it out with a puff of carbon dioxide.

Parts, stores, and equipment for a vessel and personal items for the crew can usually be shipped in free of duty. Such packages should be addressed: "USA Yacht *Whisper* in transit" plus the name of the port.

In theory there should be no customs charges for incoming packages. But each country has different procedures, best looked into when you are there. Sometimes a customs agent may be necessary; perhaps a friend in the country can help. Nevertheless, by the time such shipments actually arrive on board, the costs have often doubled or tripled and are only worthwhile for high-priority items. Steel yourself to the fact that half the time these shipments will go astray or disappear in a customs warehouse.

Another problem is that foreign representatives for an express air service (FedEx, DHL, Emery, Airborne Express, etc.) will try to extract a substantial payment from you even though the shipping costs have been paid in advance. This is unfair, of course, but you are in a bad position because the agents know that you are probably keen for the package and, in their view, are a rich yachtsman.

A possible way around all this is to ask any nearby yachts from your country whether they are changing crew members. If you can find a person who is flying in to join the yacht across the way, the person in transit may agree to bring your package as part of his or her personal luggage. Another idea is to have urgent things shipped to you in countries with simple customs procedures. In the Middle East, for instance, I would certainly opt for Cyprus over Egypt.

IMMIGRATION

This service is concerned with the flow and work status of foreigners, that is, who you are and what you're doing. Yachtsmen are generally classed as tourists or merchant seamen and are not allowed to compete with local citizens for employment. Many times you must secure permission to visit a country in advance—a visa—and in a few places you must post a bond to guarantee your exit transportation by commercial means.

To visit French Polynesia, for example, every non–European Union citizen must put up a bond equivalent to the cost of air travel out of the territory. For Americans, this anti-beachcomber guarantee is $1,000 and must be posted by the captain and each member of his crew, even though they have a perfectly good sailing vessel at hand. Incidentally, it's a good idea to get visas in advance when you visit French Polynesia; otherwise, the officials in the outer islands tend to hurry you along to Tahiti, when you might wish to linger along the way. In 2003, a visa for French Polynesia was good for three months with one renewal allowed.

Immigration regulations apply to each member of a ship's crew, for whose presence and behavior and bills the captain is entirely responsible. Sometimes it's tedious to make crew changes. If a new crew member is flying in to meet the vessel at destination X, it may be prudent to see a consular official of the country in question beforehand and get a note from him detailing any special procedures.

Each consul is a special problem, and his demands for fees must be judged according to how important his special permissions are. Some consuls are paid very little and eke out their salaries with fees. A few try to take advantage of yachtsmen. If you feel you are being victimized, you can complain to the ambassador or to the head of the department of tourism of the country in question, sometimes with startling and immediate results. Don't be too quick to complain, however. Even if you feel there has been some injustice, it's usually simpler to pay a small fee and forget it.

The sums for harbor dues, buoyage, navigation lights, and drinking water are often based on big-ship tonnage; the corresponding yacht charges are trifling. The costs for pilots and watchmen are more. But harbor regulations are always changing and are generally out of date before they can be written down. I think the best scheme is to make inquiries among foreign sailors who have been to the country you are planning to visit. People in their home country seldom realize the requirements for foreign vessels.

If you have no knowledge of a confused foreign situation and want current details, pay a personal call on the naval attaché at the country's embassy. Telephone ahead for an appointment and put on good clothes because things are formal at embassies. I've always found these to be most profitable calls. Sometimes they result in an introductory letter to a maritime official or a friend in the country. Perhaps the attaché will take an interest in your voyage and secure seasonal weather reports or other special information for you.

For example, when we were in Japan and ready to leave for the Aleutians, Margaret called on the naval attaché at the U.S. Embassy in Tokyo. (We had heard that another yacht had stopped at the U.S. Navy base at Adak the year before and unfortunately had arrived during war games.) Margaret asked the attaché to send a message informing the Adak commander that we were coming and requesting permission to stay in the harbor for a few days. By originating the request with an official, we had the system with us and a sort of quasi-authority to visit a place that we had heard was tough on transient vessels.

Another time in Peru, the Chilean attaché told us: "Wait please a few weeks before sailing south. We have a little civil commotion." (A revolution was on.)

Again, a few years later in Aden, we met an English naval officer (on holiday) who said that Port Sudan was open and safe. But he urged us to stay away from Eritrea and Yemen's northern ports.

I don't want to overemphasize this and suggest a run on attachés and others, but I think you can ask for a little assistance occasionally. Sometimes a few bits of information can lead to a slight change in plans and turn a routine passage into an exciting experience. We met a Philippine official in Ponape in the Eastern Caroline Islands who told us about the bay on southern Guam that Magellan had entered in 1521. We sailed to that little bay and our visit was memorable.

If we're unable to learn anything about a country that we want to visit, we simply throw off the dock lines and head out. If the information is conflicting, seems unreasonable, or comes from a doubtful source, we ignore it.

I often think of the wise words of Miles Smeeton regarding official clearances. "Never ask too many questions," Miles told me once. "Somebody might say no! Then what would you do? Just go, keep smiling, and the officials will have to deal with you."

HEALTH

Besides customs and immigration, a vessel must satisfy health regulations. When you enter a country for the first time and hoist the yellow Q flag (beneath the courtesy ensign of the country) to the outer part of the starboard spreader of the mainmast, the flag is signaling: "My vessel is healthy and I request free pratique." The port captain's office or the health department will send out a doctor to decide whether the people on the incoming ship are healthy and "free of plague." If your inoculations for tetanus or yellow fever or whatever have expired, you will be injected on the spot or be sent to a local hospital. Supposedly if one had the mumps or whooping cough, the vessel would be obliged to remain in a quarantine anchorage until the danger passed. (Yet you can travel by bus, plane, or automobile and never be questioned.)

When you have a health official on board, it's a good time to ask about local problems. One day we cleared into northern Australia at Thursday Island. I inquired about malaria. The doctor warned us about a deadly strain called *Plasmodium falciparum*, the cerebral form of malaria, which has a fatality rate of 15 to 25 percent.

"It will kill you stone dead," said the doctor. He sternly admonished us to take our medicine (chloroquine) on a regular weekly basis and to have a special medicine (Fansidar)* on board in case we began to show the symptoms of the cerebral variety.

Animal quarantine (for rabies) comes under health. Most countries pay no attention to dogs and cats and parrots, but Hawaii, England, New Zealand, and other places have strict rules for pets and require long quarantine periods.

Spain is a special case regarding the all-yellow Q flag, which, when seen, appears to terrify the local officials and make them believe that you have a grave infectious illness on board. Based on the experience of many yachtsmen, I would not use the Q flag in Spain.

AGRICULTURE

The inspector for agriculture is concerned with preventing harmful insects and plant diseases from entering the country. In Rarotonga in the Cook Islands, where the orange crop is of great importance, all incoming citrus fruits and their containers are routinely seized and destroyed to prevent introduction of pests. Islands that raise coconuts often have special inspections for the rhinoceros beetle. The United States prohibits any fresh meat from abroad except under closely controlled conditions because of the chance of foot-and-mouth disease in foreign cattle. And so on.

The four inspections are sometimes handled by four people, or one person may deal with several or even all of the departments. If you're anchored, the government officers will come out in a launch, or four launches. Or you may have to take your dinghy ashore to pick them up. The officials are often amused by foreign boats and like to come aboard, fantasize about yacht trips, and have a cup of coffee or maybe a small glass of rum. Since the officials live in the area, they will know about local

---

*Mefloquine or doxycycline may be preferred if the side effects are not too severe. Check with your health department for updates. Victims of cerebral malaria need intensive care in a hospital.

attractions, where to shop, security, repairs, the best anchorages, where to leave the dinghy, and so forth.

Officials expect you to have the flag of their country prominently displayed on the starboard spreader of the mainmast. Some port captains get angry if they don't see their flag and can levy fines. The countries of South America are particularly touchy on this point, especially Peru and Uruguay. We try to have 20-by-30-inch or larger courtesy flags for all the countries on our itinerary. Most flags are easy to make, and since they are viewed at a distance, the fine points of sewing (or stapling) aren't too important. The main things are the colors and general form. Brazil is hardest of all. Antigua and Barbados have complicated colors and patterns. Indonesia and Monaco are easy.

A foreign yachtsman with a ketch who visits Uruguay and is used to flying his national flag at the mizzen top (higher than the mainmast spreaders with the courtesy flag of Uruguay) soon learns that the Uruguayans want their flag higher and will stand for nothing else. No matter how illogical these demands may seem, the best thing is to agree at once and to change the flag to the local custom.

Once we were tied up in Punta Arenas, Chile, during a storm in the Strait of Magellan. Our Chilean courtesy flag was flapping violently. Already the end was gone, and as more red and white threads disappeared downwind, the flag was clearly becoming smaller. To save the flag, I took it down. A few minutes later there were two heavy knocks on the deck. I looked out. "Bandera! Bandera!" shouted a soldier, pointing to the mast.

In Turkey, Margaret made a big effort to sew the white crescent and the white star on the red background, but a local official waved his forefinger back and forth and indicated that the alignment of the crescent was faulty. I rushed out and bought a genuine article.

If you sail into a port at night or on the weekend, you may be liable for overtime charges. Generally, when you enter a country, you must go to a large port or major harbor where officials are present. It's customary not to conduct any business or for anyone to go ashore until the ship has been cleared. However, if no one comes in response to the yellow flag after a few hours, I row ashore and either telephone or walk to the port captain's office. I take a crew list, the registration paper for the ship, passports, inoculation certificates, and the outbound clearance paper (if any) from the last port. If there's a language problem, you will have to find an interpreter or fight it out with a dictionary. Officials generally speak a little English, the lingua franca of the world.

I advise keeping the ship's official registration paper or papers on board and using photocopies. Most officials accept these, and having a dozen copies on the yacht is a good plan. Also run off a dozen copies of the ship's crew list (name, position, age, ship's name, signature of captain, ship's stamp). I would make one copy of each passport in case (God forbid) the originals disappear. The copies will at least have the numbers, which will help with the issuance of new documents. Countries in the eastern Mediterranean like official-looking papers, which suggest a ship's stamp and a red ink pad. Office supply houses can easily make a ship's stamp for a few dollars and it will last forever. When I am asked for my captain's certificate, I pull out my U.S. driver's license and copy down the numbers.

I try not to pay any charges on the first day because I don't know the local rules, the "charges" may be dropped, and I generally have no local funds anyway. Just say that you have to go to the bank and will return tomorrow. I try to stall off compliance with anything that seems ridiculous until I can inquire at a yacht club or check with another yacht or the captain of a merchant ship. Sometimes officials want to keep the ship's papers and passports (they may offer you a receipt), but you should try hard to retain these documents after showing them. You can argue that if a wind comes up in the night and you have to clear out, you must have your papers. On a stop in Sudan we were obliged to surrender our papers only to discover that the next day was a religious holiday. This dragged on and we waited six days for our papers.

If all else fails, you may have to engage an agent. If this is the only way, try to find an agent or shipping company that deals with vessels from your country. It may be helpful to speak to several agents. *Be sure to settle the financial arrangements in advance.* You want to know the total charges for both your inbound and outbound transits for (1) the agent and (2) the port. Ask for a letter or an advance bill with details and a signature.

In some places the officials don't come out to you. Instead you go to the officials. Their offices may be spread all over a city or town and a stranger may have a hard time finding the principals, who may have restricted office hours. A local agent knows all the officials, can make the rounds quickly, and may be able to help you in other ways.

On the small Italian island of Pantelleria in the middle of the Mediterranean, we sailed into the harbor and tied up. It took me several hours to find out that the entrance formalities were handled at the police station, a long walk from the harbor. When I got there, I saw that the police station was like a small fortress with heavy grills on the windows and an enormous steel door at the entrance. I rang the bell several times. Finally after a long delay, a junior policeman cautiously slid back a tiny steel panel at eye level. I acted out three sets of key words: American tourist. Yacht. Stamp in passport.

The window slid shut.

A few minutes later it opened again and a senior police official in a flamboyant uniform with a red sash examined me carefully. I went through the same pantomime. The officer decided that I didn't look too dangerous and ordered the junior policeman to open up.

The big steel door was unbolted. I was taken to an office where I pointed to days on a calendar to explain what I wanted. The passports were duly stamped. We shook hands and I left the police fortress. Apparently the man I saw acted for customs, immigration, health, and agriculture.

When you leave a country, you should have an outgoing clearance of some kind if possible. Anything will do just as long as it looks vaguely official with a few stamps and signatures on it. Authorities prefer big sheets of paper with a lot of words and a countersignature or two. The last three times I have left the United States, however, the customs people have declined to give me papers of any kind. In Gibraltar, it's a big deal to have a passport stamped. Yet on leaving Guam, Western Samoa, and Bermuda, for example, I was given an outbound clearance, which is the first thing the next country's officials asked for. An Ecuadorian official told me that his country didn't issue outbound clearances; the next country, Peru, demanded an outbound clearance from my last stop and threatened me with a fine for not having one. Before a departure from California, I got a formal health certificate from the U.S. Public Health Service, which stated that I had no infected rats on board. But no one was interested in this intriguing document, and after carrying the paper around for years, I finally threw it away.

No matter what happens, don't lose your temper. If you do, you've already lost and may wind up in jail or worse because the authority rests with the officials. You're a guest in the country and should not comment on local customs, women, or politics. Certainly not on day one when you're just entering a new place.

If the preceding pages seem vague and conflicting, it's because ship's paperwork is an issue of hazy cross-purposes. The only thing certain is that there are no rules. Confusion is normal. No matter what paper you have, you need something else. In blue, green, and red. And six copies of each. Perhaps one should carry a printing press, red ribbons, a notary stamp, wax, and a signet ring. Certainly a bottle of brandy. For the captain.

Much of the fun of sailing is meeting other voyagers. This is Xavier d'Auzac, a delightful Frenchman we met in Labrador in 2000. Xavier was on his first long trip and sailing by himself on an old 38-footer. He had almost no money but a wonderful zest and enthusiasm for travel. That morning while on a walk, he had met up with a large black bear. "First I thought of shaking hands," he said. "But that seemed like a bad idea, so at the last minute I changed course." Xavier was a French Basque and had sailed to Red Bay because of the Basque whalers and fishermen who had worked there in the 17th century. Xavier was about to sail back to France, but he wanted to see icebergs, so he set off northward along the Labrador coast. "I'm thrilled to be sailing among the icebergs of Labrador," he said. "It's like a dream." Xavier was like a child in a magic forest.

29

THE DREAM AND
THE REALITY

The big secret of world travel is to do it in a sailing yacht. It's by far the best way to see the globe. You take your deluxe hotel with you, which gives you everything you need to exist pleasantly and comfortably. You have a snug berth, a writing desk, a navigation center, and a compact little galley, plus a few favorite books and clothes. All in a small and neat package.

Once you have your own boat, you can sail for years without the terrible daily costs and hassle of hotels, restaurants, and airplanes. You entirely sidestep the annoyance of reservations, standing in line, security screening, and dragging around awkward luggage. You do things at your own pace because you're in charge.

You can sail to such famous places as Venice, London, Sydney, San Francisco, and Hong Kong. You can pick an island in the middle of the Aegean or listen to green and yellow parrots in the wilds of the Amazon. Or a thousand places in between. There's the excitement of sailing from A to B at a slow and leisurely pace,

Sailing into Tasu Sound on the southwest coast of Moresby Island in the Queen Charlotte group in northwestern British Columbia, Canada.

plus the fun of meeting new people. It's even better if you take your spouse, significant other, or children with you.

In the beginning it's terrifying. The storms, the leaks, the anchors, handling the sails, deciding on the routes—so many unknowns. Fortunately, yachts travel slowly. If you're patient, do some reading, attend sailing schools, and learn from experts, you will begin to put it all together. Life aboard the yacht will suddenly begin to click. Even so, there will be a thousand exciting moments while you work through the drill from novice to sophomore to captain.

We sail for many reasons. There's the basic pleasure of traveling—to see the other side of the world, the Shangri-la on the far side of the misty ocean. To meet the people who live there and find out about their lives and occupations. To tell them how we make our living. How we pass our days. What's important to us. And by this interchange to hope that our acquaintance will grow toward friendship.

All people have a basic curiosity. I remember so well the questions that a Micronesian woman on the tiny atoll of Abemama in the Gilbert Islands in the central Pacific asked Margaret and me.

"What are the waves like beyond the horizon?" she said through a translator. "Are your storms like ours? Do you ever get scared? What do you eat? Do you have fish and coconuts in America? Why did you come to this faraway place? Tell us about yourself."

We've heard these questions many times. Though we are ordinary people, we are thought to be on a great adventure, the kind that men and women of all ages and from all countries dream of, and with which they can identify. Perhaps by talking with us, our visitors participate a little in our journey.

As a sailor, I like the adventure of using the free and easy wind to make my boat move long distances. I feel such pleasure when the wind pushes against a sail, the water swishes past the hull, and the boat hurries along at five or six knots. It's a kind of magic, a dream, a delight.

I like navigating from one place to another and arriving at a new and strange shore. I suppose that on some level, we all want to prove ourselves, to have the gratification of putting together a small expedition and making it work. Of leading others. Of finding new places and ways to see them. Of using initiative to overcome problems. Of helping people. Perhaps of telling about what we've seen and experienced.

Successful cruising in a small vessel is a heady amalgam of experiences in which all these reasons overlap and reinforce one another. An admixture of striving, satisfaction, hope, and perfection.

*   *   *

The talk that all people in the boating community hear over and over again is: "When I retire and have X dollars a month, I'm going to sail across the horizon and do such and such."

If this works, good; but what if you lose your health and ambition between now and then? Ninety-five percent of boatowners never go anywhere because after retirement, their lament changes to verse two: "I'm too old. I missed my chance. I should have gone twenty-five years ago."

Sometime in your life (before big jobs, between big jobs, or after big jobs) you can certainly snatch away a year or two. The experience will change your life. Call it a long vacation, a sabbatical year, a leavening period, or retirement sampling. Label it plan X. But don't wait too long, or the game may be up. The frail flesh lasts only so long. *Whining about the risk suggests that fear's a player.*

If extended voyages are not possible and you want a trial sail, you might try a full summer's sailing in a place that's new and different. Take your boat to a nearby coastline or set of islands—somewhere that's beyond the area you know so you'll have a fresh experience. Make an effort to arrange your sailing so it's leisurely and unhurried.

If you want to try this but lack a vessel and the expertise to sail along a distant coast, then charter a yacht somewhere exciting. If you're unsure about your skills, arrange to hire an expert local captain. If you've any aptitude for this game, you'll pick up the skills quickly, and maybe the next time you can skip the local captain.

A trial sail can be worthwhile.

Let me tell you a story about a man in Oakland, California, who built a Bill Garden–designed 46-foot Porpoise cruising ketch, a splendid yacht of its type but difficult and complicated to construct. The building went on in the man's backyard for six years. He used the finest of everything—Everdur fastenings, frames of white oak, and planking of selected mahogany.

The hull was first-class, and the saloon had some of the best joinerwork I've ever seen. Someone in the builder's family had been in the foreign service in the Far East and had brought home several intricate teak cabinets that the builder cleverly integrated into the saloon furniture.

Finally the great day came and the yacht was launched with fanfare and flags. The owner and his wife moved aboard and began buying charts and ordering stores. The excited couple invited us for cake and coffee. A few weeks later the masts were stepped, the sails bent on, and the proud owners went out for their first sail.

When the yacht heeled to the wind, the owner's wife was terrified. "It's tippy," she said. "I can't stand this. It feels to me as if the yacht is going to turn upside down." The upshot was that the vessel was sold. Six years of sacrifice and work and planning and dreaming went up in smoke. How much better it would have been to have chartered or to have crewed on other yachts to have learned about the lady's nervousness when the boat heeled.

Margaret and I have had good luck with five guidelines.

1. Throw the Calendar Away

I've mentioned this before, but it won't hurt to repeat that overprecise scheduling usually doesn't work, particularly if it involves other people. No one can predict winds and sailing speeds, and sailors are invariably too optimistic about passage times. (When was the last time that the boat was ahead of schedule?) It's simply not smart to set up a demanding itinerary with crew and friends flying in and out and substantial mileages to be covered each day. If you have an overfull yacht with lots of meals to cook and people to meet and no allowance for delays caused by calms and rainy weather, the pleasure will vanish before it's begun. If plans to exchange crew at various ports go wrong, you're liable to spoil the trip and make everyone angry.

Small-boat people think in terms of weeks, not days; airline passengers think in terms of hours and minutes. These standards are quite incompatible. Yet sailors have to take the weather and sailing breaks as they come. However, if people get locked into airline flights during the busy season, they usually can't change flights. Don't cut things too fine. Allow for flexibility by arranging rooms at a little hotel or pension (perhaps in a small, pleasant port) where your crew can stay for a few days.

Even if you're on your own in the yacht, you might get ill or decide to stay in a nice place for a day or two. You shouldn't have to justify these departures from your calendar, which, after all, is an artificial schedule.

2. Consider the Size of the Boat

We like a vessel that's 35–45 feet long because we believe this size allows both reasonable seakeeping ability and acceptable sailing speed. Plus, there's room enough for liveaboard comfort and adequate stowage space. In truth, Margaret and I like long sea passages, so we're really not in a desperate hurry when we travel; otherwise, we'd go by air.

We have the skills to sail a 60- footer, but we have no desire for a larger vessel. The concept of always the larger yacht and always the faster passage seems pointless to us. Who cares? Besides, with size, there's more concern about security, an expanded, catchall word that in the 21st century means a general uneasiness and worry about thieves in the night. It's too bad that the world has become increasingly separated into the haves and the have-nots, and that many people think that all boatowners are millionaires. In much of South America, for example, men acquire yachts only after they have become successful businessmen, built a home, raised a family, and have a summer house. *Then* they buy the boat. A yachting robbery in the eyes of a thief, therefore, means access to wealth.

Sailing vessels are generally not good targets for thieves because even at a dock, a boat is difficult and full of unknowns. Stealing yachts is almost unheard of because taking such a vessel requires special skills. Ordinary burglars are put off by the complexity of boats, which are hard to move quickly, easy to trace, and difficult to sell. (Automobiles and motorcycles make much more sense.) Special radios and radar sets are cumbersome to steal and a problem to fence; about the only readily negotiable items found aboard a boat are cash, jewelry, credit cards, and laptop computers. Nevertheless, large yachts are better targets for thieves because there is liable to be more cash, superior jewelry, higher-limit credit cards, and more salable electronics aboard.

3. Keep the Sailing Simple

With regard to equipment and complexity, I know that a bow thruster makes docking and turning easier. However, I don't care to clutter the yacht with a piece of machinery that needs to be bought, maintained, and supplied with electric power. Also, I don't like to drill holes through the hull.

Instead of an apparent-wind gauge, I use a long red ribbon at the masthead to tell the wind direction. I have learned to judge the speed of the wind by waves and whitecaps. To deliver water to the galley from the freshwater tanks, we have a simple foot pump. I prefer a saltwater-cooled engine because the cooling system is less complicated. Our hand windlass for the anchor is perfectly adequate. An electric autopilot may be handy in light airs, but I believe it should be a supplementary device, not a necessity.

Remember that anything on board that stops working will have to be repaired by the crew or sent off to the manufacturer or a specialist shop. Waiting around for packages is not fun; this is why cruising yachts carry so many tools and spare parts and favor uncomplicated systems.

But Margaret and I are not hopeless antiquarians. When I tried out the Autohelm electronic hand-bearing compass (see page 243), I immediately junked the other two hand-bearing compasses on board because the new device is clearly superior. I have a GPS set (plus a backup) because this navigation system is quick and a safety-added feature. The most important electronic device on most yachts is a depth sounder. Just try heaving a lead line on a trip every time you want to know the depth to appreciate the handiness and utility of an automatic sounding device.

I have an aluminum toerail (instead of teak) along the hull-to-deck joint because it's strong, handy to use for running rigging applications, and requires no maintenance. When we set off for the high latitudes in Canada, we mounted a radar set on the mast because of persistent fogs along the Atlantic coasts of Newfoundland and Labrador. Our reasoning was that in poorly charted areas, radar is the best way to find your way in dense fog.

The trick, it seems to me, is to judge each new item by a couple of quick questions: Does it do the job better? Will it make our life and sailing easier or simpler? Over time, is it superior? Or is it too complicated for what we'll get out of it?

When Margaret and I bought our first yacht in 1962, the vessel had cotton sails. But Dacron eclipsed cotton completely because Dacron is very strong, keeps its shape better, and is resistant to mildew. No longer did we have to dry the sails after use. It was the same story with manila line, a natural rope made from the fiber of the wild banana stalk. Manila was replaced almost overnight by three-strand Dacron line, which in turn has been taken over by the double-braided Dacron that we use today.

4. Sail to New Destinations

Try the far side of the river; the other end of the island. Visit people and scenery you haven't seen before. See the famous places, but consider small and obscure locations as well. Different sailing goals keep your senses fresh and bright.

- One example: At the western end of Canada is Vancouver Island, which measures 250 miles from top to bottom and 50 to 70 miles across. There are hundreds of yachts in the city of Victoria at the southern end of the island and in the city of Vancouver on the nearby mainland. But once you get 25 miles from either city, you seldom see a sail. Five large sounds (Quatsino, Kyuquot, Nootka, Clayoquot, and Barkley) slash the southwest coast. The sounds are ringed with tall trees and rocks, have well-protected anchorages, and are intriguing because of the salmon and the black and white killer whales (orcas). I like the Native Canadian villages with the colorful totem poles on the northeast coast.
- The main island of French Polynesia is Tahiti, which looks like a figure eight from the air and is 30 miles long and 15 miles wide. The capital city of Papeete, population 115,000, at the northwest end, is noisy, crowded, and full of snarling little automobiles and French bureaucrats. The other end of the island is isolated, peaceful, and utterly lovely; the 35-mile windward sail from Papeete to the hurricane anchorage at Port Phaeton (and the nearby Gauguin Museum) slips you neatly back in time to the era of Captains Wal-

lis, Cook, and Bougainville and gives you a chance to meet Polynesians who are not in a hurry.

- It's fun to visit *outports*, which are isolated villages supplied entirely by sea along the remote coastlines of Newfoundland. In 2001 we sailed to Grand Bruit, Gaultois, McCallum, and Francois.
- Recently we sailed to Corfu and other islands in the Ionian Sea. We've found some nice unspoiled places by heading for obscure settlements on small islands (Port Gaios on Paxos) or remote villages on big islands (Gefira on Corfu) even when there are a lot of tourists in the major centers.
- I'm a river nut and like to sail up and down long waterways. (Watch out for bridge clearances and overhead wires.) River sailing is a different world from ocean or coastal sailing. Calm, sometimes swift water. No seas. If there's any commercial traffic, there are often excellent charts. The sun-heated wind tends to blow upstream in the afternoon; cooler air may funnel downstream at night and in the morning. If you combine the wind with a suitable tidal stream, you can sometimes get a free ride both ways, but you may have to anchor occasionally. Many times there's wonderful scenery. We've played the river game in the Rio Calle-Calle in Chile, the Guadalquivir in Spain, the Guadiana in Portugal, and the mighty Columbia* in the northwest United States. We have sailed up and down the Penobscot, St. George, Kennebec, and Damariscotta Rivers in Maine; the Rappahannock on Chesapeake Bay; and the Delaware along the southwest coast of New Jersey. Sailing up a strange river or gliding past an unknown coast is like going to the library and walking along a row of bookshelves whose contents you've never seen before.

5. Have Some Fun Every Day

Gratify your senses; spoil yourself a little. I like to watch the first rosy fingers streak the dawn sky in the east. Margaret is a green-flash junkie at sunset. Whenever seabirds appear and circle the boat, everything stops while we identify the birds and add new ones to our list.

Try flying a kite from the cockpit. Or bake a cake, and plaster on some thick, delicious icing. Set aside time to read an intriguing book. Give your sweetheart a kiss.

Is it exciting to go to new places?

On the day before Christmas in 1973, we were at 38° S, in sight of the Chilean coast. We had small sails up and had been hammering southward against a relentless

---

*It's best to cross the bar of this mighty river at high slack water when the wind is down.

southwest headwind. At noon Margaret climbed on deck to take the watch.

"Go below and look at the chart and sailing directions," she said. "I think we can anchor on the northeast side of a little island named Mocha. It's about twenty miles offshore and just south of us. The Pilot says the anchorage is good in this wind."

We learned that many early explorers, including Francis Drake and William Dampier, used the northeast anchorage. In 1578, Drake had the greatest trouble from a fierce tribe of natives that lived on the island. In 1800, Amasa Delano anchored his ship *Perseverance* and wrote about the wild horses and hogs.[90] Later we read that Herman Melville may have derived the title of his novel *Moby-Dick* (1851) from Mocha Dick, the nickname of a giant white sperm whale that terrorized whaling ships in the area.[91] Mocha is the present-day breeding ground for fifteen thousand pairs of pink-footed shearwaters.

By midafternoon the wind was stronger, but we were reassured by the thin blue outline of Mocha on *Whisper*'s starboard bow. Two hours later, we were in smooth water on the northeast side of the 8-mile-long island. In front of us were mountainous wooded slopes, and we could see a tiny settlement of clapboard houses. While the angry wind whistled overhead, we let out our anchor and a long length of chain a few hundred yards from shore.

The next day, the wind blew even harder from the southwest. We were snug in our berth and made plans for a Christmas dinner. While I fired up the stove, Margaret set out a pan of bread dough for the first rising. She then consulted her storage book, burrowed in a settee locker, and pulled out a canned turkey, cranberry sauce, and a plum pudding that her sister had given us a year earlier. Soon Margaret had everything cooking. Meanwhile, I strung up a line of silver paper stars and the tiny collapsible red and green paper Christmas tree that we have hauled around for half a lifetime.

Ashore there was no sign of anyone until the hour of a daily weather forecast that was mentioned in the Chilean Pilot book. We watched a man enter a small building topped by various antennas. We tuned our old battery-powered portable Zenith radio to the frequency but heard nothing. Absolutely nothing.

All was ready by midafternoon. First Margaret and I drank a hot buttered rum. We then sang a few Christmas carols before sitting down to the steaming turkey, peppery dressing, tart cranberry sauce, candied potatoes, fresh bread, and, of course, the plum pudding. We said a prayer of thanksgiving for our good health, our happiness, our snug anchorage, and our faraway friends.

The next day the contrary wind eased and we headed south again.

Mocha Island, our Christmas Island, was soon a blur astern.

Dolphins often come alongside during the day and accompany the boat for a few minutes, or they may swim next to the cockpit in the middle of the night and startle you with their noisy breathing, splashing, and squeaky chatter. Since the days of the ancient Greeks and probably long before, dolphins have always been the friends of sailors.

Notes

Chapter 1. The Pleasure and the Freedom

1. Guy Cole, *Ocean Cruising* (London: Adlard Coles Ltd., 1959), 5–6.
2. There are dozens of editions of *Sailing Alone Around the World*, by Joshua Slocum, in print. Not only is it a good and enduring story, but because it is long out of copyright, publishers don't have to pay any royalties. My copy of Harry Pidgeon's book *Around the World Single-Handed* was published in 1960 by Rupert Hart-Davis as part of the Mariners Library. *Yachting* magazine published a long account of Pidgeon's second trip around the world in December 1938 and January 1939.
3. Figures from 1999 sales brochure for a Quest 33 built by Holby Marine of Bristol, Rhode Island.

Chapter 2. The Corpus Itself

4. Allan H. Vaitses, *Covering Wooden Boats with Fiberglass* (Camden ME: International Marine, 1981). Excellent nuts-and-bolts information from a real pro for salvaging wooden and steel boats by adding fiberglass.
5. Somewhere in Bernard Moitessier's writings (I can't find the reference) he discussed the difference between wood, plastic, and steel hulls by figuratively tossing out filing cases of these materials from a second-story window. The wooden and plastic filing cases, according to Bernard, would be smashed to bits. The steel filing case would be dented but still a filing case. Which material would you choose? asks Bernard.
6. Gilbert Klingel, *Boatbuilding with Steel* (Camden ME: International Marine, 1973). I met this Chesapeake boatbuilder in 1977 when he was constructing a yacht for the Australian sailor Blue Bradfield. There's a useful chapter (204–33) on technical aspects of aluminum construction by Tom Colvin.
7. Nigel Warren, *Metal Corrosion in Boats* (Camden ME: International Marine, 1980), 105–6. Warren provides handy technical information on steel and aluminum hulls and the problems of mixing metals. Also see Roger Pretzer, *Marine Metals Manual* (Camden ME: International Marine, 1975).
8. Bruce Bingham, *Sail* (Aug. 1973).

Chapter 3. The Magic Plastic

9. Dan Spurr, *Heart of Glass* (Camden ME: International Marine, 1999). A fascinating, well-written history of the fiberglass yacht. Outstanding research.
10. Allan Vaitses, *The Fiberglass Boat Repair Manual* (Camden ME: International Marine, 1988).
11. Ibid., 1.
12. The quote is from John Geisheker, "An Owner's View of the W 32," *Good Old Boat* 3:5 (Sept.–Oct. 2000): 9. The best summary of the Westsail story is by Lynne and Snider Vick, at http://www.tlcs.com/dms/kendall/whist2.html.
13. Eric Sponberg, "How Core Materials Make Better Boats" (Internet: Boatbuilding.com from *American Sailor* magazine, undated).
14. David Adams, *Chasing Liquid Mountains* (Sidney: Pan Macmillan, 1997), 205–9.

15. For details about C-Flex and other building ideas, see Allan Vaitses, *Boatbuilding One-Off in Fiberglass* (Camden ME: International Marine, 1984).

16. *Sail* (Aug. 1993): 27–29.

17. Vaitses, *Fiberglass Boat Repair*, 31.

18. Gougeon Brothers, *Gelcoat Blisters Diagnosis Repair and Prevention* (Bay City MI: Gougeon Brothers, 2000), 1.

19. Ibid., 8.

Chapter 4. To Find a Yacht

20. Claud Worth, *Yacht Cruising*, 4th ed. rev. (London: J. D. Potter, 1948), 515.

Chapter 5. The Search Continues

21. I interviewed Don Street at *Sail* magazine in Boston on October 23, 1979.

22. Interview with Roy Jennings (Feb. 25, 1995) regarding the Porpoise ketch incident.

Chapter 6. Three Sailing Yachts

23. The consumer price index (CPI) from the U.S. Bureau of Labor Statistics for 1965 is 31.5 and for 2001 is 178. To find the year 2001 price equivalent to $20,000, divide the CPI for the unknown price year by the CPI for the year with the known dollar value. Then multiply this number by the known dollar value: $178 \div 31.5 = 5.65 \times \$20,000 = \$113,000$.

Chapter 7. The Rig

24. Uffa Fox, *Racing, Cruising and Yacht Design* (London: Peter Davies, Ltd., 1937), 13.

25. Quoted from Van de Stadt catalog 10: 28, published by E. G. van de Stadt & Partners, Industrieweg 35, Box 193, 1520 AD Wormerveer, Holland.

26. A fuller argument is made by Eric Sponberg in "Project Amazon and the Unstayed Rig," *Professional Boatbuilder* magazine (Oct.–Nov. 1998): 44–57.

Chapter 8. How to Make Big Sails Small

27. Jeremy Howard-Williams, *Sails* (Clinton Corners NY: John de Graff, 1976), 181.

28. Lin Pardey and Larry Pardey, *The Cost-Conscious Cruiser* (Arcata CA: Pardey Books, 1999), chapter 6.

Chapter 9. Spinnakers, Light-Weather Sails, and More on Sail Handling

29. Hal Roth, *Chasing the Wind* (Dobbs Ferry NY: Sheridan House, 1994), 115–16.

Chapter 11. Planning the Trip

30. John Brown, "Searchlight on a Silent Service," *Yachting Monthly* (Sept. 1975).

Chapter 12. The Anchor Game

31. Quoted from a letter from Captain Johnson to William Stelling, dated August 27, 1973, in possession of the author.

32. Jack Coote, ed., *Total Loss* (London: Adlard Coles, 1985), 182–84.

Chapter 13. The Practice of Anchoring

33. If the depth is 20 feet, and 60 feet of cable is stretched out between the bow and a point on the seafloor, you have a triangle whose hypotenuse is 60 and height is 20. The cosine of the bow angle is 0.33 or 70.5. A scope of 5:1 with the cable stretched

tightly would mean an angle between the water and the cable of about 12 degrees.

34. See "Anchors and Anchoring" in *Yachting Monthly* (Jan. 1969); "Ground Tackle and Anchoring Techniques," by Jack West, in *Yachting* (Nov.-Dec. 1975); *Anchors and Anchoring*, by R. D. Ogg, a booklet published by the Danforth Company of Portland, Maine.

Chapter 14. Self-Steering

35. Bernard Moitessier, *The Long Way* (London: Adlard Coles, 1973), 207-11.

Chapter 15. Can You Be Seen at Night?

36. Bernard Hayman, "Can You Be Seen at Night?" *Yachting World* (Jan. 1971): 33-35.
37. Paul E. Lobo, *Sail* (Oct. 1971).
38. Quoted in Lin and Larry Pardey, "The Invisible Yachts," *Pacific Yachting* (Jan. 1973).

Chapter 16. Storm Management 1: Heaving To and Lying Ahull

39. Adlard Coles, *Heavy Weather Sailing*, 3d ed. rev. (New York: De Graff, 1975); Miles Smeeton, *Because the Horn Is There* (Sidney BC: Gray's Publishing Co., 1971); Erroll Bruce, *Deep Sea Sailing* (New York: Van Nostrand, 1953); Bernard Moitessier, *The Long Way* (New York: Doubleday, 1975).
40. Eric Hiscock, *Cruising Under Sail*, 2d ed. (London: Oxford, 1965), 338; also see Eric Hiscock, *Voyaging Under Sail* (London: Oxford University Press, 1970), 175-76. For a different view, see Larry Pardey, *Storm Tactics Handbook* (Middletown CA: Paradise Cay, 1995), 31-35.
41. Letter to the author dated February 24, 2003.
42. William V. Kielhorn, "Sea Anchors," *Sail* (May 1976). Also see "Letters to the Editor" in the September 1975 issue of *Sail*.
43. Letter to the author, July 18, 2003.
44. Coles, *Heavy Weather Sailing*, chapter 18.
45. *Telltale Compass* (June 1976). Newsletter published by Victor Jorgenson of Lake Oswego, Oregon.

Chapter 17. Storm Management 2: Running Off

46. Vito Dumas, *Alone Through the Roaring Forties* (London: Adlard Coles, 1960), 50; Bernard Moitessier, *Cape Horn: The Logical Route* (London: Adlard Coles, 1969), 169-70.
47. Moitessier, *Logical Route*, 168.
48. Ibid., 169.
49. Joshua Slocum, *Sailing Alone Around the World* (New York: Westvaco, 1969); Conor O'Brien, *Across Three Oceans* (London: Philip Allan, 1927); W. A. Robinson, *To the Great Southern Sea* (London: Peter Davies, 1957).
50. Eric Hiscock, *Voyaging Under Sail* (London: Oxford, 1970), 174-75.
51. Slocum, *Sailing Alone*, 102.
52. Thomas S. Steele, "Twice Around in *Adios*," *Yachting* (Dec. 1964), 35.
53. Robin Knox-Johnston, *A World of My Own* (London: Corgi, 1969), 108.
54. C. A. Marchaj, "Heavy Weather," *Sail* (March 1973), 29.

55. Earl Hinz, *Heavy Weather Tactics Using Sea Anchors and Drogues* (Arcata CA: Paradise Cay, 2000), 94.

56. This material is based on Miles Smeeton, *"Tzu Hang" 1957* (London: Royal Cruising Club, 1957), 67–79; Miles Smeeton, *Once Is Enough* (London: Rupert Hart-Davis, 1960), chapter 7; Miles Clark, *High Endeavours* (London: Grafton, 1992), chapter 16; John Guzzwell, *Trekka Round the World* (Bishop CA: Fine Edge, 1999), chapters 9–11. I knew the Smeetons well, and we corresponded for many years. Margaret and I spent a few days on *Tzu Hang* in British Columbia in 1971. John Guzzwell is a good friend.

57. *American Practical Navigator*, known as Bowditch (Washington: U.S. Government Printing Office, 1958), 729.

58. Willard Bascom, *Waves and Beaches* (Garden City NY: Doubleday Anchor, 1964), 43; William Van Dorn, *Oceanography and Seamanship* (New York: Dodd, Mead, 1974), 185–233.

Chapter 18. Storm Management 3: Deploying a Sea Anchor

59. J. C. Voss, *The Venturesome Voyages of Captain Voss* (London: Rupert Hart-Davis, 1955).

60. W. A. Robinson, *To the Great Southern Sea* (London: Peter Davies, 1957), 218–23.

61. Eric Hiscock, *Voyaging Under Sail* (London: Oxford, 1970), 177.

62. Lin Pardey and Larry Pardey, *Storm Tactics Handbook* (Vista CA: Pardey Books, 1995).

63. Victor Shane, *Drag Device Data Base* (Summerland CA: Para-Anchors International, 1998), 5.1.13, 5.1.20, 5.1.21.

64. Maurice Griffiths, *Yachting Monthly* (May 1967): 233.

65. Earl Hinz, *Heavy Weather Tactics Using Sea Anchors and Drogues* (Arcata CA: Paradise Cay, 2000), 67–68.

66. Erroll Bruce, *Deep Sea Sailing* (New York: Van Nostrand, 1953), 187.

67. See Jordan report CG-D-20-87 (pp. 56–57), available from the National Technical Information Service, Springfield, VA 22161. The report can also be downloaded from the sites mentioned on p. 292.

68. Victor Shane, *Drag Device*, 5.1.41–43.

69. Ibid., 5.1.41–43.

70. Peter Cumberlidge, ed., *Roving Commissions* (England: Bookcraft Midsomer Norton, 1998), 78–81.

71. Steve Dashew and Linda Dashew, *Surviving the Storm* (Tucson AZ: Beowulf, 1999), 67–77.

Chapter 19. Storm Management 4: Deploying a Stern Drogue

72. Pat Treston, "Mission Antarctica," a spectacular ten-part series in the New Zealand magazine *Sea Spray* that began in June 1971.

73. John Rousmaniere, *Fastnet Force 10* (New York: Norton, 1980), 9–10.

74. Letter from Don Jordan to the author dated September 13, 2002.

75. See the Jordan report CG-D-20-87.

76. Shane, *Drag Device*, 5.5.8–10.

77. Letters from Don Jordan to the author, June–July 2002.

78. Dashew and Dashew, *Surviving the Storm*, 465.

79. Van Dorn, *Oceanography*, 393-96; Robinson, *To the Great Southern Sea*, 68-84 and appendixes.

80. Coles, *Heavy Weather Sailing*, 218-19.

81. Willard Bascom, *Waves and Beaches*, 60-61.

Chapter 20. Managing Without Refrigeration

82. E. G. Martin, *Deepwater Cruising* (New York: Yachting, 1928), 72.

Chapter 21. What Does World Cruising Cost?

83. Betsy Hitz-Holman, *Sitting Ducks* (Newport RI: Seven Seas Press, 1983). A grim book about violence, corrupt politics, and a spoiled cruise by a former managing editor of *Cruising World* magazine.

Chapter 23. Schooling at Sea

84. John Cloud and Jodie Morse, "Home Sweet School," *Time* (Aug. 27, 2001).

85. Based on the article by Laurie Pane "Kids, School and the Cruising Life," *Sailing* (Jan. 2001): 17-20. A great, upbeat piece.

86. Carol Hogan, "The Kids Made the Cruise," *Sail* (April 1975).

Chapter 24. Heat and Cooking

87. Detailed performance guides are listed in specification A-14 by the American Boat and Yacht Council Inc., 3069 Solomons Island Road, Edgewater MD 21037-1416 or at www.abycinc.org.

Chapter 25. Nine Ideas

88. Bill King, *The Wandering Stars* (London: Faber & Faber, 1989), 36-42.

89. University of California (Berkeley) weekly press clip sheet for June 21, 1966.

Chapter 29. The Dream and the Reality

90. Walter Teller, *Five Sea Captains* (New York: Atheneum, 1960), 38-39.

91. Go to www.melville.org/mobyname.htm. This reference mentions the article by Jeremiah Reynolds titled "Mocha Dick: or The White Whale of the Pacific" in the New York *Knickerbocker* magazine for May 1839. This was 12 years before *Moby-Dick* was published, in 1851.

Glossary

Abaft. Nearer the stern than another object. "Abaft the mast."

Abeam. At right angles to the fore-and-aft line.

Aboard. On board a vessel.

About. A vessel is said to go, come, or put about when she moves from one tack to the other.

Accidental gybe. When running, to change course and cause the wind blowing from behind the vessel to swing one or more sails and booms from one side to the other. If the wind is strong, this violent movement of a boom can threaten the integrity of the rig. A heavy boom can usually be controlled by the mainsheet or with boom tackles.

Aft. Toward the stern.

Aftermost. Farthest toward the stern.

Aground. When the keel touches the seabed and motion stops.

Ahead. In front of or toward the direction of the bows.

Ahull (a storm maneuver). Lying without any sail set in a gale.

Alee. Away from the direction of the wind. To leeward.

Aloft. Up above; in the mast or the rigging.

Amidships. The middle area of a vessel; the word sometimes refers to the fore-and-aft line, that is, neither to port nor starboard. "Put the helm amidships."

Anemometer. An instrument for measuring the strength of the wind.

Apparent wind. The direction and strength of wind that is felt on a moving object. Compare with *true wind*.

Arm. To fill the hollow at the bottom of a sounding lead with grease or tallow to bring up a sample of the seafloor. "To arm the lead."

Astern. Behind or in the direction of the stern.

Athwart or Athwartships. Across; the opposite of *fore-and-aft*.

Awash. Washed over by water. "The rocks were just awash."

Aweather. To windward; toward the weather side.

Aweigh. Describes an anchor that is away from the bottom and being hoisted.

Back. To sheet or hold the clew of a sail to windward. If a jib is backed, it moves the bow of the boat to leeward. "He backed the staysail."

Backing. A term used to describe the movement of wind, which is said to *back* (say, south to southeast) when it moves counterclockwise in the Northern Hemisphere. In the Southern Hemisphere, this term is reversed and refers to a clockwise movement (say, from west to northwest). *Backing* has also been defined as moving in a direction contrary to the track of the sun. Compare with *veering*.

Backstay. A principal support, usually of wire cable, leading from a high point on a mast to a strong point on the transom or afterdeck to keep the spar from bending forward.

Baggy-wrinkle. Bulky chafing gear made from old rope that is fitted to rigging aloft.

Ballast. Weight, often of lead, iron, or stones carried low in the bilge or on the keel to give stability to a vessel.

Batten. A horizontal strip of flexible wood, metal, or plastic that is inserted in a pocket on the leech of a sail to extend and stabilize the roach to prevent curling and flapping.

Beam. 1. The extreme width of a vessel. 2. A transverse timber that supports the deck. 3. A vessel is said to be on her *beam ends* when her masts are horizontal.

Bear away. To move the helm to windward to make the vessel turn more away from the wind.

Bearing. The direction of an object in terms of compass points or degrees.

Beat. To tack, that is, to make progress to windward by a zigzag course with the wind first on one bow and then on the other.

Becalmed. When there is no wind and the sails hang limp.

Becket. An eye or loop made in wire or fiber rope.

Belay. To secure a rope on a cleat, pin, or other object. "He belayed the line on the cleat." See *cleat*.

Belly. The fullness or draft of a sail, often controlled by adjusting tension on the edges.

Bend. To fasten one rope to another, or to fix a sail in position on its spars. "The crew bent the new mainsail on the boom."

Bermudian or Marconi rig. A modern sail plan with a three-sided mainsail and jib set on a tall mast that was developed to a high state of efficiency by sailors in Bermuda. Because of the height of the mast and its complex support wires, it looked to sailors of the 1920s like the lofty antennas at a wireless, or Marconi, station. Usually written as *bermudian rig*.

Berth. A sleeping place in the cabin of a boat. It's also an area alongside a dock or in an anchorage that's occupied by a vessel.

Bight. A bend or loop in a line. Also a wide, curving bay along a coastline.

Bilge. The curve of a vessel's bottom where it merges into the sides. Also the low area inside a vessel beneath the cabin sole where water collects.

Binnacle. The stand on which the compass is mounted, usually placed just forward of the helmsman. In many yachts, it is part of the steering wheel complex.

Bitter end. The innermost part of the anchor cable.

Bitts. Short posts to which mooring lines are made fast.

Blade. The flat outer part of an oar.

Block. A device for changing the lead of a line with a minimum of friction.

Blue-water or Bluewater. Oceangoing. Offshore.

Board. A single leg or tack when sailing close-hauled.

Boat hook. A pole with a hook in the end, used to grab a line.

Bobstay. A chain, wire, or rod that runs between a low point on the hull and goes to the end of a bowsprit or bumpkin to support the spar against the upward pull of the rigging.

Boltrope. A rope sewed along the edge of a sail to strengthen it and take the strain off the cloth.

Boom. A spar to which one edge of a sail is attached.

Boomkin. A short strut extending aft from the transom to support the mizzen sheet blocks or the mizzen backstay.

Boottop. A decorative painted band, often in a contrasting color to the topsides, that runs the full length of the hull just above and parallel to the waterline.

Bosun's chair. A canvas or Dacron seat in which a crew member is hoisted aloft to inspect or work on a mast or rigging.

Bow (rhymes with *bow*). The forward-most part of the hull.

Bowsprit. A horizontal or almost horizontal spar that projects forward from the bow and from which a headstay and jib are set. The bowsprit often holds anchor fittings.

Brace. A line that controls the yard of a squaresail in a horizontal plane.

Breast line. A mooring line that leads abeam from a boat to a pier, float, or anchor.

Broach. To accidentally slew around in spite of the helmsman so that the wind is brought abeam when running before a heavy sea.

Bulkhead. A transverse partition below decks that separates parts of a vessel.

Bulwarks. A solid protection built up around the edges of a deck to prevent people or gear from being washed overboard.

Bunk. A built-in bed or berth aboard a ship.

Bunkboard. A vertically mounted device (say, 3½' long by 2' high) made of wood or canvas and mounted along the edge of a berth to keep a sleeping crew member from falling out of a windward berth when the boat heels.

Bunt. The middle part of a sail.

Burdened vessel. A boat obliged by racing or right-of-way rules to avoid other boats that have the right of way. A boat on the port tack, for example, is burdened by a vessel on the starboard tack.

By the lee. Running with the wind on the same side as the boom. It generally means that the boat is close to an accidental gybe.

Cable. 1. Measurement unit: one-tenth of a nautical mile, or 200 yards. 2. A heavy line or chain.

Camber. The athwartship curve of the deck.

Can. A plastic or metal cylinder that serves as a navigation mark along a channel. Compare with *nun*. Often nuns are on one side of a channel and cans on the other.

Canoe stern. A type of hull design with a stern that has a pointed end that projects beyond the rudderstock.

Capstan. A mechanical device with a *vertical* barrel that gives increased power when hauling on a line or chain.

Carvel-planked. Wooden hull construction in which the planking runs fore and aft and the planks are fitted against one another and usually caulked for watertightness.

Catamaran. A vessel with two separate hulls that are parallel to one another.

Catenary. The curve or sag of the cable between the vessel and her anchor.

Cat rig. A fore-and-aft rig with one mast right forward and a single sail.

Ceiling. The inside planking of a vessel.

Centerboard. A retractable flat plate of metal, wood, or fiberglass that pivots on an athwartship pin in a cavity in the boat's bottom or keel. When retracted, a centerboard reduces a yacht's draft. When lowered, the centerboard increases a boat's lateral resistance and improves her windward performance. See *daggerboard*.

Chafe. To damage or destroy by rubbing.

Chainplates. Sturdy metal straps bolted along the sides, bow, and stern of a hull, to which standing and running rigging is attached to support the mast.

Charley noble. The deck parts of a chimney coming from a galley stove or a cabin heater.

Chute. Slang for *spinnaker*. Derived from *parachute*.

Claw off. To sail toward the wind and away from a lee shore.

Cleat. A device, usually with two horizontal horns, that is bolted to the deck or cockpit area and to which a line under strain is secured. Note: Cleat is a noun, not a verb. "The woman belayed the line to the cleat," not "She cleated the line around the new fitting."

Clew. The lower after corner of a fore-and-aft sail.

Clinker. A method of hull construction in which the edges of the horizontal planks overlap slightly and are fastened to one another with glue, screws, or bolts.

Close-hauled. Sailing as close to the wind as possible commensurate with reasonable speed.

Club-footed jib. A jib with a boom along the foot of the sail.

Coachroof. A part of the deck raised to give increased headroom below.

Coaming. A small bulwark around a cockpit to stop water.

Coffee grinder. A large, powerful geared winch driven by two handles that project from a pedestal. Used to pull in sheets, halyards, and other lines.

Companionway. Steps leading below to the cabin from the deck.

Compass. A glass or plastic dome enclosing a card with a magnetic needle that indicates magnetic directions. The card floats in a liquid that dampens the card's motion.

Compass rose. A compass card printed on a nautical chart that helps a user orient the chart to true north and magnetic north.

Course. The direction sailed.

Cringle. 1. A rope eye formed on the outside of the boltrope of a sail. 2. A metal ring or eye sewn or punched into the reinforced edge of a sail, awning, cover, etc., to facilitate a control line.

Cutter. A fore-and-aft-rigged vessel with one mast. A mainsail is fitted aft and two headsails (staysail and jib) are arranged forward.

Davit or Davits. A small crane used to hoist a dinghy, anchor, outboard motor, cargo, etc. Since a davit is used at each end of a small boat, the term is often used in the plural.

Daggerboard. A flat piece of metal, wood, or fiberglass that works like a centerboard. Rather than pivoting, however, it retracts vertically in a fore-and-aft slot. When pulled up, a daggerboard reduces a yacht's draft. Lowered, it increases the boat's lateral resistance and improves windward performance. Compare with *centerboard*.

Deadlight. A metal cover that can be clamped over the glass of a portlight to increase its strength in case of a storm.

Dead reckoning or DR. The calculation of a boat's present position by advancing the previous position for the course made good and distance run over the ground.

Depth sounder. An electronic device that tells the depth of the water beneath a vessel.

Deviation. A shipboard compass error caused by the proximity of iron or other magnetic influence. The amount of error usually depends on the direction the vessel is heading.

Dismasted. To lose the mast or rig. "The wire broke and the cutter was suddenly dismasted."

Displacement. The weight of a vessel. Sometimes called *tonnage.*

Doghouse. A raised shelter forward of a cockpit or over a hatch.

Double-ender. A Scandinavian-type boat with a pointed stern, usually with an outboard rudder.

Downhaul. A line used for pulling down a sail.

Downwind. Away from the direction the wind is blowing.

Dowse. To lower quickly.

Draft. 1. The distance between the waterline and the lowest part of the keel or centerboard. Often spoken of as the amount of water that a boat draws. 2. The amount and position of fullness or curve in a sail.

Drift. To be carried by wind or current.

Drifter. A large, featherweight jib used in light airs.

Drogue. A device dragged from the stern to slow progress through the water and to keep a vessel from broaching or capsizing.

Ease. To slacken.

Ebb. The outgoing tide or tidal stream; opposite of *flood.*

Eddy. A circular current or a stream running in the opposite direction to the main tidal stream.

End-for-end. Reversing a line to equalize wear.

Eye. 1. A loop. 2. A bolt with an eye at one end into which a shackle can be secured.

Fairlead. A fitting through which a line is passed to alter the direction of its lead or to keep it clear of other gear.

Fairway. The middle of a channel.

Fake down or Flake down. A scheme in which a person runs his hands along the length of a line to remove kinks and twists and then arranges the line on deck with each loop (fake or flake) just overlapping the one under it so that the line will run out without fouling.

Fall. The hauling part of a line.

Fathom. Six feet.

Fetch. 1. (verb) To reach a desired point of land or buoy. 2. (noun) A contributing factor of wave height, specifically, the straight-line distance the wind has blown over the surface, generally from a windward shore to the vessel.

Flood. The incoming, rising, upstream tide. Opposite of *ebb.*

Floors (hull construction). Athwartship strengthening pieces that connect the frames or ribs on the starboard side of the vessel to the frames or ribs on the port side. In yachts, the cabin sole (never called "the floor") usually rests on the floors.

Fluke. The pointed part of an anchor that digs into the ground.

Flying. A triangular sail is set flying when its luff is not fastened to a stay but is held by the tack (at the forward lower corner), the head (at the top), and the clew (back bottom corner).

Foot. The lower edge of a sail.

Fore-and-aft. In line with the keel.

Forefoot. The most forward part of the underbody of a hull.

Forereach (storm management). To make headway when hove to.

Foresail. The fore-and-aft sail set on the aft side of a schooner's foremast.

Free. Not close-hauled. "The yacht was running free."

Freeboard. Height of the topsides of a hull.

Full and by. Sailing close-hauled with all sails full.

Furl. To fold a sail side-to-side along a spar and to secure it with ties. A harbor furl is particularly neat, with the folds even and wrinkle-free, and is considered a sign of good seamanship.

Gaff. The upper spar to which a quadrilateral mainsail, foresail, or mizzen is bent.

Gaff jaws. The fitting at the inboard end of a gaff, often covered with leather, that slides up and down the mast. Generally used in the plural.

Gaff sail. A quadrilateral sail fitted with a gaff boom at the upper end.

Galley. A seagoing kitchen.

Gallows. A permanent framework that supports the main or foresail boom when the sail is lowered.

Galvanize. To coat iron or steel with zinc to protect it from corrosion. Usually done by hot dipping after the metal has been cleaned with acid.

Garboard or Garboards. The fore-and-aft plank next to the keel in a carvel-built wooden boat. By extension, this general area in a hull built of other materials.

Genoa (pronounced *JEN-o-ah*). A large jib that overlaps the mainsail.

Gimbals. Mounting arrangements that use gravity to permit a weighted table, stove, berth, or compass to pivot so their tops remain horizontal when the boat heels.

Gipsy or Gypsy. The horizontal drum of a winch around which line or chain is turned to heave in the anchor. Sometimes called a *wildcat*.

Gooseneck. The universal joint that holds the forward part of a boom to a mast.

Grapnel. A small anchor with four or more arms designed to hook around strong points on the seafloor.

Great circle route. A sailing route calculated to follow the curvature of the earth. It saves distance on long passages but requires the course to be changed from time to time. A piece of string pulled tight between two points on a globe makes a great circle route. Generally used on passages of 200 miles or more. Compare with *rhumb line*.

Green water. Solid water from a wave that's shipped aboard.

Grommet. A metal ring punched or sewed into a sail or canvaswork, often at the corners.

Gunwale (pronounced *gun'l*). The rail of a boat where the deck meets the topsides.

Guy. A steadying line attached to one end of a spar.

Gybe (noun or verb). Gybing and tacking are the two basic maneuvers of sailing. If a vessel is running before the wind, and the helmsman turns the boat so that the wind blowing against a sail is changed from one side to the other, he is said to have gybed or completed a gybe. It usually means changing the wind from one quarter to the other. If the sail is on a boom, this heavy spar sometimes swings across violently. See *accidental gybe*. Also spelled *jibe*.

Halyard. A line used for hoisting a sail or flag. Generally, it's vertical and works through a block mounted high on a mast.

Hand. 1. (verb) To lower a sail or spar. 2. (noun) A crew member.

Handy billy. A tackle used to give extra pulling power on a line.

Hank. 1. (noun) A clip, usually of metal, used to hold the luff of a sail to a stay. 2. (verb) To install a sail with a hanked luff on a stay. "He hanked the staysail to the forestay."

Hard or On the hard. The paved area of a boatyard where small vessels are hauled ashore and blocked up for storage. "The blue yawl was on the hard for the winter."

Harden or Harden up. To trim a sail almost flat for windward work.

Hard up or Hard down. To shove the tiller as far as possible to windward or to leeward, respectively. "Put the tiller hard up."

Head. 1. (noun) Toilet room on a vessel. 2. (noun) The upper corner of a triangular sail. 3. (verb) To aim a boat in a direction. "Head into the wind."

Headboard. A special piece of wood, aluminum, or many thicknesses of fabric at the head of a mainsail or mizzen to assist with the mounting and hoisting. It often has extra mast slides for security.

Headroom. The height measurement inside a cabin.

Headsail. The triangular sail that is set in front of the mainmast or the forward-most mast.

Headway. A boat's forward motion.

Heave-to (storm management). To trim shortened sails and the helm so that the vessel almost stops.

Heel. To lay over or list.

Helm. The steering position. "Susan, take the helm."

Hoist. 1. (verb) To raise a sail. 2. (noun) The length of a sail's luff.

Hull. The body of a vessel exclusive of her masts and gear.

In irons. Headed directly into the wind with no headway and with the sails fluttering so the boat cannot bear off on either tack. If the vessel begins to drift backward, she is said to be "making a sternboard."

Jib. The foremost headsail. Not to be confused with *jibe* (see *gybe*).

Jumpers or Jumper struts. A method of reinforcing the upper front portion of a mast to take the pull of a small jib whose head does not reach the masthead, a common arrangement in many one-design fleets.

Jury rig. A makeshift or substitute rig.

Kedge. A light, general-purpose anchor that can be carried out in a dinghy and used to haul a vessel off when she has gone aground.

Kellet. A weight, usually of lead, lowered along an anchor line to increase the holding power of an anchor. A kellet can also be used to lower the height of a cable in a shallow anchorage when propellers are a hazard.

Ketch. A two-masted fore-and-aft-rigged boat whose smaller mizzenmast is stepped forward of the rudder post.

Knee. A triangular-shaped wooden or metal support that joins a beam to a frame.

Lanyard. A small line used to secure an object.

Lead (rhymes with *said*) line. A light line, weighted at one end with a piece of lead and marked in feet, fathoms, or meters that is used to determine the depth of water.

Leech. The aftermost part of a sail.

Leech line. A light adjustable line sewed into the tabling along a sail's leech to control flutter and shaking.

Lee cloth. A rectangle of canvas (say, $3\frac{1}{2}'$ long by 2' high) hung vertically along the inside edge of a fore-and-aft berth to keep the occupant from falling out when the boat heels to leeward.

Lee helm. The tendency of a vessel to turn her bow away from the wind. Considered to be dangerous. Compare with its opposite: *weather helm*.

Lee shore. A coastline onto which the wind is blowing from the water.

Leeway. The amount that a boat slides to leeward while she is sailing.

Lifelines. Strong wires that are strung from the bow pulpit through stanchions mounted along the deck to the stern pulpit and which make a safety fence for the crew working on deck.

Limber holes (hull). Fore-and-aft holes drilled through the floors connecting the frames (beneath the cabin sole) to permit water to drain to the deepest part of the bilge where it can be pumped out.

LOA. Length overall. The on-deck length of a boat from transom to stem.

Loom. 1. The part of an oar that is in the boat when rowing. Said by some to be the part from the blade to the handle or grip. 2. The distant glow of a lighthouse or city lights.

LP. The longest perpendicular line on a triangular sail. The LP refers to a line at right angles to the luff that runs through the clew and is used in headsail measurements.

Luff. 1. (noun) The forward part of a fore-and-aft sail. 2. (verb) To alter course toward the wind, to head up, which makes the sails flap.

Mainsail. The principal sail on the mainmast.

Make fast. To secure or belay a line.

Marconi or Bermudian rig. A modern sail plan with a three-sided mainsail and jib set on a tall mast that was developed to a high state of efficiency by sailors in Bermuda. Because of the height of the mast and its complex support wires, it looked to sailors of the 1920s like the lofty antennas at a wireless, or Marconi, station.

Mast. A vertical spar to support rigging, yards, and sails.

Mast step. A frame or slot to secure the lower end of the mast, often on the keel.

Meat hook (slang). A broken (and often unseen) strand of rigging wire that sticks out and can rip a sail or a finger.

Mercator chart. A system of chart drawing based on the earth's globe. The meridians and parallels of latitude appear as lines crossing at right angles. The converging meridians of the sphere have been spread to parallel lines on the chart; the parallels of latitude are still parallel, but instead of being equidistant, the distance between them increases poleward while keeping proportional with the spreading of the meridians. Thus, islands near the equator are shown normal size, but toward the poles, land masses are increasingly enlarged. This is of no practical importance until you reach latitudes of 60 degrees or higher. With a few exceptions, all charts in use are Mercator projections. A straight-line course on such a chart is called a *rhumb line*. It's important to remember that all distances measured on a Mercator chart *must always be taken on the latitude scale* (along the sides). If you measure distances on the top or bottom along the longitude scales, your navigation will have serious errors.

Mizzenmast or Mizzen sail. The aftermost mast or sail on a ketch or yawl.

Monkey's fist. A specially tied large knot with an enclosed weight at the end of a heaving line.

Monohull. A boat with one hull.

Moor. 1. To tie up or make a vessel fast alongside a pier or between two posts or buoys. 2. To anchor with one anchor ahead and one behind so that the boat lies between the anchors.

Multihull. A boat with two (catamaran) or three (trimaran) hulls.

Navel pipe. The fitting on the foredeck through which the anchor chain or cable passes.

Neap tides. Tides that occur at the quarter moon. They have less range at this time of the month, with the high water being lower than average and the low water higher than average.

Nip. A sharp bend in a rope, where it passes over a sheave or through a fairlead. "It's a good plan to change the nip every morning."

Nun. A plastic or metal cone-shaped fairway buoy. See *can*.

Nylon. A synthetic fiber used in making strong, stretchy line and tough, lightweight cloth. Sailors favor nylon lines for many anchoring situations and nylon cloth for spinnakers and lightweight sails.

Oarlock or Rowlock. A crutch or holder into which an oar is shipped when rowing.

Ocean current. Consistent movement of water in the open sea not produced or affected by tides.

Off soundings. Beyond the 100-fathom depth mark.

Off the wind. Downwind, on a broad reach or run.

Offing. Position at a distance from the shore.

Oil bag. A sack made of thick cloth through which holes are pricked with a sail needle or an ice pick so that oil can drip overboard to calm rough seas.

On soundings. Inshore of the 100-fathom depth mark.

On the wind. Sailing close-hauled.

Outhaul. A line that adjusts the position of the clew and controls the foot tension on a boomed sail.

Overfalls. Violently upset water and breaking waves caused by tidal action. Areas best avoided by small vessels. Compare with *race* or *tidal race*.

Overhang. The amount a vessel extends beyond the waterline at the bow and stern.

Pad eye. A small metal oval- or diamond-shaped plate bolted to the deck or elsewhere that has an upstanding eye to take a block or fitting.

Painter. A short towing or docking line secured to a dinghy's bow.

Partner or Partners. The opening in the deck through which the mast passes.

Pawl. A small wedge of metal that moves back and forth on a pivot and locks the gears of a winch or capstan to keep it from turning in an undesired direction.

Pay out. To ease chain or line.

Pelican hook. A hinged hook with a retaining link often used on lifelines.

Pendant. Any short control line, such as a reefing pendant, which hangs from the reef cringle on the leech of a mainsail. Also used to describe a short length of wire attached to the head of a small jib to adjust the halyard length. The word is frequently confused with *pennant*, which is a flag, not a control line.

Pennant. A decorative, signal, or identifying flag, frequently triangular in shape. Do not confuse this word with *pendant*.

Pinch. To sail too close to the wind so that the sails luff and the speed drops.

Pitchpole (storm management). A rare accident that causes a boat to pitch into a violent forward somersault when her stern is lifted suddenly by an enormous breaking wave.

Point. To sail close-hauled. "Good pointing ability" means a boat is able to sail well to windward.

Pooped. Describes a vessel over whose stern a wave has broken and filled the cockpit.

Port. The left-hand side of a vessel when looking forward.

Portlight or Porthole. A small pane of glass or plastic, sometimes arranged to open, that is set in a strong frame along the sides of the cabin or topsides to allow light below. The preferred term is *portlight*.

Preventer. A control line fastened to the end of a movable boom that pivots in a horizontal direction. Often used to describe the line rigged between the end of the mainsail (or foresail or mizzen) boom and the stem. This line "prevents" an accidental gybe when running with the after end of the mainsail boom well outside the hull.

Pulpit. A high metal guardrail made of tubing or pipe built around the bow or stern. *Lifelines* run between the bow and stern pulpits via stanchions that are spaced along the edges of the deck.

Purchase or Tackle (pronounced *TAY-cul*). An arrangement of a line and two or more blocks to increase pulling power. "He clapped a four-part purchase between the halyard and the deck and easily tightened the line."

Quarter. The areas on either side of a vessel between amidships and the transom. Usually described as the *port quarter* or *starboard quarter*.

Race or Tidal race. Strong and swift upset water movements caused by a tidal stream in shallow water or conflicting tidal streams. Usually a localized occurrence. Compare with *overfalls*.

Racking seizing. A seizing made with figure-of-eight turns to prevent lines or knots from slipping.

Rake. The angle a mast, transom, or bow makes with the perpendicular.

Range. 1. A beacon or other marker that, when lined up with a second marker, indicates a channel. 2. The difference in level between the high and low water of a tide.

Reach. A course sailed across the wind. If the wind is at 90 degrees to the long dimension of the hull, the boat is sailing a beam reach. If the wind is forward of 90 degrees, the boat is on a close reach. If sailing with the wind aft of 90 degrees, it's a broad reach.

Reaching. Sailing with the wind coming from the side.

Ready about. An order to prepare for a tack. It is followed by the command "helm's alee" or "hard alee."

Reef. To reduce sail area.

Reeve. To pass a line through a hole, ring, sheave, or block. "He climbed the mast and reeved a new main halyard."

Rhumb line. A straight-line compass course between two points on commonly used Mercator charts. Rhumb line courses are generally used for trips of 200 miles or less. Compare with *great circle route*.

Rig. A vessel's sail and mast arrangement.

Roach. The curve along the edges of a sail.

Roller furling. A scheme that rolls the luff of a sail around a wire or rod instead of furling the sail by lowering it.

Round up. To bring a vessel's head to wind.

Rowlock or Oarlock. A crutch or holder into which an oar is shipped when rowing.

Run or Running. To sail before the wind.

Running backstay. A movable stay that supports a mast from aft against the force of a sail or sails.

Running by the lee. Running with the wind on the same quarter as the boom. See *accidental gybe*.

Running rigging. Halyards, sheets, lifts, and other adjustable lines and wires that are used to hoist and control sails and spars. Compare with *standing rigging*.

Sag or Sag off. To make excessive leeway.

Scantlings. The dimensions of the frames, planks, plating, fiberglass layup, etc., that are used in a vessel.

Schooner. A fore-and-aft-rigged vessel, usually with two masts, in which the mainmast (aft) is taller than the foremast.

Scope. The length or sweep of an anchor cable. Often described in comparative terms. "She anchored with a scope of 5 to 1" (which means that in a depth of 5 meters she had 25 meters of chain out).

Scull. To propel a boat by working a single oar from side to side over the stern while the angle of the blade is changed with each stroke.

Scuppers. Overboard drains on deck or in the cockpit.

Seacock. A valve, usually hand-operated, that opens and closes a pipe that passes through the hull and prevents unwanted water from entering the boat.

Seizing. The secure binding together of two lines or two parts of the same line.

Self-bailing. Describes a boat cockpit with *drains* or *scuppers* that empties itself of unwanted water because it is above the waterline.

Serve. A process that protects line from chafe or the elements by spirally binding it round and round with marline or light cord.

Set. 1. (verb) To raise a sail. 2. (verb) To cause an anchor to dig into the holding ground. 3. (noun) The carrying of a boat by current or tidal stream

Shackle. A U- or D-shaped metal fitting with an eye in each arm through which a pin is screwed or driven.

Shake out. To let out a reef.

Sheave (pronounced *shiv*). The grooved roller over which a line passes when it goes through a block.

Sheer. The curve of the gunwale when viewed from abeam in profile. A straight sheer has no curve between stern and bow; a normal sheer is concave; a reverse sheer is convex. A broken sheer reflects poor design or construction. A hogged sheer suggests that the hull is collapsing from age. Sailors and boat aficionados generally favor a normal (or concave) sheer and spend much time discussing this aspect of boat design.

Sheet. A line attached to the clew of a sail to control its trim or setting.

Shell. The outer casing of a block.

Shroud. A wire or rod giving athwartship support to a mast, bowsprit, or bumpkin.

Slack water. Period between flood and ebb tide when the tidal stream stops.

Slick (storm management). The smooth patch left to windward on the surface of the sea when a vessel is driven broadside to leeward by the wind.

Sloop. A single-masted fore-and-aft-rigged sailing boat with a mainsail and one headsail.

Small stuff. Short lengths of light line (marline, spunyarn, string, cord, twine, etc.) that sailors carry in their pockets and use to tie up large coils of line and for a hundred other purposes. I find that 24-inch lengths of $\frac{1}{8}$-inch-diameter Dacron are ideal and I always have half a dozen pieces in my pocket.

Snapshackle. A special shackle with a hinged closure bar held by a spring-loaded pin instead of a threaded bolt-type closure.

Snatchblock. A block with an opening in one side of the shell so that a line can be inserted without having to thread it through the block.

Snub. To cause sudden tension on a line or anchor cable by taking a turn or two around a strong point (capstan, winch, etc.).

Snugged down. Well reefed; under a small or comfortable area of sail for the existing wind and point of sail.

Sole or Cabin sole. The floor of a cabin or cockpit. The term *floor* is not used.

Sound. To measure the depth of water with a marked stick or lead line.

Soundings or In soundings or On soundings. A measurement of water depth as marked on charts. Generally considered to be 100 fathoms or less.

Spinnaker. A large lightweight nylon sail set forward of the mast on downwind legs and reaches.

Spinnaker sock. A long collapsible tube of light cloth used to control a spinnaker when setting or furling the sail.

Splice. A method of joining lines by interlacing the strands from the ends of two lines.

Spreader or Spreaders (mast rigging). Wooden or metal struts that hold wire shrouds at a carefully designed distance from the mast so that adequate angles (generally 10° to 14°) can be maintained at the masthead for good athwartship mast staying.

Spring line. A docking line that runs at an acute angle from the pier to the boat to help stop fore-and-aft surging. Generally, boats need a forward spring and a back spring along with the usual bow and stern docklines. Four lines in all.

Spring tides. Water movements at the time of the full and the new moon. The tides have greater ranges; the high water is higher than average and the low water is lower than average.

Spritsail. A quadrilateral sail whose peak is held aloft by a long slim pole or *sprit* that goes from tack to peak. This one-sail rig is often used on small boats and dinghies.

Stanchions. Vertically mounted stainless steel or aluminum rods or pipes mounted along the deck to support lifelines. Together with *lifelines* and *pulpits*, they make a fence to help keep the crew from falling overboard.

Standing part. That part of a line that is made fast and not hauled upon.

Standing rigging. Shrouds and stays that support the mast and spars and are not handled during the sailing of the vessel. Compare with *running rigging*.

Starboard. The right-hand side of a vessel when facing forward.

Starboard tack. A vessel is on the starboard tack when the wind is blowing over her starboard side.

Stay. A length of wire or rod giving fore-and-aft support to a mast. Hence: headstay, forestay, *backstay*.

Staysail. A fore-and-aft working sail set forward of a mast and hanked to a forestay.

Steerageway. Enough speed to make the steering function.

Stem. The forward part of the bow.

Stern. The aftermost end of a hull.

Sternboard. Going backward. The boat was caught *in irons* and making a sternboard.

Stiff. A vessel is stiff when she does not heel easily. The opposite of *tender*.

Stopper knot. A knot at the end of a line to stop it from going through a block.

Stud-link chain. Chain in which each link has a crossbar to prevent the sides from pulling together and collapsing under great strain.

Stuffing box. A special fitting around the propeller shaft on the inside of the hull to stop incoming water.

Swell. Long, usually low waves caused by a distant storm.

Tabling. Cloth reinforcement along the edge of a sail.

Tack. 1. (noun or verb) Tacking and *gybing* are the two basic maneuvers of sailing. When a sailing vessel with forward motion tacks, she turns into the wind and a little beyond. This causes the wind to go from pressing on one side of the sails to the other. After a successful tack, the boat moves ahead on a new course that is 90 to 110 degrees from the old course. The result is a zigzag course to windward. 2. (noun) The lower forward corner of a fore-and-aft sail.

Tackle (pronounced *TAY-cul*) or Purchase. An arrangement of a line and two or more blocks to increase pulling power. "He clapped the tackle between the halyard and the deck and easily tightened the line."

Taffrail. The rail along the deck that runs across or around the stern.

Tail. To haul on a line around a winch or capstan that is being turned by one or more crew members.

Tang. A metal strap fastened to a strong point to which standing or running rigging is attached.

Telltale. A short length of thread or ribbon tied to a stay to indicate wind direction.

Tender. 1. A vessel that heels easily (opposite of *stiff*). 2. A yacht's dinghy or small boat.

Thimble (rigging). A round or oval metal eye with a concave outer surface into which metal cable or fiber line fits smoothly to reduce chafe and point loading.

Tholepins. An arrangement to hold oars in a rowing boat. Short hardwood dowels (say, ¾" dia. or 18 mm) are fitted vertically along a boat's midship gunwale area. The oars are loosely tied to the tholepins with a turn or two of thin line. A traditional arrangement that uses no metal, is cheap, and works well.

Through-hulls. Plumbing pipes that pierce the hull below the waterline for various drains and inlets. Each through-hull should have a seacock just inside the hull in case of a plumbing failure. Through-hull functions are often combined to minimize their number, upkeep, and expense. Boats that go to sea all keep a tapered wooden plug next to each through-hull in case the seacock or through-hull fails.

Tide or Tides. The periodic vertical rise and fall in the surface level of oceans and lakes caused by the gravitational forces of the sun and moon.

Tidal stream. The horizontal movement of water caused by changing tides. The times of tides and tidal streams are usually different and are found by consulting tide tables, tidal atlases, and special marks on charts. Since a current is a flow of water that continues for a long period, it is incorrect to speak of tidal currents. The proper term is *tidal stream*, which refers to a short-term horizontal water movement.

Tiller. A wooden or metal bar used by the helmsman to turn the rudder.

Toerail. A low wooden or aluminum rail built along the edge of a deck to provide footing when the boat is heeled. Often this rail has a series of holes into which blocks can be shackled for use with running rigging.

Topping lift. An adjustable line that holds up the end of a boom or pole.

Topside or Topsides. 1. (noun) The side of the hull above the waterline. 2. (adverb) A word used to describe the movement of a person from a below-deck cabin to the deck. "The two women went topsides."

Transducer. A small electronic fitting in a vessel's bottom from which sound waves are sent to and from the seafloor. This information is converted to readings on the cockpit dial of a *depth sounder*.

Transom. The athwartship surface at the farthest aft point of a vessel.

Transverse. Across, athwartships, at right angles to fore and aft.

Traveler. A track or bar with a sliding adjustment that permits athwartship control of running rigging.

Trim. To take in. "He trimmed the sheet on the winch." The commands to the winch grinder are usually *trim* (to take in) and *ease* (to let out).

Trimaran. An unballasted vessel with three hulls.

True wind. The direction and strength of wind felt on a vessel that is not moving. *Apparent wind* is the wind felt on a moving object.

Trysail. A small stormsail set in place of the mainsail in heavy weather.

Turnbuckle. A tension-adjusting device made of threaded rods that screw into a threaded barrel.

Under bare poles or Bare pole (storm management). Sailing or blowing along with no sails hoisted in extremely strong winds. The word choice depends on the number of masts.

Under way. Moving under power or sail.

Upwind. The direction from which the wind is blowing.

Vang. 1. A line led aloft from the deck to the end of a gaff boom or sprit to control the spar. 2. One or more tackles used to keep a boom from lifting on downwind or reaching legs. Sometimes called a kicking strap.

Variation. The difference between true and magnetic north in a given area. Every nautical chart shows the variation for the region covered by the chart. Compass courses need to be corrected for both *variation* (area adjustment) and *deviation* (shipboard adjustment).

Veer or Veering. A term used to describe the movement of wind, which is said to veer (say, west to northwest) when it moves clockwise in the Northern Hemisphere. In the Southern Hemisphere, this term is reversed and refers to a counterclockwise movement (say, from west to southwest). Veering has also been defined as moving in a direction that follows the track of the sun. Compare with *backing*.

Wake. The water turbulence that follows a moving vessel.

Warp. An anchor or mooring line.

Washboards. Two or three strong boards placed horizontally in fitted vertical slots on either side of the companionway to close the entrance to the cabin of a sailing yacht.

Way. The movement of a vessel through the water.

Wear. The act of turning a boat to the other tack by maneuvering her away from the wind and gybing instead of tacking. In this maneuver, the stern of the vessel is taken through the eye of the wind. Wearing is sometimes done when it is impossible to tack a boat because of head seas or poor forward speed.

Weather helm. The basic design of a sailing vessel that causes her to head into the wind when the tiller is released. Considered a safety measure.

Weather shore. A shore to windward of a vessel that offers shelter from waves and seas.

Weigh. To raise an anchor. "The two sailors weighed the 100-pound anchor." One does not *way* an anchor.

Whip. 1. (noun) A single block with a line rove through it that gives a 2:1 purchase. 2. (verb) To secure the loose strands at the end of a line by tightly wrapping turns of heavy thread or light cord at right angles to the line. Often called a whipping (noun).

Whisker pole. A small-diameter spar attached between the mast and the clew of a jib to hold the sail out against a following wind when running *wing and wing*.

Winch. A mechanical device for tensioning lines. Two or three turns of the line to be tightened are taken around a drum that is turned by gears driven by a handle or an electric or hydraulic motor.

Windlass. A powerful winch, usually placed at the bow, for hauling anchors. A windlass has a horizontal drum; a *capstan* has a vertical drum.

Wishbone or Wishbone rig. A fore-and-aft boom structure used behind a mast. It has two opposing curved arms shaped like a wishbone between which a sail is hoisted. The clew of the sail is tensioned by an adjustable line taken to the after end of the wishbone.

Wing and wing. Sailing on a run with the eased mainsail on one side of the boat and the jib on the other, with the clew of the jib stretched before the wind with a spinnaker or whisker pole.

Working sails. Sails that are easy to set and use in ordinary weather.

Yaw. A vessel whose bow swings from side to side, usually when running, is said to yaw.

Yawl. A two-masted fore-and-aft-rigged sailing vessel whose aftermost (mizzen) mast is located behind or abaft the rudder post.

Acknowledgments

My thanks to Ed Boden and John Letcher, long-time friends, veteran small-boat sailors, and technical experts par excellence. And to Carol Hasse of Port Townsend, Washington, a sailmaker of great skill, who is my confidante in all matters pertaining to rigs and sails. To Ed Zacko for his assistance with the photographs of the Tinker dinghies. To Earl Hines for information about riding sails. Finally to my editor, Jon Eaton.

My thanks and gratitude to the expert photographers who helped with the illustrations. The credits:

Frontispiece: Russell Turiak
Pages xvi, 88, 118, 153, 273, 328, 334, 335, 376, 385, 398, 416: Margaret Roth
Page 10: Harry Pidgeon
Page 22: Tee Jennings
Page 30: Beken of Cowes
Page 65: courtesy Armada de Chile
Page 87: Eric Sponberg
Page 96: Lisa Pittoors
Page 105: Jean Knocker
Page 110: Eileen Ramsay
Page 114: Tom Wylie
Page 115: courtesy Garry Hoyt
Pages 137, 138: Jim Sollers, based on Henry Hill illustrations
Page 207: W. A. Robinson
Page 266: courtesy Henry H. Anderson Jr.
Page 354: Bournemouth News Agency

Index